'Modern politics has been shaped both by specific understandings of the temporality of human existence and by enormous forces demanding either amnesia about temporality or its translation into overbearing narratives of a linear history. The consequences can be read through our prevailing accounts of sovereign states, international relations, modernization, development, citizenship and the status of humanity as such. While still resilient, these accounts are being challenged at every turn. Shaped especially by postcolonial critiques of international relations, this remarkable and provocative collection of essays reports from many sites at which the politics of temporality and the temporalities of novel forms of politics press against the waning authority of all spatialized categories.'

R. B. J. Walker, University of Victoria, Canada

'An exceptional assemblage of essays written by an impressive array of critical theorists, artists and poets. The contributors lay down a powerful intellectual challenge aimed at disrupting dominant theorizations in IR, to "unhinge time from its presumed neutrality", and provoke engagement with the temporal structure of the relationship of politics and violence. The authors expand the anticolonial and postcolonial critique of the project of Modernity and the West or Global North as the primary temporal analytical site against which all else is to be measured or interpreted. The book provokes its readers to transform assumptions and re-imagine possibilities of an anti-racist and decolonial vision of world politics, focused on "the politics of life" and immanent transformations of social relations.'

Barry Gills, University of Helsinki, Finland

'*Time, Temporality, and Violence in International Relations: (De)fatalizing the Present, Forging Radical Alternatives* is an obligatory reading for anyone interested in understanding how space and time constitutes the unyielding forms (sovereignty, the state, etc) that are the staple of research International Relations. Exploring *time*'s transformative promises, the texts assembled in this volume dare to unsettle the spatializing political categories of world politics, which hide how and why colonial and racial violence have constituted the global present.'

Denise Ferreira da Silva, Queen Mary University of London, UK

Time, Temporality and Violence in International Relations

Time transforms the way we see world politics and insinuates itself into the ways we act. In this groundbreaking volume, Agathangelou and Killian bring together scholars from a range of disciplines to tackle time and temporality in international relations. The authors – critical theorists, artists and poets – theorize and speak from the vantage point of the anticolonial, postcolonial and decolonial event. They investigate an array of experiences and structures of violence – oppression, neocolonization, slavery, war, poverty and exploitation – focusing on the tensions produced by histories of slavery and colonization and disrupting dominant modes of how we understand present times.

This edited volume takes IR in a new direction, defatalizing the ways in which we think about dominant narratives of violence, 'peace' and 'liberation' and renewing what it means to decolonize today's world. It challenges us to confront violence and suffering and articulates another way to think about the world, arguing for an understanding of the 'present' as a vulnerable space through which radically different temporal experiences appear. And it calls for a disruption of the 'everyday politics of expediency' in the guise of neoliberalism and security.

This volume reorients the ethical and political assumptions that affectively, imaginatively and practically captivate us, simultaneously unsettling the familiar, but dubious, promises of a modernity that decimates political life. Re-animating an international political, the authors evoke people's struggles and movements that are neither about redemption nor erasure, but a suspension of time for radical new beginnings.

Anna M. Agathangelou is Associate Professor in political science and women's studies at York University, Toronto, and co-director of Global Change Institute, Nicosia. Her academic interests include postcolonial and Marxist theory; transnational feminisms; critical theories of empire, colonization and slavery, race, sex and bodies; militarization of global relations; Marxist epistemologies; and poetics of transformation.

Kyle D. Killian is a family therapist and core faculty in the Marriage and Family Therapy Program at Capella University. He has published on intercultural and interracial couples, refugee families, trauma and self-care and vicarious resilience in helping professionals. A blogger at *Psychology Today*, Dr. Killian has developed measures of traumatic stress, critical thinking, cultural identity, vicarious resilience, and emotional intelligence.

Interventions
Edited by Jenny Edkins, Aberystwyth University, and
Nick Vaughan-Williams, University of Warwick

The Series provides a forum for innovative and interdisciplinary work that engages with alternative critical, post-structural, feminist, postcolonial, psychoanalytic and cultural approaches to international relations and global politics. In our first five years we have published sixty volumes.

We aim to advance understanding of the key areas in which scholars working within broad critical post-structural traditions have chosen to make their interventions, and to present innovative analyses of important topics. Titles in the series engage with critical thinkers in philosophy, sociology, politics and other disciplines and provide situated historical, empirical and textual studies in international politics.

We are very happy to discuss your ideas at any stage of the project: just contact us for advice or proposal guidelines. Proposals should be submitted directly to the Series editors:

- Jenny Edkins (jennyedkins@hotmail.com) and
- Nick Vaughan-Williams (n.vaughan-williams@warwick.ac.uk).

'As Michel Foucault has famously stated, "knowledge is not made for understanding; it is made for cutting." In this spirit The Edkins – Vaughan-Williams Interventions series solicits cutting edge, critical works that challenge mainstream understandings in international relations. It is the best place to contribute post disciplinary works that think rather than merely recognize and affirm the world recycled in IR's traditional geopolitical imaginary.'

Michael J. Shapiro, University of Hawai'i at Manoa, USA

Critical Theorists and International Relations
Edited by Jenny Edkins and Nick Vaughan-Williams

Ethics as Foreign Policy
Britain, the EU and the other
Dan Bulley

Universality, Ethics and International Relations
A grammatical reading
Véronique Pin-Fat

The Time of the City
Politics, philosophy, and genre
Michael J. Shapiro

Governing Sustainable Development
Partnership, protest and power at the world summit
Carl Death

Insuring Security
Biopolitics, security and risk
Luis Lobo-Guerrero

Foucault and International Relations
New critical engagements
Edited by Nicholas J. Kiersey and Doug Stokes

International Relations and Non-Western Thought
Imperialism, colonialism and investigations of global modernity
Edited by Robbie Shilliam

Autobiographical International Relations
I, IR
Edited by Naeem Inayatullah

War and Rape
Law, memory and justice
Nicola Henry

Madness in International Relations
Psychology, security and the global governance of mental health
Alison Howell

Spatiality, Sovereignty and Carl Schmitt
Geographies of the nomos
Edited by Stephen Legg

Politics of Urbanism
Seeing like a city
Warren Magnusson

Beyond Biopolitics
Theory, violence and horror in world politics
François Debrix and Alexander D. Barder

The Politics of Speed
Capitalism, the state and war in an accelerating world
Simon Glezos

Politics and the Art of Commemoration
Memorials to struggle in Latin America and Spain
Katherine Hite

Indian Foreign Policy
The politics of postcolonial identity
Priya Chacko

Politics of the Event
Time, movement, becoming
Tom Lundborg

Theorising Post-Conflict Reconciliation
Agonism, restitution and repair
Edited by Alexander Keller Hirsch

Europe's Encounter with Islam
The secular and the postsecular
Luca Mavelli

Re-Thinking International Relations Theory via Deconstruction
Badredine Arfi

The New Violent Cartography
Geo-analysis after the aesthetic turn
Edited by Sam Okoth Opondo and Michael J. Shapiro

Insuring War
Sovereignty, security and risk
Luis Lobo-Guerrero

International Relations, Meaning and Mimesis
Necati Polat

The Postcolonial Subject
Claiming politics/governing others in late modernity
Vivienne Jabri

Foucault and the Politics of Hearing
Lauri Siisiäinen

Volunteer Tourism in the Global South
Giving back in neoliberal times
Wanda Vrasti

Cosmopolitan Government in Europe
Citizens and entrepreneurs in postnational politics
Owen Parker

Studies in the Trans-Disciplinary Method
After the aesthetic turn
Michael J. Shapiro

Alternative Accountabilities in Global Politics
The scars of violence
Brent J. Steele

Celebrity Humanitarianism
The ideology of global charity
Ilan Kapoor

Deconstructing International Politics
Michael Dillon

The Politics of Exile
Elizabeth Dauphinee

Democratic Futures
Revisioning democracy promotion
Milja Kurki

Postcolonial Theory
A critical introduction
Edited by Sanjay Seth

More than Just War
Narratives of the just war and military life
Charles A. Jones

Deleuze & Fascism
Security: war: aesthetics
Edited by Brad Evans and Julian Reid

Feminist International Relations
'Exquisite Corpse'
Marysia Zalewski

The Persistence of Nationalism
From imagined communities
to urban encounters
Angharad Closs Stephens

Interpretive Approaches to Global Climate Governance
Reconstructing the greenhouse
Edited by Chris Methmann, Delf Rothe and Benjamin Stephan

Postcolonial Encounters in International Relations
The politics of transgression
in the Maghred
Alina Sajed

Post-Tsunami Reconstruction in Indonesia
Negotiating normativity through gender mainstreaming initiatives in Aceh
Marjaana Jauhola

Leo Strauss and the Invasion of Iraq
Encountering the Abyss
Aggie Hirst

Production of Postcolonial India and Pakistan
Meanings of partition
Ted Svensson

War, Identity and the Liberal State
Everyday experiences of the geopolitical in the armed forces
Victoria M. Basham

Writing Global Trade Governance
Discourse and the WTO
Michael Strange

Politics of Violence
Militancy, international politics, killing in the name
Charlotte Heath-Kelly

Ontology and World Politics
Void Universalism I
Sergei Prozorov

Theory of the Political Subject
Void Universalism II
Sergei Prozorov

Visual Politics and North Korea
Seeing is believing
David Shim

Globalization, Difference and Human Security
Edited by Mustapha Kamal Pasha

Imagining World Politics
Sihar & Shenya, a fable for our times
L.H.M Ling

International Politics and Performance
Critical aesthetics and
Creative practice
Edited by Jenny Edkins and Adrian Kear

Memory and Trauma in International Relations
Theories, cases, and debates
Edited by Erica Resende and Dovile Budryte

Critical Environmental Politics
Edited by Carl Death

Democracy Promotion
A critical introduction
Jeff Bridoux and Milja Kurki

International Intervention in a Secular Age
Re-enchanting Humanity?
Audra Mitchell

The Politics of Haunting and Memory in International Relations
Jessica Auchter

European-East Asian Borders in Translation
Edited by Joyce C.H. Liu and Nick Vaughan-Williams

Genre and the (Post)Communist Woman
Analyzing transformations of the Central and Eastern European female ideal
Edited by Florentina C. Andreescu and Michael Shapiro

Studying the Agency of being Governed
Edited by Stina Hansson, Sofie Hellberg Maria Stern

Politics of Emotion
The song of Telangana
Himadeep Muppidi

Ruling the Margins
Colonial power and administrative rule in the past and present
Prem Kumar Rajaram

Race and Racism in International Relations
Confronting the global colour line
Alexander Anievas, Nivi Manchanda and Robbie Shilliam

The Grammar of Politics and Performance
Edited by Shirin M. Rai and Janelle Reinelt

War, Police and Assemblages of Intervention
Edited by Jan Bachman, Colleen Bell and Caroline Holmqvist

Re-Imagining North Korea in International Politics
Problematizations and alternatives
Shine Choi

On Schmitt and Space
Claudio Minca and Rory Rowan

Face Politics
Jenny Edkins

Empire Within
International hierarchy and its imperial laboratories of governance
Alexander D. Barder

Sexual Politics and International Relations
How LGBTQ claims shape International Relations
Edited by Manuela Lavinas Picq and Markus Thiel

Emotions, Politics and War
Edited by Linda Åhäll and Thomas Gregory

Jacques Lacan: Between Psychoanalysis and Politics
Edited by Samo Tomšič and Andreja Zevnik

The Value of Resilience: Securing Life in the 21st Century
Chris Zebrowski

Political Aesthetics: Culture, Critique and the Everyday
Arundhati Virmani

Walzer, Just War and Iraq: Ethics as Response
Ronan O'Callaghan

Politics and Suicide
The philosophy of political self-destruction
Nicholas Michelsen

Late Modern Palestine
The subject and representation of the second intifada
Junka-Aikio

Negotiating Corruption
NGOs, governance and hybridity in West Africa
Laura Routley

The Biopolitics of Lifestyle
Foucault, ethics and healthy choices
Christopher Mayes

Critical Imaginations in International Relations
Aoileann Ní Mhurchú and Reiko Shindo

Time, Temporality and Violence in International Relations
(De)fatalizing the present, forging radical alternatives
Edited by Anna M. Agathangelou and Kyle D. Killian

Time, Temporality and Violence in International Relations

(De)fatalizing the present, forging radical alternatives

Edited by Anna M. Agathangelou and Kyle D. Killian

LONDON AND NEW YORK

First published 2016
by Routledge
2 Park Square, Milton Park, Abingdon, Oxon OX14 4RN

and by Routledge
711 Third Avenue, New York, NY 10017

Routledge is an imprint of the Taylor & Francis Group, an informa business

© 2016 selection and editorial material, Anna M. Agathangelou and Kyle D. Killian; individual chapters, the contributors

The right of Anna M. Agathangelou and Kyle D. Killian to be identified as authors of the editorial material, and of the individual authors as authors of their contributions, has been asserted by them in accordance with sections 77 and 78 of the Copyright, Designs and Patents Act 1988.

All rights reserved. No part of this book may be reprinted or reproduced or utilised in any form or by any electronic, mechanical, or other means, now known or hereafter invented, including photocopying and recording, or in any information storage or retrieval system, without permission in writing from the publishers.

Trademark notice: Product or corporate names may be trademarks or registered trademarks, and are used only for identification and explanation without intent to infringe.

British Library Cataloguing in Publication Data
A catalogue record for this book is available from the British Library

Library of Congress Cataloging-in-Publication Data
A catalog record for the book has been requested

ISBN: 978-0-415-71271-2 (hbk)
ISBN: 978-1-315-88370-0 (ebk)

Typeset in Times New Roman
by Apex CoVantage, LLC

Dedicated to:

**Kostas Evangelou
our godfather
whose life, magnanimity and being
continue on as music, poetry and dance**

**Captain David Charles Foley
best man, and brother,
thank you for four-and-a-half decades
of friendship and fellowship**

and

**Geeta Chowdhry
feminist, anti-colonial true social revolutionary,
with a deep love and belief in people**

Contents

Illustrations — xviii
Acknowledgments — xxi
Contributor biographies — xxii

Introduction: Of time and temporality in world politics — 1
ANNA M. AGATHANGELOU AND KYLE D. KILLIAN

1 **International relations as a vulnerable space: A conversation with Fanon and Hartman about temporality and violence** — 23
ANNA M. AGATHANGELOU AND KYLE D. KILLIAN

SECTION I
Contemporary problematics: Tensions, slavery, colonization and accumulation — 43

2 **Time, technology, and the imperial eye: Perdition on the road to redemption in international relations theory** — 45
SIBA N. GROVOGUI

3 **The social life of social death: On afro-pessimism and black optimism** — 61
JARED SEXTON

4 **Temporality and insecurity in international practices** — 76
TY SOLOMON

5 **Doing time in the (psychic) commons: Black insurgency and the unconscious** — 87
FRANK B. WILDERSON III

xvi Contents

6 **Outside of time: Salvage ethnography, self-representation and performing culture** — 104
WANDA NANIBUSH

7 **Impolitical mandate: De-fatalizing a port city** — 119
SUVENDRINI PERERA AND ANNETTE SEEMAN

8 **The productive ambivalences of post-revolutionary time: Discourse, aesthetics, and the political subject of the Palestinian present** — 129
NASSER ABOURAHME

SECTION II
Neoliberal temporalities — 157

9 **Migrant day laborers, the violence of work, and the politics of time** — 159
PAUL APOSTOLIDIS

10 **Atemporal dwelling: Heterotopias of homelessness in contemporary Japan** — 172
RITU VIJ

11 **Child's play: Temporal discourse, counterpower, and environmental politics** — 189
ANDREW R. HOM AND BRENT J. STEELE

12 **Childhood, redemption and the prosaics of waiting** — 205
SAM OKOTH OPONDO

13 **Temporalizing security: Securing the citizen, insecuring the immigrant in the Mediterranean** — 221
PINAR BILGIN

14 **Killing time: Writing the temporality of global politics** — 233
ASLI ÇALKIVIK

15 **Hurricane Katrina and bio-temporalities: Media representations of 'environmental' disasters** — 246
MICHAEL J. SHAPIRO

16 **Re-Imagining the anonymous city: Defatalizing the digital present through analog photography** 260
    CLIFF DAVIDSON

SECTION III
Poetic interventions for social transformation 275

17 **Freedom telling on time: The Arab Revolt's poems** 277
    NATHALIE HANDAL

18 **Poetry: Blunt Balm and Dust to Dust** 284
    TSITSI JAJI

19 ***From the Bed & Breakfast Notebooks*** 288
    ALEXANDRA HANDAL

   Bibliography 295
   Index 327

Illustrations

1.1	Africa, then and now	37
7.1	Annette Seeman, *Impolitical Mandate*, 2012	119
7.2	Annette Seeman, *A Working Port 1*, 2012	120
7.3	Annette Seeman, *A Working Port 2*, 2012	121
7.4	Annette Seeman, *A Working Port 3*, 2012	121
7.5	Annette Seeman, *A Working Port 4*, 2012	122
7.6	Annette Seeman, *Another's Telling*, 2012	124
7.7	Annette Seeman, *Another's Telling 2*, 2012	125
7.8	John Teschendorff, *Ship of Fools (Tampa Drawing)*, 2010, reproduced with the kind permission of the artist	125
7.9	Annette Seeman, *Dead Garden 1*, 2012	126
7.10	Annette Seeman, *Dead Garden 2*, 2012	127
8.1	Advertising billboard, Nablus, in front of a building partially destroyed during the suppression of the 2000 Second Intifada uprising, 2011	133
8.2	A purpose-built suburban neighbourhood on the northern fringes of Ramallah	133
8.3	Police publicity images cover part of a street in Ramallah	134
8.4	Police publicity images cover part of a street in Ramallah	134
8.5	Advertising billboard, Nablus, 2011	136
8.6	Advertising billboard, Ramallah, 2010	137
8.7	'The land belongs to the hands that liberate it', Abed al-Rahman al-Muzayin, 1978, PLO Unified Information	140
8.8	Land Day commemoration, Abed al-Rahman al-Muzayin, 1985, PLO Unified Information	141
8.9	'Passion is not bound by tools', image of Jawwal poster advertisement, Bir Zeit, 2011	142
8.10	'We are all with you oh fida'i', advertisement, Ramallah, 2014	143
8.11	'We are all fida'iyun', Emile Menhem, 1977, Palestinian National Liberation Movement (FATAH)	144
8.12	Marc Rudin, 1984, Joint Leadership PFLP and DFLP	145
8.13	The 2011–2013 National Development Plan, Palestinian National Authority (PNA)	146

8.14	Land Day commemoration, Jamal al-Afghani, 1985, PLO Unified Information	147
8.15	Billboard advertising for cellular phone corporation, Ramallah, 2011	148
8.16	Billboard of Yasser Arafat echoed by Bank of Palestine advertisement, Ramallah, 2012; the aesthetic reverb is again striking – the outward, horizon-seeking gaze, the determined posture are repeated in a kind of slippage between the two images	149
8.17	Shifting forms of the feminine: New advertising and old mural juxtaposed in downtown Ramallah, 2009	149
8.18	Billboard heralding Palestine's rebirth at the United Nations, Ramallah	152
16.1	Happy lucky chow time	263
16.2	Table for none	265
16.3	Worst hiding spot ever	266
16.4	Disconnected	266
16.5	Country house, city house	267
16.6	Sketchy	268
16.7	Welcome to Chinatown – keep right	268
16.8	The new/old tears	270
16.9	Lonely short board	271
16.10	Spadina Dundas snow smile	271
16.11	99¢ hot dogs	272
16.12	New Year's subway pigeon	272

Acknowledgments

We thank the contributors for their intellectual engagement through the stages of the book's development: Friends, colleagues and comrades in generating a (de)fatalized world. Many other colleagues were sources of inspiration. We are grateful to Gamal Abdel-Shehid, Lissa Chiu, Ena Dua, Alberto Guevara, Bernie Lightman, Karen Murray, Stephen Newman, Elyse Nouvet and Ann Porter. At the University of Toronto we are grateful to Rinaldo Walcott and Ayesha Basit. Special thanks also to Caroline Kennedy, Sophia Dingli, Noël K. O'Sullivan and Margo. Both Noël and Margo were the most incredible hosts, with dinners and dancing. At Harvard special thanks go to Sheila Jasanoff and co-fellows of 2014–2015. At Kobe University special thanks go to Hiroyuki Tosa, Ronni Alexander, Popoki and the graduate students. We are thankful for their ongoing support, and this book we hope embodies their vision and what they do every day to make our world a less fatal one. We thank all of our friends and interlocutors-in-life over the years: Chris Achilleos, Apostolos Apostolou, Christalla Christofi, Shampa Biswas, Maria Hadjipavlou, Aida Hozic, Kostantin Kilibarda, Emily Merson, Sheila Nair, Mustapha Kamal Pasha, Nicos and Maria Peristianis, Randolph Persaud, Giorgio Shani, Sankaran Krishna, Robbie Shilliam, Simona Sharoni, Nicos Trimikliniotis, Heather Turcotte, Tamara Spira, Sevgül Uludağ and Magda Zenon.

Thanks to Elizabeth Thompson and Emily Merson for their invaluable assistance with editing and bibliographic research. Thanks to our families, and our second sets of parents and siblings: Kostas and Neophyta Evangelou, Evaggelos, Stelios, Elena, Katia, Antonis, Ioanna, Neophytos, Evi, Phoebe and Maria.

A special note of appreciation goes to our sons, Mikael Lawrence and Aleksi Christos, who are often, but not always, patient while waiting for their mom and dad to put the finishing touches on 'urgent' matters on their computer screens. Thank you to Lydia de Cruz, Jenny Edkins and Nick Vaughan-Williams at Taylor & Francis, whose enthusiasm, energy and insights shepherded this project to fruition. Thanks also to the journal *InTensions*, which published earlier versions of several chapters in Volume 5, 2011. And thanks to our mothers, Artemis Christofi and Sallie Ann Clayton Killian, for not consuming alcohol or smoking during their pregnancies.

Anna M. Agathangelou and Kyle D. Killian
May 27, 2015

Contributor biographies

Nasser Abourahme is a doctoral candidate at Columbia University, where he works between political theory and urban studies in the department of Middle Eastern, South Asian, and African Studies. He is an assistant editor at the journal *CITY*.

Anna M. Agathangelou is associate professor in political science and women's studies at York University, Toronto, Canada, and former research fellow in Science and Technology Studies at Harvard. Her current book project examines the global and political dimensions of post-conflict DNA identification of the missing and disappeared in a variety of sites, including Cyprus.

Paul Apostolidis is professor in the political science department at Whitman College in Walla Walla, Washington, and teaches community-based research, politics of race and immigration and Latino politics. He is author of *Breaks in the Chain: What Immigrant Workers Can Teach America About Democracy* (University of Minnesota 2010).

Pinar Bilgin, associate professor in the department of international relations at Bilkent University, Ankara, Turkey, specializes in critical approaches to security studies and is an associate member of the Turkish Academy of Sciences.

Aslı Çalkıvik is assistant professor in the Department of Humanities and Social Sciences at Istanbul Technical University, where she teaches international political theory, security and the politics of knowledge production.

Cliff Davidson is a PhD candidate in sociology at the University of Western Ontario. His research interests include commodification and sociology of education, social processes in urban spaces and visual sociology.

Siba N. Grovogui is professor of Africana Studies and Research Center at Cornell University and teaches international relations and political theory. He is author of *Sovereigns, Quasi-Sovereigns, and Africans: Race and Self-Determination in International Law* (University of Minnesota Press 1996) and *Beyond Eurocentrism and Anarchy: Memories of International Order and Institutions* (Palgrave Macmillan 2006).

Alexandra Handal is an artist and filmmaker who lives and works between London and Jerusalem. Her short film, *From the Bed & Breakfast Notebooks* (2008), was selected for the prestigious New Contemporaries 2009 internationally juried exhibition. She completed a practice/theory PhD in fine art at Chelsea College of Art and Design, London.

Nathalie Handal is a professor at the Center for the Study of Ethnicity and Race at Columbia University and a poet, playwright and the author of *Poet in Andalucía* and *Love and Strange Horses* and editor of *The Poetry of Arab Women: A Contemporary Anthology* and co-editor of the W.W. Norton landmark anthology *Language for a New Century: Contemporary Poetry from the Middle East, Asia & Beyond*.

Andrew R. Hom is research associate in politics at the University of Glasgow, Scotland, and writes about IR theories as narrative responses to various challenges associated with time's flow.

Tsitsi Jali teaches about global black literatures, cinema, and music at Duke University. Her book *Africa in Stereo: Modernism, Music and Pan-African Solidarity* (2014) examines the impact of African American music and literature in Ghana, Senegal and South Africa on African notions of solidarity in the twentieth century.

Kyle D. Killian is a family therapist and on faculty at the Marriage and Family Therapy Program at Capella University. Dr. Killian researches multiracial families, resilience and trauma. His books include *Interracial Couples, Intimacy and Therapy* (Columbia University Press 2013) and *Intercultural Couples: Exploring Diversity in Intimate Relationships* (Routledge 2008).

Wanda Nanibush is an Anishinaabe-kwe curator, word and image warrior from Beausoleil First Nations. She has a masters in visual studies and is a PhD candidate at the University of Toronto, is curating independently and is working for the Art Gallery of Ontario.

Sam Okoth Opondo is assistant professor in comparative politics and Africana studies at Vassar College, New York, and writes on the often-overlooked amateur diplomacies of everyday life, postcolonial cities, aesthetics, ethics and cultural translation in Africa and the dynamics of 'mediating estrangement' and co-habitation. He is co-editor of *The New Violent Cartography: Geo-Analysis After the Aesthetic Turn* (Routledge 2012).

Suvendrini Perera is professor in the Department of Cultural Studies at Curtin University and has published on issues of race, ethnicity and multiculturalism, refugee topics, critical whiteness studies and Asian Australian studies. She is author/editor of seven books, including *Australia and the Insular Imagination: Beaches, Borders, Boats and Bodies*, and the anthology *At the Limits of Justice: Women of Colour on Terror*.

Annette Seeman is an artist and senior lecturer in the Faculty of Built Environment Art & Design at Curtin University, and her research explores the public and private influences that constitute meaning for domesticity and sanctuary (or the lack thereof). She has exhibited in New Zealand, Cambodia, Thailand, Japan, Indonesia and Malaysia.

Jared Sexton is associate professor and director of African American studies at University of California, Irvine, and his research interests include critical theory, race and sexuality, coalition politics and contemporary U.S. cinema. He is author of *Amalgamation Schemes: Antiblackness and the Critique of Multiracialism* (University of Minnesota Press 2008).

Michael J. Shapiro is professor of political science at the University of Hawaii, Manoa. His research draws from international relations, cultural studies, political philosophy, critical theory, psychoanalysis, gender studies and aesthetics. He is author of over ten books, including *Violent Cartographies*, *Cinematic Political Thought*, *For Moral Ambiguity*, *Reading 'Adam Smith'*, *Methods and Nations*, *Deforming American Political Thought*, *Cinematic Geopolitics*, and *The Time of the City*.

Ty Solomon is lecturer in international relations at the University of Glasgow, Scotland, and author of *The Politics of Subjectivity in American Foreign Policy Discourses* (University of Michigan Press 2015). His research examines affect, security and use of the concept of weapons of mass destruction.

Brent J. Steele is professor of the Political Science Department, University of Utah, and author of five books, including *Alternative Accountabilities in Global Politics: The Scars of Violence* (Routledge 2013), *Defacing Power: The Aesthetics of Insecurity in Global Politics* (University of Michigan Press 2012) and *Ontological Security in International Relations* (Routledge 2008).

Ritu Vij is senior lecturer in the Department of Politics and International Relations at the University of Aberdeen. She has been affiliated with Kobe, Meiji Gakuin, Meiji, Ritsumeikan and Tokyo Universities.

Frank B. Wilderson III is professor of African American studies and drama at the University of California, Irvine. His books include *Red, White & Black: Cinema and the Structure of U.S. Antagonism* (Duke University Press 2009) and *Incognegro: From Black Power to Apartheid and Back: A Memoir of Exile* (South End Press 2008).

Introduction

Of time and temporality in world politics

Anna M. Agathangelou and Kyle D. Killian

Time transforms the way we see world politics and insinuates itself into the way we act. Yet its centrality is largely undocumented. Time's force as a lens through which to think about possibilities of an anti-racist, decolonial vision of world politics in the twenty-first century has been equally evaded, with its relevance for the understanding of international relations (IR) bracketed. Except for a few notable examples (Blaney and Inayatullah 2010; Edkins 2001; Hutchings 2007, 2008; Jarvis 2009; Shapiro 2000; Walker 1993, 2010), temporality is 'all but absent' (Hutchings 2008: 11), making it possible for major strands of theories in realism, institutionalism, constructivism, liberalism, Marxism, and poststructuralism to craft an 'international' – that is, a site of knowledge intervention – by *transcending time*. Masking time and spatializing it within their texts, theorists imagine certain kinds of bodies reading their text with particular kinds of assumptions about time and temporality.

If this is the way theorists in IR are trained to epistemically orient themselves, and if this orientation becomes a material temporal energy that constitutes the world, those of us who focus on the spatial aspect of the projects emerging as the 'state' and the 'market' inevitably ask ourselves: what are the stakes in ordering projects like the state and the market in their 'international' iterations if we mask and spatialize notions of time?

The first section of this introduction explores these questions and explains how and why time and temporality must be an integral part of theorizing IR and world politics more broadly. It grapples with time and temporality as a way to think and imagine a 'present' whose inscription of violence is not masked or spatialized through debt deferred promises. Thinking about the 'present' requires us to consider the ways time and temporality are articulated next to figures of promises and freedom.

The second section grapples with iterations of time and temporality in postcolonial event. Insisting on understanding time in its ontological, epistemological, and institutional arrangements, postcolonial studies argues temporal reformulations are pivotal to political projects interested in rupturing a present whose inflection is violence and fatalism. Writers focus on the immanent transformations of social relations, bringing temporal questions to the fore: at the heart of their projects, even for those most focused on the historical past, we find questions of how the violent past and its persistence in the present might be negotiated. Rather than understanding time as a backdrop before which the present passes into a shadowy history, postcolonial projects seek to unhinge time from its presumed neutrality; at their most creative, they maintain an unwavering commitment to thinking about temporality in relation to an indeterminate future.

The final section outlines the contributions of each of the authors to this volume.

Time, temporality and international relations

Kimberley Hutchings argues the 'end' of the Cold War saw the emergence of a new time and a new world order, raising questions about the nature and orientation of time. 'Is time moving toward a progressive end point? Is world political time destined to become a continual 'clash of civilizations'? Do specters haunt the present and the future?' In explaining the meaning of her third question, Hutchings says mainstream theory draws on contending conceptions of *chronos* (linear time from the ancients) and *kairos* (change in *chronos*-time either by humans or divine Fortune). The specter haunting modern political philosophers, she says, is the belief that politics is a project of controlling time as *chronos* and creating a different kind of time through *kairos*. Such an endeavor leads to a notion that the political ought to be inscribed with an assumed singular time, thereby blocking out anything and anybody that does not fit (Hutchings 2008: 159).

If theorizing time and temporality is a specter for IR scholars evading the emergence of authoritarian capitalist states, radical religious formations, non-Western persistent practices, gender, reproduction, and colonization, what does IR turn itself into? This specter haunting IR embodies a dogmatic rationality in the form of liberal and property society (a capitalist market, historical formations, social contracts). In Hutchings's view, if the Cold War is taken as an event, both incorporeal and material, it becomes a provocation to action that can propel us to become open to the force of time while remaining attuned to the discursive and material constraints of the present. It demands a struggle of engagement to problematize its archives, memories and specters and puts the event up for grabs. But if it is taken as a given event and a 'transition' to a progressive point whose materiality can come in the form of a 'clash of civilizations', or a point that brings with it the specters and the violence with which the present or future must grapple, provocations to action may be limited instead of being reframed.

Becoming open to the force of time while remaining attuned to discursive and material constraints of the present demands problematizing a kind of historicism that recapitulates politics in the terrestrial matrix (Sivin 1976: 516). This historicism emerges as an issue in several IR static, narrativizations, and phenomenological readings because of the structure of violence itself: a teleological orientation, with peace as the end. This structure is transposed onto an assumed dichotomy of a 'war against all' (state of nature, anarchy) and peace (civil society, social contract).

Even when teleology sits in the genres of historiography and its subject evades teleological designs, IR registers such accounts as proof of anarchy, calling forth projects programmed by 'a history of the present' where sovereign-bound subjects control their passions. The production of this 'history' requires making a kind of time out of *kairos* by controlling *chronos* (dividing and sequencing time in a linear manner). In this way, politics for IR turns into a teleological historicized outcome of what went before, eradicating indeterminacy, historical invention, and creativity.

IR turns politics into a historicist fiction that presumably knows the end (bringing God into politics through the back door). There is nothing more linear than the presumption that the possibility of peace could ever be explained linearly. If IR's theorizing relies on a stabilization that centers peace as an always inhabited present and the determinations of past and futures as mere modifications, no wonder it is haunted and in crisis, unable to understand the emergence of world phenomena, including the rise of authoritarian capitalist regimes, insurgent movements in the Middle East and North Africa (MENA), and ecological concerns.

Hutchings's work enables theorists of IR to grapple with time, temporality, violence, and decolonial projects beyond messianic claims to communities like nationhood or the market or to more revolutionary projects where freedom and order are bound with the teleological movement of violence and force. If both crisis and control are recognized as naturalized attitudes toward time and mystified expressions of time, the change of *kairos* to control indeterminacy in the future, through and outside the verifiable, becomes problematized, even abandoned.

In a study of time and temporality, Hom maps the instantiations of temporality in IR (2013: 83). Citing a series of different authors, first dead and then alive, Hom argues the field identifies and prioritizes space as a vantage point of analysis without tending to time. By conjuncting metaphors that embody this dichotomization of time and eternity, IR flirts with time without explicitly grappling with it. For him, the evasion of theorizing time is material; it materializes a manner through which we read, understand, and bind concepts. We agree.

IR draws on a multiplicity of temporal metaphors, strategically creating a haphazard way of speaking about or describing time. IR's identity, representation, social imaginaries and discourses stabilize themselves by spatializing time or masking it. One answer to this choice of deploying metaphors is to argue that even in their most historical forms, IR metaphors are exemplars of an attitude towards 'real' time, even if not explicitly so. Or IR scholars may simply be more concerned with thinking about the question of the political by giving accounts of violence and sovereignty, phenomena behind all political philosophies. It may not be always clear whether IR scholars think about time 'thoroughly enough' (Hom 2013: 19), but it is apparent that the politics of sovereignty is both convivial and violent, generating intense sensual pleasure for both rulers and ruled (Marriott 2011: 58; Mbembe 2001). Equally generative and imprisoning is the sensual pleasure in the co-producing of knowledge and order, even if IR reads incoherently and inconsistently.

To approach something as dangerous or to suspend engaging with time because it may be destructive, the 'assassin of stability,' 'disturbing' relations, constantly 'revolutionizing,' 'profaning' and 'melting' all that is 'fixed and consecrated' (Russ 2013: 114), seems anti-intellectual and arbitrary. Perhaps, it is this arbitrariness of suturing the present that turns into the most erotic timely event that makes IR. Consumed with complex and violent relations undermining peace or permanence, IR theorists, with intrepid bravado, beckon impending conflicts but are unable to hide their disdain for what they think they are witnessing: the acceleration of time in increasingly violent sovereign relations from the perspective of an upcoming timelessness or eternity. The abolition of violence and conflict in civil society seems tantamount to the abolition of time itself, yet such a future state can only be carried forward by time. Time is enlisted in the fight against itself but never explicitly, always metaphorically and analogically.

If time is the methodological starting point of all thought, as theorists like Blaney and Inayatullah, Walker, Shapiro, Hutchings and Hom argue, we ought to engage with it as a force, a set of discourses, a device, an ontology, and an institution of governance, rather than 'indiscriminately applying its omnipotence and ravages' to those with whom we disagree (Russ 2013: 114). Facets of human experience and political life deconstruct spatial and temporal binaries associated with the pre-modern versus modern differentiations in various texts yet are unnecessarily ossified. It is curious what effort goes into conceiving questions of violence, political authority, obligation, will and freedom in terms of competing spatial representations of political order, even when we can productively think about such phenomena in terms of time, especially in terms of lived experience (i.e., temporality) and perceptions of time (Hoy 2009).

Hom (2013: 19), Walker (1993) and Hutchings (2008) trace IR's problem with time, imagining a political and politics otherwise. This is a political whose knowledge and social order are co-produced, as Jasanoff notes, speaking of science: '[It] . . . involves the crafting of future states of being and forms of life – indeed, imagined communities – which depend in turn on acquiring (and occasionally rejecting) scientific knowledge and the life-changing commodities that science delivers' (2004: 4). IR's narratives of time are written not vis-à-vis some transcendental essence but as something with its own time; work and knowledge produced transform the flow and flux of time into perceptions of space, often habitually and at times without realizing this is being done.

If space and time are immanent, flexible constitutive aspects of the politics of our lives and the world we transform to give purpose to our actions, how do IR theorists explain not engaging explicitly with time?

When we rethink in terms of time and temporality, the parameters of conceptualization and terms of debate over the politics of life change dramatically. At the broadest level, this shift allows greater fidelity to the complexities of lived human experience, highlighting dimensions IR theorists generally take as given and transforms assumptions about the politics of life. Rather than conceiving the state as a given and the primary object of analysis and the subject of politics as an autonomous, propertied masculine human with pre-selected preferences and values, we could think of it as a concrete, complex international arrangement undergoing change within a variety of overlapping social spaces, power dynamics and discourses and with the use of multiple devices and institutions of governance to secure a certain international order. Instead of asking if states 'fail,' we can re-orient our imaginations to see how in concrete moments, the production of knowledge (science) and politics interact in co-producing the normative, epistemic, ontological, practical and technological aspects of life in modern societies. We can ask about the role of temporality in mutable projects and frames through which people come to imagine and direct their daily lives.

Our work ought to be oriented not to find the essence of a 'thing' (in this case IR), but to probe the formation of phenomena to see how social imaginaries point to new existences and to ask what activates them. The paradox we must confront is not simply that the evasion of time treats the state, the national, the interstate, the civilizational, the global and the ecological as givens. More crucially, mystifying the question of time, rather than historicizing how it becomes an object of analysis, excludes its historicity.

Defining and allocating prospective values within certain sovereign boundaries while setting bounds on imagined enemies is the stuff of a certain reasoning in IR, 'with associated demands, . . . rules of evidence, argument and adjudication' (Jasanoff 2004: 4). This theorizing is limiting and cannot be addressed without asking questions about the politics of time and temporality. Accordingly, Hom grapples with 'the simultaneous and seemingly contradictory visions of Western Standard time, or clock time, and the problem of Time, understood as time's natural propensity for bringing dissolution, discord, and death to human experience' (Hom 2013: iii). In using IR as a site of a narrative vocation whose response to change is a particular orientation, self-reflectivity and lived experience, he argues that in both theories and methodologies, even quantitative ones, IR is a 'narrative timing project whose viability hinges on its ability to placate, manage, or tame the problem of Time' (ibid: iii).

IR makes a series of philosophical assumptions about the world, including time and temporality. Instead of seeing temporal aspects as vestigial 'to the core "scientific" concerns of stability and structure, order, synchronic comparison, and parsimony or elegance' (Hom 2013: 63), it is important to recognize in international politics that time and temporality, even when they are not theorized, are co-produced with spatiality (Valverde 2015).

Hom articulates an analytical toolbox to read IR's account of time, reinvigorating debates around temporal aspects like change, violence, disorder, process, history and complexity. Systematically, though implicitly, IR produces institutional practices that constitute the different approaches of academic discourse. The 'experimental laboratory,' Hom argues (2013: 135), 'poses an alternative to natural observation which provides prolific empirical data' by preventing any interference from the outside chaotic world and 'reducing the interaction of natural change' (ibid: 132). Paradoxically, the laboratory doors are closed, making it a space '*unbound*' by the problem of Time' (ibid: 133).

This unboundedness from the problem of time and its antithesis to eternity are enforced in the relationship between problems of knowledge and problems of social order. There are differences in how concerns about time are articulated in concepts of the international such as 'state of nature,' 'social contract,' 'balance of power,' 'containment' and 'order.' Yet a reading of IR scholarship as lacking the desire or as unable to theorize time evaporates into a narrative that is neither humane nor peaceful when it concerns global governance or reflexive modes of scientific analysis. But reading this evasion as a narrative activity may re-insert a schema that would reduce its activities to final meanings.

If IR produces a multiplicity of narratives showing how different theories embody 'unilinear' understandings of history while constituting 'othering devices,' the question remains: how can such a process be effected without a schematic of relations that is itself already established? Dominant IR's narratives of its birth rely on the 'story' of its 'origin,' therefore relying on the exterior of such a story, something that could initiate the story but is not included in the story as such. In this sense, both time and the temporality of that constituted as outside or other must always be the erased or recoded lever or pivot according to which the schematic division of inside and outside can be established, maintained and cyclically returned to the origin so that the raw outside or accident can appear as a necessary historical precondition for the 'logical' developmental narrative to emerge.

Our unresolved question in this introduction is whether it is possible to consider IR from the standpoint of time without being committed to narratives of inclusion, and a present with an end in linear, dialectical or existential resolution, and whether it is possible to think of world politics as political moments of living and active theoretical forms of life 'not surreptitiously mortgaged to a thought of racism in [their] understanding of the politics of life' (Marriott 2011: 37).

Perhaps more important for thinking of time, temporality, and the present (i.e., the future of our century as Fanon would say) in relation to the political are accounts of the problem of violence and sovereignty. Hobbes (1996 [1651]), Little (2007) and Bull (2002 [1977]) engage with time, even when their understanding operates at two distinct registers. Dominant readings of IR empty these registers by articulating a social secular order (albeit theological) at the level of the functioning of the state and the operation of sovereign power. In that sense, time seems sublated in a social articulated in macropolitical terms that lack time and are forever eternal. But that is a function, we may argue, of the subject matter of IR theory. It is impossible to write about Hobbes, for instance, or Bull's idea of 'order' without considering macropolitical questions of a sovereign power that does not entangle itself with the time and the temporality of the theological-secular.

Hobbes is dealing with a foundational moment where questions of governance and political form are laid bare. Knowledge production is directly related to questions of the political. This brings up the question of sovereign power and crucial related questions: what constitutes and at what moment science and the *public* for this sovereign power? What notion of time is being bounded and unbounded and how so? Who gets to be the authoritative producer of knowledge, how so, when? Whose witnessing counts as timely and credible? With Hobbes's ideas of science and the public, we can imagine a universal assent of a subject whose transcendence is made possible once and for all; we can even begin to rethink the question of time if we return to the paradox implicit in his theory of violence from which theorists, like Kant, depart (2008 [1755]).

Hobbes' temporality is rarely engaged. But temporality allows a different reading of his view of nature as articulated in *Leviathan* (1996 [1651]), namely, the manner through which a certain politics is co-produced with a secular order Leviathan, as the state, may involve itself in the use of force, is in some sense a substitute for nature. The use of force is is some way the art of undoing the old, of unraveling the natural, and of severing the present from the past. Politics, is thus, both a stand-in for nature and its opposite, anti-nature. Further, the fictions that postulate the existence of a 'before' and an 'after' allow time to become the determining factor (Hobbes 1969: 101) of the racialization of the world. Hobbes's idea of civil society is conjuncted with the condition where there is no society, thereby no time or danger or violent death. In the end, however, Hobbes's dichotomization of the uncivil/civil does not exhaust the problem of the relationship between temporality and the making of subjects (Mbembe 2001: 15).

In *De Cive*, Hobbes invokes temporality to 'suggest that the state of nature occupies an earlier, more primitive historical register than the more developed civil state' (Nyquist 2013: 258). Even though Hobbes engages with the uncivil conditions in Europe, he says about native Americans, 'Europeans encounter the "savages" as their contemporary ancestors' (Nyquist 2013: 259). Hobbes uses Indigenous peoples 'as a referent for natural liberty,' equating them with the state of nature to argue for the absolute freedom of individuals who 'enjoy the security and prosperity that their subjection to a sovereign produce[s]' (Moloney 2011: 189). In so doing, he prepares the ground for a new time and a new political order, with the Leviathan his example of a firmly controlled, explicitly political present.

The state is not just a kind of a solution, according to Hobbes. It is *the* solution. It imposes a political time on its subjects or de-subjects them from the multiplicity of spiritual and religious temporalities. But leveraging the temporal regime of a Leviathan against the referent of the indigenous subject does not resolve the question of violence. The respective temporalities he ascribes to his subjects and to his social contract clash, implying the inevitability of violence as a necessary means to secure a timely order. The time of the political order of Hobbes is itself constituted with an explicit violence that takes assumptions about notions of time and Western Europeans to the nth degree; as 'Greco-Roman civility's rightful heirs,' they are 'peculiarly equipped to transmit the antique arts and knowledge that Christianity has refined to nations unable to govern themselves' (Nyquist 2013: 260). And *these* heirs are not just any heirs. They are immanent ones who can fight from European spheres in the 'new' world arena of conflict and conquest. Of course, these fights are fabulated as gendered; if America was a woman, the fight over her body and the conquest, sexual and otherwise, could be the way to secure the winner (Agathangelou 2014) and cosmic time.

With the encounters between Europeans and the inhabitants of the Americas and Africa, debates sparked over how to reconcile the Bible with the existence of these 'others.' Two opposing positions developed: polygeny, whereby differing races belong to separate species, and monogeny, whereby all races are descended from a single ancestor but have developed in differing ways. This dichotomization/displacement was and is not politically neutral. The displacement of the other from the 'present' and the relegating of such a 'body' into 'areas' are devices of the inter-state system, the coloniality of power characterizing the contemporary world, and the historiographical 'proving' of backwardness based on the notion of 'area.' This distinction also plays itself out in the division and hierarchization of knowledge labor: production of discipline, as opposed to area studies. These devices are generative of inequality and violence, with inequality coded as distance in time. Denying shared time makes possible the denial of the status of the other as an acting and speaking agent who shares the present with the reasoned (masculine, white) subject. The 'time-distancing discourse of evolutionism,' for example, naturalizes and legitimates ideas of primitive and inferior others living in other times (Fabian 1983: 5).

If Hobbes is hailed as the major author of how we think and organize our scientific enterprise, what does this say about our temporal literacy of and on time? What are the implications of such easy reads and displacements of the nuanced experiments and fabulations undertaken by authors like Hobbes? Shouldn't we be considering the relations of our scientific enterprise, indeed our literacy itself, as a question of time?

Many metaphors deployed in IR embody a finite mode explained in terms of tempus and duration (cyclical violence vs. linear progress, progressive vs. degenerative world etc.), so the substance of IR ends up requiring an explanation in terms of eternity and timelessness. If the existence of the finite mode (i.e., regime) is duration, then taking away its duration (i.e., violence) will not make it eternal but will take away violence's (durational) existence. Key metaphors embodying such moves include: 'real "structures" (Buzan 1993: 93; Waltz 1979; cf. Suganami 1999: 383), "levels of analysis" (Singer 1961; Wendt 1992; Wight 2006), "spill-over" in "resurgent" regionalism (Hurrell 1995: 348), theories as "models" (Kilgour and Wolinsky-Nahmias 2004; Kremeniuk and Sjostedt 2000), scholarship as an "intervention" (see Routledge's *Interventions* series), "ruptures" (Nolin 2006; Walker 1993: 2, 27), "state as person" (Wendt 2004), international politics as a "game" with "rules" (Kratochwil 1989; Onuf 2012; Putnam 1988), norm "cascades" (Finnemore and Sikkink 1998), some instances of "scars" (Steele 2012), the "Anglosphere" (Vucetic 2011) and "economic man"' (Hom 2013: 83n31).

Problematizing IR's evasion of time by pointing to the metaphors impressed upon world politics, Hom suggests such cognitions flatten the understanding of world politics. The imagining of IR as a tension between time and eternity makes it impossible to narrate IR as a timing activity. Hom narrativizes IR as a timing activity so that the field can take time seriously: 'Narrative propounds a timing standard by which people orient themselves and act in the world, but is also itself the product of timing operations resulting in a temporal vision' (Hom 2013: 56). This narrativization of time in IR exposes its social construction and the timing standards deployed to make timing activities possible.

Even if IR is read as a narrative activity, questions of community membership and narrative order orient us toward the question of difference, which is at the forefront of theorizing time in debates on the state, war, capitalism, knowledge production and labor power. Take, for instance, the brush strokes in Genesis, where the division of the world into darkness and light, day and night, good and bad is articulated: 'And God said, "Let there be light": and there was light And God saw the light, that it was good; and God divided the light from the darkness. And God called the light Day, and the darkness he called Night. And the evening and the morning were the first day' (Genesis 1: 3–5). Adam and Eve who are (initially) free of the relations of reproduction and generations are also atemporal.

To be free of judgment and shame is to be free of stories about before and after, to be free of anxiety about what time it is or what is to come. Without knowledge, the present cannot be delineated from past or future. But knowledge changes everything, and Eve is the cause of human time in Genesis. She is a transgressor (Genesis 3: 22–24) pointing to the two dimensions of being godlike: gendered knowledge and gendered time.

The co-constitution of dominant IR as field and discipline depends on a series of symbolic representations to achieve its goal of understanding and explaining change. The telling of the constitution of IR is not easily assembled in a simple narrative of temporal activity, and the co-constitution of time with these narratives remains perplexing for many. The co-production of dominant IR presumes a stable point of reference in eternity, and by comparison, human time – and everything associated with it – is always deficient. In effect, this stability of eternity identifies, explains and naturalizes hierarchy. Power stems from where/when the world is viewed. It may sound peculiar that dominant IR theorists experience their own mental faculties as unsettling while perceiving overtly divine terms (e.g., being present in all times and places) as less troubling and more compelling. For most, time as a human condition of change and loss invalidates what they know and what they are. By contrast, eternity's static (and accessible) conceptual formulation has the power to smooth over or encompass the improbable. In this sense, *divine temporality* is less enigmatic than human temporality. If this is the case, does the narrativization of IR as a temporal activity or the use of narrative as time activity address the problem?

From Hom's perspective, the response is possibly no. The narrative of time activity expressed by neopositivists on one side of the spectrum has a utilitarian calculus, while on the other side, critical realists use an ontological calculus to gauge time against eternity as the ultimate measurement. This kind of narrative timing activity defines theorists in relation to each other and in reference to an eternity through which they comprehend their own desires for change and the ordering of the world. Differences in the theological/fictional point of reference (God) cause trouble in IR theorizing. Much theorizing paints a God at peace with himself and his timelessness condition, but IR theorists must come to terms with a present guilt incurred in the past in the garden of Eden and with an unknown future. Critchley (2009) articulates this guilt and debt by citing Heidegger: "'Life is a business whether or not it covers its costs'. Debt is a way of being. I owe therefore I am."

Narrative theorizing as an activity of time may become a form of confession, compelling us to tell a story that makes sense of our own story. Arguably, telling such a story alleviates a human temporality of loss (forgetting) and reduction (having our sense of self warped by selective outstanding moments). Importantly, the constitution of much IR theory depends on social imaginaries of temporal difference in its racialized, gendered, classed, sexuality, and ability iterations. As the epistemologically more attractive concept, eternity is more satisfying to assume or speak about than time with its multiple contingencies and uncertainties emerging from constituted hierarchies and difference. Eternity offers a model for what the present might be. For Hom, neopositivists, critical realists and interpretivists end up 'recapitulating narrativised responses to the flow of Time' (Hom 2013: 163), depending on 'methodologies [that] claim ... the mantle of scientific facts' instead of recognizing they 'are actually doing something more like science fiction' (ibid: 163, 165).

Hom narrativizes IR *accurately* and *elegantly* (as one of our graduate school professors who was obsessed with modeling used to say) and in a timely fashion, but occasionally leans toward historicism or atemporal narratives. Much of the analysis remains an internal critique, leveraging one problematic construction against another to show what political differences might result if IR were thought and narrativized temporally. Hutchings's work (2008) rests on the force of narration and counter-discursive utterances that might break through official accounts of the sovereign state and change, reducing time's force to competing signs or internal struggles within theoretical frameworks and theorists.

Postcolonial theorists chart struggles to dismantle fictions based on linear narrations and the movement of global capital. Chakrabarty insists if the present is to direct the future, 'critique has to figure out the now' (2004: 458). Grappling with two schemas of history of modernity (History 1 (the logic of capital) and History 2 (practices not inhering in capital), Chakrabarty argues we must historicize the present while understanding that our periodization of the present is directly linked to our understanding of the political, which is never without a particular understanding of the *now*. This demands a self-reflexive examination of both the situatedness and the assemblages pivotal for the production of knowledge, capital and violence. Temporality is a register where multiple relations can be drawn; critics should become an active part of 'configur[ing] a now so plural as not to be exhausted by any single definition' (Chakrabarty 2004: 462).

Chakrabarty is not alone in this postcolonial move. Others challenge dominant temporal divisions of the world (locals, natives, etc. vs. global capitalists) (Scott 2008; Tanpinar 2014) and modernity's attempts to ontologize the world as Western, modern, and secular (Khayyat 2014; Tanpinar 2014). For them, such moves are paradoxical: instead of being able 'to merge with the life in this world and go about [our] business,' 'all [we] can see is a wall of secularized Christian civil societal institutions' (Khayyat 2014: 4).

Ontologizing the 'world' as Western, modern, and secular?

In his *Critique of Reason*, Kant articulates time as the transcendental condition of all experience. For him, all humans are endowed with reason, and reason's ultimate goal, to synthesize and complete knowledge, is always a problem of time. In its attempt to complete knowledge, reason uses three major ideas, God, Freedom and Immortality, to fill the hole created by the indeterminacy of time.

This transcendental reason was quickly deleted from scientifically based fields as it does not easily map onto scientificity. Foucault's *The Order of Things* (1973) outlines this historical production of *secular finitude*. For Foucault, the introduction of a sense of finitude, the elimination of the transcendental, makes this an 'order,' not a cosmology. Approaches to mortality have changed with changes in the conditions of knowledge and experience. Before the nineteenth century, he says, notions of mortality and finite time were more about earthly 'limitations'; 'man' was destined to work, was destined to die and would never come to understand the world in its infinity.

In reading Foucault's understanding of time and the changes of the idea of infinity, we are not suggesting these changes were caused by the secular transformation of life and death. Rather, different eschatological frames and conceptions of the afterlife (or lack of it) have a material effect on notions of lived time and vice versa. The afterlife is experienced and used as a temporal strategy. Simultaneously, a political doctrine insists that separating the institutions of religious authority from political and scientific authority changes the conditions under which people are supposed to carry out their activities, including the ways they are supposed to act in relation to the sovereign and the way the sovereign is supposed to act on its subjects, especially with respect to violence.

Drawing on Foucault and Benjamin, Asad argues secular modern politics seeks to homogenize time into a proper history, wherein secular refers to a set of sensibilities, concepts and practices producing a kind of human and a set of social institutional arrangements in the form of modernity, the ultimate time machine.

Secularization involves both the production of difference and the deployment of violence in sieving who the subject of history is and who can potentially become temporalized. By applying an exception to the rule of the secular law, it finds its bases in the grammar of fatalism (those who can reason scientifically and take responsibility as opposed to those who are attributing everything to God, stars or causes). The challenge to this fatalism (i.e., the conclusion that all things happen in their best and proper time, without any human officiousness) depends on a set of technologies, and modern projects whose ultimate and supposed goal is '(de)fatalization' (freeing people from necessity and determinism) at any cost possible.

Secularization and temporalization co-constitute that modern capitalist order and 'divine sovereignty' systematically with violence by producing a series of fictions. Time, that force that is never fully present to itself and our lives, subjectivity, competing histories, or *dispositif* of regulatory power, becomes the very standard of hitching value to empty it of those who are out of joint; this process reduces "life to a final meaning" (Marriott 2012: 57), that fictional eternity, the teleological illusion, which itself depends on the constitution of homogeneous time.

> 'Modernity' is neither a totally coherent object no a clearly bounded one, and that many of its elements originate in relations with the histories of peoples outside Europe. Modernity is a project – or, rather, a series of interlinked projects – that certain people in power seek to achieve. The homogeneous time of state bureaucracies, and markets, is central to the calculations of modern political economy. It allows temporalities – immediate and mediated, reversible and nonreversible – by which individuals in a heterogeneous society live and by which their political responses are shaped. . . .
>
> (Asad 2003: 3)

These technologies of violence are configured in this political schema so as to perpetuate the secular modern project and its homogenizing capacities. Violence, in turn, is deemed acceptable or unacceptable, depending on the criteria of organizing time into a politically hegemonic proper history. Death works in secular modern politics in a way that perpetuates and stabilizes this secular time. For (secular) liberals, violence is acceptable when it makes possible an imaginary of the project of modernity. Death is acceptable where it is the property of the state, triggering the question why some violence (outside history) is considered a threat while other violence (within secular history) is not (ibid: 4)[1].

Going back to the major thematic of this book, the (de)fatalization of the 'present', how can such inscriptions of time with violence be grappled with? How do notions of fatalism become technologies of violence even when paradoxically such fictions inscribe themselves on modernity, the time machine par excellence? How are those moments occupied by events and figures that remain trenchantly beyond the grasp or recollection of the great historical narratives to be engaged with? The attempt to devise a form of writing sufficiently broad to include such forgotten fragments of 'real history' involves the dislocation of received forms of writing and the undermining of extant genres and styles predicated upon an originary violence. How ought we to disrupt the constitutional arrangements that aim at forgetting?

Agamben's more recent genealogical account of governmentality (2011) infuses Catholic theology into an understanding of contemporary politics. Elsewhere, engaging with early debates in Judeo-Christian theology (2005), he focuses on the relationship between the ontological position of God and the choices made to bring into existence humanity as a starting point. For him, the idea of economy shapes and is shaped by how political theorists and theologians understand the presence of the transcendent in the immanent practices of governmentality: 'Immanent and transcendent order once again refer back to each other . . . only as a perpetual oikonomia, as a continuous activity of government of the world, on what implies a fracture between being and praxis and, at the same time, tries to heal it' (Agamben 2011: 89). He argues the history of power within Western theories of progress can be understood as a transcendental model of time managed and administered within the bounds of the world of politics. Thus, questions of temporality emerge from the economy of progress (ibid: 19).

Explaining the manner in which progress gains cultural currency yields insight into the crucial relationship between it and poetic temporality. Subjectification requires violence and appropriation of the body. While Foucault argues discipline could not be possible without a corporeal punishment of some kind, he also says modernity is modernity simply because there is no need for the appropriation of subjects or violence. Rather, the modern order's fulcrum is its governmental machinery. Foucault, of course, is ambivalent about the liberal order's violence and 'allows the timelessness of the [liberal] will to christen an eternalized present as history' (Russ 2013: 286)[2]. Pratt asks rhetorically: 'What were the slave trade and the plantation system if not massive experiments in social engineering and discipline, serial production, the systematizing of human life, the standardizing of persons?' (1992: 204).

Some critical and postcolonial theorists articulate schematics and alternative histories and narratives as the way to resist the fatal and flattening forms of life accompanying the anticipatory logics of capital (Kapoor 2002). Others deploy 'universalist' positions, arguing capital can compute any difference in its own internal calculus (Basu 2007). Fanon challenges such theorizations; the question of the colonial is a question of time, he says, and the precise moment when the imperialists and racialists attempt to eradicate those incommensurable to the social order, we ought to join them "in the fluctuating movement they are just giving shape to . . . the signal for everything to be called into question" (Fanon 1967: 227). Joining them at this moment in the space of instability (Ibid), opens up the possibility for "a movement of temporalization that is not simply present, or timely" (Marriott 2011: 54). This is precisely why colonial violence changes the way we examine IR questions such as war and capital. Accordingly, Fanon calls for a politics of a 'real leap' of invention (1967: 58).

Interrogations of time from the vantage point of the colonial, slavery, and settler colonialism point to temporal disjunctions accompanying narration, in conflicting or silenced histories or as symptoms of processes of global capital. In narration, time is said to be out of joint, as writing out of signification provides a critical and temporal lag in identity: personal, sovereign, international. Political subjects require moments in which to live – not just conceptions of time – and moments in which politics can happen. But how does the co-production of 'time' and 'political order' become imagined and possible? What if the readings of critiques of colonialism and imaginings of a decolonial future are inventions, the real leaps (the disjunctures and ruptures) of our times?

The moment and event of the postcolonial

Michael Shapiro engages theorists who turn the idea of time into a mechanism of colonization. Against Hegel who universalizes European time, Shapiro moves to 'alternative experiential bases for the acts that produce parallel temporalities', or the 'nowtime as city-time' (Shapiro 2011: 39). There are three ways of thinking and theorizing time from the vantage point of those who think, understand and experience the world otherwise:

> The way people inhabit time has a powerful ontological significance, so that to disrupt their temporal existence is to disturb their way of being. Second, linguistic practices directly reflect a people's temporal habitus. And third, one strategy by which peoples construct collective coherence relies on disassembling temporal contingencies as people and states spatialize temporality, transforming a dynamic of existence into a territorial fixity.
>
> (Shapiro 2011: 113)

These violent existential modalities of disassembling and territorial fixity speak much to the way IR and political science think, imagine and embody the political.

Such embodied modern knowledge production communicates significant information about the assemblage of the other and the time of the other, frozen in a 'tableau vivant,' a static, eternal primitive laid out on a graph, 'packed,' as Fabian writes, 'into a spatial matrix' (1991: 58). The use of time as a neutral, universal variable in ideologies of imperialism (or globalization) cloaks a system that carefully preserves spatial distance and separation. Placing all the world within a neutral, empty time, Fabian argues, 'may look incorporative' in that it creates 'a universal frame of reference' (ibid: 69). But the universality of time creates spatial barriers within which a temporally distant other remains carefully classified and ripe for exploitation. By circumventing or preempting coevalness, modernity draws lines zoning the world, conjoining color and time and placing the political function of time as a limit, a resource, a site of exploitation and ultimately antagonism.

We insist *the fiction of time* as a force coproduces subjectivity or competing histories or is deployed within a dispositif of regulatory power, be it colonial, neocolonial, imperial or otherwise. Time's persistence as a force, however, does not mean it is a graspable object. It is never fully present to itself or to us, yet it is imbricated with all living beings and materialities, inhabiting life as an internal, constitutive, imperceptible force (Grosz 2005: 5).

The most important initial criticism we bring to bear in our understanding of IR is simply stated, even if its implications are not. We have conceptualized IR and the political in IR in spatialized terms; this spatialization poses theoretical limitations and practical problems in its masking and naturalizing of notions of time in the formation of empire. Existing logics and techniques, such as science and the clock, have been central in the commercial, military, political and jurisdictional domination of the world. IR theorizations seem to have no use for time, thereby cathecting the field in projects that do not deem relevant the materiality of notions of time in projects of violence such as slavery, colonization, settler colonialism and imperialism (Agathangelou 2014; Blaney and Inayatullah 2010).

IR scholars have explicitly or implicitly evaded temporality in their analyses of sovereign governmentalities naturalizing, universalizing and secularizing time as a variable and, most of the time, emptying it of content, turning it into a dummy variable. The secularization of 'universal time' was crucial to the development of a Cartesian system of space-time coordinates because Judeo-Christian models of time insisted on its intrinsically qualitative and variable nature. Emptying time of its biblical dimensions rendered it neutral, a universal grid onto which, eventually, Levi-Strauss could map his 'cultural isolates' (1966: 256) in an eternal present. This treatment of time ostentatiously denies time's status as a socially constructed object with a technologically induced political agency, allowing the theorist to use it as a resource through which controversial events and political processes can be viewed.

We problematize this technologically induced political agency and its use as a source of knowledge. Political, social and global elaborations and complications unfold nonlinearly, as do our actions within them. Faced with these complications, these provocations, we are able to reconstitute and understand problems attending to conceptualizations of time; because we cannot fully apprehend and control the present, we make the real leap, the invention that affirms indeterminacy and the much feared excessive force of time, the world and life.

Overview and outline

This volume brings together critical theorists, artists and poets to engage systematically the temporal structure of the relationship of politics and violence, with a focus on the tensions between slavery, colonization, settler colonialism and the postcolonial event. As these theorists show, a disruption of dominant theorizations and their generated contingent affects begins by recognizing slavery, anticoloniality, settler colonialism and postcoloniality that persist as a series of events in time. Together, their work expands the anticolonial and postcolonial critique challenging the idea of the West and the Global North as primary temporal analytical sites and their citizens as the agents of politics against which everybody else is to be temporally sequenced. Such critiques open up the space for us to take time as the primary focus in our analyses of the global, world politics, ethics and revolutionary practices.

Much theorization of the 'past' and the 'future' has been undertaken in world politics, some of it seeking, in the name of ethics, to make the multiplicity of social relations present and visible and, therefore, intelligible and governable (Weber 2010; Zaloom 2009). Yet many explanations generated in different sites (state, market, university) violate the principles of ethical reason that claims to desire the eradication of violence. Guided by a desire to maintain a 'jurisdiction' in the production of knowledge in time, theorists turn their approaches/theories into sharpened prediction tools binding with, and feeding into, accrued commonsensical and dominant circulating narratives, models and affects that insert people, desires and even requests into familiar systems and categories. Instead of starting a conversation about a ruptured *present*, its 'nicks, disruptions or upheavals' (Grosz 2005:5) problematizing what it means to 'tell the truth' (Brugués 2011) about current problems, this theorization takes temporal 'breaks' for granted. The presumed interruption in the flow of historical social relations turns past and present into discreet temporalities, each possessing distinct regimes of order: pre-colonial and colonial, slavery and colonization, liberal and neo-liberal. These dominant approaches to treating life literally take for granted a 'totalized metaphysics of order' as their starting point of analysis without creatively accounting for the role that certain notions of time play in articulating problems or asymmetrical power relations and violences (Sahlins 2005).

This volume grapples with what it means to defatalize the present, that is, to stop pretending to know the end both in terms of eradicating colonialism and also liberating those who are subject to it. It brings scholars and artists together who creatively look at different worlding expressions (Agathangelou 2011; Agathangelou and Ling 2009), showing how people participate in and disrupt such violent strategies and methods of expediency as the laws, constitutions and democracies that abstract their everyday struggles, betraying them and their lives. By starting with an examination of these shattering experiences of betrayal (Mbembe 2010) and avowed promises, we can trace how imaginations become captive and how the everyday politics of expediency re-animates dead paradigms, modifying the reified substrate logics that turn sites into disaster zones marked with death.

In this volume we call for a notion of a defatalizing the present as that decolonial moment that similarly to Fanon is the "collapse and abandonment of all given meanings, all compensatory forms of commitment, including that of tragedy itself" (Marriott 2011: 57). The contributors ask about the production of the earthly, from the vantage of time and temporality of the anti-colonial and postcolonial event. What is the time of the anti-colonial and postcolonial event as it is inflected through the earthly? What does it look like? What does it enable us to do? Are the times of the anti-colonial and the postcolonial event and the earthly indissolubly related, so that to speak of these entanglements is to speak of a specific mode of temporality? Is there an anti-colonial and postcolonial event without its own time? How do people invent meaningful approaches that do not turn their lives fatal amidst the multiple violences they inhabit? What can those persons interested in (de)fatalizing the present draw upon to develop a radical earthly politics?

This book is divided into three sections. In the first, 'Contemporary Problematics: Tensions, Slavery, Colonization and Accumulation,' all authors grapple with tensions of the neo-colonial and postcolonial event, pointing to the untimeliness of their readings. In 'International Relations as a Vulnerable Space: A Conversation with Fanon and Hartman on Temporality and Violence,' we show the ways time and temporality inflect our imagination and engagement with time and vulnerability in world politics. We explore temporality as co-produced with a system of global raciality, and entangled with capital, and stretch our understanding of the sovereign and its historicity. In 'Time, Technology, and the Imperial Eye: Perdition on the Road to Redemption in International Relations Theory,' Siba N. Grovogui addresses celestial time and earthly time, showing how *possession* of time became crucial to the separation of sovereign powers and allowed the fiction of establishing distinct forms of legitimacy. He elucidates how historically produced sacral understandings and instrumentalizations of violence have emerged as an essential technique of life. He addresses how the pursuit and production of knowledge – in the technical, social and humanistic sciences – have become accessory to this violence.

In 'The Social Life of Social Death: On Afro-pessimism and Black Optimism,' Jared Sexton explores a tension emergent in the field of African American studies regarding the theoretical status of the concept of social death. Social death has recently been revived as useful for the critical theory of racial slavery as a matrix of social, political and economic relations surviving the era of abolition. This 'afterlife of slavery,' as Saidiya Hartman terms it (2008), challenges practitioners to question the prevailing understanding of a post-emancipation society and revisit basic questions about the structural conditions of anti-blackness. Sexton demonstrates how afro-pessimism intervenes in this global formation of discursive material, an economy of enunciation that resists the attenuation of the struggle for black freedom.

In 'Temporality and Insecurity in International Practices,' Ty Solomon critically analyzes practice theory, which focuses on the ground-level practices and background knowledge that make up much of everyday international politics. Recent critics suggest practice theory in IR lacks an adequate understanding of meaning-making and the subject. This chapter argues such concerns can be enveloped into the broader yet under-explored role of temporality in practices and urges practice theory to grapple with the fundamental insecurity of subjectivity by theorizing the interweaving of temporality and subjectivity as productive of such practices.

In 'Doing Time in the (Psychic) Commons: Black Insurgency and the Unconscious,' Frank Wilderson III introduces the concept of objective vertigo against the backdrop of the guerilla war waged by the Black Liberation Army (BLA) against the United States in the late 1960s, 1970s and early 1980s. Reading the BLA accounts and the narrative strategies of police confessions, he shows the complexity expressed by BLA writers about the violence committed upon them. He concludes with some thoughts on Gramsci, the strategy of the War of Position and the harvest of the BLA sacrifice.

In 'Outside of Time: Salvage Ethnography, Self-Representation and Performing Culture,' Wanda Nanibush analyzes Curtis's film *In the Land of the Head Hunters: A Drama of Primitive Life on the Shores of the North Pacific* (1914) and its multiple re-constructions. She grapples with time in the ways attitudes shift in film. Ranging from romantic representations of Indigeneity and the possibility of Indigenous resistance to the colonial gaze, to new meanings, this film becomes a different cultural object for both the more recent Kwakwaka'wakw communities and its intended non-Indigenous interlocutors.

In 'Impolitical Mandate: De-fatalizing a Port City,' Suvendrini Perera and Annette Seeman present visual and verbal fragments, scraps of autobiographical and historical stories, images and narratives that both cohere and diverge, communicating how 'temporalities layer upon, transect and inscribe one another along a coastline that is no timeless landscape, but an ecology that is, precisely, *in and of time*: a port-scape of human, animal and mineral freights, of multiple occupations and arrivals, historical and asynchronous, living and dead'.

In the final chapter of section I, 'The Productive Ambivalences of Post-Revolutionary Time: Discourse, Aesthetics, and the Political Subject of the Palestinian Present,' Nasser Abourahme engages a critical emerging notion of the Palestinian political subject. Reading the contemporary image in the West Bank in the form of posters and advertising against a re-staging of the revolutionary political posters of the 1970s and 1980s, he argues post-revolutionary Palestine, defined by a constitutive blurring of temporal markers, might be the site from which to rethink the nature of our separations of the colonial and postcolonial.

Section II, 'Neoliberal Temporalities,' addresses different temporalities and the ways they provide insights to think and understand a defatal present beyond the fatalisms of neoliberalism. In 'Migrant Day Laborers, Neoliberal Temporality, and the Politics of Time,' Paul Apostolidis juxtaposes Postone's and Gorz's accounts of time with comments from precarious workers in Seattle and Portland to show the jarring time fluctuations entailed in laboring, searching for work and dealing with violence on the street and on the job. Worker centers radically reorient day laborers' fragmented non-work-time toward cooperative political and educational endeavors, but broader alliances with industrial workers are needed to confront neoliberal violence in its full temporal complexity.

In 'Atemporal Dwelling: Heterotopias of Homelessness in Contemporary Japan,' Ritu Vij examines heterotopias of homelessness in contemporary Japan. Against a recuperative politics oriented to folding 'the homeless' back into the care of the self, state or community, homelessness, re-figured here as a practice of atemporal dwelling, outlines an alternative conceptual register of politics. Inverting dominant understandings of home and homelessness, atemporal dwelling practices defatalize the putatively abject zone of homelessness by constituting a social otherwise. In "Child's Play: Temporal Discourse, Counterpower and Environmental Politics", Andrew Hom and Brent Steele examine discourses about differentiated responsibilities related to environmental equity and capacity as instantiations of temporality in international politics. Temporality serves as a legitimating and Othering device, quarantining the 'underdeveloped' in unique and powerful ways. However, the temporality they identify is one of the multiple sites of struggle informing this volume, providing an opportunity to challenge Western hegemony via environmental issues, and counter-power.

'Childhood, Redemption and the Prosaics of Waiting' by Sam Okoth Opondo juxtaposes two child-centered short stories by E. C. Osondu, 'Waiting' (2008) and 'Janjaweed Wife' (2010), and Noviolet Bulawayo's 'Hitting Budapest' (2010) with historical and theoretical texts elucidating the critical locus of enunciation supplied by fictional children. In contrast with sentimental narratives and moral imaginaries treating children as foils for adult anxieties or those seeing them as innocent human victims in whose name we need to act 'now,' the children in these stories offer politically perspicuous account of forms of waiting, entanglements and everyday practices that politicize children's time.

In 'Temporalizing Security: Securing the Citizen, Insecuring the Immigrant in the Mediterranean,' Pinar Bilgin discusses how European actors have increasingly adopted security practices vis-à-vis the Mediterranean, portraying insecurities of the South as a passing phase in the search for security and justifying violent practices. This chapter suggests by temporalizing difference, one's contemporaries are relegated to a past where security dynamics are presumed to work differently. By spatializing time, one's contemporaries living in other parts of the world are relegated to a past world.

Aslı Çalkıvik, in 'Killing Time: Writing the Temporality of Global Politics,' engages with how the temporality of the present and the future are ignored within disciplinary discussions in IR, even though history in/of the present is acknowledged by critical approaches. Drawing on historical materialist accounts, she explores a different sense of a politics of time – a politics that takes as its object the structure of time that mediates social experience. She argues contemporary developments in global political life, especially the increasing speed in global transactions and the transformation in security practices toward preemptive action, are changing the tendency to evade time, opening up discussions about nascent conceptions of politics of time.

Next, in 'Hurricane Katrina and Bio-Temporalities: Media Representations of "Environmental" Disasters,' Michael Shapiro engages the interpretive frames within which environmental disasters are understood. Setting the early official and media representations of Hurricane Katrina against Spike Lee's *When the Levees*

Broke and David Simon's HBO series *Treme*, he reads for difference between the temporal trajectory of macropolitics (the changing official policy responses) and micropolitics of the event (the experiences and coping responses of victims over time).

Closing section II with 'Re-Imagining the Anonymous City: Defatalizing the Digital Present through Analog Photography,' Cliff Davidson engages how contemporary cities are constructed to be systematic. Timespace in the city controls individual trajectories and sequenced practices. Similarly, digital photography has been subsumed by the timespace of a continual present, with a resulting mass of generic images transferred across the globe instantaneously. The digital present fatalizes (controls, shapes, annihilates) individual trajectories and creative agency through a continual present. This chapter asks how *flânerie* (aimless wandering) and analog photography can defatalize the timespace of the anonymous city and digital present.

Section III, 'Poetic Interventions for Social Transformation,' features poetry by Nathalie Handal and Tsitsi Jaji and film stills and text from Alexandra Handal. Nathalie Handal begins with the poem 'Freedom.' Poetically, each word and each line constitute the instant of a relationship between two modalities of temporalization: the temporality of an irreducible creative life and the temporality that demands again and again the instilling of fear, regimes of legality and silence to evade the presence of revolutionaries as non-existent even when their temporality may be what enables the 'human' and the 'global' to be, that is, multiple-wording(s)/relations. Next, Tsitsi Jaji speaks and sings of the problems that intimate virile power configurations make possible. For her, pharmaceutical companies draw on people's energies and lives to co-constitute profitability and social order. Profitability as the organizing principle of life and the global configures an architecture inscribed with multiple global health crises. Finally, Alexandra Handal offers stills from her film *From the Bed & Breakfast Notebooks* narrating the border between east and west in the divided city of Jerusalem. Her contribution conjuncts the constitution of city soundscapes, the production of oral history of Palestinian refugees and her own video footage from east and west Musrara with a body search at the airport.

Together these final three authors show how the colonized body takes hold in a universality of time and a universality of relations of time to disrupt the project of particularity that has never been the concern of the colonized. Even in the most loving of all eroticisms, slavery and colonization are events of intimacy at particular moments that cannot be imaginatively transcended (Agathangelou 2011; Grovogui 2011), but rather ruptured for the real leap.

Notes

[1] To answer this question, we can draw a connection with Asad's idea of how temporal experience is made to be a political mechanism for the constitution of subjects. Such a bounded 'presence' of a world and a subject is not risky, dangerous or destabilizing to the configuration of the nation-state or capital. Bodily operations though such as

suicide bombing are considered destabilizing in the sense that their presence challenges this order including the problem of the limit of death.
2   Elsewhere Foucault's contemplation of death, and of a body that dies as an ascetic practice and a temporal orientation, allows him to suggest this neutralizes "both the future and the evil." See Michel Foucault (2000) "Hermeutic of the Subject," The Essential Works of Foucault 1954–1984. Ed. Paul Rabinow, Trans. Robert Harley and Others. New York: the New York Press, p. 103.

Bibliography

Agamben, G. (2005) *The Time That Remains: A Commentary on the Letter to the Romans*, Stanford, CA: Stanford University Press.

———. (2011) *The Kingdom and the Glory: For a Theological Genealogy of Economy and Government*, Stanford, CA: Stanford University Press.

Agathangelou, A. M. (2011) 'Making Anew an Arab Regional Order? On Poetry, Sex, and Revolution,' *Globalizations*, 8(5):581–594.

———. (2014) 'Wither Anarchy? Harvesting the 'Global' Bio-tech Body, Indian Markets and Biomedical Technologies,' in M. Mayer, M. Carpes and R. Knoblich (eds.), *The Global Politics of Science and Technology*, 179–204, Berlin, HG: Springer-Verlag.

Agathangelou, A. M. and L. H. M. Ling (2009) *Transforming World Politics: From Empire to Multiple Worlds*, New York, NY: Routledge.

Asad, T. (2003) *Formations of the Secular: Christianity, Islam, and Modernity*, Stanford, CA: Stanford University Press.

Basu, P. (2007) 'Political Economy of Land Grab,' *Economic and Political Weekly*, April 7:1281–1288.

Blaney, D. and N. Inayatullah (2010) *Savage Economics: Wealth, Poverty and the Temporal Walls of Capitalism*. New York, NY and London, UK: Routledge.

Brugués, A. (2011) *Interview with Jian Ghomeshi* on *Q*, December 21. Available online: <www.cbc.ca/q/>.

Bull, H. (2002 [1977]) *The Anarchical Society: A Study of Order in World Politics*, New York, NY: Columbia University Press.

Buzan, B. (1993) 'International Political Economy and Globalization,' in A. J. Bellamy (ed.), *International Society and Its Critics*, 115–133, Oxford, UK: Oxford University Press.

Chakrabarty, D. (2004) 'Where Is the Now?' *Critical Inquiry*, 30(2):458–462.

Critchley, Simon. (2009) 'Being and Time, part 7: Conscience' *The Guardian*, July 20, 2009. http://www.theguardian.com/commentisfree/belief/2009/jul/20/heidegger-being-time-critchley

Edkins, J. (2001) 'Time, Personhood, and Politics,' in G. Buelens, S. Durrant and R. Eaglestone (eds.), *The Future of Trauma Theory: Contemporary Literary and Cultural Criticism*, 127–139, London, UK: Routledge.

Fabian, J. (1983) *Time and the Other: How Anthropology Makes Its Object*, New York, NY: Columbia University Press.

———. (1991) *Time and the Other: How Anthropology Makes Its Object*, New York, NY: Columbia University Press.

Fanon, F. (1967) *The Wretched of the Earth*, New York, NY: Grove.

———. (2008 [1952]) *Black Skin/White Masks*, London, UK: Pluto.

Finnemore, M. and K. Sikkink (1998) 'International Norm Dynamics and Political Change,' *International Organization*, 52(4):887–917.

Foucault, M. (1973) *The Order of Things: An Archaeology of the Human Sciences*, New York, NY: Vintage.
Grosz, E. (2005) *The Nick of Time: Politics, Evolution, and the Untimely*, Durham, NC: Duke University Press.
Grovogui, S. N. (2011) 'To the Orphaned, Dispossessed, and Illegitimate Children: Human Rights Beyond Republican and Liberal Traditions,' *Indiana Journal of Global Legal Studies*, 18(1):41–63.
Hartman, S. (2008) *Lose Your Mother: A Journey along the Atlantic Slave Route*, New York, NY: Farrar, Straus, Giroux.
Hobbes, T. (1969) *The Elements of Law Natural and Politic*, 2nd edn., F. Tönnies (ed.), New York, NY: Barnes and Noble.
———. (1996 [1651]) *Leviathan*, R. Tuck (ed.), Cambridge, UK: Cambridge University Press.
Hom, A. (2013) *'Reckoning Ruin: International Relations Theorising and the Problem of Time,'* Ph.D. Dissertation, Wales, UK: Aberystwyth University.
Hoy, D. C. (2009) *The Time of Our Lives: A Critical History of Temporality*, Cambridge, MA: MIT Press.
Hurrell, A. (1995) 'Explaining the Resurgence of Regionalism in World Politics,' *Review of International Studies*, 21:331–388.
Hutchings, K. (2007) 'Happy Anniversary! Time and Critique in International Relations Theory,' *Review of International Studies*, 33:71–89.
———. (2008) *Time and World Politics: Thinking the Present*, Manchester, UK: University of Manchester Press.
Jaji, T. (2009) 'Sound Effects: Synaesthesia as Purposeful Distortion in Keorapetse Kgositsile's Poetry,' *Comparative Literature Studies*, 46(2):287–310.
Jarvis, L. (2009) *Times of Terror: Discourse, Temporality, and the War on Terror*, Basingstoke, England: Palgrave Macmillan.
Jasanoff, S. (ed.) (2004) *States of Knowledge: The Co-Production of Science and Social Order*, New York, NY: Routledge.
Kant, I. (2008 [1755]) *Critique of Pure Reason*, M. Muller (ed.), New York, NY: Penguin.
———. (2008 [1689]) *Universal Natural History and Theory of the Heavens*, Arlington, VA: Richer Resources.
Khayyat, E. (2014) 'How to Turn Turk?' *Eurozine*, September 17. Online. Available HTTP: <http://www.eurozine.com/authors/khayyat.html>
Kilgour, D. M. and Y. Wolinsky-Nahmias (2004) 'Game Theory and International Environmental Policy,' in D. F. Sprinz and Y. Wolinsky-Nahmias (eds.), *Models, Numbers, and Cases: Methods for Studying International Relations*, 317–343, Ann Arbor, MI: University of Michigan Press.
Kratochwil, F. V. (1989) *Rules, Norms and Decisions: On the Conditions of Practical and Legal Reasoning in International Relations and Domestic Affairs*, New York, NY: Cambridge University Press.
Kremeniuk, V. A. and G. Sjostedt (eds.) (2000) *International Economic Negotiation: Models vs. Reality*, Cheltenham, UK: Edward Elgar.
Levi-Strauss, C. (1966) *The Savage Mind*, Chicago, IL: University of Chicago Press.
Little, R. (2007) *The Balance of Power in International Relations: Metaphors, Myths and Models*, Cambridge, UK: Cambridge University Press.
Locke, J. (2008 [1689]) *Second Treatise of Government*, London, UK: Penguin Classics.
Marriott, D. (2011) 'Whither Fanon?' *Textual Practice*, 25(1):33–69.
Mbembe, A. (2001) *On the Postcolony*, Berkeley, CA: University of California Press.

―――. (2010) 'Africa in Theory: A Conversation between Jean Comaroff and Achille Mbembe,' *Anthropological Quarterly*, 83(3):653–678.
Moloney, P. (2011) 'Hobbes, Savagery, and International Anarchy,' *American Political Science Review*, 105(1):189–204.
Nolin, C. (2006) *Transnational Ruptures: Gender and Forced Migration*, Hampshire, UK: Ashgate.
Nyquist, M. (2013) *Arbitrary Rule: Slavery, Tyranny, and the Power of Life and Death*, Chicago, IL: University of Chicago Press.
Onuf, N. G. (2012) *World of Our Making: Rules and Rule in Social Theory and International Relations*, Columbia, SC: University of South Carolina.
Pratt, M. L. (1992) *Imperial Eyes: Travel Writing and Transculturation*, New York, London: Routledge.
Putnam, R. (1988) 'Diplomacy and Domestic Politics: The Logic of Two-Level Games,' *International Organization*, 42:427–460.
Russ, A. R. (2013) *The Illusion of History: Time and the Radical Political Imagination*, Washington, DC: Catholic University of America Press.
Sahlins, M. (2005) 'Hierarchy, Equality, and the Sublimation of Anarchy: The Western Illusion of Human Nature,' *Tanner Lectures on Human Values*, November 4, Ann Arbor, MI: University of Michigan.
Scott, D. (2008) 'Tragedy's Time: Post Emancipation Futures Past and Present,' in R. Felski (ed.), *Rethinking Tragedy*, 199–218. Baltimore, MD: John Hopkins University.
Shapiro, M. J. (2000) 'National Times and Other Times: Re-thinking Citizenship,' *Cultural Studies*, 14(1):79–98.
―――. (2011) *The Time of the City: Politics, Philosophy and Genre*, New York, NY: Routledge.
Singer, J. D. (1961) 'The Level of Analysis Problem,' *World Politics*, 14(1):77–92.
Steele, B. J. (2012) *Alternative Accountabilities in Global Politics: The Scars of Violence*, Abingdon, UK: Routledge.
Suganami, H. (1999) 'Agents, Structures, Narratives,' *European Journal of International Relations*, 5(3):365–386.
Tanpinar, A. H. (2014) *The Regulation of Time Institute*, New York, NY: Penguin.
Valverde, M. (2015) *Chronotopes of Law: Jurisdiction, Scale and Governance*, New York, NY: Routledge.
Vucetic, S. (2011) *The Anglosphere: A Geneaology of a Racialized Identity in International Relations*, Stanford, CA: Stanford University Press.
Walker, R.B.J. (1993) *Inside/Outside: International Relations as Political Theory*, Cambridge, UK: Cambridge University Press.
―――. (2010) *After the Globe/Before the World*, London, UK: Routledge.
Waltz, K. (1979) *Theory of International Politics*, Reading, MA: Addison-Wesley.
Weber, R. (2010) 'Selling City Futures: The Financialization of Urban Redevelopment Policy,' *Economic Geography*, 85(3):251–274.
Wendt, A. (1992) 'Anarchy is What States Make of it: The Social Construction of Power Politics,' *International Organization*, 46(2):391–425.
―――. (2004) 'The State as Person in International Theory,' *Review of International Studies*, 30:289–316.
Wight, C. (2006) *Agents, Structures and International Relations: Politics as Ontology*, Cambridge, UK: Cambridge University Press.
Zaloom, C. (2009) 'How to Read the Future: The Yield Curve, Affect and Financial Prediction,' *Public Culture*, 21(2):245–268.

1 International relations as a vulnerable space

A conversation with Fanon and Hartman about temporality and violence

Anna M. Agathangelou and Kyle D. Killian

Introduction

In the introduction to this book, we explored how dominant IR has conceptualized sovereignty and war (Hobbes 1996; also Ireland and Carvounas 2008) in spatialized terms. This spatialization poses theoretical limitations and practical problems, including masking and displacing time and implicating temporality. In spite of their ostensible differences, realists *and* critical theorists of sovereignty maintain their existing parameters when spatializing time (Walzer 1977). In this sense, the conventional dichotomy of space and time and the contours of their discourse obscure their shared assumptions and common blind spots.

Many realists present sovereignty as a formal, stable representation of an idealized vision of political order, a solution to war or brute violence; though embodied, these historical relations are rife with tensions (Krasner 2001; Morgenthau 1951; Waltz 1979). They contain an implicit or explicit axiological hierarchy, extrapolate an account of desirable political arrangements, and posit a stable and unified conception of the state and institutional arrangements and subjectivity primed to bring about that order. When sovereignty and war are used to produce certain behaviors, perspectives, or political outcomes, they work together as a particular kind of disciplinary construct that evades time, even though time binds them. The uncritical acceptance of this displacement of time from our conceptualization of the sovereign and war generates problems for our narration of history, the sovereign, war, violence, and political subjects. We must ask whether such limited and politically circumscribed accounts become the drivers of petrified relations and the mark of death, even when espoused otherwise.

Engaging with theorists who problematize the narrowly punctuated understandings of sovereignty, war, capital, and subjectivity (Hartman 2007; Marriott 2014; Mbembe 1992; Wilderson 2010) ought to yield insights. Even more important are Saidiya Hartman's narration of the entanglements of time and slavery and Fanon's account of violence, sovereignty, and capital. By superimposing time onto various other given states and racialized situations to show their 'difference,' both grapple with time in relation to slavery, colonization, and capitalism. They open up questions about sovereignty by creating theoretical concepts that traverse the gaps among theorists of sovereignty, history, war, violence, and capital.

When we think in terms of time and temporality, the parameters of the conceptualization of violence and fatalization of the present change dramatically, allowing us to consider the complexities of lived human experience and highlight dimensions of social life that IR and certain critical postcolonial theorists have seen as irrelevant. In this chapter, in conversation with Fanon and Hartman, we point to the ruptures/tensions accompanying material technologies/the inventions, the 'real leap's in Fanon's words (Fanon 1952: 229). Fanon's real leaps are radically untimely (Marriott 2014: 518). They cannot be *speculated* or preempted. They are a creative invention of a grammar that grapples with the 'form of antinomies of redemption (a salvational principle that will help us overcome the injury of slavery and the long history of defeat) and irreparability' (Hartman 2002: 759). Thinking of the force of time and the event via Hartman on slavery and colonization stretches our narrow understandings of sovereign power and forces of capture, allowing us to consider imaginaries, as well as the ways institutions such as the state and market consider some subjects mere flesh outside the dialectical movement of history or capital.

Although we cannot fully represent or narrate them, forces of time and the event produce problems. To a greater or lesser extent, we can mark their interjections and irruptions into life otherwise experienced as continuity: we can perceive their qualities, analyze indices of their interjection, and even make them somewhat predictable. We are affected by them; we intensify their force; we even precipitate their transformation.

This chapter takes seriously Fanon's idea that 'the problem to be considered here is one of time' (Fanon 1952: 226–227). In conversation with Fanon and Hartman, we show the ways time and temporality inflect our imagination and engagement with time and *vulnerability* in international relations and world politics. One theorist takes the idea of *time as a problem* of time (Fanon 1952) and *as a force*, 'arbitrary and violent, that positions [the racialized subject] globally' (Murillo 2013). The other ruptures a linear understanding of the sovereign and the ways we narrate violence to exclude slavery and colonization in its gendered forms: her notion of an 'original generative act,' with the 'centrality' of its 'blood-stained gate,' posits the ontological destruction of the black woman as the 'inaugurating moment in the formation of the enslaved' within modernity's violent arena of value (Hartman 2007: 18). Both authors take seriously the way the concept of time becomes a producer of a globality whose 'ontological horizon is manufactured by scientific signifiers' (the sovereign as analogy or anarchy as metaphor) and 'the political-symbolic weapons' (da Silva 1997: 5) that produce non-Europeans as non-existent 'untimely' subjects. Those 'who thrive in the mark of death' (ibid: 5) are not covered by the ethical principles governing post-Enlightenment social configurations.

In the first section, we explore temporality co-produced with a system of global raciality entangled with capital, stretching our understanding of the sovereign and its historicity. This global raciality encodes and embodies multiple orders of violence, with time a problem and a force, 'basically a fundamental feature' (Murillo 2013: 4) of politics that should not be taken for granted. In the second section, we consider colonial and postcolonial events that disrupt immersions into 'temporal continuity,' challenging easy conceptualizations of temporality and co-constituting a material indeterminacy. Slavery, coloniality, and multiple postcolonial struggles inflect the operating forces that disrupt, problematizing a present saturated with ideas about life as derivatives (i.e., financial investing in the future). We conclude with questions devised to contribute to the unthinking and untimeliness of the world, necessary to the collective designing of a decolonial project that recognizes and dismantles the mark of a fatalism and death.

Speculative times or speculations of the times?

We live in times of speculation and preemption. Time, slavery, and colonization are interrelated and co-constituted with the world and world economy. Temporal relations can be drawn on to determine the value of subjects (as commodities) and labor (in Marx's abstract sense) in terms of market principles. Paradoxically, while modernity projects consistently argue their vision is of freedom, security, independence, and democracy for all by means of progress in science and technology, capital is a temporality seeking constant innovation at any price. This market is currently in crisis. Or so we are told. Financial derivatives dominate market scandals, and, in turn, the temporality and politics of debates about the financial crisis and the anthropocene stem from financial derivatives (Agathangelou 2013).

There was a time before capital's spectacular self-imagining had fully colonized modern practices of knowledge, politics, and representation; still in the process of constituting its world, capitalism-to-be could not claim to have reached all natural or social limits to its self-actualization. Karl Marx calls this stage 'primitive accumulation' or the 'historical process of divorcing the producer from the means of production' (1990: 874–875). Outside Europe, 'primitive' accumulation came as direct force and theft: 'the treasures captured was undisguised looting, enslavement and murder flowed back to the mother-country and were turned into capital there' (ibid: 924, 917). As van Fossen perceptively notes, part of the primitive accumulation of capital is the use of time to exploit people:

> Accelerating production, exchange, and consumption raises profits and gives a comparative (or survival) advantage over competitors. The annihilation of spatial boundaries and the movement into new territories are particularly emphasized in crises, when the rate of change increases. In this 'annihilation of space and time' capitalism globalizes further and aggressively socializes new and existing workers into new time disciplines, while imposing novel conceptions of space.
> (van Fossen 1998: 66–67, cited in Russ 2013: 168)

For Marx, as Russ points out, capitalism is the degradation of human time on two registers; one 'corresponds to the history of our social relations and the other to the opposite history of our productive progress' (Russ 2013: 170). Marx reads capitalism as the theft of the workers' labor time and the 'extraction of surplus time, converted into profit, which is used to massively expand our productive capacities and infrastructure' (ibid: 170). Marx's argument is circular, Russ says; it reinserts the dichotomy of time and timelessness by focusing on the future, generating what he calls the illusions of history or 'privileged attempts by the timeless mind to transcend or annul history' (ibid: 4).

The division of intellectual labor among the forefathers of modern reason (Rousseau, Kant, Hegel, Marx, Foucault) allows punctuations of linearity, hierarchizations, and divisions of past, present, and future. At the same time, it permits dichotomized distinctions between time and space, masculine and feminine, mind and body to be mapped onto the anarchy/sovereign/interstate structure. These produced binaries exist as analogical correlates of time/timelessness, material/transcendental, mind/body, state of nature/sovereign, and security/insecurity, ultimately associating time and mind with order, health, and purity and associating timelessness with disorder, disease, and impurity. The projection of the sovereign's time imaginary onto a territory and onto the territory of its 'bodies' produces intersecting borders dividing mind from body, modernity from non-modernity, and order from disorder. When time is a linear movement from segmented and bounded 'past' into 'present' and on to the 'future' and vice versa, a progressive or developmental model 'convert[s] historically specific regimes of asymmetrical power into seemingly ordinary bodily tempos and routines, which in turn organize the value and meaning of time' (Freeman 2007: 3). To problematize this linear understanding of time is to acknowledge that within the lost moments of official history, slavery time generates a discontinuous history best told through the entanglements of multiple 'time[s] out of joint,' 'heterogeneit[ies that] can be felt in the bones, as a kind of skeletal dislocation.' Of course, in 'this metaphor, time has, indeed is, a body' (Freeman 2007: 1).

In its newer iterations, IR has systematically evaded grappling with slavery except for a few notable postcolonial theorists (Agathangelou 2009, 2011; Blaney and Inayatullah 2010; Du Bois 1999; Fanon 1967; Persuad and Walker 2001; Shilliam 2004, 2015; Vitalis 2010). Several scholars in other disciplines have written on the 'Middle Passage' as a form through which we can understand capitalism. Some work in the humanities argues the slave trade still haunts the market logic of the twentieth century; Baucom says temporality accumulates rather than recedes, and the 'Middle Passage' represents a passage into modernity (2005: 313). Thus, the slave ship, with all its overtones of illness, bodily corruption, and violence, is originary. A *lieu de mémoire*, it is the birthplace of a modern subjectivity at the junction of slavery and finance capital:

> [It] needed not only a standard set of exchange mechanisms, but a standard imaginary, a standard grammar of trust, a standard 'habit' of crediting the 'real' existence of abstract values, such as credit, with abstract 'slaves' functioning as 'a standard measure' through which to express the value of the range of commodities and currencies available for exchange.
>
> (ibid: 89–90)

He connects this to the Zong case, when the ship's captain murdered African captives by throwing them into the sea so as to translate their bodies and their potential for labor via insurance into currency and evacuated them of their singular characteristics by turning them into abstract (and universal) units of exchange. This facet makes it a 'truth event,' identifying 'not a marginal or local abnormality within the system but the global abnormality of the system itself' (ibid: 118–22). Baucom's reading places the historian as a melanchoic witness to history's aggrieved. History, he says, is not a 'property of the past but the property the present inherits as its structuring material and the property (both affective and instrumental) the past holds in the present' (ibid: 330).

The body politics and power relations made possible by working with time, then, link temporality and raciality, temporality and sexuality. As categories, raciality and sexuality are more complex when we think them from the vantage of the slave and slavery, especially the flesh of the enslaved woman. Spillers tells us:

> I would make a distinction . . . between 'body' and 'flesh' and impose that distinction as the central one between captive and liberated subject positions. In that sense, before the 'body' there is the 'flesh,' that zero degree of social conceptualization that does not escape concealment under the brush of discourse, or the reflexes of iconography . . . If we think of the 'flesh' as a primary narrative, then we mean its seared, divided, ripped-apartness, riveted to the ship's hole, fallen, or 'escaped' overboard.
>
> (1987: 66)

Making these distinctions depends on the gratuitous violence upon the slave, the object to whom anything anytime can be done and whose life can be squandered. The timely erection of this New World Order, with its human sequence written in blood, represents for its African and Indigenous peoples a scene of *actual* mutilation, dismemberment, and exile. The enslavement *marks* a theft of the body and land and the willfully violent *severing of the captive body from its motive will* and its active desire, all the while generating fortunes for the captor. This gratuitous intimacy may take the form of a capture of a body, a source of irresistible, destructive sensuality, its translation into potential pornotroping, a thing, and/or property, as attempts to 'emplot the slave in a narrative' (Hartman and Wilderson 2003: 184) or to incorporate slaves as sovereign subjects within official nationalist discourses (Spillers 1987: 66–69) may obliterate them.

This distinction between body and flesh (the captive body) is significant for knowledge/power and has a temporal politics in the form of evolutionary notions of flesh, such as throwbacks or 'remnants,' with (white) sexuality's development following a linear trajectory of heterosexual reproduction (Freeman 2007). What precipitates the possibility of a coherent story, Wilderson tells us, following Hartman, is the act of murder and enslavement. The only means of entry into civil society, history, and temporality are entitlements, sovereignty, and immigration or 'narratives of arrival' (Wilderson 2003: 236). However, within these narratives the 'black American subject does not generate historical categories of Entitlement, Sovereignty, and/or Immigration for the record,' as if this 'flesh' constituted through gratuitous violence is 'off the record' (Hartman 1997: 24; Wilderson 2003: 236). So how do we write those 'impossibilities to illuminate those practices that speak to the limits of most available narratives to explain the position of the enslaved' (Hartman and Wilderson 2003: 184)?

There is, in other words, a temporal gap in the production of a narrative that explains how discourses always articulate the slave as 'lagging' humanity, unable to be co-constituted even with work (Wilderson 2003) or integrated into civil society as a sovereign subject or sovereign laborer. These narrations bind labor in a way that keeps the afterlives of slavery (Hartman 1997) animated. How the black body is narrated has implications for the manner in which temporality becomes a dividing barometer of raciality: 'From the very beginning, we were meant to be accumulated and die' (Wilderson 2003: 238). The theoretical slippages from singular conditions to particularities or identities are one and the same, but Wilderson ruptures them, arguing beginnings in narratives do not entail the same kinds of ends for the slave (Wilderson 2010, 2003).

The 'time of slavery,' that is, 'the relation between the past and the present, the horizon of loss, the extant legacy of slavery, the antinomies of redemption (a salvational principle that will help us overcome the injury of slavery and the long history of defeat) and irreparability' (Hartman 1997: 759), has an afterlife. In assembling and narrating the 'primal scene' (Farley 2005: 54), the master inflicts violence on this almost-gone subject, turning it into flesh by appropriating it and transfiguring it into a 'fiction of power' (Hartman and Wilderson 2003: 184). In 'narrat[ing] a certain impossibility,' Hartman speaks to the 'limits of most available narratives' (ibid: 184). It is important that the writing of history not sneak in a liberal sequential registering of more slave entities that could potentially become integrated into a raciality matrix. By bringing the position of the unthought into 'view without making it a locus of positive value,' 'without trying to fill in the void' (ibid: 185), Hartman makes her own work, her own cultural history/literary genre, experiential rather than teleological, simultaneously challenging familiar stories and historical teleological accounts that presume slavery is a memory.

Devices such as focalizing the 'unthought' violences toward the making of slaves, the emphasis on the fifteenth century's ongoing effect on the present, and graphic descriptions of the brutality on the ships from Africa to the Americas and Europe are pivotal in making the past present. A description of how the positionality of black and white women was understood and approached differently during the slave trade has implications for how their positionalities are read today, including their rights and possibilities of freedom. Certain technologies of governance consolidated around this time included the evolution of juridical, philosophical, and narrative structures, without taking into account the slave trade. Take the notion of consent, philosophically articulated as universal but apparently disarticulated by blackness. More specifically, descriptions of the lives of slave women in the United States point to how female slaves as fungible objects differed ontologically from white women who might be house servants – subordinated but with the possibility of being free:

> Being forced to submit to the will of the master in all things defines the predicament of slavery. The opportunity for nonconsent [in this case, sex] is required to establish consent, for consent is meaningless if refusal is not an option . . . Consent is unseemly in a context in which the very notion of subjectivity is predicated upon the negation of will.
>
> (Hartman 1997: 111)

Slavery's temporality does not register in many of our accounts of juridical and international frameworks. Yet the ontological destruction of the body is achieved by violence, while value is formed to effect a complete disavowal of the body's existence. The key to grasping the originary (violent and occluded) moment of the transmutation of flesh into some commodity and value into subjectivity is found in the reconciliation of the binarism that produces and is produced by value.

Discussing slavery is important for recognizing the procedural modalities functioning within the ontological disposition of modernity as it relates to blackness: the primacy of carnality and the denial of the flesh structurally. This distinction is nuanced and elusive, but it is important to understanding liberalism as a set of politico-economic discourses that mediate a kind of sovereignty, as well as an experiential protocol that, through its specified *a priori* version of sovereignty, animates and translates property relations. 'Like women,' writes McClintock, 'Africans (both men and women) are figured not as historic agents but as frames for the commodity, valued for their exhibition alone' (1994: 215). To this, she adds: 'Value, beside itself, finds itself if only for a moment in the place of the Other, who or which is always without value' (1994: 216). Value, then, as both form and force enters the world accompanied by its fungible commodity, but this commodity is effaced by violences of value, thereby suggesting 'value is violence' and 'value is violence disguised or dis-figured' (Barrett 1999: 219; also Marx 1965).

The 'commodification of humanity' was 'grotesquely revealed' in the colonials' attempts to define the economic exchanges and ritual beliefs of other cultures as 'irrational' and without time, disavowing 'them as legitimate systems' (McClintock 1994: 228). The 'systematic undervaluation' of African systems 'with respect to merchant capitalism and market values in the European metropolis' (ibid: 231) obtained a kind of violence not easily framed by the knowledge systems of Enlightenment. Farley says:

> The zero hour of exploitation, that moment, the moment of capture, was the moment we were marked as Black. Thus classified, marked, as Black, we became a class, white-overblack. That moment, the moment of white-overblack, is the moment in which we were constituted as a race.
>
> (Farley 2005: 52)

This moment proffers the 'dual existence of the slave as person and property' (ibid: 52), when submission is required of the slave, not just to the will of his or her master but to all white persons. At this time, the penal codes of the slave-holding states weighed much more heavily on slaves than on whites. The enslaved, captive body had no rights, no humanity, not only before the law but also within civic existence.

Today, the extent to which the racially marked body was formerly given no means of redress in civil society has been forgotten, as has the extent to which ownership was extended to every white person. Yet the Middle Passage represents the primal 'scene that became these United States . . . Without the colorline there is no market. The market requires ownership and this ownership is an ownership of people that is displaced onto an ownership of things . . . The Black is capital's faculty of imagination' (Farley: 58–59). Similarly, Hartman notes the submission of the slave to all whites, 'prefigured' an exacting submission that extended to 'bloodshed and murder' and 'furnish[ed] a pretext' and an inducement to 'patiently endure every species of personal injury, which a white person, however brutal or ferocious his disposition . . . may choose to offer' (Hartman 1997: 24).

From the vantage of the temporal co-theorization of the continuity of slavery and black 'flesh' as producing social value rather than its resolution, Hartman says 'if the past is another country,' she is part of it: 'I, too, live in the time of slavery, by which I mean I am living in the future created by it. It is the ongoing crisis of citizenship . . . If the ghost of slavery still haunts our present, it is because we are still looking for an exit from the prison' (1997: 133). For some, slavery is an event of the past, especially those who punctuate a linear progressive developmental unfolding of events, but Hartman insists slavery's afterlives are present in all our governance approaches and structures.

Hartman journeys to Ghana in the 1990s to understand her formation as a subject and what it means to become expendable. She begins her autobiography with concepts of herself as 'alien,' 'stranger,' '*obruni.*' Yet she finds the United States inescapable, even in Ghana's sacred sites. US economic freedom and wealth offer a different kind of mobility to which local Ghanaians have no access. She feels scrutinized by an exclusionary and Othering gaze, assigning her to a national category she does not or cannot claim. Hartman becomes apprehensive about the direction of the journey back, marked by privilege not available to the Africans with whom US citizens seek to develop a familial relationship.

In her exploration of the Atlantic slave trade and the Middle Passage, she traces these historical originary acts to their effects on twentieth-century flesh, bodies, and subjects: 'I was born in another country, where I also felt like an alien and which in part determined why I had come to Ghana. I had grown weary of being stateless. Secretly I wanted to belong somewhere or, at least, I wanted a convenient explanation of why I felt like a stranger' (Hartman 2007: 4). Her feeling of statelessness in the United States sends her on a quest to identify a 'country' of belonging. But in visiting the textual and physical archives, she finds gravesites (ibid: 17). In the figures and texts, she locates only death; travels to memorials of the slave trade cannot answer her questions or rid her of disconnection, displacement, and loss: 'Monuments, like graves, are intended to preserve the dead and to suspend the past.

But everything I could see refuted this. I still thought of the castle as a tomb, but if it were, then where were the mourners? Didn't a gravesite require the company of the bereaved?' (ibid: 70). Standing in the slave dungeon, she realizes sites of torture do not necessarily constitute sacred spaces. Her body rejects the knowledge that the dungeon does not continue to be marked by the remnants of the bodies kept there. Her impossible desire 'to reach through time and touch the prisoners' is met by headaches, nausea, and the feeling that her body can no longer contain her or protect her from the accumulated filth (ibid: 118–119).

Hartman insists on the accumulation of knowledge about the slave trade and complicates the narrative. She highlights how Ghana's merchants first imported slaves, with Portuguese acting as the middlemen; they later became exporters of slaves for the American slave trade. She argues it is necessary to face the unfaceable but on the terms offered – the existing historical terms, not the desired ones. Yet in reflecting on her time in Ghana, she explains she will continue to lay claim to the accounts of resistance she uncovered: 'If after a year in Ghana I could still call myself an African American, it was because my Africa had its source in the commons created by fugitives and rebels, in the courage of suicidal girls aboard slave ships, and in the efforts, thwarted and realized' (Hartman 2007: 234).

Rereading the slave ship as a site of the fugitive is itself simultaneously a defatalizing (i.e., rupturing a temporality that relegates slavery as an event of the past) and an invention in time. It allows us to understand the formation of capitalism, value, and the subject within time by deconstructing, denaturing, and de-designing the relationship between 'the West and the Rest' (Hall 1992: 276) and allowing us to discover new ways of thinking through the complexities of the past and present. Speaking of Africa and diaspora, Quayson tells us:

> We must be prepared in our own thought to contemplate the total negation of what Africa means – before we can put it to good use post-slavery, colonialism, and apartheid. And this negation has to be assimilated into our own thought, not as an internalization of absolute victimhood, but as a productive means by which we simultaneously let go of and assert our identities.
> (2002: 586)

What Quayson calls 'negation' is being invented as a bodily repossession, rupturing the time of the sovereign and the time/boundary of value to point to the continuities of violence and to creative acts of challenging and re-designing institutions and the world; Quayson offers an argument for the slave ship as a temporal embodiment that re-opens our practices of reading, orienting us epistemologically to challenge the impulse to violently name and categorize difference in order to enslave and contain.

From fugitive to real leaps

In different corners of the world, finance capital is pushing for unprecedented domination, leaving people vulnerable with its multiplicities of speculation. However, the constitution of such speculation depends on a narrated radical temporality of the capitalist subject. Russ says: 'Timelessness is a branding iron used like a weapon to protect international relations and political economists (the most radical of all, Karl Marx) and their claims from similar accusations' (2013: 164). Speaking of how Marx works with the space between time and eternity in theory, he adds:

> The enlargement of the scope of Marx's project and science is directly proportional to the universality of transcendence, and the more things that are dragged from the transcendent, the more they help to widen the worldwide ambitions of Marxism.
>
> (Russ 2013: 165)

This 'dragging in' of transcendence has serious implications for the ways time and eternity become laid equally across the horizontal plane of notions of society and time.

We see this dragging in today through speculation. Speculation depends on a *salto mortale*, the 'fatal leap' Karl Marx borrowed from Kant (1793), who was referring to the 'death-defying leap' of boundless subjectivism to describe speculative capital's leaps into a risky future. A socio-political and economic process with a certain conjectural thought co-produces what we come to know as speculation, that is, to think imaginatively and hypothetically about the uncertain and yet-to-come future in innovative ways to constitute more surplus and profits.

To speak of 'credit' is always to speak of faith: the faith required to lend money and expect to receive it back with interest and the faith required to use 'money' – that is, paper whose value is credited by the state. 'Genres of credit crisis' denaturalize by making total and all-encompassing the fundamental uncertainty of an economic order in which risk is not distributed but exploited, not managed but created. Whereas the early writing in international political economy (i.e., Marx) defines property and labor, today's theories in IR and political economy respond to a world where ownership itself is increasingly unstable. Theorists are charged with describing the hegemony of a financial system in which vast sums of money and debt are 'bundled' into strictly impersonal 'securities,' sold and re-sold, divided and rejoined like so many Frankenstein monsters. No wonder the genres of credit crisis are characterized by terror and catastrophe. Much of the writing today in IR is concerned with those who dominate the economy by participating in financialization risks.

In contrast to the fatal leap Marx uses to describe finance capital, Fanon says a 'real leap consists in introducing invention into existence' (1952: 229). He can make this leap because, he says, 'I am not a prisoner of History . . . I should not seek there for the meaning of my destiny' (ibid: 229). In his brilliant argument on the 'time-lag, or difference of rhythm, between the leaders of a nationalist party and the mass of the people' (ibid: 87), Fanon reveals the underlying seriousness in European imperialism. The colonized are constantly battered down by militaristic and police forces and essentialized through stereotypes, which reify 'absolute evil' in the bodily form of the 'native' (Fanon 1963: 6). In other words, the colonizers are morally obligated to control, violently if necessary, the 'malevolent powers' of the colonized; this becomes the norm in a contrived Manichean struggle.

Fanon argues violence is inevitable in oppression. It is a mechanism in the language of the oppressors and, indeed, in all forms of oppression (Fanon 1963: 4, 8, 27, 34, 57). Jean Paul Sartre makes similar claims (1976: 720, 731) about the inevitable exploitation of economic markets, the violence of racism, and the colonized people of Algeria whose every action/reaction is constrained by the oppressive colonizer. Virtually every thought is affected by belligerent colonizers in some way, on the register of capital and in the global raciality matrix whose leadership is white. In a speech 'Racism and Culture,' Fanon contends 'the apparition of racism is not fundamentally determining' (1967: 133). Rather, racism is a means of camouflaging exploitation, and 'military and economic oppression most frequently precedes, makes possible and legitimates racism' (ibid:134). This emphasis on economics is not meant to belittle the significance of white racism. Rejecting shades of gradation, Fanon insists that, inescapably, 'a colonial country is a racist country' (ibid: 135). Like Césaire (2000 [1955]) and unlike Wright (1994 [1956]), Fanon draws a line between the perpetuators and the objects of imperialism while deploying a nuanced timely analysis of colonization and temporality that also informs his critique of neocolonial elites in *The Wretched of the Earth*.

In *Black Skin, White Masks*, Fanon calls for an understanding of the lived condition of blackness. Blacks' exclusion and violence is rooted in a politics of time, thereby demanding we focus on sovereign and capital violence from the vantage point of time: 'Every human problem must be considered from the standpoint of time' (Fanon 1952: 12). The understanding and the possibility of the invention come in understanding these violences (sequencing, ordering, subjugating and annihilating) in the present which cannot continue: 'Ideally, the present will always contribute to the future' (ibid: 12). In recognizing he belongs to his time and lives from that time, he pushes for this invention, especially when 'the now must be claimed as a place of belonging and self-inscription; but it must also be recognized as the gathering of all pressures that deny the black subjectivity' (Gikandi 2008: 3). Fanon shows global raciality is produced through a series of scientific signifiers, producing, enslaving, and colonizing the black and colonized body from a fictional conception that of petrifying blackness.

The forced exclusion and enslavement of Africans was co-constituted with an enshrined European modernity, whereby the African black was existentially and experimentally non-existent, with the European white becoming the pivotal figure in the possession of time. Indeed, the black is imprisoned with no sense of time in 'crushing objecthood' (Gikandi 2008: 21) and depends on the other for recognition:

> And then the occasion arose when I had to meet the white man's eyes. An unfamiliar weight burdened me. The real world challenged my claims. In the white world the man of color encounters difficulties in the development of his bodily schema. Consciousness of the body is solely a negating activity. It is a third-person consciousness. The body is surrounded by a certain uncertainty . . . A slow composition of myself as a body in the middle of the spatial and temporal world – such seems to be the schema.
>
> (Fanon 1952: 110–111)

Fanon challenges Hegel's idea that all subjects' awareness of alienation and separation is part of a dialectical synthesis with a higher self-consciousness and subjectivity. The slave is enforced in a community to which he does not belong: 'Every step into the structure of time leads into further negativity, death, and dissolution' (Gikandi 2008: 22).

In *The Wretched of the Earth* Fanon says the colonial encounter – specifically slavery and colonization – turns the Other into a commodity, with the slave exchangeable, just like any other commodity. But the slave also comes to measure and mean exchange, and at this point, he/she is fully born as an economic subject, although Hartman and Wilderson suggest the slave does not even register as a subject. The economic subject is also immediately a *semiotic* subject. The colonial encounter exposes the co-existence of a commodity-based epistemology (and constant threat of reification), with a value-based epistemology of race.

In other words, for Fanon, the Manichean colonial world is not only ideological but also profoundly material. There is nothing abstract or atemporal about colonialism: 'All that the native has seen in his country is that they can freely arrest him, beat him, starve him . . . Morality is very concrete' (Fanon 1963: 43). For him, unlike Lukács (1989) or Western Marxists, the colonial situation, including its economic, ideological, and geographical structure, does not offer the possibility of a higher synthesis in the now: the Kasbah and the colonial town are opposed 'and follow the principle of reciprocal exclusivity. No conciliation is possible, for of the two terms one is superfluous' (Fanon 1963: 38). And where time and eternity are written on the social landscape, Fanon rejects Hegel's master-slave dialectic, noting that what the master wants from the slave 'is not recognition, but work' (Fanon 1963: 6).

Real leap's creative force: Unhinging time?

Fanon insists 'every human problem must be considered from the standpoint of time' (1952: 13). Our temporal considerations must begin in bodily action in the present, a living present directed toward an immediate future that necessarily exceeds its own conditions. To explore the force of time, Fanon mobilizes dialectical thought to interrogate subjective and structural conditions of racialized existence, national culture, artistic representation, and historical transformation. As he grapples with the fatalism of his time, he comes in touch with contesting forces in the passing present. Consequently, he shifts his language to wrest bodily action and modes of identification from problems of dialectical thought, wittingly and unwittingly bound to colonial history.

While Fanon asserts time is at the heart of social transformation and the upheaval of race relations, re-thinking time and understanding temporality in a way that it is not immediately captured by colonial discourses and dialectical, phenomenological, and humanist categories remains elusive. He knows the traps of the intellectual history that wed subjectivity and history to an unrelenting dialectic, where the movement of history defines the human, time, and being as such; within a dialectic of being and nothingness, *the black, but also the Jew and the Arab, is on the side of nothing*, always making his or her appearance as the antithesis to the human. Even knowing himself to be otherwise, in this structure, Fanon cannot 'know himself' except through recognition by the Other, and the Other always responds with predetermined misrecognition, recapitulating a racist past even as he attempts to act against those terms. Whether turning to science, philosophy, or an aesthetics of subjective experience to ground his being in this dialectical 'framework of the world,' he finds himself reduced to a minor mechanism in the history of the world's unfolding of time.

Soaring, albeit briefly, on the heights of an 'unhappy romanticism,' losing himself 'completely in Négritude,' Fanon describes his dismay at realizing the potentiality of the 'unforeseeable' future (1952: 135) promised by Négritude, a movement 'designed to have afforded a sense of being, agency and a black consciousness immanent in its own eyes,' remains a figure of negation in modernist history. The affirmation of his immanence of being is devastated by Sartre in *Orphée noir* (1948), 'a date in the intellectualization of the experience of being black' (ibid: 134):

> [At] the very moment when I was trying to grasp my own being, Sartre, who remained the Other, gave me a name and thus shattered my last illusion. While I was saying to him: 'My Négritude is neither a tower nor a cathedral, / it thrusts into the red flesh of the sun' . . . while I was shouting that, in the paroxysm of my being and my fury, he was reminding me that my blackness was only a minor term . . . Without a Negro past, without a Negro future, it was impossible for me to live my Negrohood. Not yet white, no longer wholly black, I was damned.
>
> (Fanon 1952: 137–138)

Within this philosophical schema, Fanon foregrounds the inability of the Other (master), and himself (slave), to recognize a black/colonized consciousness that might be deemed autonomous, or at the very least, outside the mechanisms of historical time and Manichean race relations. By extension, the internal processes necessary to dialectical transformation are blocked. Reciprocity does not turn back to go forward; according to Fanon, there is no mediation, no labor of the negative enabling movement beyond the structure of a present that will not pass.

This critique of the dialectic is repeated in Fanon's biting analysis of Hegel in *Black Skin, White Masks*. It is difficult to misconstrue Fanon's tone in his scathing critique of a system of thought from which he is distancing himself. Even so, he adds helpful footnotes: 'I hope I have shown that here the master differs basically from the master described by Hegel. For Hegel, there is reciprocity; here, the master laughs at the consciousness of the slave' (Fanon 1952: 220). He laments: 'Without responsibility, straddling Nothingness and Infinity, I began to weep' (ibid: 140). To be active despite this damnation becomes Fanon's life project.

For Fanon, as for Hartman, the notion of temporality is tied to the unthought of modernity, the slave, the theft of land, the colonized. Notions of temporality in global structures, including capital, and modernity's institutions figured as a movement between dialectical terms and accompanying modes of existence, imagine and write the colonized and African as unthought and non-existent. Fanon's words express the effect of these notions on black and African bodies: 'A feeling of inferiority? NO, a feeling of nonexistence' (Fanon 1952: 139). This repeats racialized representations in the present, amputating the transformation of the present by generating the conditions for the reproduction of global capitalism's raciality (Chakravarty and da Silva 2012).

It is not a coincidence that the recent financial crises have mobilized racist knowledges to displace the 'predatory targeting of economically dispossessed communities,' with major events like the 'bailout of the nation's [US] largest investment banks instantly and volubly, recast as a problem caused by the racial other "illegal immigrants" and "state-dependent minorities"' (Chakravarty and da Silva 2012: 364). Problematically, this moment of financial crisis becomes an opportunity for further speculations to generate more profits. Mbembe comments:

> Questions concerning the place of race in capitalism and capitalism's intrinsic capacity to generate 'the human' as waste are being raised anew, at a time when radical shifts can be observed in the way neo-liberalism operates. In many places, the Continent is witnessing the consolidation of rapacious and predatory modes of wealth extraction . . . Both the logic of privatization and that of extraction are underpinned and buttressed by various processes of militarization.
>
> (2011: 189)

These modalities of approaching the present are based on speculative logics in the form of military or economic preemption, as in the MENA region and Greece in ongoing geopolitical reconfigurations. Uncertainty of the future seems a source for military, legal, and economic doctrines of preemption. Each site draws on a series of representations of future enemies to preemptively and predatorily penetrate the future to change it. Uncertainty becomes a site of gambling, of speculation, of possible investments for future profits and further thefts. Some politicians go so far (Greece, the TROIKA) as to say these penetrations are empty of political content and unmoored from the historical past. Each and every event is 'like no other,' a blank slate to statistics and the neoliberal speculative imagination.

These logics are maintained in the seemingly innocuous discourses and representations of everyday life, appearing in cartoons and other popularized visualities. Consider the following depiction of Africa's debt and its reproduction of dominant and easy conjunctions of the past and present.

The solidified and stratifying discourses of supposedly apoliticized tradition and nationalism are Fanon's target for analysis as he tries to help us make our way out of this capture: 'Intellectual alienation is a creation of middle-class society. What I call middle-class society is any society that becomes rigidified in predetermined

IR as a vulnerable space 37

Figure 1.1 Africa, then and now
Source: © 2012 Zapiro (All Rights Reserved) Printed/used with permission from www.zapiro.com

forms, forbidding all evolution, all gains, all progress, all discovery' (Fanon 1952: 224). Middle-class practices keep the present repeating historical divisions and Manichean structures:

> It is tradition, it is that long historical past, that is invoked when the Jew is told, 'there is no possibility of your finding a place in society.' Not long ago, one of those good Frenchmen said in a train where I was sitting: 'just let the real French virtues keep going and the race is safe. Now more than ever, national union must be made a reality. Let's have an end to internal strife! Let's face up to the foreigners (here he turned toward my corner) no matter who they are.'
>
> (Fanon 1952: 121)

Here we understand Fanon's expansion of 'his' international time: 'his century, his country, his time,' his 'present' (ibid: 121), sadly expanded sixty years later into France's time: time in these terms is kept from passing, relegated to turning over on itself.

Fanon does not limit his critique of national culture and the rigidification of time to criticisms of European national culture; he targets the bifurcating anti-colonial, middle-class nationalism of indigenous elites faced with uneven development of international commerce. In his view, although they initially offered a compelling level of potential recognition, the twentieth-century recuperation of black history, politics, and culture and conscious attempts to produce a black aesthetics expressing a shared heritage to counter colonial racisms, as exemplified through Négritude, fall prey to the historical apparatus of capture. These projects always produce a compounded alienation in which the 'native intellectual' is 'not yet white' but 'no longer wholly black.' When the European 'educated Negro' is not busy 'enlarging [his necessary] difference . . . incomprehension, [and] disharmony' between himself and his people through his preoccupation with European modernity, he attempts 'a forced belonging with them' (Fanon 1958: 77–78). Unfortunately, 'this attitude, so heroically absolute, renounces the present and the future in the name of a mythical past' (ibid: 14).

This failure to achieve the 'human' through dialectical recognition will always be two-fold. First, the colonized will fail to take a substantial place in Western European histories (Fanon 1952: 223). Second, this project will fail to express the people accurately: 'At the very moment when the native intellectual is anxiously trying to create a cultural work he fails to realize that he is utilizing techniques and language which are borrowed from the stranger in his country' (ibid: 224). The construction of a mythic or political past belonging to Africa will always remain a minor term in historical and ontological dialectics; a 'stock of particularisms' subordinated to universal being, it will operate as a rigidification of a 'materialized tower of the past' (ibid: 226) where we are sealed away, with our alienation hindering action, perception, and innovation.

According to Fanon, genuine transformation of the present requires the ability 'to *liquidate the past*,' not reify it (Fanon 1952: 121; emphasis added). Fanon is interested in a 'much more fundamental substance' of the people, a present perpetually in motion, 'which itself is continually being renewed' (Fanon 1952: 224). A relevant relationship of the past, according to Fanon, is intimately linked with bodily action and the unfolding of the present. Put simply, a politics of recognition, representation, and historical redress obfuscates the present lived reality and the immediacy of the future for which we should act (Fanon 1952: 227).

Political action, then, is the attempt to grapple with the theft of land, the colonial, and slavery in the present. Discourses of financial and military preemption and speculation (war in Iraq, financial crisis in Greece, global war on terror) attempt to contain global risk but participate in creating it. Narrative prolepsis and mystical narrations about pure presence or cultural and religious experiences lay bare the perversity of preempting the future in advance of its arrival, going back and forth between an eschatology of apocalyptic fictions, mystical experiences, political ideologies of the end of history, and financial speculations about the global crisis.

Hartman and Fanon grapple with the 'unthought,' the non-existent, the interruptions within experiences of continuity, and neocolonial, anti-colonial, and postcolonial events. They point to that which demands expansion of the ways we think, recognize, hear, feel, sense, embody, and act. Their recognition of time challenges the enslavement of temporality, without evading that such temporality adheres to the living with a force we have to reckon with, a force whose elaboration points to the power of history and our 'present' lives, not as determined or overdetermined but 'as signs of a new meaning-bearing event[s]' (Marriott 2011: 42) and radically indeterminate.

In thinking about time with Hartman and Fanon and in reading with them historical considerations of the past, whether official or critical histories, testimonies, or aesthetic productions, we recognize that the failures of representation, of narration, and of discourses have more to do with philosophical expectations that fit *a priori* institutional criticality and self-reflexivity. Marriott says:

> Fanonian real has no 'double' or mirror-reflection and authorizes nothing other than what it is: the absence at the centre of each representation or image. The real, in brief, cannot be presented nor written – and thus made recognizable – for, lacking any double, it remains resistant to any identification.
>
> (2011: 62)

This is the moment that takes seriously the vulnerability of our times while making real leaps 'towards the new nation whose time is always liberatory and whose arrival in general leads to a paradoxical suspension of time or tabula rasa that is also radically new' (ibid: 33).

Fanon's idea of decolonization, of a tabula rasa, comes from his recognition of the vulnerability expressed by the present. Pushing asunder intellectual and political understandings, tabula rasa is the figure that evades containment, enslavement, and capture. The only way to begin to acknowledge this is through bodily engagement directed at the future: the present is exceeded by a leap, an action that can neither fit into categories of history nor be eclipsed by its predetermined forms constraining present recognition:

> It is not enough to try to get back to the people in that past out of which they have already emerged; rather we must join them in the fluctuating movement which they are just giving shape to, and which, as soon as it has started, will be the signal for everything to be called into question.
>
> (Fanon 1952: 227)

By way of conclusion

Tellingly, *Black Skin, White Masks* concludes at the moment of responding to the crisis of Man – his inability to rise to the status of a God, coupled with the danger of becoming trapped in a 'stock of particularisms' (Fanon 1952: 226). Fanon emphatically but unpredictably evokes Nietzsche to shift his focus from dialectical formations to invention. This provocation toward a real leap and, therefore, a new humanity and away from either individual or national identification is reiterated in the conclusion to *The Wretched of the Earth*. Repeating his emphasis on the crisis of Man – in particular, appropriately, European Man – Fanon writes: 'When I search for Man in the technique and the style of Europe, I see only a succession of negations of man, and an avalanche of murders' (1952: 312). Fanon calls for a recognition of the unfolding of forces of time and the virtual in conjunction with unexpected tendencies of material forces in the world. This demands a shift in our recognition and our action. Provocations from the world, from the unfolding and folding of a continual passing present, coupled with the movement of time's interval, prompt creativity, divergence, and a capacity to 'combine our muscles and our brains in a new direction' (Fanon 1952: 313).

Bibliography

Agathangelou, A. M. (2009) 'Necro-(neo) Colonizations and Economies of Blackness: Of Slaughters, 'Accidents,' 'Disasters' and Captive Flesh,' in S. Nair and S. Biswas (eds.), *International Relations and States of Exception: Margins, Peripheries and Excluded Bodies*, 186–209, New York, NY: Routledge.

———. (2011) 'Bodies to the Slaughter: Slavery, Reconstruction, Fanon's Combat Breath, and Wrestling for Life,' *Somatechnics Journal*, 1(1):209–248.

———. (2013) 'Slavery Remains in Reconstruction and Development,' in M. K. Pasha (ed.), *Globalization, Difference, and Human Security*, 152–165, New York, NY: Routledge.

Barrett, L. (1999) *Blackness and Value: Seeing Double*, Cambridge, UK: Cambridge University Press.

Baucom, I. (2005) *Specters of the Atlantic: Finance Capital, Slavery, and the Philosophy of History*, Durham, NC: Duke University Press.

Blaney, D. and N. Inayatullah (2010) 'Undressing the Wound of Wealth: Political Economy as a Cultural Project,' in J. Best and M. Patterson (eds.), *Cultural Political Economy*, 29–47, New York, NY: Routledge.

Césaire, A. (2000 [1955]) *Discourse on Colonialism*, New York, NY: Monthly Review Press.

Chakravarty, P. and D. F. da Silva (2012) 'Accumulation, Dispossession, and Debt: The Racial Logic of Global Capitalism – An Introduction,' *American Quarterly*, 64(3):361–385.

da Silva, D. F. (1997) *Toward A Global Idea of Race*, Minneapolis, MN: University of Minnesota Press.

Deleuze, G. (1988) *Foucault*, S. Hand (trans.), Minneapolis, MN: University of Minnesota Press.

Du Bois, W. E. B. (1999 [1903]) 'The Souls of Black Folk,' in H. L. Gates and T. H. Oliver (eds), *The Souls of Black Folk: Authoritative Text, Contexts, Criticism*, New York, NY: W.W. Norton.

Fanon, F. (1952) *Black Skin, White Masks*, New York, NY: Grove.

———. (1963) *Wretched of the Earth*, New York, NY: Grove.

———. (1967) *Toward the African Revolution*, New York, NY: Grove.

Farley, A. (2005) 'Accumulation,' *Michigan Journal of Race and Law*, 11(51):51–73.

Freeman, E. (2007) 'Introduction,' *GLQ: A Journal of Lesbian and Gay Studies*, 13(2/3):159–176.

Gikandi, S. (2008) *'Unhappy Consciousness: The Black Atlantic and the Phenomenology of Modern Time,'* Paul Gilroy Conference, Institute of Arts and Humanities, University of North Carolina at Chapel Hill, 19 January.

Hall, S. (1992) 'The West and the Rest: Discourse and Power,' in S. Hall and B. Gieben (eds.), *Formations of Modernity: Understanding Modern Societies*, 275–331, Cambridge, Oxford: Open University and Polity Press.

Hartman, S. (1997) *Scenes of Subjection: Terror, Slavery, and Self-Making in Nineteenth Century America*, New York, NY: Oxford University Press.

———. (2007) *Lose Your Mother: A Journey along the Atlantic Slave Route*, New York, NY: Farrar, Straus and Giroux.

Hartman, S. and F. Wilderson (2003) 'The Position of the Unthought,' *Qui Parle*, 13(2):183–201.

Hobbes, T. (1996) *Leviathan*, R. Tuck (ed.), Cambridge, UK: Cambridge University Press.

Ireland, C. and D. Carvounas. (2008) 'Unpredictability, the Economically Secured Present, and the Open Future of Modernity: Learning from Koselleck and Extrapolating from Elias,' *Time & Society*, 17(2/3):155–178.

Krasner, S. (2001) *Sovereignty*. Online. Available HTTP: <http://www.globalpolicyorg/nations/realism.htm> (Accessed 30 May 2015).

Lukács, G. (1989) *The Historical Novel*, London, UK: Merlin Press.

Marriott, D. (2011) "Wither Fanon?" *Textual Practice*, 25(1):33–69

Marriott, D. (2014) 'No Lords A-Leaping: Fanon, C.L.R. James, and the Politics of Invention,' *Humanities*, 3:517–545.

Marx, K. (1965) *Pre-Capitalist Economic Formations*, New York, NY: International.

———. (1990) *Capital Volume 1*, New York, NY: Penguin Classics.

Mbembe, A. (1992) 'Provisional Notes on the Postcolony,' *Africa: Journal of the International African Institute*, 62(1):3–34.

———. (2011) 'Democracy as a Community Life,' in J. W. De Gruchy (ed.) *The Humanist Imperative in South Africa*, 187–194, Stellenbosch, South Africa: Sun Press.

McClintock, A. (1994) *Imperial Leather: Race, Gender and Sexuality in the Colonial Contest*, New York, NY: Routledge.

Morgenthau, H. J. (1951) *In Defense of the National Interest: A Critical Examination of American Foreign Policy*, New York, NY: Alfred A. Knop.

Murillo, J. III (2013) 'Black (in) Time – Untimely Blackness,' in *Quantum Blackanics*, 1–51, unpublished dissertation, Providence, RI: Brown University.

Persuad, R. and R. B. J. Walker (2001) 'Apertura: Race in International Relations,' *Alternatives: Global, Local, Political*, 26:373–376.

Quayson, A. (2002) 'Obverse Denominations: Africa?' *Public Culture*, 14(3):585–588.

Russ, A. (2013) *The Illusion of History: Time and Radical Political Imagination*, Washington, DC: Catholic University of America Press.

Sartre, J. P. (1976 [1960]) *Critique of Dialectical Reason, Volume I: Theory of Practical Ensembles*, London, UK: NLB.

Shilliam, R. (2015) *The Black Pacific: Anti-Colonial Struggles and Oceanic Connections*, New York, New Dehli, Sydney and London: Bloomsbury.

———. (2004) 'Hegemony and the Unfashionable Problematic of 'Primitive Accumulation',' *Millennium: Journal of International Studies*, 33(1):59–88.

Spillers, H. (1987) "Mama's Baby, Papa's Maybe: An American Grammar Book,' *Diacritics*, 17(2):64–81.

van Fossen, A. (1998) 'Globalisation,' in G. Dow and G. Lafferty (eds.), *Everlasting Uncertainty: Interrogating the Communist Manifesto 1848–1998*, 60–67, Annandale, NSW: Pluto Press.

Vitalis, R. (2010) 'The Noble American Science of Imperial Relations and its Laws of Race Development,' *Comparative Studies in Society and History*, 52(4):909–938.

Waltz, K. N. (1979) *Theory of International Politics*, Reading, MA: Addison Wesley.

Walzer, M. (1977) *Just and Unjust Wars: A Moral Argument with Historical Illustrations*, New York, NY: Basic Books.

Wilderson, F. (2003) 'The Prison Slave as Hegemony's (Silent) Scandal,' *Social Justice*, 30(2):18–27.

———. (2010) *Red, White & Black: Cinema and the Structure of US Antagonisms*, Durham, NC: Duke University Press.

Wright, R. (1994 [1956]) *The Color Curtain: A Report on the Bandung Conference*, Jackson, MS: University of Mississippi Press.

Section I
Contemporary problematics

Tensions, slavery, colonization and accumulation

2 Time, technology, and the imperial eye

Perdition on the road to redemption in international relations theory

Siba N. Grovogui

Introduction: Time, violence, and technology

The discipline of international relations has determinate and indeterminate relations with time, space, and morality left largely unexamined for equally determinate and indeterminate reasons. This silence is surprising because the *possibility* of the discipline itself is a function of time: its perception, construction, unfolding, and effects. These, in turn, are related to space. The perceptions of time traversing disciplinary discourses originated in Europe, leaving out other regional or cultural conceptions, forms, and formulations. This chapter considers the implications of the discipline's dependence on European perceptions of time. For a number of reasons – related to the relationships between Western Christendom, Europe, and modern imperialism – I will refer to these conceptions as Western. They brought with them the assumptions that humans could shape their fate through progress and social order based on determinate rationality and scientific laws. Human progress and civilization could, thus, be measured and indexed according to fixed standards of measurement and indexation of human actions and according to set terms of political legitimacy and moral acceptability of actions. On these accounts, IR represents manifestations in time-space of other equally time-related events: consciousness (resonance of time in the psyche); sovereignty (ownership of time through power); freedom (ranges and degrees of allowable or permissible actions); and sanctions for such actions (granting legitimacy or interdiction through violence) (Smythies 2002).

By focusing on the impact of historical developments flowing from Europe, I will highlight two things. First, the time-space distinction does not operate everywhere in the same manner in either thought or action. Second, the conception of the time-space binary and its modes of operations occurred along axes imagined in Europe, first under Christianity and then, following the Renaissance, during the Enlightenment. At these moments, European attitudes toward time become indistinguishable from attitudes toward space and toward non-European others. Unsurprisingly, this erasure proceeded from the erasure of other (non-European) conceptions of time and space, guaranteeing the removal of their psychic and intellectual resources from modern consciousness.

This erasure manifests itself in nearly all discourses of all perspectives in the discipline of international relations, particularly in the evolution and trajectory of IR, the production of value (or laws and norms), and the dispensation of justice (through war, peace, or other forms of melioration). In other words, whether the outlook be thematic (security, peace, war) or programmatic (realism, liberalism, constructivism), theories of international relations are steeped in European-born time and space distinctions. So much so that certain crucial dimensions of IR cannot be understood without them. The same may be said of disciplinary perspectives across the world, especially the English and Northern European schools of thought. This, in itself, is not an indictment. Problematically, the discipline of IR has endeavored to justify it.

A defining moment of our time occurred during the Renaissance with the secular appropriation of time. While this move distinguished between ecclesiastic and secular pronouncements on time, it conceded the possibility of relegating control of the operation of time to the sovereign authority of the Papacy while imagining secular time to be left to political sovereignty. This was merely a re-actualization of the compact between Pope Leo III and Carolus Magnus (Charlemagne) in the ninth century, whereby celestial time and earthly time devolved into two different kinds of sovereignty: the pope and the emperor. The possession of time became crucial to the separation of sovereign powers and allowed the fiction of establishing distinct forms of legitimacy. The possessor of time could also determine for its subjects (the flock or the population) the acceptable form of livable life, conditions of justice, and, for the emperor, the end of civil order. It is from the vantage point of the civil order that all forms of freedom, liberty, justice, and social peace could be imagined.

The religious connotations of time, particularly its coincidence with the sovereign, never left secular European imperial ambitions. One crucial area of convergence is the use of violence as a technique of life. In either the religious or secular realm, the possession of time rendered the sovereign responsible for it and gave him (yes, him) the power to allow life, determine life forms, and end life, if necessary, for the preservation of the realm. Sovereign violence – that is, sacred violence or violence without appeal – emerged as a necessary means by which time was given force and stability. Sacred violence became the exclusive means of self-professed masters of the universe to protect themselves and their pre-ordained destiny as inheritors of the Kingdom; dispense with illegitimate and false sovereigns who would endanger the Kingdom; and conquer and subordinate heathens and other 'unknowing' sinners. This outlook is a key structuring event of international relations, morality, and existence.

The entangled relations of time, empire, and subjectivity have been obscured for a number of reasons. One is epistemological and may revert to the question of differences between Being as the theologically derived ontology of existence, prevalent in Christianity and monotheism generally (Heidegger 1962), and the biological fact of life: a plural and multifaceted physical and moral existence in need of nurturing and sustenance, requiring access to requisite resources. Into this conjecture, violence intercedes a mode of differentiation and organization and, therefore, of subjectivity. In its association with empire, violence has emerged as the primary mode of allocation of power and value, making the pursuit of the technologies of violence central to the pursuit of scientific and moral thought.

The historically produced sacral understanding and instrumentalization of violence has emerged as an essential technique of life, with the pursuit and production of knowledge becoming accessory to this violence. The resulting 'militarization' of thought has shaped perceptions of technology, with implications for moral and political aesthetics and the possibility of adjudication of international ethics. Post-Enlightenment stipulations on the phenomenon of violence, judgment, and aesthetics lack sufficient distance from the fact of empire, or the secular appropriation by post-Christian entities of the mantle of 'eternal' and 'omniscient' sovereign with an indivisible, legitimate, and exclusive claim to the 'realm.' In effect, the Western ego has emerged as the sovereign and the realm, with privilege of force reflected in the ethical, strategic, and moral visions characterizing modern international relations.

The story of modern IR is one of a succession of international orders, each structured around sets of principles, norms, and juridico-political regimes provided by either a single hegemon or a coalition of the same, whether in cooperation or competition. Historically, hegemonic powers have proclaimed the justness of their instituted orders and, as such, instituted historical forms of justice to entice rivals into cooperation and appease 'weaker' entities through a rhetorical formulation of the common good. Regardless of the correspondences between rhetoric and reality, modern hegemons re-actualize the notion of *suprema potestas*, whereby the sovereign is the unparalleled authority. In this secular claim, kings, emperors, and their more republican counterparts are only a shade removed from 'eternal' in their pretension to exclusive 'omniscience' and the sovereign and indivisible privilege to define and enforce the rules serving as foundations for the interactions of all within the realm.

These simple predicates drive the maxims of the relevant social knowledge and orient the science of technology. Away from fundamental knowledge of the inner workings of nature and natural law, technology is on a course to an operational pragmatism (*techne*). The mission of the providers of technology is to imitate nature, not necessarily by replicating it, but by creating (an)other natural order in which the power behind technology finds a 'natural' home to express itself according to its own internal teleology. In *techne*, disinterested understanding gives way to context-dependent situations. Regardless of how it is understood (necessity, engineering, inevitability, etc.), *techne* is implicated in the crafting of empire in association or complicity with the strategic instrumental predilections of imperial powers toward domination. Disguised as necessity, hegemonic powers – much like the sovereign in the domestic realm – seek to possess a superior power of violence through the monopoly of the means to it. This presents itself as a guarantor of international stability but, paradoxically, reveals itself as destabilizing. The underlying arrangements secure a stable order only if other entities are convinced of the justice of the juridico-political regime the technology of violence is intended to uphold and, correspondingly, if the hegemon is perceived to act justly.

Herein lies the paradox: the dominant leadership is trusted to limitlessly amass and perfect the means (or technology) of violence while appealing to others to forgo the same. Put otherwise, on the one hand, the sovereign must keep pace with potential threats to itself and the order upon which it is predicated because it cannot give up vigilance by *simply* trusting others. On the other hand, the sovereign insists on being trusted by others who must dispense with the 'eternal' logic enunciated by the hegemon in its own cause.

This paradox lies in a space between justificatory predicates of hegemonic ascension and logical rationalization of the function of trust and remains a primary source of violence and instability in modern international existence. The two sides of this paradox express themselves in distinct fashions. The drive to hegemony is predicated on the need to produce the commons (spaces, values, destiny) in the interest of the deliverance of peace, stability, and, lately, prosperity. Yet the means to establishing the commons is conquest and empire. This imperial phenomenon is neither natural nor unavoidable. It presents itself as necessary only because of theological conceptions of life and destiny in which God's chosen must deliver all others through conversion by all means. For spaces outside Europe, the modern imperial phenomenon has interrupted other less drastic and dramatic processes of integration of regions into common spaces of interactions.

Divine violence, ordained and pre-ordained

There is a unique set of relations in the modern international order between the manners in which order is imagined, the extent of the allowable violence, and the end of violence unique to it. This is not to say similar configurations are not found elsewhere. Rather, the underlying dimensions of international existence are particular to the order attained from Europe. This may explain the apparent success of the European ethos of international relations, but no evidence suggests an inherent moral or constitutional superiority of the European model. Again, the discipline has given resonance to this model by purposefully gleaning from past authors' maxims, assumptions, deductions, and hypotheses to create the disciplinary canons.

This is not the place to test the validity of the implied theories, but many assumptions are internally coherent. The themes of anarchy, state of nature, human nature, and the associated promises of deliverance have generated legitimate and compelling discourses, analogies, tropes, and symbols that may be justified within the orientations of the base anthologies of ideas and facts used by those who formulated them: Niccolo Machiavelli, Dante Alighieri, Thomas Hobbes, John Locke, Hugo Grotius, Immanuel Kant, F.G.W. Hegel, to name a few, and their Greek and Roman predecessors, including but not limited to Plato, Aristotle, Homer, and Cicero. Of course, they are all mindful of the dilemmas, anxieties, and tragedies associated with life. For the purposes of this chapter, I am satisfied by the rigor of their analyses and the legitimacy of the ideological inflections inherent in the resulting theories of international relations.

Much melody may be derived from the tones and motifs of the modern theories flowing from the aforementioned – they are enchanting and continue to appeal to scholars. The tone was set at the so-called discovery of the Americas, which ushered in faith in European superiority, followed by ascendancy, and non-European inferiority, followed by subordination. The tone has been adjusted over time but has never repudiated the essential notes: the West must remain the paramount if not the sole proprietor of the will of the international community; the desire of others must be subordinated to Western hegemons; the will of others is substantively and constitutionally inferior to the West; by nature and the order of things, the West in exclusivity may define its interests to encompass things and relations in spaces inhabited by others with no fear of reciprocity. The question was never *whether* others should surrender their will, blood, and materials to the West; it was always by what amount.

Nor did it matter that the modes of evidence, particularly ethnographic and sociological, used to give substance and sustenance to Western imperial ventures were often dubious. Western canons have emulated the Bible: faith created its own certainty as myth became social science, and a form equivalent to methodology emerged to define its methods. One functional myth was that European (later Western) ascent was pre-ordained, if not on account of the Christian faith, at least on account of science, technology, and reason, with the latter becoming evidence for the former. Although the manner in which this 'faith' was arrived at matters, it clouds the most important dimension of international relations where others are concerned: the West determines the requirements of international existence, defines morality, and decides what instruments to apply to attain conformity or compliance. This is the case whether the matter concerns treaties or interventions.

Language, legal institutions, and armament work in this context as technologies of power. The purpose of intervention has been described as salvation (Las Casas – Sepulveda contest); legitimate commerce (Grotius's *Mare Liberum*); restoring dignity (to which natural law is said to apply); mutual benefits (Lord Lugard's dual mandate); guardianship (Mandate system); technical assistance (Truman's Point Four technical assistance program for 'developing countries'), and development and democracy. None can be contested *prima facie*, except in its implementation in the institutional instance. Here, the legal instruments regulating relationships between the West and others stand on their own: among them, capitulation, protectorate, empire, and trusteeship.

Importantly, the predicates underlying this ideological formulation of the relationship between the West and others suggests necessity and enforcement through cooperation or confrontation. In either case, the contemporaneous Western language of geopolitics has provided pre-ordained answers: redress through treaty enforcement, wars of attrition, and enforcement through military interventions. As a result, from the discovery of the New World through the slave trade and colonialism and decolonization, the relations between, on the one hand, continental Europe states and European entities dispersed through the world and, on the other, political and cultural entities elsewhere have been mediated by a language of command unilaterally directed at others: the assumption of the sovereign right to defend the 'national interest' and unidirectional extra-territoriality.

There is no standard of violence in this context other than that deemed necessary or sufficient by those with the sovereign right to intervene. Hence, it is almost an article of faith that anyone disrupting the prescribed order must pay in discomfort (military coercion), materials (expropriation under occupation), and sovereignty (stripping local sovereignties of the essential dimensions of sovereignty allowable to the hegemon).

This predetermination of the terms of the relationships between Europe and others has necessarily prescribed a commensurate commitment to the requisite technologies of intervention. One need not endorse Vijay Prashad's *The Darker Nations* (2008) to concur with him that European violence in non-European empires has been deliberately wedded to the ideology of pre-ordainment: if no longer the path of God, it is still the path of *reason and pragmatism*. In any case, to reprise an earlier statement, the idea that the West has a right of intervention is given, as is the determination to intervene. Related without dispute are the following: by faith or reason (or today's rule of law), Europe is responsible for those who might be outside it; the West is answerable for, and by right concerned with, what happens all over the globe; the West will generate (when necessary in consultation with others) the principles, norms, and symbols of communications through which assurances are given to the self and others; the West alone determines the values or standards by which conformity with and transgressions of its proclaimed universal values are measured.

'Just' use of violence in this context is measured by its propriety as technique, coterminous with an imperial desire, to bring pagans, miscreants, and other metaphorically fallen entities back into the fold. This can only be done through intervention by self-professed masters of the universe to protect themselves and their pre-ordained destiny as inheritors of the Kingdom, dispense with illegitimate sovereigns who endanger the Kingdom, and conquer and subordinate (once in God's name and now by reason) heathens and other 'unknowing' sinners for their redemption. This outlook remains central to modern empires and is a key structuring event of international relations, morality, and existence.

Time, consciousness, affectivity, and law

The right to intervene has ideational, constitutional, and institutional requirements. These operate mostly in the domestic realm when life decisions are made, particularly in security, access of resources, and their production, distribution, and consumption. In these latter instances, questions of the constitution and institutions such as the state are not merely standards for determining the propriety of conduct of national officialdom or measures of the satisfaction of citizens with the nature of their relationships with the state. Appreciation of the law, morality, and ethics appears in the national context differently than in IR where clarification is demanded in the relationships between self and others, between the freedom and security of nationals and of other nationals, between the security of one state and other states. The responses to these demands depend on intangibles and tangibles. The intangibles include psychic dispositions (toward fear, for instance), psychological factors (pertaining to, say, consciousness or awareness, feeling, and motivation) and symbolic resources (intellectual assets, knowledges). Together, these define the sense individuals and collectives have of the physical and moral landscape of international relations. By landscape, I mean not only regions and the mechanisms and institutions connecting them but also the flows and dynamics traversing them. The natural corporeal and non-corporeal endowments providing access to this landscape do so through the senses and are expressed through the faculty by which the body perceives external entities.

From the prior formulation, two kinds of sense are implicated into one another. The first is an historical sense (or appreciation) of the operation of the senses (or faculties) on its objects. This is determined by the psychology and other sciences of the brain. The second is a sense producing the faculties that is itself the product of their operations. One such product is consciousness, also a faculty. Each influences the other (Jay 2011). It is often assumed consciousness is formed through the interactions of fundamental entities: time, space, and matter. Each entity has unique properties, but all are intricately connected in the manners in which knowledge operates, previously by psychology and now by neuroscience and psychophysics.

To be precise, the relation relevant to me is not one implicated in the physicality of space-time or time-space. Rather, it is phenomenological – that is, the manners in which time-space relations are experienced in concrete circumstances. In this context, consciousness manifests itself as a factor of appreciation of time and space and as a means to integrate the dynamics and flows of time and within space. Consciousness is not the sum of all knowledges available to the individual mind as it synthesizes the landscape of social relations, regional connections, and human activities in conjunction with temporal and cultural understandings of the requirement of life for self and others. What is it then?

International relations does not depend on either constitutional self-understandings by states or observances of international legal stipulations on global coexistence. Rather, the existing constitutional and legal dispositions are augmented by temporal factors, including the imperial drive to conquer and colonize and related spatial affects. Whether these may be called national cultures or not, spatially defined entities historically internalize feelings toward self and others that leave significant impressions on the mind, shaping reflexes and moving intellect and body at the time of decision. These affects, the way they shape responses, and the extent to which they characterize actions can be filed under the rubric of affectivity.

Affects and affectivity are not so much the motivation or justification of policy as they are *sensory filters* that help process information expeditiously and proficiently. They are neither constant nor stable. They are as subject to change and adaptation as they are to manipulation and transformation. Two significant modern events have had lasting effects on Western feelings toward others. The first is actually a cluster of events occurring in what Queen Isabella of Spain called the Miracle Year of 1492: the simultaneous defeat of the Moors, the expulsion of Jews, the end of the Andalusian experiment in Christian-Muslim cohabitation, and the discovery of the New World. To Catholic Spain, the miracle of 1492 restored a balance among the faiths hitherto lost to the Crusades, giving ascendency to Christianity and Christians. The other event, dating from the Renaissance, is the advent of the idea of Man in the humanities and social sciences as endowed with reason, science, and rationality. The paradox of this Man was that it was very particular. I do not mean to say the attributes of Man were particular to the European; rather, Europe envisaged its own forms of reason, science, and rationality as universal and others as not (Trouillot 1997). Related theoretical constructions, deductions, and implications are not difficult to guess. They appealed to populaces because they rekindled in secular forms the idea that Christian Europe was chosen by God to deliver the rest from sin. Hence, in the New World, missionaries and secularists could all agree on the broad outline of conquest: a mission to convert native populations from their own ways to ensure their inclusion in new modes of organization based on new faiths.

Each event generated experiences validating emotive dispositions and altering underlying psychic states. The senses were the first victims. They were bent through false and actual facts to generate positive responses to the emergent imperial agendas through representations of self and others more propaganda than science. These shifts recruited even those Europeans at the margins into projects of violence and against the 'savages' (see Pagden 1993: 117; Pagden 1988; Starobinski 1993: 3). To justify colonization, native populations were presented as lacking kings, laws, and faiths (*sans roi, ni loi, ni foi*). The legal designation of subsequent administration arrangements attest to a supposed goodness and empathy or humanitarian underpinning of the colonial project: trusteeship (*encomienda*) and protectorates. When native resistance countered the colonial plan, the end of repression was presented in multiple ways, depending on the imperial power. For the Spanish, it was seen as necessary to preserve the self from threat to identity and survival; the British employed fictions of superior and inferior civilization in which key concepts (property, society, government) emphasized the 'deficiencies' and illegitimacy of indigenous governing systems (Buchan 2001; Thomas 1994: 14). Equally, ideas such as vacant lands, or improper use of the land, or claims that indigenes had no laws but 'custome,' and subjection to English rule would bring them to 'civilitie,' allowed a denial of legitimacy of existing governing structures in colonial spaces (Purchas 1906 [1625]: 224–238; Smith 1969 [1612]: 369–374, 438). Overnight, native populations became aggressors on their own land threatening to undermine God's work or civilization. Locke argued their forms of social and political organization were inferior, primitive and undeveloped (Tuck 1999: 42–45), thereby contributing to

Spanish ideas and practices whereby indigenous peoples ought not have rights. In any case, local resistance was registered as an obstacle to the realization of providential goals.

Much about the Renaissance and the Enlightenment is universal and positive. Consider art, science, technology, ideas and articulations of freedom, public and private liberties, republicanism, and human rights. Yet the related standards of goodness, beauty, sexuality, happiness, legality, and ethics acted as processing sensors for ideologies casting hierarchies of region, gender, and race along the lines of a patriarchal (if not misogynist) and racialized (if not racist) imperial project. No domains of knowledge escaped the tragic developments in methods and analyses. The mind was subjected to the moral likeness of sensory disorder. The senses, or affect and affectations, took over, leaving out evidence: erasure occurred in plain sight (Locke's idea that natives had no relation to their environment constitutive of property); narcissism contorted visuality (Kant's anthropology as it relates to the sublime); prejudice distorted observation (Hegel's philosophy of history, which succumbed to natural history). Hence, science and reason succumbed to ideological conceit, intellectual hubris, and imperial desire. While conceit and hubris may be attributed to the excitement of Europe's rediscovery of itself (renaissance), imperial desire directed the production of knowledge away from observation, inquiry, and understanding. The destination was now modes of understanding human or social developments, together with scientific and technological achievements across space, as natural and constitutive of, or in the essence of, time. In this perspective, ontology, epistemes, and methodologies became invested in designing time-specific moralities and ethics as timely and in the essence of time.

This suggests affect and affectivity are not without history or material foundations. Nor are they without consequences. For instance, in relation to the Arab world, it may be deduced that historical events from the Crusades to date – spanning the defeat of the Moors, Arab nationalism and revolts upon the demise of the Ottoman empire, and the Israeli-Palestinian conflict – have been narrated in conjunction with one another to nurture antagonistic feelings toward regional and/or national professions of independence, sovereignty, and self-determination in the Middle East. These feelings color the sense (Orientalist) analysts make of events; more problematically, they are often the only way to make sense of things Middle Eastern and North African to separate regional allies from those who are anti-Western, a sentiment barely disguised by euphemisms of autocracy, anti-democratic, rights abuse, and the like. In all instances, prejudices and clichés determine the range of possible actions.

Technology, violence, and ethics

In theory, the violence of confrontation has been ascribed to anarchy and the requirements of life in the proverbial state of nature, while the effects of this violence are frequently filed under tragedy. The label of tragedy masks responsibility for actions leading to confrontation and obfuscates the role of judgment in the decisions related to the means of violence deployed. In fact, there is much freedom in the selection and design of the means of violence preceding the moment of its deployment. The development of the means of war depends, first, on technology, or the application of scientific knowledge to practical purposes, and, second, on design, or the intentional planning of the use of devices, based on determinate understandings of their functions.

Technology does not merely offer possibilities for action. It requires the freedom to choose it, preceded by the will to design it. The advent of technology may, at times, be happenstance but, more often than not, depends on heterogeneous knowledges requiring assembly and purposeful design with an eye toward use. The base knowledges of and about technology are always relatable to experiences and, therefore, to political, moral, and ethical sensibilities, which together define the type of sensitivity an entity holds toward life and life forms. This is why technology is understood as almost always coterminous with a negotiated outcome or, more properly, a negotiation of the boundaries of the acceptable. Take, for instance, the appeal of drone technology. While it is difficult to ascertain whether drone technology has passed the threshold of the morally acceptable, US officialdom has promoted it for a number of reasons: it is cost-effective, it confines the battlefield to regions beyond the national shore, it is central to the ethical question for the US military about where it belongs, and it protects the lives of soldiers – *our* soldiers.

It is hard to quarrel with this predicate of the ethical when taken solely in the context of its constitutional formulation. Such predicates are constitutive of the responsibility of the state toward its protectors and the commitment any government makes to the soldiers it recruits. However, two questions are worth asking.

First, does providing the best equipment entail inflicting maximum harm on others? Second, are there other moralities and, therefore, possible ethical commitments involved in wars that exceed their national formulation? The answer to the first question is unequivocally no, unless we are ready to dispense with the ideas of proportionality of war and the necessary limits to war's ends. The answer to the second has multiple parts. For one thing, the quality of weapons bears no relation to the rightness, legality, or legitimacy of the cause. For another, equally important under international law, winning a war might require one set of combatants to dispense with the capacities of another to fight. This principle is not just understood in constitutional terms, but falls under the purview of international law. Since the Geneva Conventions, international jurisprudence holds there are no justifications for exposing non-combatants and inoffensive entities to harm during war. This principle clearly conflicts with the avowed purpose of drones to make the enemies (combatants) and surrounding populations bear the cost of war as a necessary trade-off for the peace of one nation, region, or group of nation-states.

The co-constitution of technology and subjectivity is disguised in the language of cost, efficiency, and progress. Its reality is revealed in decisions on and distinctions in citizenship and foreignness that revert to the question of eternal life chosenness, on the one hand, and necessarily dispensable life, on the other. The privilege of life is tied to the preservation of time, while the fate of death is bequeathed to the enemies of the eternal: time as unending goodness or, in a more secular index, property-dependent civil society; rule-of-law good governance; reason-bound morality; capitalist-induced progress; liberal democracy; and so forth. This is not hyperbole. Two reactions to drone warfare prove this point. The first was Americans' reactions to the US government's acknowledgment it had *inadvertently* killed Western hostages: US citizen Warren Weinstein and Italian citizen Giovanni Lo Porto. The other was the scandal when it was revealed police across the US were increasingly deploying military-style equipment in cities to quell riots. The outrage was not in the use of killer drones (despite the cost to bystanders) or that armored vehicles and rocket-propelled grenades could be used in urban settings. It was not even that such weapons should be developed. It was that these weapons belong to combats in different spaces (non-Western), where the terms of morality and ethics function differently and lives lived do not accord with the principles of 'our time.'

Similar decisions are made about smart bombs, designed to wage a kind of war about which there have been longstanding prohibitions. Urban warfare must be avoided at all costs for fear of its indiscriminateness and unpredictable consequences. Pablo Picasso's *Guernica*, a mural-size canvas, demonstrates its transgression during the Spanish Civil War, movingly relating the horrors of indiscriminate war. The work retains its poignancy: it was covered by a blue curtain during Colin Powell's presentation leading to the US invasion of Iraq. Obliterating it from consciousness through disguise or removal from public spaces portends something more sinister. Discomfort and the ensuing erasure of *Guernica* coincided with the advent of laser-guided weapons, a technology able to dispense with moral prohibitions against urban warfare. In this case, technology emerged as the means to fix a moral quandary. Smart weapons and their laser-guided targeting systems brought the promise of pinpointing a target in cities and large urban agglomerations with little damage beyond their target. The citizenry could relax as the civilian populations surrounding such targets would be unscathed. As the US invasion of Iraq and Israeli interventions in the West Bank and Gaza have shown, smart bombs are not always smart; they can be defective or the target misidentified. Luckily for the users of such bombs, and sadly for the victims, there is no commensurate international jurisprudence to deter their use to date. These weapons pose a moral quandary: either they are smart, and all their victims are deliberately targeted, or they are not sufficiently smart and do not justify dispensing with prohibitions against urban warfare.

It is an interesting question to ask how citizens of Western states accommodate the new technologies of war. One answer might be cultural recruitment; due to Western faith in science and technology, such technologies are branded as offering easy solutions to difficult questions. Respect for technology becomes a convenient pedagogical tool to collapse the analytical walls between, first, virtue and skill (a la Aristotle) and, second, between *virtù* as fortitude and *fortuna* as chance (Machiavelli). With each subsequent conflation, we inch closer to dispensing with longstanding philosophical formulations of the relationships between humans, science, and technology that set technical life (Heidegger) apart from praxis, a non-technical conception of moral life. The other answer to the question of accommodation is that citizens overcome moral squeamishness through their 'certainty' that these weapons will be used appropriately, only against those deserving death on account of their sinful ways against life and its requirements (as determined by Western expectations) and terms. Again, these terms are proposed as conditions of war where the other reforms, surrenders, or dies!

The open opportunity to embrace military technology and to instigate its deployment is a defining feature of our time. It has led to over-reliance on military solutions in foreign policy where once diplomacy was the first recourse. It has led to the militarization of thought: faith in the inevitability of military action and participation in rendering such solutions palatable to the senses and effective on the ground. The militarization of science and technology is only matched by a parallel militarization of society, whereby social networks and human activities either contribute to or are oriented toward the production, distribution, and consumption of military goods, values, and services. In this manner, the systems of production, distribution, and consumption within society are undistinguishable from military necessities.

There is a contradiction in the manner in which the imperial will is inserted in the operations of time: deliverance (through reform or conversion to Western ways) requires acceptance by the others of the inscriptions of time in technology and vice versa. In the first instance, the others must appreciate and understand Western understandings of time and their relations to the technologies and sciences of life and death as proper, eternal, and universal. In the second, the others must accept this universal time on cultural terms that are essentially Western. In fact, these terms are the conditions of legitimacy of proselytism: time proper (as opposed to proper time) is properly so because it was Christened and legitimately bequeathed to the West through, first, Christianity and, then, reason and science. Under the terms of time thusly defined, there is no deliverance without uniform understandings of time as eternal, uninterrupted, uninterruptible, Christened, and Western. The paradox erupts upon conversion to the very cultural Western notion of time. Conversion is necessary to assure mutual legibility of the requirements of time: the converted are guaranteed salvation as equal members of the realm. It promises the same path to paradise: the promises of the realm to lead a secured life and to defend such life with the same passion and technology as reason and science allow. This path requires vigilance against temptations and the possibility of corruption. Corruption and temptation are universal problems; all faithful would do well to guard against them and prepare to confront their primary purveyor: Satan. This is a call to arms and a call to prepare to surpass Satan technologically as a means of preserving time.

Conclusion: Technology and aesthetic experiences

It is a puzzle and a paradox that so much debate and energy are spent on the dangers of non-normative use of violence by entities that, however cruel, produce neither the means of violence nor the legitimacy for their uses. Besides condemning terrorist groups and other non-state and irregular forces, the discipline of IR should concern itself with the objective and subjective features of human existence. To be sure, life is not characterized merely by biological processes, and these processes are not independent of the social realities constructed around them to support them or potentially end them. Related questions – whether formulated as moral, legal, political, or ethical issues – hold the key to life, the quality of life, and possible life-forms.

Technology demarcates (biological) existence from productive life and in so doing is a key determinant of the ways humans live life. It determines whether processes of life are self-sustaining or autoimmune and bent on self-destruction. From this perspective, technology is not inanimate. Much like an actant in linguistics enables conjugation of the main verb, technology acts as a window into the function assigned to moral thought that anticipates actions. Analogically, the function of technology may be to surrender to viruses, pernicious forms of thought undermining the deployment of knowledge of techniques, processes, and resulting machines, computers, and other devices toward the betterment of the species over time, not the satisfaction of temporal needs in the short term.

One sad, hopefully provisional, conclusion is that modern humans have been enamored with the technologies of violence for such a long time that the intentional use of physical force to end life has become a plausible solution to crises. This plausibility rests in temporality, whereby solutions to conflicts can only be contemplated preemptively to coordinate and secure a 'now.' Without leaving room for future engagements, the interests of others and the collective, any collective, must be subordinated to instant gains, no matter the likelihood of grave physical and psychological harms. Technology has become its own episteme, ontology, and teleology. Military technology, for instance, is designed with an inclusive intentionality to inflict maximum harm on specified targets, pinpointed via radars, satellites, positioning devices, and microchips. The incorporated time scale is calculated on the basis of the moment of decision when the trigger is engaged and 'enemies' meet their end.

From a political perspective, this vision of time and the relations between it and life eliminate certain forms of politics, including provisions for infinity in diplomacy: infinite permutations of situations or infinite opportunities to change course. This invites the indeterminacy of responsibility to self and others, not to mention future generations and nature itself. Specifically, security politics must be construed against the backdrop of a possible apocalypse or the possibility of the end of time as the end of politics. This possibility of the impossibility of a politics of life (of restoration and preservation of life) negatively fixes relations between the fact of tragedy (the original sin or conflict context of life) and the deliverance of hope (or the collective ability to produce a philosophy of life that is at least minimally redemptive) in favor of doom, abuses of power, evasion of responsibility toward others, subordination of life to the requirements of the ego, enslavement to a conjured-up necessity of survival (as opposed to being bound by necessity), and surrender to fear.

The latter has already occurred and is the principal affective feature of international relations. Since September 11, 2001, in the US, thought has been in the grip of fear of mortal enemies of life and civilization. This clouds discussions of national and international life, the rights of citizens, and civil liberties – in short, obfuscating political and moral subjectivity. This affectivity, although predictable, could not have lasted without factors discussed earlier. It has structured how US officialdom and academics imagine sovereignty and civic life. In the name of sovereignty, the Patriot Act sanctions acts bordering on international illegality, including the confirmation of the categories of illegal combatants and preemptive deterrence, as well as a prison for war crimes outside national jurisdiction.

Historically, the right to respond to threat is an exercise in the art of life: life must be defended for its sustenance. To respond to threat is not necessarily to put life in danger, even the life of the enemy. Threat is often topical and precise, so in international law and theology, the response to threat is legitimate when proportionate and timely. Preemptive deterrence, by contrast, approximates a politics of death. Since the nature of the threat is never clear and must be assumed to persist as long as the enemy is alive, there is no commensurate protection against its potential (evil) act but to eliminate the source. Hence the fear of drones and future killer or self-triggered robots designed to operate on the basis of pre-programmed algorithms of suspect behavior to sniff out and eliminate potential threats before they materialize.

Theories of IR must propose a philosophy of life that offers more than cynicism. The cultural spaces of the production of knowledge and technology cannot be the sole province of the initiates. Although they may be the product of the labor of initiates, their infrastructure and end must be provided by the larger collective. The latter may initiate and control the processes of production but must share the networks of distribution with fellow citizens. Further, the initiates must not control the processes of consumption or uses of technology. This last point is a cautionary note to theorists and engineers. Technology is always ultimately inserted into symbolic spaces of life of which all members of society are aware and for which they collectively bear responsibility. Producers of knowledge and technology are not unaware of social processes and their hierarchies of values and norms. They know the status of social bodies within and without national borders. They know what laws exist and how they set people apart or together.

The means of war – weapons, ammunitions, tracking devices, and surveillance technologies – affect morality, identity, and life. Technology is a governing temporal modality. It helps control, confine, and even destroy life. Everything that matters in life matters in relation to life. The oaths of loyalty to country, national ideologies, and propaganda matter to the context of production of knowledge. Rightly so. But they cannot unite everyone into a single subject while desiring to circumvent the tensions of seemingly irreducible differences in favor of a fiction of a stable, unified persistence across time. They cannot, and ought not to, deter from the larger responsibility to contribute that which is right and, in the process, build the commensurate collective attitude about what it means to live a moral and purposeful life. In this regard, engineers operate in different domains than social scientists. We have different kinds of responsibility. As social scientists, ours is shedding light on the cultural determinants of the aesthetic life across the planet, investigating other peoples' sensibilities commensurate with their modes of existence, accurately representing the nature of relationships among the entities that constitute the international order, offering parameters for conflict resolutions, and proposing principles of interactions whose predicates, assumptions, and teleologies inspire the confidence and trust of others – or their contempt and fear. This last point is important because the legitimacy and translatability of discourses do not depend solely on reason. They exceed the limits of reason and play within the limits of reason. What matters is that theory for our (pre-apocalyptic) time offers resources to sustain life everywhere and institutions to guarantee access to life for all. This is the only way toward a modicum of salvation.

Alternatively, we can continue to shroud our theoretical edifices within scaffoldings of myths, self-serving moral axioms, convenient ethical injunctions, and untenable political privileges. This may be soothing. But it is not the science of the times, as it may easily dispense with all the requirements of knowledge. Nor is it wisdom. Rather, it is the road to perdition.

Bibliography

Buchan, B. (2001) 'Subjecting the Natives: Aborigines, Property and Possession under Early Colonial Rule,' *Social Analysis* 45(2):143–162.

Heidegger, M. (1962) *Being and Time*, John Macquarrie and Edward Robinson (trans.), New York, NY: Harper & Row.

Jay, M. (2011) 'In the Realm of the Senses: An Introduction,' *American Historical Review*, 116(2):307–315.

Locke, J. (1970 [1690]) *An Essay Concerning Human Understanding*, J. Yolton (ed.), London, UK: J. M. Dent.

———. (1988 [1690]) *Two Treatises of Government*, P. Laslett (ed.), Cambridge, UK: Cambridge University Press.

———. (1993) 'Credit, Disgrace,' in D. Wootton (ed.), *Political Writings of John Locke*, 39–67, New York, NY: Mentor.

Pagden, A. (1988) 'The 'Defence of Civilisation' in Eighteenth-Century Social Theory,' *History of the Human Sciences*, 1(1):33–45.

———. (1993) *European Encounters with the New World: From Renaissance to Romanticism*, New Haven, CT: Yale University Press.

———. (1995) *Lords of All the World*, New Haven, CT: Yale University Press.

Prashad, V. (2008) *The Darker Nations: A People's History of the Third World*, New York, NY: New Press.

Purchas, S. (1906 [1625]) *Hakluytus Posthumus or Purchas His Pilgrimes*, Vol. 19, Glasgow, Scotland, UK: James MacLehose.

Smith, J. (1969 [1612]) 'A Map of Virginia,' in P. L. Barvour (ed.), *The Jamestown Voyages under the First Charter 1606–1609*, Vol. 2, 369–374, Cambridge, MA: Hakluyt Society.

Starobinski, J. (1993) *Blessings in Disguise; Or, the Morality of Evil*, A. Goldhammer (trans.), Cambridge, Oxford: Polity.

Trouillot, M. R. (1997) *Silencing the Past: Power and the Production of History*, Boston, MA: Allyn and Bacon.

3 The social life of social death
On afro-pessimism and black optimism

Jared Sexton

> What's at stake is fugitive movement in and out of the frame, bar, or whatever externally imposed social logic – a movement of escape, the stealth of the stolen that can be said . . . to break *every* enclosure. This fugitive movement is stolen life, and its relation to law is reducible neither to simple interdiction nor bare transgression.
>
> (Moten 2008b: 179)

> Such gatherings are always haunted by a sense that violence and captivity are the grammar and ghosts of our *every* gesture. This is where performance meets ontology.
>
> (Wilderson 2009: 122–123)

1.

In his finest and most distressing role, Sidney Poitier plays Virgil Tibbs, a Philadelphia police detective, in Norman Jewison's *In the Heat of the Night* (1967). Mr. Tibbs is commandeered by the police chief of Sparta, Mississippi, to solve the murder of Philip Colbert, a Chicago industrialist whose business plan for the development of the local economy is jeopardized by his untimely death. Chief Gillespie has justice on his mind as well as the rate of unemployment of his rural, working-class, white constituency. Closing the case to the satisfaction of the industrialist's widow ensures the job creation essential to the maintenance of law and order on *this* side of the tracks. Identifying a black perpetrator ensures individualized disorder stays on *that* side of the tracks. It's a two-for-one deal that keeps everything on track and keeps the tracks in place: the built environment of segregation and the mythos of Jim Crow.

Taken together, this chain of events might otherwise be known as a favorable business climate. More relevant to our present engagement, however, is the pivotal scene in which Tibbs uncovers the final clue: 'a man's name' (*In the Heat of the Night*). Snubbed at every turn, harassed, threatened, demeaned, and assaulted by every white person considered to be a lead in the case, Tibbs is interrogating Mama Caleba (played by Beah Richards). He leans in and says:

TIBBS: Now listen. Hear me good, Mama, please. Don't make *me* have to send *you* to jail.
MAMA CALEBA: A lot you care!
TIBBS: There's white time in jail, and colored time. The worst kind you can do is colored time.

'Colored time' enters the drama, 'this maniacal tale emerging at the century's apex of black radicalism' (Sexton 2009: 44), with the force of dread: interminable, perhaps even incalculable, stalled time. And it enters as an intramural affair, across the conflicted relational aspirations of male and female gender, as a form of strife and striving at cross-purposes internal to the black (radical) tradition.[1]

The projected image of black masculinity inscribed, impossibly, in the function of police power is maneuvering within the claustrophobic space between the law and its extra-legal supplement and leveraging against a black feminist sexual politics a threat of incarceration that it is neither authorized to enlist nor armed to enforce. In desperation, this captive of an everyday, social incarceration reaches for a pivot point: the prison within the prison, a *solitary* confinement. This is the slow time of captivity, the dilated time of the event horizon, the eternal time of the unconscious.

2.

To speak of 'simple interdiction' and 'bare transgression' implies what today must be considered a naïve understanding of law requiring an untenably strict delimitation of inside and out (Moten 2008b: 179). Yet the idea of the epigraph of law as 'frame, bar, or whatever externally imposed social logic' or as even 'enclosure' can be read as an involvement with just such an understanding (ibid). In a way it cannot be otherwise, as the language of this difference between inside and out must be used to demonstrate why it is not what it seems or claims to be. If we could sum it up in advance, we might say captivity is always an unsettled condition, open to an outside about which it will not know anything and about which it can never stop thinking, a nervous system in pursuit of the fugitive movement it cannot afford to lose and cannot live without, if it is to go on existing in and as a mode of capturing.

In 'The Case of Blackness,' Moten is concerned with a strife internal to the field formation of black studies, internal, moreover, to the black (radical) tradition that black studies is or seeks out as institutional inscription, a 'strife between normativity and the deconstruction of norms' that he argues 'is essential not only to contemporary black academic discourse but also to the discourses of the barbershop, the beauty shop, and the bookstore' (Moten 2008b: 178). Put differently, there is strife within the black (radical) tradition between 'radicalism (here understood as the performance of a general critique of the proper)' and a 'normative striving against the grain of the very radicalism from which the desire for norms is derived' (Moten 2008b: 177). If radicalism gives rise to the desire for norms, if the general critique of the proper gives rise to the desire for propriety and not vice versa, the prevailing notion of critique – and the forms and sources of our critical activity – is put into question. It would mean that we could not analytically presuppose 'the system in which the subordination takes place' and then insert the subjects or objects of that system 'into this pre-established matrix to engage in their functional articulation of the permutations prescribed therein' (Chandler 2000: 261). Instead, we would have to account for 'the *constitution* of general system or structure [emphasis added]' and not just its *operational* dynamics (ibid).

Moten finds examples of this notion of critique in a certain moment of Fanon and in a citation of Fanon in 'Raw Life,' (Sexton and Copeland 2003). There are references to an interview with Saidiya Hartman conducted by Frank B. Wilderson III under the title, 'The Position of the Unthought' (Hartman and Wilderson 2003) and, by extension, to Hartman's *Scenes of Subjection* (1997) and *Lose Your Mother* (2007) and to Wilderson's *Red, White and Black* (2008), as well as to some of the sources the latter draws upon: Kara Keeling's *The Witch's Flight* (2007), David Marriott's *On Black Men* (2000), and Achille Mbembe's *On the Postcolony* (2001). These works share 'an epistemological consensus broad enough to include Fanon, on the one hand, and Daniel Patrick Moynihan, on the other – encompassing formulations that might be said not only to characterize but also to initiate and continually re-initialize the philosophy of the human sciences' (Moten 2008b: 188).

In the same vein, and based on reading 'raw life' as a synonym rather than an opening of another frame of reference, Moten writes against what he sees in 'a certain American reception of Agamben' as a 'critical obsession with bare life' that 'fetishizes the bareness of it all' (Moten 2008b: 216). This 'constant repetition of bare life' the troubled and troubling reading of Fanon *avec* Agamben fails to engage with Agamben's (affirmative) notion of 'form of life' (Moten 2008b). Here one is unfaithful to the best of Agamben if one's theorization 'separates life from the form of life,' just as one is unfaithful to the best of Foucault if one overlooks his 'constant and unconcealed assumptions of life's fugitivity' in support of a conviction that misattributes to his thought a thesis about the absoluteness of power (ibid).

A relation of mutual implication links these two observations – strife internal to black studies and failure in the understanding of power. 'The Case of Blackness' cautions against the tendency to depart from the faulty premise of black pathology and carry the discourse being criticized within the assumptions of the critique. If one misunderstands the nature of power in this way, one will likely assume the pathology of blackness and vice versa. Wilderson warns against the tendency to 'fortify and extend the interlocutory life of widely accepted political common sense' and its theoretical underpinnings (Wilderson 2008: 36).

Before we adjudicate whether Fanon suffers from 'an explicatory velocity that threatens to abolish the distance between – which is also to say the nearness of' – a whole range of conceptual pairs requiring a finer attunement to 'their difference and its modalities' (Moten 2008b: 182), we should adjudicate whether the fact that 'blackness has been associated with a certain sense of decay' is something we ought to strain against as it strains against us. If we stay the course, need we mobilize a philosophy of life to do so?

Donna Jones makes a powerful intervention to that end in *The Racial Discourses of Life Philosophy* (2010). In the perennial skirmishes between the conceptual touchstones of lack and surplus, negation and affirmation, transcendence and immanence, she cuts a theoretical bias that moves at times obliquely, at times directly, zooming in to the finest of detail and pulling back to survey the sweeping vista. In her careful and daring exploration of the emergence of life philosophy in late nineteenth- and early twentieth-century Europe – and its appropriation by leading lights of the contemporaneous but non-synchronous Négritude movement – she finds not a coherent intellectual history, or a dialectal movement or a simple contest of meaning, but a profound convolution of thought, a convolution that the current discussion inhabits. A convolution arising in the wake of Marx and of Darwin about the nature of nature, about the essence of life and living insofar as such questions were raised, excitedly or ominously, by industrialization and urbanization and the institutional projections of modern science attendant to a globalizing capitalist world system in crisis; attendant to the twilight of Europe's vast colonial enterprise, in the intermezzo between the international abolitionist movement and the movements for civil rights and decolonization that move in and across the black (radical) tradition.

Looking back at Henri Bergson's 1907 *Creative Evolution* and the milieu of philosophical debate against which it inveighed, we see with Jones how the sustained effort that garnered the 1927 Nobel Prize in Literature added to this convolution of thought a certain confabulation about life, a life force set against the machine, the mechanical, and the mechanistic. Jones's research tracks the subtle and often muddled distinctions at work in Darwin and his critics and defenders, in Marx and his interlocutors, in Nietzsche, in Bergson – in the whole field of inquiry established by vitalism and its lasting impact on contemporary thought. Shot through this theoretical tangle is the vexed and vexing question: *What is freedom?* This is more than a notion, depending on your vantage. 'My mouth shall be the mouth of those calamities that have no mouth,' Aimé Césaire writes; 'my voice the freedom of those who break down in the solitary confinement of despair' (Césaire 1983: 45).

To interrogate 'the *racial* discourses of life philosophy' (Jones 2010) is to demonstrate the question of life cannot be pried apart from that thorniest of problems: that dubious and doubtless 'fact of blackness' (Fanon 1967), or what I call the social life of social death. This is as much an inquiry about the nature of nature as it is about the politics of nature and the nature of politics; it is meta-political no less than it is meta-physical. In charting the intellectual prehistory of the theorization of biopolitics, Jones forecasts – and reframes – the biotechnological anxiety or euphoria provoked by the prospect of engineered life in our own time *and* the way it is powerfully associated with notions of social, economic, and political possibility. Reading Deleuze and Guattari, Foucault or Agamben cannot be the same, to the degree that we have engaged the tragic-comic complexities of existence in black. Moten might follow the long qualification of vitalism accomplished by Jones in her text, just as he might read skeptically the implications of an affirmative biopolitics. The remaining question is whether a politics, an aesthetics, that affirms (social) life can avoid the thanatological dead end if it does not will its own (social) death. Marriott might call this 'the need to affirm affirmation through negation . . . not as a moral imperative . . . but as a psychopolitical necessity' (Marriott 2007: 273).[2]

In this chapter, I preface the exploration of a tension emergent in the field of black studies, not unrelated to the strife in Moten's writing on the theoretical status of the concept of social death. This sort of prefatory note implicates how we formulate notions of social life and, in a fundamental way, the tension regards the emphasis on or orientation toward life or death, or the thought of the *relation* between the two, as it plays out within a global history of slavery and freedom. Social death might be thought of as another name for slavery and what it comprises; social life, then, is another name for freedom and an attempt to think about what it entails. Though slavery is an ancient institution with provenance in nearly every human society, we are concerned with the historical emergence of *freedom* – as economic value, political category, legal right, cultural practice, lived experience – from the modern transformation of slavery into what Robin Blackburn (1997) terms the 'Great Captivity': the convergence of the private property regime and the invention of racial blackness. The meditation is at once structural and historical and seeks to displace a binary understanding of structure and history, asking what the most robust understanding of slavery might consist of and how the practice of writing history might proceed. We want to think about what makes racial slavery to pursue that future anteriority that, being both within it and irreducible to it, will have unmade it and that anterior futurity which always already unmakes it.

Orlando Patterson developed the concept for an academic audience in his encyclopedic 1982 survey, *Slavery and Social Death: A Comparative Study*; surprisingly little elaboration followed in the wake of his intellectual contribution and the minor controversy it spurred. That debate played out in book reviews and passing references in scholarly articles and books; it generally invoked a caricature of the concept as already debunked. Not that there isn't much in Patterson to worry about, especially if we are interested in examining how aspects of the neoliberalism he came to embrace are embedded in prototypical form in his *magnum opus* and in earlier writings from *before* the commencement of the Reagan/Bush era proper. Consider comments by V. P. Franklin in the *Journal of Negro History*:

> The large gap in our knowledge of global slavery 'from the perspective of the dominated' still needs to be filled. Orlando Patterson's *Slavery and Social Death* provides us with a great deal of information on the legal status of slaves and freed people from ancient times to the present, but his lack of knowledge of ancient and modern languages and his dependence upon secondary sources limits the value of the work for researchers who have moved beyond 'the World the Slaveholders Made' to an analysis of what it was like 'To Be A Slave'. And his inadequate and outdated discussion of slave life and

culture in this country makes the work of questionable value to historians and social scientists interested in the Afro-American experience in the United States.

(Franklin 1983: 215–216)

The negative estimation is two-fold: on the one hand, Patterson is unable and uninterested in writing history from the perspective of the dominated; on the other, Patterson takes the liberty of speaking about the dominated, and the result is travesty.

Franklin draws up an earlier review article Patterson penned for the *New Republic* to establish in Patterson an acute condescension toward the career of the African American in the United States that suggests something about the conceptual framework more generally. In registering profound disagreement with one of the principal arguments of Eugene Genovese's 1974 *Roll, Jordan, Roll*, Patterson denounces the 'Afro-American cultural system' as a 'limited creed – indulgently pedestrian and immediate in its concerns, lacking in prophetic idealism, a total betrayal of the profound eschatology and heroic ideals of their African ancestors' (quoted in ibid: 215). Patterson adds: 'It was not a heritage to be passed on. Like their moral compromises, this was a social adaptation with no potential for change, a total adjustment to the demands of plantation life and the authoritarian dictates of the masters' (ibid). He concludes: 'A people, to deserve the respect of their descendents, must do more than merely survive spiritually and physically. There is no intrinsic value in survival, no virtue in the reflexes of the cornered rat' (ibid). I will call Patterson's verdict here an instance of the universal tendency to debasement in the sphere of analysis, insofar as that analysis posits the presupposition of its object. One might think, with Franklin, that a shift in perspective from slaveholder to slave slips the knot of the hermeneutic circle. But the question of the constitution of the system, as Chandler reminds us, is the question of the constitution of those subjects or objects whose functional distribution plots the operations of the system.

Whereas Patterson's detractors take to task his historical sociology for its inability and unwillingness to fully countenance the agency of the perspective and self-predicating activity of the slave, those engaging his work remark on the fact that the concept of social death cannot be generalized. It is indexed to slavery and does not travel. The concept cannot be transposed, willy-nilly, to the description and analysis of the varieties or variations of oppression or persecution, whether in the historic instance or in the contemporary moment. There are problems in the formulation of the relation of power from which slavery arises; there are problems in the formulation of the relation of this relation of power to other relations of power.

In a contemporaneous review, Ross Baker observes, against the neoconservative backlash politics of 'angry white males' and the ascendance of another racialized immigration discourse alternating, *post*-civil rights, between model minority and barbarians at the gate: 'The mere fact of slavery makes black Americans different. No amount of tortured logic could permit the analogy to be drawn between a former slave population and an immigrant population, no matter how low-flung the latter group' (Baker 1983: 21). Baker's refusal of analogy is pegged to a realization 'brought home by the daunting force of Patterson's description of the bleak totality of the slave experience' (ibid). I hold onto this perhaps unwitting distinction Baker draws between the mere *fact* of slavery, on the one hand, and the daunting force of description of the slave *experience*, on the other. In this distinction, Baker echoes the problem identified by Moten as a conflation of the fact of blackness with the lived experience of the black (Moten 2008b: 179) and the problem identified by Hartman as a conflation of witness and spectator before the scenes of subjection at the heart of slavery (Hartman 1997: 4). Moten's delineation is precise and encourages a sophisticated theoretical practice, but Hartman's conclusion is also accurate in a sort of non-contradictory coincidence or overlap that situates black studies in a relation field that remains under-theorized. Rather than approaching (the theorization of) social death and (the theorization of) social life as an 'either/or' proposition, why not attempt to think of them as a matter of 'both/and'? Why not articulate them through the supplementary logic of the copula?

Social death has emerged from a latency period as a notion useful for the critical theory of racial slavery as a social, political, and economic matrix surviving the nineteenth-century era of abolition, 'a racial calculus and a political arithmetic that were entrenched centuries ago' (Hartman 2008: 6). This 'afterlife of slavery,' as Saidiya Hartman terms it, challenges practitioners to question the established understanding of a post-emancipation society and to revisit basic questions about the structural conditions of anti-blackness in the modern world. For Wilderson, the principal implication of slavery's afterlife is to warrant an intellectual disposition of 'afro-pessimism' that posits a political ontology dividing the Slave from the Human in a *constitutive* way, a complication of the assumptive logic of black cultural studies in general and black performance studies in particular (Wilderson 2009). This critical move has been misconstrued as a negation of the historical agency of black performance, even a denial of black social life; a number of scholars have reasserted the earlier assumptive logic in a gesture that hypostatizes afro-pessimism (see Brooks 2006; Brown 2008; Johnson 2003; Munoz 1999; Weheliye 2005).

What I find intriguing about the argument of 'The Case of Blackness,' and the black optimism it articulates, is how it works away from a discourse of black pathology only to swerve right back into it as an ascription to those found to be taking up and holding themselves in 'the stance of the pathologist' in relation to black folks. There is recourse to psychoanalytic terminology (fetishization, obsession, repetition), and at the heart of the matter a rhetorical question establishes both the bad advice of a wild analysis and a tacit diagnosis: 'So why is it repressed?' The 'it' afflicted by the psychopathology of obsessional neurosis is the understanding, which is also to say the celebration, of the ontological priority or previousness of blackness relative to the anti-blackness that establishes itself against it, a priority or previousness termed 'knowledge of freedom.'

What does not occur is a consideration of the possibility that something might be unfolding in the project or projections of afro-pessimism 'knowing full well the danger of a kind of negative reification' associated with its analytical claims to the paradigmatic (Moten 2004: 279). Arguably, an object lesson in the phenomenology of the thing is a gratuity that folds a new encounter into older habits of thought through a re-inscription of (black) pathology that reassigns its cause and relocates its source without ever really getting inside it. In a way, this relates not to a disagreement about 'unthought positions' (and their de-formation) but to a disagreement, or discrepancy, about 'unthought dispositions' (and their in-formation). I maintain this insofar as the misrecognition at work in the reading of that motley crew listed in the ninth footnote regards, perhaps ironically, the performative dimension or signifying aspect of a 'generalized impropriety' so improper as to appear as the same old propriety returning through the back door. Without sufficient consideration of the gap between statement and enunciation here, to say nothing of context or audience or historical conjuncture, the discourse of afropessimism, even as it approaches otherwise important questions, can only seem like a 'tragically neurotic' instance of 'certain discourse on the relation between blackness and death' (Moten 2007: 9).

Fanon and his interlocutors, or what appear rather as his fateful adherents, would seem to have a problem embracing black social life because they never really come to believe in it, because they cannot acknowledge the social life from which they speak and of which they speak (as negation and impossibility) as their own (Moten 2008b: 192). Another way of putting this might be to say that they are caught in a performative contradiction enabled by disavowal. But are things even this clear in Fanon and the readings his thought might facilitate? Lewis Gordon's sustained engagement with Fanon finds him situated in an ethical stance grounded in the affirmation of blackness in the historic anti-black world. Responding to the discourse of multiracialism emergent in the late twentieth-century United States, Gordon writes, following Fanon:

> There is no way to reject the thesis that there is something wrong with being black beyond the willingness to 'be' black – not in terms of convenient fads of playing blackness, but in paying the costs of anti-blackness on a global scale. Against the raceless credo, then, racism cannot be rejected without a dialectic in which humanity experiences a blackened world.
>
> (Gordon 1997: 67)

What is this willingness to 'be' black, of choosing to be black affirmatively rather than reluctantly, that Gordon finds as the key ethical moment in Fanon?

Elsewhere, in a discussion of Du Bois on the study of black folk, Gordon restates an existential phenomenological conception of the anti-black world developed across his first several books: 'Blacks here suffer the phobogenic reality posed by the spirit of racial seriousness. In effect, they more than symbolize or signify various social pathologies – they become them. In our anti-black world, blacks *are* pathology' (Gordon 2000: 87). This conception supports Moten's contention that much radical black studies scholarship sustains the association of blackness with a sense of decay, fortifying and extending the interlocutory life of widely accepted political common sense. In fact, it seem that Gordon deepens the already problematic association to the level of identity. Yet this is precisely what Gordon argues is the value and insight of Fanon: he accepts the definition of himself as pathological as it is imposed by a world that knows *itself* through that imposition, rather than remaining in a reactive stance that insists on the (temporal, moral, etc.) heterogeneity between a self and an imago originating in culture. Though it may appear counter-intuitive, or rather because it is counter-intuitive, this acceptance or affirmation is active; it is a willing or willingness to pay whatever social costs accrue to being black, to inhabiting blackness, to living a black social life under the shadow of social death. This is not an accommodation to the dictates of the anti-black world. The affirmation of blackness, which is to say an affirmation of pathological being, is a refusal to distance oneself from blackness in a valorization of minor differences that bring one closer to health, to life, to sociality.

Fanon writes in 'The Black Man and Language': 'A Senegalese who learns Creole to pass for Antillean is a case of alienation. The Antilleans who make a mockery out of him are lacking in judgment' (Fanon 2008: 21). In a world structured by the twin axioms of white superiority and black inferiority, of white existence and black non-existence, a world structured by a negative categorical imperative, Gordon advises: 'Above all, don't be black' (Gordon 1997: 63). In this world, the zero degree of transformation is the turn toward blackness, a turn toward the shame that 'resides in the idea that "I am thought of as less than human"' (Nyong'o 2002: 389). In this we might create a transvaluation of pathology itself, an embrace of pathology without pathos.

To speak of black social life *and* black social death, black social life *against* black social death, black social life *as* black social death, black social life *in* black social death is to find oneself in the midst of an argument that is also a profound agreement taking shape in (between) *meconnaissance* and (dis)belief. Black optimism is not the negation of the negation that is afro-pessimism, just as black social life does not negate black social death by inhabiting it and vitalizing it. A living death is as much a death as it is a living. Nothing in afro-pessimism suggests there is no black (social) life, only that black life is not social life in the universe formed by the codes of state and civil society, of citizen and subject, of nation and culture, of people and place, of history and heritage, of all that colonial society has in common with the colonized, of all that capital has in common with labor – the modern world system. Black life is not lived in the world that the world lives in, but underground, in outer space. This is agreed. That is to say, what Moten asserts against afro-pessimism is a point already affirmed by afro-pessimism and is one of the most polemical dimensions of afro-pessimism as a project: black life is not social, or rather black life is *lived* in social *death*, which is also *social* death. That's the point of the enterprise at some level. It is all about the implications of this agreed upon point where arguments (should) begin, but cannot (yet) proceed.

3.

Those writing in a critical vein in the human sciences often refer to 'relations of power' yet gloss over the complexity of the idea of relation itself, especially regarding the relation it has with power, or, rather, regarding the way in which power obtains *in* and *as* relation. We are not afraid to say relations of power are complex, but we have less to offer when faced with the stubborn fact that relation itself is complex, that it does not simply suggest a linkage or interaction between one thing and another, between subjects, say, or between objects, or between subjects and objects, or persons and things. The attention to relation Christina Sharpe (2010) sustains across her intellectual enterprise puts pressure on any static notion of each term. This is an interrogation of power in its most intimate dimension. We learn not just that power operates intimately (which it does) or that intimacy is inextricable from the question of power (which it is), but that the relation between the two – when it is brought into view, within earshot, when it enters language – deranges what we mean, or what we thought we understood, by the former *and* the latter. And where or when are these questions, and their relation, posed with greater *force* – political force, psychic force, historical force – than within the precincts of the New World slave estate, and within the time of New World slavery? We still must ask: 'What is slavery?' 'What is the time of slavery?' (see Hartman 2002; Hanchard 1999).

The answer, or the address, to this battery of questions involves a strange and maddening itinerary that would circumnavigate the entire coastline or maritime borders of the Atlantic world, enabling the fabrication and conquest of every interior – bodily, territorial, and conceptual. To address all of this is to speak the name of race *in the first place*, to speak its first word. What is slavery? And what does it mean to us, and for us? What does slavery mean for the very conception, the history and future, of the objective pronoun *us*?

If the intimacy of power suggests the sheer difficulty of difference, the trouble endemic to determining where the white imagination ends and the black imagination begins, then the power of intimacy suggests, with no less tenacity and no less significance, that our grand involvement across the color line is structured like the figure of an envelope, folds folded within folds: a black letter law whose message is obscured, enveloped, turned about, reversed. Here a structure of violence is inscribed problematically in narrative, an inscription that can only struggle and fail to be something other than a writing-off, or a writing-over. The massive violence that founds and opens a structure of vulnerability, a world-making enjoyment of that violence of enjoyment disappears into the *telos* of resolution, the closure of family romance, the drive for kinship, where insistence replaces imposition. Black rage converts magically to black therapeutics, a white mythology that disavows its points of origin in the theft that creates the crime and its alibi at once. This illegible word, where affect drops away only to remain, is what Sharpe terms '*monstrous* intimacy' (Sharpe 2010), 'a memory for *forgetting*.'[3] And what would we do without it? Indeed, what might we do?

What kind of politics might be possible across this gap, as wide as a river, as thin as a veil? It is a powerful misrecognition that enables an understanding of afro-pessimism as moving against black life, in other words, of pathologizing blackness. Blackness is not the pathogen in the afro-pessimist imagination, and it is a wonder how one could read it so even as it is no wonder at all. No, blackness is not the pathogen in afro-pessimism, the world is. Not the earth, but the world, and maybe even the whole possibility of and desire for a world. This is not to say blackness is the cure, either. It is and it isn't. If, as Moten suggests, radicalism is the general critique of the proper and blackness is radicalism in the split difference between experience and fact, then afro-pessimism, in its general critique of the myriad recuperations of the proper at the singular expense of blackness (blackness in some ways as that expense of the proper) is, in fact, the celebration (of the experience) of blackness as (the) performance (of) study.

This chapter thinks through an ambivalence investing the differentiated field of black studies, a meditation on the conditions of an intellectual practice among those posing the greatest problem for intellectual practice. I have only been able to outline two associated points: 1) the paradigmatic analysis of afro-pessimism and the black optimism of performance studies relate through a set-theoretic difference rather than dialectical opposition or deconstruction; 2) afro-pessimism remains illegible – and unduly susceptible to dismissal – without attending to the economy of enunciation that sustains it and to the discursive-material formation in which it intervenes. That discursive-material formation is global in scale, approximating the terms of 'the anti-black world' (Gordon 2000); that economy of enunciation resists the attenuation of black freedom struggle against what I introduce as 'people-of-color-blindness' (Sexton 2010b). There is a rule of inverse proportion at work here: how radical a reconstruction you seek relates to how fully you regard the absoluteness of power, whether you conceive of the constituted power of the slave estate as actively productive or understand it as a reactive apparatus of capture. Insofar as we understand the time of slavery as a coeval temporality of past, present, and future, insofar as we understand the truly global scale of slavery as a fundament, perhaps even the privileged one, of something like a modern epoch as such, then we cannot but reconstruct the world as we know it, if we are going to remain 'absolute about abolition' (Harney and Moten 2013: 82). In short, slavery must be theorized maximally, in ways that rupture dominant understandings of time and its contingent relations of power, if its abolition is to reach the proper level. The singularity of slavery is the prerequisite of its universality.[4] The 'colored time' of the anti-black world entails the endless waiting of an interminable captivity; that very timelessness is also freedom from the strictures of historical being as progress. That freedom, suffered in the form of enjoyment, or joy, is the real movement of movements, the free base. Get with it or succumb to the forces of mitigation that would change the world through a baseless coalition of a thousand tiny causes.

As a way of concluding with anticipation, I'll ask directly: 'Are the epigraphs in contradiction? Do we have here two incommensurable approaches to black studies, or perhaps some other relation?' Let us assume, with Wilderson, it is the case that *every* gesture, *every* performance of blackness, *every* act or action, critical or creative, rhetorical or aesthetic, is haunted by this sense of grammar and ghosts, of a structure and a memory of its (still) coming into being through and as violence. Does this haunting imply, much less ensure, that there is no, and can be no, fugitive movement of escape, as Moten has it? Does afro-pessimism fail to hear the resonance of black optimism? Or might something else be at work? Of course, when Wilderson writes that 'performance meets ontology,' he is saying more than that. Though he is attempting to think the two registers together (the performative and the ontological), he does not deny the performative in the ontological, but rather insists that performance does not, in fact, have disruptive power at the level or in the way that it has been theorized to date. More radically still, he suggests this theorization remains insufficiently elaborated. That, at least, is how I read the animating gesture of the intervention and interlocution.

Adjudicating the question may require that this sense of permanent violence, if not the violence itself, become intelligible. But can it be rendered available to thought or even become knowledge? This is Wilderson's intervention: to illuminate the ways in which we do not, cannot, or will not know anything about this violence, the ways in which our analyses miss the paradigm for the instance, the example, the incident, the anecdote. Is this knowledge, or sense, something that operates at the point where thought breaks down, at its limit? Some may chafe at the notion of permanence here because it seems not to admit of historicity or, more radically, of a certain impossibility of permanence. But we are talking about permanence in the pedestrian sense that something 'lasts or remains without *essential* change.' It is the logic of change as permutation. The contention arises, then, over what it means to inhabit this permanence and, in related fashion, how it is to be inhabited. Can there be knowledge of a grammar (of suffering), of a structure (of vulnerability)? If so, is it available to articulation, can it be said, or is it an unbearable, unspeakable knowledge? Can it even be experienced as such, expressed, accounted for practically or theoretically? Or is there only 'knowledge of the *experience* of freedom [from grammar, structure, or ghosts], even when that knowledge precedes experience' (Moten 2004: 303)?

This is another way of bringing into the open a question that might otherwise be choked out by whispering campaign or low-intensity conflict or depoliticizing collegiality: Does (the theorization of) social death negate (the theorization of) social life, and is social life the negation (in theory) of that negation (in theory)? Put differently, does the persistence of a prior – but originally displaced and heterogeneous – (black) social life against the (anti-black) social death that establishes itself against it demand more than the fullness of an account? I'm asking a question of procedure here, of course, but also one of politics. Must one always think blackness to think anti-blackness, as it were, a blackness that is against and before anti-blackness, an *anti*-anti-blackness that is also an *ante*-anti-blackness? Can one gain adequate understanding of anti-blackness – its history and politics, its mythos, its psychodynamics – if one does not appreciate how blackness, so to speak, calls it into being? Can one mount a critique of anti-blackness without also celebrating blackness? Can one pursue the object of black studies without also affirming its aim?

What I take to be a certain aggression, or perhaps anxiety, in the deconstruction of the structure of vulnerability and the grammar of suffering that undergird afro-pessimism is not a sign of pathology in the moral register, but a matter of the apprehension of psychic – and political – reality in the properly psychoanalytic sense: an effect of misrecognition, a problem of register and symbolization, an optical illusion or echo that dissimulates the source and force of the propagation. It is a confusion of one for two and two for one, the projection of an internal differentiation onto an external surface, the conversion of impossibility into prohibition. Wilderson's is an analysis of the law in its operation as 'police power and racial prerogative both under and after slavery' (Wagner 2009: 243). So too is Moten's analysis, at least that portion of the intellectual labor committed to the object of black studies as critique of (the anti-blackness of) Western civilization. But Moten is just that much more interested in how black social life steals away or escapes from the law, how it frustrates the police power and, in so doing, calls that very policing into being *in the first instance*.

The policing of black freedom is aimed less at its dreaded prospect, apocalyptic rhetoric notwithstanding, than at its irreducible precedence. The logical and ontological priority of the unorthodox self-predicating activity of blackness, the 'improvisational immanence' that blackness is, renders the law dependent upon and belated to what it polices. The blackness affirmed in and as black social life is always *before* the anti-blackness confirmed in and as black social death. Blackness the *ante*; anti-blackness the *post*. The latter reads black be-ing as being black and finds such being a scandal to what Hortense Spillers calls 'the dynamic principle of the living that distinguishes the subject from his/her objectification' (Spillers 2003: 302). This is not the noble agency of resistance. It is an ineluctable reticence that we might not discern if it were not pushing back, so long as we know that this pushing back is really a pushing forward. And yet, the 'blackness that evades the natal occasion with a peculiarly insistent previousness' (Nyong'o 2009) does not thereby have the last word. Whereas blackness precedes and precipitates anti-blackness, anti-blackness presumes and presupposes blackness. Call them blackness1 and blackness2, with the key qualification that the strange temporality of retroaction disallows the possibility of any strict chronology. In this *perverse* sense, then, black social death is black social life. The object of black studies is the aim of black studies. The most radical negation of the anti-black world is the most radical affirmation of a blackened world. Afro-pessimism is 'not but nothing other than' black optimism.[5]

Notes

1 This notion is an amalgamation of Cedric Robinson's well-known theorization of 'the black radical tradition' in his classic text, Black Marxism, and the concept of 'the black tradition' theorized in Bryan Wagner's Disturbing the Peace.
2 On the notion of biopolitics, see Lemke (2011) and on affirmative biopolitics, see Esposito (2008). Cf. Marriott (2007), especially his 'Afterword: Ice Cold.'
3 'Memory for Forgetting' is the tentative title of Sharpe's forthcoming second book.
4 On the universal singular, see Zizek (2002). What the 'thousand tiny causes' mentioned in the following lack, pace Zizek, is precisely 'the dimension of universality; they do not relate to the social totality' on a global scale (558).
5 I may be simply returning Moten's message in inverted form when he writes: 'How can we fathom a social life that tends toward death, that enacts a kind of being-toward-death, and which, because of such tendency and enactment, maintains a terribly beautiful vitality?' (Moten 2008a: 188).

Bibliography

Baker, R. K. (1983) 'Review of *Slavery and Social Death: A Comparative Study*,' *Worldview Magazine*, 26(4):20–21.

Bergson, H. (1998) *Creative Evolution*. Unabridged edition. Mineola, NY: Dover Publications.

Blackburn, R. (1997) *The Making of New World Slavery: From the Baroque to the Modern, 1492–1800*, New York, NY: Verso.

Brooks, D. (2006) *Bodies in Dissent: Spectacular Performances of Race and Freedom, 1850–1910*, Durham, NC: Duke University Press.

Brown, J. (2008) *Babylon Girls: Black Women Performers and the Shaping of the Modern*, Durham, NC: Duke University Press.

Césaire, A. (1983) *Notebook of a Return to a Native Land*, Berkeley, CA: University of California Press.

Chandler, N. (2000) 'Originary Displacement', *boundary 2*, 27(3):249–286.

———. (2008) 'Of Exorbitance: The Problem of the Negro as a Problem for Thought,' *Criticism*, 50(3):345–410.

Esposito, R. (2008) *Bíos: Biopolitics and Philosophy*, Timothy Campbell (trans.), Minneapolis, MN: University of Minnesota Press.

Fanon, F. (1967) *Black Skin, White Masks*, New York, NY: Grove Press.

Franklin, V. P. (1983) 'Reviewed Work(s): *Slavery and Social Death* by Orlando Patterson,' *Journal of Negro History*, 68(2):212–216.

Gordon, L. (2000) *Existentia Africana: Understanding Africana Existential Thought*, New York, NY: Routledge.

Hanchard, M. (1999) 'Afro-Modernity: Temporality, Politics, and the African Diaspora,' *Public Culture*, 11(1):245–268.

Harney, S. and F. Moten (2013) *The Undercommons: Fugitive Planning and Black Study*, New York, NY: Minor Compositions.

Hartman, S. (1997) *Scenes of Subjection: Terror, Slavery and Self-Making in Nineteenth-Century America*, New York, NY: Oxford University Press.

———. (2002) 'The Time of Slavery,' *The South Atlantic Quarterly*, 101(4):757–777.

———. (2007) *Lose Your Mother: A Journey along the Atlantic Slave Route*, New York, NY: Macmillan.

Hartman, S. and F. B. Wilderson III. (2003) 'The Position of the Unthought,' *Qui Parle*, 13(2):183–201.

In the Heat of the Night. (1967) Film. Directed by Norman Jewison, USA: United Artists.

Johnson, E. P. (2003) *Appropriating Blackness: Performance and the Politics of Authenticity*, Durham, NC: Duke University Press.

Jones, D. V. (2010) *The Racial Discourses of Life Philosophy: Vitalism, Négritude, and Modernity*, New York, NY: Columbia University Press.

Judy, R. (1996) 'Fanon's Body of Black Experience', in L. R. Gordon, T. D. Sharpley-Whiting and R. T. White (eds.), *Fanon: A Critical Reader*, 53–73, New York, NY: Wiley-Blackwell.

Keeling, K. (2007) *The Witch's Flight: The Cinematic, the Black Femme, and the Image of Common Sense*, Durham, NC: Duke University Press.

Lemke, T. (2011) *Biopolitics: An Advanced Introduction*, New York, NY: NYU Press.

Lewis, M. (2008) *Derrida and Lacan: Another Writing*, Edinburgh, UK: Edinburgh University Press.

Marriott, D. (2000) *On Black Men*, New York, NY: Columbia University Press.

———. (2011) 'Whither Fanon?' *Textual Practices*, 25(1):33–69.
Mbembe, A. (2001) *On the Postcolony*, Berkeley, CA: University of California Press.
———. (2003) 'Necropolitics,' Libby Meintjes (trans.), *Public Culture*, 15(1):11–40.
Moten, F. (1994) 'Music Against the Law of Reading the Future and *Rodney King*,' *Journal of the Midwest Modern Language Association*, 27(1):51–64.
———. (2003) *In the Break: The Aesthetics of the Black Radical Tradition*, Minneapolis, MN: University of Minnesota Press.
———. (2004) 'Knowledge of Freedom,' *CR: The New Centennial Review*, 4(2):269–310.
———. (2007) *'Black Optimism/Black Operation'*, Unpublished paper on file with the author.
———. (2008a) 'Black Op,' *PMLA*, 123(5):1743–1747.
———. (2008b) 'The Case of Blackness,' *Criticism*, 50(2):177–218.
Muller, J. and W. Richardson (eds.) (1988) *The Purloined Poe: Lacan, Derrida and Psychoanalytic Reading*, Baltimore, MD: Johns Hopkins University Press.
Muñoz, J. E. (1999) *Disidentifications: Queers of Color and the Performance of Politics*, Minneapolis, MN: University of Minnesota Press.
Nyong'o, T. (2002) 'Racist Kitsch and Black Performance,' *Yale Journal of Criticism*, 15(2):371–391.
———. (2009) 'Barack Hussein Obama, Or the Name of the Father,' *The Scholar & Feminist Online*, 7(2), New York, NY: Barnard Centre for Research on Women. Online. Available HTTP: <http://sfonline.barnard.edu/africana/print_nyongo.htm>. (Accessed 26 March 2015).
Patterson, O. (1982) *Slavery and Social Death*, Cambridge, MA: Harvard University Press.
Robinson, C. (2000) *Black Marxism: The Making of the Black Radical Tradition*, Durham, NC: University of North Carolina Press.
Sexton, J. (2009) 'The Ruse of Engagement: Black Masculinity and the Cinema of Policing,' *American Quarterly*, 61(1):39–63.
———. (2010a) 'African American Studies,' in John Carlos Rowe (ed.), *A Concise Companion to American Studies*, 210–228, Malden, MA: Wiley-Blackwell.
———. (2010b) 'People-of-Color-Blindness: Notes on the Afterlife of Slavery,' *Social Text* 28(2):31–56.
Sexton, J. and H. Copeland. (2003) 'Raw Life: An Introduction,' *Qui Parle*, 13(2):53–62.
Sharpe, C. (2010) *Monstrous Intimacies: Making Post-Slavery Subjects*, Durham, NC: Duke University Press.
Spillers, H. (2003) *Black, White and In Color: Essays on American Literature and Culture*, Chicago, IL: University of Chicago Press.
Wagner, B. (2009) *Disturbing the Peace: Black Culture and the Police Power after Slavery*, Cambridge, MA: Harvard University Press.
Weheliye, A. (2005) *Phonographies: Grooves in Sonic Afro-Modernity*, Durham, NC: Duke University Press.
Wilderson, F. B. III (2008) *Red, White and Black: Cinema and the Structure of U.S. Antagonisms*, Durham, NC: Duke University Press.
———. (2009) 'Grammar and Ghosts: The Performative Limits of African Freedom,' *Theater Survey*, 50(1):119–125.
Wolfe, G. C. (1985) *The Colored Museum: A Play*, New York, NY: Grove Press.
Zizek, S. (2002) 'A Plea for Leninist Intolerance,' *Critical Inquiry*, 28(2):542–566.

4 Temporality and insecurity in international practices

Ty Solomon

Introduction

Time is rarely used as a framework for analyzing world politics. Yet as the contributors to this volume attest, temporality is a lens through which to critically interrogate the present. Acknowledging the multiple temporalities that comprise the present is to recognize 'the' present is never fixed, homogenous, or uncontestable. It is often through everyday practices that the ultimately contestable present is made to seem natural. Oftentimes practices – routinized, embodied, material, discursive – make the politics of the present seem normalized and beyond contestation. The recent work in the 'practice turn' in international relations theory raises questions about the role of practices in global politics (Adler 2008; Adler and Pouliot 2011a, 2011b; Leander 2011; Neumann 2002; Pouliot 2008, 2010). Practice theory focuses on the ground-level practices and background knowledge comprising much of everyday international politics. While promising, a notable theoretical oversight in the literature that points directly to the heart of what practices do is the implicit dependence upon a strong notion of the *subject*. Insofar as practices are defined as 'competent performances' within a particular intersubjective context (Adler and Pouliot 2011b), practice theory in IR has operated within a *subject*-centered analytical framework. But if practice theory is to grasp the key performative aspects of practices, it must more comprehensively theorize the subject of practices (Duvall and Chowdhury 2011).

This chapter suggests IR practice theory must contend with the fundamental *insecurity* of meaning and subjectivity. Drawing on Jacques Lacan and Slavoj Žižek, I argue temporality plays a central role in the construction of meaning and subjectivity. Perhaps part of the reason for the neglect of time in practice theory's conceptualization of subjectivity is its downplaying of time in the production of meaning that itself is temporally registered. As the production of meaning and subjectivity are constitutive of social practices, their interweaving with temporality suggests a richer understanding of practice than hitherto offered in IR.

In what follows, I explore the role of temporality in the constitution of practices. First, I follow recent critiques and make explicit key theoretical gaps in the 'practice turn,' focusing on the shortcomings of a subject-centered approach and noting how current practice research may benefit from work on the issue of subjectivity.

Second, I outline relevant concepts from Lacanian theory on the temporal production of meaning and the constitution of subjectivity. Although this framework is extensive, I focus on arguments on the role of retroactive time in meaning-making and subjectivity. Third, I outline how these ideas may be incorporated into a more conceptually comprehensive account of practices in global politics.

Practices in IR theory

The past decade has seen a flurry of work constituting what has been termed a 'practice turn' in IR theory, following such a turn in social theory more generally (Schatzki, Cetina, and Savigny 2001). This movement was initiated in part by Neumann's (2002) contention that extant discursive approaches in IR focused too much on language and neglected others kinds of social actions and lived experiences of agents. Much of this recent 'turn' has come to be associated with the work of Emmanuel Adler and Vincent Pouliot (Adler 2008; Adler and Pouliot 2011a, 2011b; Pouliot 2008, 2010). Taken together, the major claim of the practice literature is that 'it is not only who we are that drives what we do; it is also what we do that determines who we are' (Pouliot 2010: 5). Or as stated by Iver B. Neumann, practice theory offers 'general and abstract accounts of incorporated and material patterns of action that are organized around the common implicit understandings of the actors' (2002: 629). Instead of following the more common constructivist causal arrow running from identity and pointing to the formation of interests that leads to behavior, the concept of practice reverses this causal chain. Practice entails the background knowledge that actors habitually draw upon in their behavior. Translated into international politics, practice is the 'contingent alignment between the practitioners' [diplomats, etc.] dispositions (the stock of background knowledge accumulated from experience) and their positions in the field of international security (defined by evolving rules of the game and stocks of valued resources)' (Pouliot 2010: 1).

Adler and Pouliot break down practice into five components (Adler and Pouliot 2011a). First, a practice is 'a performance – that is, a process of doing something' (ibid: 7). Neither strictly action nor idea, practice entails both simultaneously through the enactment of the process itself. Second, practices are patterned and iterable (ibid: 7). Similar to routine, practice is typically regularized over time and socially recognized as such within a given context. This patterned regularity becomes meaningful in given contexts because of the recognized frequency. Third, practices are 'more or less competent in a socially meaningful and recognizable way' (ibid: 7), as they are appraised along similar standards within groups of people and presumably enacted with some audience in mind. Such actions become meaningful in a given context through social recognition of competency. Fourth, 'practice rests on background knowledge, which it embodies, enacts, and reifies all at once' (ibid: 8). Background knowledge, in this sense, is not necessarily rational calculations of interests but, rather, a kind of intuitive know-how that guides behavior in a given context. It is 'practical' and 'often resembles skill much more than types of knowledge that can be brandished or represented, such as norms or ideas' (ibid: 8). Finally, practices bring together the discursive and the material aspects of interaction. Practices require the use of language as the main channel through which social meaning is expressed; they entail enactments that manipulate and change the physical world and collective understandings about the world (ibid: 8).

While a focus on practices offers insights, several aspects remain under-theorized. In their concluding chapter to Adler and Pouliot's edited volume, Raymond Duvall and Arjun Chowdhury (2011) offer a sympathetic yet critical assessment of the practice turn. In their view, its biggest theoretical challenges concern the conceptualization of the subject and meaning-making.

First, they contend that as the focus on practices locates 'front and center' these materially situated beings *doing* practices, we can safely say analyzing practices in IR center the subject, manifested in his or her 'competent performances' (Duvall and Chowdhury 2011: 337). As Adler, Pouliot, and others argue, practices are 'competent' insofar as their meaning coincides with the existing shared beliefs and background knowledge of a relevance audience, becoming meaningful for that audience in that particular context. But for Duvall and Chowdhury, practices 'are not just performances of subjects, they are competencies through which they act in the world and do things. The social context of competent performances means that *practices are also the means through which subjects are produced as such*' (Duvall and Chowdhury 2011: 338; emphasis added). In other words, much practice research places 'the agent "front and center" as "practitioner" and thus begins with a pre-constituted subject – thereby neglecting the key notion that through 'particular kinds of performances (the deed), the doer is produced – a subject's social identities are established' (ibid: 338). Duvall and Chowdhury take issue with the notion of practices as 'competent performances' (Adler and Pouliot 2011b), contending an approach conceptualizing practices as subject-forming performative enactments would offer a more comprehensive understanding of how beings *become* subjects through their practical doings.

Second, they argue IR practice research lacks an adequate theory of meaning. Meaning is a defining element of practices according to Adler and Pouliot; practices are 'socially meaningful patterns of action which, in being performed more or less competently, simultaneously embody, act out, and possibly reify background knowledge and discourse in and on the material world' (Adler and Pouliot 2011b: 6). Consequently, interpretive methodologies are employed to recover subjective meanings through careful contextualization (Pouliot 2010). Yet as Duvall and Chowdhury note, 'the meaning of practices may not necessarily be self-evident or transparent to their author or their recipient' (Duvall and Chowdhury 2011: 343). Insofar as practices are defined as competent performances, this implies a 'proper' interpretation of 'competency' by the group interpreting the practice in question. While this accounts for many kinds of practices in global politics, it suggests a level of linguistic stability at odds with the slippery and over-determined aspects of language that many in IR have shown (Hansen 2006; Milliken 1999). In a similar vein, Anna Leander argues many practice theorists take a too-rigid view of the linguistic 'scripts' guiding agents' practices (Leander 2011). For Leander, Bourdieu's practice theory neglects the 'multiplicity of scripts that coexist' within a single agent or act (Leander 2011: 304). We need to acknowledge 'that for any given situation, actors mix scripts . . . and perhaps even abandon them altogether, performing new hierarchies into being' by resisting the scripts of the powerful' (ibid: 304).

What these critiques suggest, Duvall and Chowdhury argue, 'is that meaning is far more unstable than can be inferred from the [act of a] practice itself' (Duvall and Chowdhury 2011: 344). Here, they draw upon Lene Hansen to point out that agents often engage in practices they perceive as having meaning before the practical act is carried out, even if it is only through the act itself that meaning is produced (Hansen 2011). Practices 'work to anchor a particular set of meanings that are taken as self-evident and *prior to the practices themselves*' (Duvall and Chowdhury 2011: 344). Duvall and Chowdhury briefly mention Lacan's notion of retroactive causality as a way to think about how, for example, a worker's participation in a strike is believed by the worker to be driven by his/her pre-existing identity as 'worker,' yet it is only with the actual material participation in a strike that this identity is inscribed, embodied, and enacted (ibid: 344). Thus, 'what needs theorization is the linguistic structure to which [the practice in question] refers' (ibid: 344).

Duvall and Chowdhury's critique draws on views of subjectivity and meaning prevalent in IR for some time: 'Our concerns draw heavily on theories of signification and subject formation and, as such, may appear to rest on poststructural meta-theoretic bases often understood as antithetical to the empirical analysis of practices' (Duvall and Chowdhury 2011: 337). Such a perception would be mistaken, they argue.

Adler and Pouliot concur that their conceptualization of practices is at least partly indebted to poststructuralist scholars (Der Derian 1987; Doty 1996), even while they diverge from this approach: 'In contrast to poststructuralists, who typically endeavor to expose the contingency, openness, and instability of discourse, we want to explain how, on the ground, most political dynamics come to rest on the fixation of meanings – a hard work in which practices come to play a prominent role' (Adler and Pouliot 2011b: 3). Yet they too quickly dismiss the intimate links between these key concerns. Although they rightly focus upon the practices that do the 'hard work' of solidifying meanings, such an analysis cannot be divorced from the ontological instabilities and contingencies that necessitate this work in the first place.

Given these gaps in theorizing subjectivity and meaning, we need a framework that can draw together these concerns to interrogate and strengthen the ontological foundations of practice theory. The analysis that follows weaves these core issues into a single framework under the broader theoretical question of the role of temporality in social practices. The psychoanalytic framework theorizes the insecurity of meaning and subjectivity while simultaneously integrating the role of temporality and desire in subject formation through practices.

Retroactive time in meaning-making and subject formation

When meaning-making and subjectivity in global politics is emphasized, scholars tend to focus on the 'slippery' aspects of the discourses within which both are produced. That is, much critically oriented research in IR emphasizes how the ungrounded 'nature' of discourse produces the conditions of possibility of meaning and the conditions for its undermining. Practice theory would benefit from a deeper engagement with the problem of temporality in meaning and subject formation.

IR scholars analyzing meaning-making often focus on the role of difference. Following the work of Ferdinand de Saussure and others, discourses are understood as symbolic systems within which signifiers draw their meaning not from their 'intrinsic' meaning, but from their relationship to other signifiers (Saussure 2011). Words do not have 'natural' meaning, but meanings are produced through the discursive linking of signifiers and signifieds, or words and the objects or concepts that words purport to represent. Or as Jacques Lacan argues, there is a 'sliding of the signified under the signifier' (Lacan 2006: 419). For instance, this produces the meaning of 'dog' not through any natural linking of the animal and the signifier 'dog,' but because 'dog' is always placed in a sign system alongside other signifiers from which it is contrasted. 'Dog' is meaningful because it is different from 'cat,' which is different from 'bat,' and so on. This meaning is produced through the contrasting 'play of differences' between the relations of signifiers in the sign system in which they are found (Epstein 2008: 6–8; Hansen 2006: 18–23; Milliken 1999: 229). In US security discourses after 9/11, the subject 'America' was constructed as 'good' in reference to an 'evil' terrorist enemy. 'America' as a subject within the signification system of the 'war on terror' became meaningful in contrast to 'evil' others (Jackson 2005).

There is another crucial aspect to meaning-making and subject formation according to Lacanian theory. Difference is essential for meaning and subjectivity yet is only *one* aspect of how meaning is produced, and the tensions of difference are continually bound to the workings of time in the unfolding of meaning. Consider a simple example. Take the sentence: 'Dick and Jane were exposed, when they were young children and in a repeated manner, to harmful radiation.' In conventional understandings, the meaning of the sentence develops linearly as the sentence is articulated. In other words, the meaning of the sentence is produced chronologically – and understanding proceeds linearly – as the meaning of each term is added together to finally compose the entire sentence. In contrast, Lacan argues there are certain key moments in which meaning is constructed temporally by either anticipation or retroaction. In this example, when 'to harmful radiation' ends the sentence, the previous two clauses ('Dick and Jane were exposed, when they were young children and in a repeated manner') retroactively take on a particular meaning. This becomes more apparent when another phrase is substituted to conclude the sentence, such as 'to classical music.' The earlier portion of the sentence, even while containing the same grouping and ordering of signifiers, takes on a drastically different meaning. In this view, the relationship between temporality and meaning in the sentence is not linear but projected *retroactively* once the final signifier is articulated. As Lacan has it, a 'sentence closes its signification only with its last term, each term being anticipated in the construction constituted by the other terms and, inversely, sealing their meaning by its retroactive effect' (Lacan 2006: 682).

For Lacan, the movement through which the meaning of a chain of signifiers is retroactively produced is also the temporal movement through which an 'individual' is positioned as a 'subject' in socio-symbolic relations. In political discourse, for example, our most prominent anchoring signifiers often perform this work. For example, in a political field of unfixed signifiers – such as 'welfare' and 'freedom' – different powerful signifiers retroactively project different meanings upon them, depending upon the particular discourse within which they are articulated. In a discourse of American 'conservatism,' 'welfare' may have negative connotations ('government dependency'), and 'freedom' may have an economic ('free market') sense. In contrast, in a discourse of American 'liberalism,' 'welfare' might represent worthwhile public efforts toward social justice, while 'freedom' may be understood as expanding minority rights. Only after the articulation of a prominent anchoring signifier ('conservative,' 'liberal') do the other terms become politically meaningful. The key political illusion here, as Žižek points out, is that 'the meaning' of the chain appears to have 'been there' all along (Žižek 1989: 102). It is the false impression that 'the meaning' of any of the elements of the discourse ('welfare,' 'freedom') is intrinsic or 'natural' to the terms themselves, rather than having been retroactively projected backward by the intervention of a prominent signifier (Žižek 1989: 102). This stitching together is 'successful only in so far as it effaces its own traces' (ibid: 102). The contingency of meaning and subjectivity are erased through the retroactive temporal movement.

For these reasons the subject is not only discursively unfixed but is also *temporally* insecure. The subject is never fully 'present,' not only in a differential sense insofar as its identity is never located 'in' itself but in broader socio-symbolic structures. The subject is never fully 'present' in a temporal sense. As Lacan argues, what 'is realized in my history is neither the past definite as what was, since it is no more, nor even the [present] perfect as what has been in what I am, but the future anterior as what I will have been, given what I am in the process of becoming' (Lacan 2006: 247). The insecurity of subjectivity is due to the subject 'not having fully been' in the past and 'not quite yet being' in the future. The subject only ever 'will have been' (future anterior tense), since it never fully arrives at the future image of stability, security, and wholeness toward which it strives in social practices aimed at securing a fixed identity.

Yet *desire* for this (ultimately illusory) security sparks identification practices in the first place. Just as constructivists argue that public policies are ultimately rooted in states' identities, Lacanian theory contends many (if not most) of a subject's actions are oriented toward fulfilling a 'whole' sense of self or image of a fixed identity that is nevertheless impossible. For Lacan, desire drives the subject's identifications toward the image of fixity and security that collective symbols seem to promise. Given the intrinsic instability of such symbols (their meanings can never be fully pinned down), subjects can never attain the wholeness to which they aspire; hence, desire remains unfulfilled and ongoing. Just as meaning can never be fixed, meaningful subjectivities produced in discourse can never be secured, and desire is unstable and perpetual.

The subject is caught among these 'backward' and 'forward' temporalities. As Malcolm Bowie explains, the subject 'comes into being at the point of intersection between an irrecoverable past and an unattainable future; its structure is that of a ceaseless cross-stitching, in language, between what-is-no-longer-the-case and what-is-not-yet-the-case' (Bowie 1991: 184). Put another way, Žižek argues the 'subject becomes at every stage "what it always already was": a retroactive effect is experienced as something which was already there from the beginning' (Žižek 1989: 104). Politically, this is often seen in nationalist myths of origins. The various political forces within a country continually re-narrate the nation's 'origins' to discursively claim they represent 'the true meaning' of the nation, and this meaning is to be recovered in a nation's 'pure' founding. However, such 'origins' are never self-evident or grounded in an extra-discursive or unambiguous reality. National origins 'are never simple given facts: we can never refer to them as a found condition, context, or presupposition of our activity. Precisely as presuppositions, such narratives are always-already "posited" by us. Tradition is tradition insofar as we constitute it as such' (Žižek 1993: 127).

'We' retrospectively constitute and constantly re-imagine who 'we' are as the nation. Subjects become subjects not merely through 'competent performances,' which are socially meaningful and recognizable (Adler and Pouliot 2011a: 6). Subjectivity emerges as subjects continually presuppose themselves 'as having always been,' as always retrospectively positing their origins, effacing (or seeming to efface without ever fully doing so) the traces of contingency and lack around which identification practices cohere.

This fundamental insecurity of subjectivity on these intimate levels – the temporal and the discursive – spark subjects' identity practices in the first place. In Lacanian terms, the simultaneous lack of a 'full' self and the desire for a centered and temporally secure self stimulate identification practices.

Temporality and practices

A key problem of identity practices with which Lacanian theory grapples is insecurity and contingency. This framework can offer a more comprehensive approach to practices. An example from Žižek suggests how temporality and practices are interwoven. Like Adler and Pouliot, Žižek insists the ideational and the material are inevitably drawn together through a social practice. For instance, a common explanation for religious practice is that beliefs lead to practice. That is, because of one's pre-existing belief in a higher power, one gets down on one's knees to pray.

However, Žižek suggests belief is not always prior to material practice. Belief, he argues, 'is definitely not to be conceived at the "psychological" level: it is embodied, materialized, in the effective functioning of the social field' (Žižek

1989: 36). Belief often comes through or after the institution of a practice. To doubters of religion, Žižek suggests: 'Leave rational argumentation and submit yourself simply to ideological ritual, stupefy yourself by repeating the meaningless gestures, act *as if* you already believe, and the belief will come by itself' (ibid: 39). The belief will appear to have been there 'all along'; the belief itself will have been retrospectively projected backward and will be seen as having caused the practice. This temporally informed conceptualization has potential for thinking more comprehensively about what it is that practices 'do' in international politics.

A useful way to begin to think about how temporality may enrich a practice framework is to return to Adler and Pouliot's elaboration of the constituent aspects of practices. Recall their broad definition that practices 'are socially meaningful patterns of action which, in being performed more or less competently, simultaneously embody, act out, and possibly reify background knowledge and discourse in and on the material world' (Adler and Pouliot 2011a: 6). A practice is a performance, with 'no existence other than in their unfolding or process' (ibid: 7). As straightforward as this claim is, a Lacanian perspective directs our attention to the roles of temporality and desire in the performance and constitution of practices. Practices entail much more than an agent 'doing something'; they include the performative construction of the agent's very subjectivity. In this sense, performances 'do' more constitutive work than Adler and Pouliot give them credit for.

As David Campbell argues, entities such as states 'have no ontological status apart from the various acts which constitute [their] reality' (Campbell 1998: 10). Yet neither Adler and Pouliot nor Campbell theorize or show the role of temporality in the performative constitution of the subject. Such performances involve continual discursive practices of retrospectively presupposing a 'pure origin,' a retroactive projection of security and wholeness the subject posits as constituting its past and therefore grounding its present, even if such a stable past is illusory. As Žižek contends, the 'subject becomes at every stage "what it always already was": a retroactive effect is experienced as something which was already there from the beginning' (Žižek 1989: 104). In this sense, practices as performances of subjectivity entail this temporal movement as constitutive since subjectivity is never fully temporally secure. Desire for wholeness necessitates this retrospective presupposing of the subject's identity because it offers a sense of security that aims to cover its constitutive insecurity.

Adler and Pouliot explain practices have a patterned regularity and are socially recognized as 'competent' (Adler and Pouliot 2011a: 7–8). Much of Duvall and Chowdhury's critique rests on this notion of 'competence' in that it may entail an interpretation by the analyst that could downplay the importance of what may at first appear to be 'incompetent' performances, but only appear so in relation to the status quo (Duvall and Chowdhury 2011). As Adler and Pouliot note, social recognition 'is thus a fundamental aspect of practice: its (in)competence is never inherent but attributed in and through social relations' (Adler and Pouliot 2011a: 7). Social recognition of a practice as either competent or incompetent entails interpretation and attribution of meaning, yet neither is divorced from temporal movements.

Through a Lacanian lens, interpretation and meaning-making are often constituted through the same kind of retroactive temporality through which the subject itself is produced. Meaningful discursive practices are produced by interventions of powerful cultural symbols ('freedom,' 'democracy,' etc.) that both anchor and project meaning retroactively back onto a grouping of signifiers. The meaning of a discursive practice, therefore, is never clear to an audience until the final signifier has been offered. In this sense, not only is interpretation a kind of appraisal by an audience of whether a particular practice is competent or incompetent, as Adler and Pouliot emphasize. Such interpretations involve a continual 'back and forth' temporality, a retroactive and anticipatory reading and implicit attempts to pin down 'a meaning' that cannot be fully fixed due to signifiers' temporal instability. What is deemed a 'competent' or 'incompetent' practice by an audience is itself never fully pinned down.

This discussion suggests a focus on practices can enhance efforts to defatalize the present and critique practices of power and violence. An emphasis on the temporality of performative practices illustrates the key political illusion of practices – their apparent natural-ness – and a way to counter them. The intrinsic insecurity of meaning is seemingly covered over through the retroactive production of meaning-making. As Žižek points out, that 'the meaning' of a discourse or practice appears to have 'been there' all along is itself the result of retrospective presupposing of a stability and security that was never fully present (Žižek 1989: 102). The production – through practices – of seemingly stable meanings and subjects is 'successful only in so far as it effaces its own traces' (Žižek 1989: 102) through the movements of retroactive temporality. Through the politics of these movements power often attempts to suppress difference according to dominant narratives. The projection of an imagined whole subject as 'having always existed' has long been deployed to stamp out difference said to threaten 'our' present. Immigrants, political dissent, and religious differences are frequent scapegoats said to threaten the imaginary 'nation,' the collective 'us,' a pure collective subject assumed to have existed in the past, yet a retroactive presupposition by powerful political forces.

Thinking through the role of temporality in the inherently unstable constitution of meaning-making and (collective) subjectivity offers a way to more thoroughly disrupt discursive practices which – often violently – hail back to the 'origins.' If the temporal contingency of discourses of power can be revealed, their inherent unfixity and ambiguity may be further contested. Such contestation opens alternative practices, understandings, and temporal experiences.

Conclusion

This chapter raises the issue of time/temporality as it relates to current conceptualizations of social practices in IR. In doing so, it follows recent critiques of the IR practice turn and recent work in the field that argues for the relevance of time to understanding global politics more broadly. Specifically, the chapter critiques and conceptually elaborates two of the key aspects of practices: meaning-making and subjectivity. Using the lens of temporality to view the 'practice turn' in IR is an effective way to critique practices of violence and power which present themselves as 'natural.' It contributes a deeper understanding of what makes practices unstable and never finished, and it suggests critical leverage that may be deployed to disrupt the façade of invulnerability that powerful practices nearly always present to audiences.

In drawing on Lacan and Žižek, the chapter introduces the notion of retroactive temporality in the production of meaning and the formation of the subject. While IR has thoroughly explored the role of difference in subject formation, its temporal dimensions are often neglected; such gaps are evident in contemporary practice research. The outline here represents a first step in this direction; the concept of practice can be enriched and more rigorously theorized by bringing in the issue of temporality as an aspect of both meaning-making and subject-formation. In outlining how temporality offers a more comprehensive and conceptually rich conceptualization of practices, the chapter bolsters some of the theoretical foundations of this promising line of work.

The issues examined here suggest avenues for further research. There may be grounds for more work in the complex relationship between practices, temporality, and affects or emotions. Following Janice Bially Mattern's outline of an emotion-based approach to practices (2011), the framework suggests desire for (full) subjectivity is intimately linked to the subject's temporal insecurity. This may be the first in a series of larger questions about the role of emotions and temporality. Although desire (as discussed here) is bound up with temporality, the temporal aspects of a range of emotions seem ripe for analysis. Questions about the duration of emotions and emotional responses, or how temporality functions in the rising or fading of particular emotions, may be of interest. In other words, the notion that subjectivity itself may be composed of multiple intersecting and even conflicting temporalities raises broader questions about the relationship between the insecurity of subject-formation processes and unstable social-discursive structures.

Bibliography

Adler, E. (2008) 'The Spread of Security Communities: Communities of Practice, Self-Restraint, and NATO's Post Cold War Transformation,' *European Journal of International Relations*, 14(2):195–230.

Adler, E. and V. Pouliot (eds) (2011a) *International Practices*, Cambridge, UK: Cambridge University Press.

———. (2011b) 'International Practices,' *International Theory*, 3(1):1–36.

Bially Mattern, J. (2011) 'A practice theory of emotion for International Relations,' in E. Adler and V. Pouliot (eds.), *International Practices*, 63–86, Cambridge, UK: Cambridge University Press.

Bowie, M. (1991) *Lacan*, Cambridge, MA: Harvard University Press.

Campbell, D. (1998) *Writing Security: United States Foreign Policy and the Politics of Identity*, Revised Edition, Minneapolis, MN: University of Minnesota Press.

Der Derian, J. (1987) *On Diplomacy: A Genealogy of Western Estrangement*, Oxford, UK: Blackwell.

Doty, R. (1996) *Imperial Encounters: The Politics of Representation in North-South Relations*, Minneapolis, MN: University of Minnesota Press.

Duvall, R. D. and A. Chowdhury (2011) 'Practices of Theory,' in E. Adler and V. Pouliot (eds) *International Practices*, 334–354, Cambridge, UK: Cambridge University Press.

Epstein, C. (2008) *The Power of Words in International Relations: Birth of an Anti-Whaling Discourse*, Cambridge, MA: MIT Press.

Hansen, L. (2006) *Security as Practice: Discourse Analysis and the Bosnian War*, New York, NY: Routledge.

——. (2011) 'Performing Practices: a poststructuralist analysis of the Muhammed cartoon crisis,' in E. Adler and V. Pouliot (eds) *International Practices*, 280–309, Cambridge, UK: Cambridge University Press.

Jackson, R. (2005) *Writing the War on Terrorism: Language, Politics, and Counter-terrorism*, Manchester and New York: Manchester University Press.

Lacan, J. (2006) *Ecrits*, Bruce Fink (trans.), New York and London: W.W. Norton.

Leander, A. (2011) 'The Promises, Problems, and Potentials of a Bourdieu-Inspired Staging of International Relations,' *International Political Sociology*, 5(3):294–313.

Milliken, J. (1999) 'The Study of Discourse in International Relations,' *European Journal of International Relations*, 5(2):225–254.

Neumann, I. (2002) 'Returning Practice to the Linguistic Turn: The Case of Diplomacy,' *Millennium*, 31(3):627–651.

Pouliot V. (2008) 'The Logic of Practicality: A Theory of Practice of Security Communities,' *International Organization*, 62(2):257–288.

——. (2010) *International Security in Practice*, Cambridge, UK: Cambridge University Press.

Saussure, F. (2011) *Course in General Linguistics*, W. Baskin (trans.), P. Meisel and H. Saussy (eds.). New York, NY: Columbia University Press.

Schatzki, T. R., K. K. Cetina and E. von Savigny (eds.) (2001) *The Practice Turn in Contemporary Theory*, New York, NY: Routledge.

Solomon, T. (2013) 'Time and Subjectivity in World Politics,' *International Studies Quarterly*, 58(4):671–681.

Žižek, S. (1989) *The Sublime Object of Ideology*, London and New York: Verso.

——. (1993) *Tarrying with the Negative: Kant, Hegel, and the Critique of Ideology*, Durham, NC: Duke University Press.

5 Doing time in the (psychic) commons

Black insurgency and the unconscious[1]

Frank B. Wilderson III

> Death is such an essential and revelatory future moment, not because it is a non-arbitrary end point of life, but because it is the one part of the subject's life that cannot be taken away from the subject: one's death is unavoidably one's own.
>
> (Lee 1990: 92)

> The slave dies, it is true, but he dies in the master.
>
> (Patterson 1982: 98)

No time in the court's unconscious

The armed resistance of paramilitary organizations disrupts the temporal stability of civil society and the state, opening up the possibility of new temporalities – new, and presumably more ethical, criteria for chronicling stasis and change. The time of the settler gives way to that of the postcolonial subject; the time of capital succumbs to the time of labor. Revolutionary armed struggle attempts to blow the lid off the temporal hegemony of the state and civil society to replace it with a new and ethical criterion for instantiating the time of subjectivity. This process is vital for the renewal or restoration of the subaltern's political community. This was the intention at the root of the Black Liberation Army's (BLA) and the Irish Republican Army's (IRA) motivations when they fought against, respectively, the US's security forces and British security forces in the 1970s and 1980s.

The guerilla war waged by the BLA against the US in the late 1960s, 1970s, and early 1980s was part of a multifaceted struggle ongoing since the first Africans landed in the 'New' World to redress Black dispossession. But the political trials of BLA soldiers marked an unprecedented moment in the history of that struggle; it became *de rigueur* for revolutionaries to refuse the role of defendant and assume the role of prosecutor and judge (while still in custody and often handcuffed), with the public gallery as jury. This shift comprised an unparalleled inversion of jurisprudential casting in which the court (and by extension the US government) became defendant. Assata Shakur recalls how brothers and sisters came to her trial every day to 'watch the circus' (1987: 212): a courtroom of people joining the defendants in their refusal to rise when the judge came in; folks giving the Black Power salute in full view of US marshals; Black Muslim men and women spreading their prayer rugs in the corridors of the court; Black parents explaining the racism of the American legal system to their children. As the judge entered the courtroom, one child looked up and said, 'Mommy, is that the fascist pig?' to the laughter and applause of the gallery (Shakur 1987: 212).

With only small arms and crude explosives at their disposal, with little logistical support, with no liberated zone to claim or reclaim, and with no more than a vague knowledge of a few hundred other insurgents scattered throughout the US operating in largely uncoordinated and decentralized units,[2] the BLA launched sixty-six operations[3] against the largest police state in the world.

The value of the BLA's armed insurgency is found not in the stated intentions of their Marxist and postcolonial discourse, but in the ways their unflinching revolutionary efforts pushed the envelope beyond what could be assimilated by such humanist discourses, beyond, that is, the political agenda they espoused. The Slave confronted civil society on terms civil society could not accommodate because the terms were not authorized by those elements that allow communal legibility, elements constituting the 'universal' unconscious and notions of the political commons. The violent response of the state and civil society provide a deeper understanding of how and why Black subjugation cannot be explained by the logic of humanist discourse, whether political or psychoanalytic. The state refused to assign BLA paramilitaries the status of political prisoners, and it refused their entreaties to articulate the *rationale* for their insurgency. The average citizen simply refused any rubric of analogy through which BLA paramilitaries in particular, and Black people in general, could be imagined as kin. This injunction against Black people's assimilation into the space and time of political community is deeper than the conscious discourse articulating filial and affilial ensembles of community. Without this injunction, the integrity of community would be lost; hence the relentlessness of the violence mobilized to snuff out Black resistance regardless of how that resistance frames its intentions. In short, this is a violent response dedicated to the salvation of the Human race.

Postcolonial and Marxist paramilitaries, *in contradistinction to Black insurgents like the BLA*, are assimilated by a range of transindividual icons, images, and concepts that secure their coherence. Consider Seán Mac Stíofáin's (first chief of staff of the Provisional IRA) message printed in *Hands off Ireland!*:

> The *nationally minded*, the Irish-minded people of the North know that the IRA is their army, is the revolutionary army of the Irish people, and they know that many IRA volunteers have died fighting in defence of their areas. They know they will never be able to lead a normal, peaceful and happy life until the British imperialist presence has been removed from this country.
> (O'Boyle 2002: 32)

Mac Stíofáin's land, as a transindividual third term, mediates a dialogical situation, enabling him to enter the lists of similarities and differences more indicative of the Symbolic push and pull of hegemonic struggle, over the status of national identity, the value of political martyrdom, and the restoration of civil society, all of which ground his discourse in a kind of political *sanity* the BLA's insurgents could never attain because the violence subsuming the Irish has temporal limits (from the late 1960s to the 1998 Good Friday Agreement) and spatial limits (the urban North).

Black people, in contradistinction, exist in what historian David Eltis calls 'violence beyond the limit' (1993: 1423), by which he means: (a) in *libidinal* economy there are no forms of violence considered too cruel to inflict upon Blacks; (b) in *political* economy there are no rational explanations to make sense of this violence. Whereas the Human's relationship to violence is contingent, triggered by her transgressions against the regulatory prohibitions of the Symbolic Order or by macro-economic shifts in her social context, the Slave's is open-ended, gratuitous, and unconstrained. The violence inflicted upon Black people is an extension of the master's prerogative. Orlando Patterson clarifies this distinction between violence that positions the Human (worker, postcolonial subject, woman, or queer, for example) and violence that positions the Slave (the Black) by emphasizing the difference between the violence that constitutes capitalism and slavery, respectively:

> The worker who is fired remains a worker, to be hired elsewhere. The slave who was freed was no longer a slave. Thus it was necessary continually to repeat the original, violent act of transforming free man into slave. This act of violence constitutes the prehistory of all stratified societies . . . *but it determines both the prehistory and (concurrent) history of slavery.*
> (Patterson 1982: 3; emphasis added)

The violence that inaugurates the Slave is comprehensive, with the temporality of social life quashed by the temporality of social death. Whereas in social life one is a victim of violence if one transgresses the codes and customs of the order into which one was born, in social death the threat of violence is prelogical, open to violence based upon the whim of any member of civil society who is not Black. Whereas in social life one is dishonored as a result of being found guilty of transgression, in social death one is dishonored *a priori*, in one's being. Whereas in social life, one's kinship structure is recognized *as* a kinship structure, even if degraded (i.e., the Irish), in social death, one is a 'genealogical isolate.' Patterson says:

> Formally isolated in his social relations with those who lived, he [the Slave] also was culturally isolated from the social heritage of his ancestors. He had a past, to be sure. But a past is not a heritage. Everything has a history, including sticks and stones. Slaves differed from other human beings in that they were not allowed freely to integrate the experience of their ancestors into their lives, to inform their understanding of social reality with the inherited meanings of their natural forebears, or to anchor the living present in any *conscious community of memory*. That they reached back for the past, as they reached out for the related living, there can be no doubt. *Unlike other persons*, doing

>so meant struggling with and penetrating the iron curtain of the master, his community, his laws, his policemen or patrollers, and his heritage.
>
>(Patterson 1982: 15; emphasis added)

Blackness is often misconstrued as an identity (cultural, economic, gendered) of the Human community, but no Black temporality is antecedent to the temporality of the Slave. Africa's spatial coherence is temporally coterminous with the Arab and then European slave trade. The time of Blackness is the time of the paradigm; it is not a temporality grasped with the epistemological tools at our disposal. The time of Blackness is no time at all because one cannot know a plenitude of Blackness distinct from Slaveness. The prior references of the worker (a time before the Enclosures) or of the postcolonial subject (a time before the settler) are simply not available to Black people:

>For the Slave, historical time is no more viable a temporality of emancipation than biographical time – the time of empathy. Thus, neither the analytic aesthetic nor the empathetic aesthetic [the demystifying cure of the analytic encounter] can accompany a theory of change that restores Black people to relationality. The social and political time of emancipation proclamations should not be confused with the ontological and epistemological time of modernity itself, in which Blackness and Slaveness are imbricated ab initio . . . [Blacks are] constituted by a 'violence that separates ontological time (the time of the paradigm) from historical time (the time in the paradigm).'
>
>(Wilderson 2010: 339–340)

The violence of slavery inaugurates a socially dead sentient being whose temporal resonances can never be transposed into temporal events. When the Slave attacks civil society and the state, as the BLA did in the 1960s, 1970s, and early 1980s, and frames her incursions with a list of temporal episodes that *cannot* be reconciled with social death, the result is an 'impossible and unanticipatable' text that 'shatter[s] its expression, rendering that expression suddenly unrecognizable and incomprehensible' (Keeling 2003: 107). The violence meted out to the BLA bore none of the hallmarks of political reciprocation borne by the same intensity of violence against Native Americans and Puerto Ricans. No treaties. No negotiations. No recognition of demands. No recognition of Black political or domestic community.

David Gilbert and Judy Clark, two former members of the Weather Underground, stood trial with Kuwasi Balagoon in what is commonly called the Brinks Trial.[4] They sat out much of the trial, arguing that 'to participate would be to recognize the legitimacy of the court to criminalize *political* acts. When they did appear, it was to make statements condemning white supremacy and U.S. imperialism' (Berger 2006: 252). They sought to short-circuit the court's disciplinary logic by exploiting their trial as an opportunity to shift the terms of adjudication from moral questions of guilt and innocence to ethical questions of state power and political legitimacy.

Evelyn Williams comments, 'Political prisoners scrutinize each motion their attorney files with an eye not for its legal competence or consequences but for its political ramifications in the overall unceasing need to expose the society in its true light, not to extricate themselves from its grip' (1993: 84). She characterizes BLA courtroom tactics as part of an overarching strategy to disrupt the spatial paradigm of jurisprudence: at the lowest level of cartographic abstraction, the bodies that accuse become the objects of prosecution; at a higher level of abstraction, the space of punishment becomes the space of pedagogy. This strategy included instantiating a new paradigm of temporality on the proceedings themselves, with the temporal logic of morality subordinated to the temporal logic of ethics. The paramilitary operated through a narrative of class redemption unfolding over a longer imaginary continuum than a narrative of personal redemption, helping the 'defendant' see and perform beyond the consequence of her/his own life and death.

Evelyn Williams implies that this overarching strategy is founded upon an unflinching paradigmatic analysis, undeterred by state violence and buttressed by a desire to restore relational logic to the idea of the court and thus consider it as a political institution within a political constellation. Representing Assata Shakur, Williams says: 'So we made a pact: I would do my legal thing and she would do her necessary thing' (1993: 84). The 'necessary thing' ran the gamut from taking judges and officers of the court hostage, as Jonathan Jackson did in Marin, to refusing to stand when the judge entered the room, to commandeering the court as a liberation school, to refusing to testify or testifying in ways that shunned decorum and the rules of evidence.

Consider the statement Kuwasi Balagoon read before he was sentenced to life imprisonment:

Your honor

your honor
since i've been convicted of murder
and have taken time to digest
just what that means
after noting what it means to my family
and how it affects people who read the newspapers
and all
i see now that i've made a terrible mistake!
and didn't approach this trial
in a respectful, deliberate or thoughtful manner
didn't take advantage of the best legal advice
and based my actions on irrelevant matters
which i can see now in a much more sober mind
had nothing to do with this case
i must have been legally insane thinking about:
the twenty five murders of children in atlanta since

>   Wayne Williams' capture
>   the recent murder of a man in boston by the police
>   the recent murders of two in chicago by the police
>   the shooting of a five-year-old little boy in suburban calif[ornia]
>   the lynching in alabama
>   the mob murder of a transit worker in brooklyn
>   the murders of fourteen women in boston
>   feeling that this is evidence of something
>   and that there must
>   be a lesson in all of this—I thought
>   murder was legal.
>
> (Balagoon 2003: 95)

Balagoon's poem is an example of the 'necessary thing' – the kind of performative gesture for which the BLA political prisoners were famous. The poem supports, through the narration of systematic and legal state murders, examples of Balagoon's 'untimely' death. It explodes and exposes the position of the law and the state.[5]

But as a *testimony* of an ongoing Black holocaust, Balagoon's poem is incomplete; not in quantity, but in quality. Its deepest insight is that the law is a White technology that kills Black people because they are Black,[6] coupled with the inference that Balagoon was guilty before the Brinks expropriation. His innocence cannot be vouchsafed until all semblance of the law has been eradicated. The poem's closing line, 'I thought murder was legal,' locates the court at the end of a metonymic chain of hate crimes and politicizes the presumed impartiality of the pending violence – the life sentence about to be handed down. Such counter-hegemonic gestures are part of a process Gramsci calls the War of Position's isolation and emasculation of ruling-class values. But the Gramscian model breaks down because the subjects of the poem (Black people) are not Gramscian subjects (Wilderson 2002). A spanner in the Gramscian works is evident in the *way* the deaths are narrated. The body count Balagoon offers reads like a report on holocaust atrocities; we get no sense of the people who existed before the holocaust or the impacts on their polity, cosmology, or structures of feeling.

I am humbled by the courage it took to use the space and time allotted to read atrocities into the public record, often at the expense of adjudicating the charges levied against them. But the reportage of atrocities is just that, reportage: laden with spectacle and lights on sustained meditations on trauma. How can a sense of redress (juridical or political) emerge from a context where sustained meditations on trauma have no purchase, where the spatial and temporal resonances of the trauma Black people experience is barred from being recognized by and incorporated into the corpus of Human events?

There are important continuities between the ethical dilemmas raised when a Slave stood before the bar in the nineteenth century and when the BLA stood before the bar in the 1970s and early 1980s. The Dred Scott trials are exemplary of this. Arguably, Dred Scott was pushing in the opposite direction from the BLA;

he wanted to *depoliticize* the court so it would focus on a narrow (and just) interpretation of existing law. But I am not asserting historical continuity of courtroom strategies. The historical continuity of the Dred Scott case and the BLA trials isn't a continuity of performance but a continuity of position.

Chief Justice Taney's 1857 majority decision was an early rejoinder to the BLA's demand 124 years later that their standing before the court be recognized as political rather than juridical. Taney returned Dred Scott to slavery by arguing in the opposite direction, from the juridical to the political. Taney argues that Dred Scott has no standing as a juridical subject because he has no standing as a political subject. 'The question is simply this,' Taney writes, 'Can a negro whose ancestors were imported and sold as slaves, become a member of the political community?'[7] Taney is compelled to compare the Black to the Indian as a necessary prerequisite to legitimating the court's decision to re-enslave Dred Scott. In so doing, he triangulates the dyad between the Human and the Black with the Indian:

> The situation of [the Black] population was altogether unlike that of the Indian race. The latter, it is true, formed no part of the colonial communities and never amalgamated with them in social connections or in government. But although they were uncivilized, they were yet free and independent people, associated together in nations or tribes, and governed by their own laws. Many of the political communities were situated in territories to which the white race claimed the ultimate right of dominion.[8]

From the opening of Taney's tangential pursuit of Native Americans, it seems they constitute a defeated and denigrated identity within the Human race, devalued Humanity as opposed to the embodiment of social death (Blacks). Taney's writing speaks of a being with subjective presence and of a community with the capacity for 'perspective of consciousness,' '[u]ncivilized . . . yet free and independent . . . associated together in nations or tribes, and governed by their own laws' (Gordon 1995: 183). Furthermore, Indians are not natally alienated because their claims to their offspring are recognized by and incorporated into the world. By extension, their right to govern is acknowledged beyond their circle (temporal recognition), just as their place names have resistance in the eyes of the Other (spatial recognition): 'Many of the political communities were situated in territories to which the white race claimed the ultimate right of dominion' (Gordon 1995: 184).

Taney imposes imaginary and fantastic formulations on what heretofore in the ruling has been sober and realist prose buttressed by relational (albeit racist) logic:

> Indian Governments were regarded and treated as foreign Governments, *as much so as if an ocean had separated the red man from the white*; and their freedom has constantly been acknowledged, from the time of the first emigration to the English colonies to the present day, by the different Governments which succeeded each other.
>
> (Neale 1990: 27)

Through a process of condensation and displacement, or jurisprudential dreamwork, Taney maps the imagery of settlerism onto the body of Indigenism. Like the dreamer who brings his own water to the beach, Justice Taney has to *manufacture* an ocean out of dry land, lest the analogy between Whites and Indians crumble. The declaration that Africa is void of political community, coupled with the fantasy of immigration the court's unconscious mobilized to situate the Indian within political community, was a vital intervention that reminded the lower courts that general dishonor and natal alienation are two of the three constitutive elements of slavery, not proprietary claims. Dred Scott has no juridical standing because he is not a member of political community; he is not a member of political community because he is a genealogical isolate; his status as a genealogical isolate is an effect of his subsumption by structural violence unique to his paradigmatic position. To hear his case on the basis of proprietary claims or, more to the point, *to hear it at all*, is to breach the divide between the living and the dead – those who can mediate their existence through transindividual objects and those who, at best, can only *be* a mediating object.

This paradox of existence in which one can never be the subject of symbolic mediation even though one is always already an object of symbolic mediation is the quandary encountered by Kuwasi Balagoon and Dred Scott when they went to trial. The textual heat of Kuwasi Balagoon's poem is not cathected by transindividual concepts like land or labor power, but dispersed throughout an array of bodily violations, horrifying images indexical of the absence of his capacity to lay claim to mediating concepts. In Balagoon's case, we do not get a picture of someone whose native land has been stolen, whose labor power has been usurped, or whose culture has been quashed and corrupted, but of someone whose condition of possibility is elaborated by violence too comprehensive to comprehend, violence so totalizing it reenacts its prehistory, repeatedly, in the present (Patterson 1982).

Dying on time

In 1976 Margaret Thatcher took political prisoner status away from Irish Republican paramilitaries incarcerated in British prisons.[9] Her government recast them as social prisoners, or ODCs, ordinary decent criminals, in the vernacular of the Yard. They were told to wear normal prison uniforms instead of their own civilian clothes or the uniforms of their respective armies (IRA or ORIA). The incarcerated Republicans fought back with a politics of refusal, which unfolded in stages: First, with a refusal to wear anything at all, except for the blankets they were given for their beds. Second, with a refusal to bathe or to be bathed, resulting in forced baths and forced shaves – naked, unwashed, and unshaven Republicans fighting with fists, feet, and head-butts against heavily armored, truncheon-wielding guards. Third, smuggling the names of guards out of the prison so they could be targeted for assassination by outside paramilitaries. When the guards responded by denying them their toilet privileges, they initiated the fourth phase, in which they poured their urine through the crack beneath their cell doors and smeared their feces on the walls (see Feldman 1991; McQueen 2008).

In all this, we see the contours of a narrative arc that remains *formally* intact, even though the story takes place in prison where time stands still, where one's incorporation within the flow of Human events has been all but usurped. That is to say, a temporal progression from equilibrium to disequilibrium to equilibrium restored can still be discerned. Their status as political prisoners is the moment of equilibrium. The Thatcher government's denial of that status and their resistance to that denial constitutes disequilibrium. For Republican paramilitaries, prison time disturbs and usurps the content of the political narratives they author. At the level of form nothing quite so cataclysmic has occurred. What we have instead is no more than a lateral move, wherein the generic arc of narrative is retained but filled in with new content.

The vestimentary codes of military community were also the markers of political community. Thatcher attempted to rescind that which her government and the British people had heretofore acknowledged. This is a very different move than the court's denial of the BLA's political status or Justice Taney's denial of Dred Scott's juridical status. Thatcher's dictum was up against a prior plenitude, a political status and rationale, that she had recognized and incorporated. In the case of the BLA paramilitaries, no such precedent existed. And Taney makes it clear that the absence of precedent in the case of the Slave lends temporal coherence to a heritage of conflict between Humans. The connection between temporality and atemporality is crucial: it allows some to think about coherence whereas the Slave does not register at all. The Slave is ultimately a problem of time, not of identity.

At the core of any form of community are episodes so elemental that they are unavailable to conscious discourse. They can only be apprehended through analysis or in the aftermath of severe and traumatic upheaval, and even then as traces or symptoms. In the IRA's prison struggle for the renewal of recognition as political prisoners we can see Lacan's concrete discourse in this complicated palimpsest. There is the body, naked but refusing to be clothed, the sphincter and urinary track rejecting childhood training and, in the last stages of disequilibrium, the mouth refusing to be fed. These episodes of Lacan's first and second elements of the unconscious ('this is my body' and 'these are my childhood memories') undergo a radical form of violence, an assault on and by the self that, at first blush, bears resemblance to the violent labor of the Black unconscious: 'an unconscious which appears to hate you' (Marriott 2000: 79). Here 'appears' has two meanings: first, a spatial violence against the psyche from which there is no territorial respite, or a self-inflicted disturbance at the level of one's organs and most intimate practices; second, a temporal violence because prison time is not simply the instantiation of a kind of stillness, but the activation and reactivation of reversals that seek to return the subject to that moment before his induction into subjectivity, before proper zoning of his body, when he was not a subject but an *infans*. It seems the Republicans' response to the Thatcher government was so radical as to blow the lid off the unconscious by way of a repeated and sustained violence against the unconscious's capacity for corporeal inscription.

The denouement to the third moment on the narrative arc, equilibrium restored, can lead to no more than a further expansion of psychic and physical deracination, the flowering of disequilibrium, as when the Republican paramilitaries went on a hunger strike and sent twenty-two corpses out from the prison into the world. But just the opposite occurred (Feldman 1991). Why, in other words, did the trajectory of the Republicans' resistance lead to greater temporal coherence given that death was the inevitable outcome? Why didn't these activities lead to social death? Why does the subject's death register, discursively, but the murder that produces a Slave does not? By what paradox did the flow of corpses, like the flow of urine and feces, reinforce their capacity for corporeal inscription, strengthen the bonds of political community, and protect Republicans from the abyss of genealogical isolation into which BLA insurgents were born?

In *Ecrits*, Jacques Lacan makes a striking assertion about the role of death in the formation of the subject:

> The death instinct essentially express[es] the limit of the historical function of the subject. This limit is death – not as an eventual coming-to-term of the life of the individual, nor as the empirical certainty of the subject, but, as Heidegger's formulation puts it, as that 'possibility which is one's own most, unconditional, unsupersedable, certain and as such indeterminable . . .' for the subject – 'subject' understood as meaning the subject defined by his historicity.
>
> (Lacan 1966: 103)

Death vouchsafes the subject's relational capacity. Death bestows meaning and enables coherence in the manner of a punctuation mark at the end of a sentence. Death, Lacan seems to say, enables narration. Lacan eschews empirical time, the 'the coming-to-term,' for a kind of time par excellence. Death, for Lacan, is as constitutive of subjectivity as is the transition from an *infans* (an amorphous being without language, the means to distinguish her- or himself from the Real) to a proper subject (a void papered over with discourse). Death is not that which jettisons one from the Symbolic Order. Rather, it seals the subject's instantiation as a subject because it guarantees the subject's historicity. This is what makes (a Human) death, as the epigraph from Jonathan Lee indicates, 'a revelatory future moment . . . the one part of the subject's life that cannot be taken away from the subject' (Lee 1990: 92).

The problem with Lacan's claim is its presumed ubiquity. Discourse, rather than violence, is thought to be the generative mechanism of *everyone's* elaboration as relational beings. But not all sentient beings are subjects because historicity is not a universal possession. The violence of slavery bars Blacks from the psychic commons of the state and civil society, *ab initio*. Only for the Lacanian subject is death a coherent and sense-making *event* (an element of the psychic *commons*) at the end of long, metonymic chain of events, whereas for the Slave, as Patterson argues, death is not the moment on a metonymic continuum that secures the meaning of the moments that have come before, but is more akin to a metaphor, a crushing anvil that *obliterates* the capacity of the Slave to know s/he is alive.

A Slave's death, like everything else a Slave experiences, expresses, and encounters is an extension of the master's prerogative. Patterson explains:

> The master's existence is enhanced by the slave's, for in addition to existing on his own account his consciousness is mediated through another consciousness, that of the slave. In other words, another person lives through and by him – becomes his surrogate – and the master's power and honor is thereby enhanced. The master's independence becomes the real – the only – basis of the slave's thralldom. By negating the slave's existence, the master seems to solve one of the most pressing problems of a free and equal relationship: the frustration that the other, if he is free, is also strongly desirous of winning confirmation of his identity from ego. Both are struggling to gain the other's confirmation of their superior identity. All free relationships amount to a 'life-and-death struggle.'
>
> (Patterson 1982: 97–98)

Here, Patterson echoes Frantz Fanon's interpretation of the violence subsuming the Black, the Slave, as a structural violence that turns a body into flesh (Spillers 2003), ripped apart literally and imaginatively. This violence destroys the possibility of ontology because it positions the Black within an indeterminately horrifying vulnerability. As such, 'the black has no ontological resistance in the eyes of the white man' (Fanon 1968: 110) or, more precisely, in the eyes of Humanity:

> Slavery appears to solve the dilemma of ontological resistance (or recognition and incorporation) which is necessary for intersubjective relations but anathema to the Human/Slave relation. The slave cannot negate the master, for whatever he does is done on behalf of the master. *The slave dies, it is true, but he dies in the master; so the master becomes autoconfirming, so to speak.*
>
> (Patterson 1982: 98; emphasis added)

The absence of 'ontological resistance' frees the master from the messiness of having to consider and struggle with the Slave's life-affirming proclamations. Those proclamations are simply folded into that which affirms the master. The Hegelian dialectic (which, like Heideggerian 'possibility,' is foundational to Lacan's theory of the subject) is subsumed by the violence of slavery so that it might be incorporated in the master's prerogative. Patterson continues: '[The master] cannot be sure even of his own existence, since the reality of his domination rests on the unreality of that which he masters: the slave, whom he has socially killed and rendered non-essential by making him a mere extension of himself' (1982: 98).

Although the meaning of the master's life is secured in important ways through his/her death (the end of the Lacanian chain of metonyms), it is secured in *essential* ways, that is to say, in the first ontological instance, through the murder of the Slave. As Patterson points out, this metaphoric violence – a violence that murders the Slave's subjective *capacity* – needs to be repeated through the 'history' of the Slave. The subject, then, does not exist by herself or for herself, but for and through another: 'For in this labor which he undertakes to reconstruct for another, he rediscovers the fundamental alienation that made him construct it [his identity] like another; and which has always destined it to be taken from him by another' (Lacan 1966: 42).

The fundamental alienation to which Lacan alerts us is the subject's alienation in language, his assimilation by and of a transindividual modality, language. To 'rediscover' this fundamental alienation is to come to grips with the fact that one is not one's mirror image, and the imago of the other is not the sum total of the other, thus putting one on the road to healthy relationships with one's 'contemporaries' (Lacan 1966: 47). Subjectivity is not fixed, like a mirror image, but dynamic because its fundamental objects, the tools of alienation and language, do not belong to any one being, but are every subject's common inheritance.

Without mediating objects the subject's relational capacity folds in on itself; the result is a slide from the Symbolic into the Imaginary, that is, acute forms of neurosis, though not psychosis, which would involve a loss of representational relations altogether. For Human relations, this slide from healthy triangulation between subjects and symbols into unhealthy dyadic contact between imagoes can be debilitating. But debilitating effects can be addressed and redressed by a progressive return to the Symbolic. In this process, the psyche subordinates its reliance on imagoes to a reliance on language, Symbolic representation of a higher order; the return lifts the psyche out of severe neurosis into a healthier form of neurosis in which one is able to live in a deconstructive relation to egoic monumentalization (Wilderson 2010: 306).

The third term with transindividual capacity is for Lacan (and others) the unconscious: 'It is . . . in the position of a *third term* that the Freudian discovery of the unconscious becomes clear as to its true grounding . . . The unconscious is that part of the concrete discourse, in so far as it is *transindividual*, that is not at the disposal of the subject in re-establishing the continuity of his conscious discourse' (Lacan 1966: 49; emphasis added). This unconscious is constituted by a temporal coherence that cannot be reconciled with slavery. This is a tricky point because neither Lacan nor I would argue that the generic and constitutive elements allowing for temporal resonance in the unconscious are absent in the Black psyche. Blacks are sentient beings who have drives and desires and suffer somatic compliance, the residual effects of trauma, much like other sentient beings. But there is a difference between temporal resonance and temporal coherence. A resonance is like the sound of a tree falling in the forest. Coherence is the *event* of recognition by someone who not only hears and/or sees it fall but who can incorporate it into a lexicon of events to be shared and acknowledged by others. Slaves have no auditors for their temporal resonances, no 'contemporaries' in Lacan's vernacular, who can recognize and incorporate those temporal resonances as events.

Lacan tells us 'the unconscious is that part of the concrete discourse, in so far as it is *transindividual*, that is not at the disposal of the subject in re-establishing the continuity of his *conscious* discourse' (1966: 49; emphasis added). The Human subject has assimilated this 'common' discourse of the unconscious so effectively that it is almost impossible for it to be brought to consciousness without a protracted intervention such as psychoanalysis. As such, it participates more powerfully in the formulation of thought and ideas than do conscious constructs with transindividual qualities.

Lacan identifies five elements that constitute the unconscious that, when read against natal alienation and general dishonor, two of Orlando Patterson's three constitutive elements of slavery,[10] lose their innocence as qualities that constitute the commons of the mind. They are: the body (in the mind's eye), childhood memories, semantic evolution, traditions, and 'the traces that are inevitably preserved by the distortions necessitated by the linking of the unadulterated chapter to the chapters surrounding it [i.e., the socius], and whose meaning will be re-established by my exegesis [the working of words, presumably in psychoanalysis]' (Lacan 1966: 50). But Slaves are prohibited from integrating the experiences of their forbearers into their lives or 'anchor[ing] the living present in any conscious community of memory' (Patterson 1982: 15). One could argue that the unconscious is just that – unconscious. There is no way for the juggernaut of social death to prohibit the Slave from being a bona fide member of the all-but-inaccessible *unconscious* community of memories; the gratuitous violence that alienates the Slave's natality empirically cannot alienate her from the elements of natality as they appear in the discourse of her unconscious. But this amounts to an unwillingness to look the violence of social death in the face, which is worse than Lacan's complete inattention to the role of violence in psychic life.

The first of the five elements of the unconscious can be found 'in moments: this is my body. That is to say, the hysterical nucleus of the neurosis in which the hysterical symptom reveals the structure of a language, and is deciphered like an inscription which, once recovered, can without serious loss be destroyed' (Lacan 1966: 50). This is all well and good for a non-Black person, because his/her lack of honor, what Patterson calls 'general dishonor' (1982: 15), is not embedded in the language *ab initio*. In other words, as language unfolds over time (in spoken and written discourse), the hysterical and neurotic subject can be positioned in a wide range of inscriptions, some honorable, some dishonorable, many in between and/or unfazed by the binary. But slavery is an intrusion into language at the level of structure, as well as in its discursive performance. Were Slaves to lose their inscription of 'general dishonor,' they would lose their status as Slaves and become Human beings.[11] The problem with this for Blacks is that the violence of the paradigmatic shift elaborating Blackness did so *through* Slaveness – through which, by way of contradistinction, the Human is then elaborated. For Humans, the range of inscriptions within the unconscious remains open-ended, pregnant with futurity. But the legibility of subjectivity is constituted as absence for a sentient being elaborated by social death.

The phrase 'this is my body' (Lacan 1966: 50) has no valence in slavery. The Slave is 'flesh,' not body (Spillers 2003). Even the timeline of the Slave's hysterical symptoms does not belong to her. This prompted Frantz Fanon to write (in a corrective aimed at Jung but just as pertinent for our interrogation of Lacan), 'The unconscious is not governed by cerebral heredity: it is the consequence of . . . an impulsive cultural imposition' (Fanon 1968: 167). Lacan's taxonomy of the unconscious is not hobbled by Jung's mysticism and essentialism because he organizes his definition of the unconscious around the concept of history rather than heredity. But, like Jung, Lacan starts from the premise that temporal coherence is a universal possession. That is to say, his theory of the unconscious is itself unconscious of the degree to which temporal coherence is not a Black capacity and of the degree to which the unconscious is, in the first ontological instance, an effect (or beneficiary) of social death – unconscious of the fact that, only in the second instance, *after species division*, is the unconscious an effect of language. Fanon writes:

> The Antillean is a slave to this cultural imposition [what Patterson would call a genealogical isolate] . . . At the age of twenty – i.e., at the time when the collective unconscious is more or less lost or at least difficult to bring to the realm of the conscious [the transindividual nature of the unconscious: the fact that it is lost to consciousness means that it is more deeply entrenched in the psyche than if it was available to consciousness] – the Antillean realizes that he has been living a mistake. Why is that? Quite simply because (and this is very important) the Antillean knows he is black, but because of an ethical shift, he realizes (the collective unconscious) that one is black as a result of being wicked, spineless, evil, and instinctual. Everything that is the opposite of this black behavior is white.
>
> (Fanon 1968: 167)

'What do you do,' Marriott asks, 'with an unconscious which appears to hate you?' (Marriott 2000: 79). We see how, for the Slave, a Lacanian recovery of the unconscious, in its 'structure of language,' would not lead to the Slave's ability to, 'without serious loss,' jettison his/her 'hysterical nucleus of neurosis' (Lacan 1966: 50).

For the Lacanian subject, a therapeutically assisted encounter with the unconscious reveals the transindividual nature of language. But the Black

> must enter into combat not only with presentiments and premonitions of a world condemning him to nonexistence, he must also enter the lists against his own image. That battle, though principally conceived in grand metaphysical terms as a Hegelian war over 'reciprocal recognitions,' an ontological war in which existence 'is always a question of annihilation or triumph,' is also a tenacious street war over the simple right to live.
>
> (Marriott 2000: 88)

We are back in the realm of social death. Marriott's tenacious street war over the simple right to live is the performative manifestation of Patterson's first constituent element of slavery, 'naked violence' (Patterson 1982). This unmediated exposure to the whims of others is the violence that subtends general dishonor, the 'presentiments and premonitions of a world condemning him to nonexistence'

(Marriot 2000: 88). The structural violence of social death (for which the phrase 'Black existence' is a euphemism) saturates language itself so that a Black person must 'enter the lists against his own image' (Marriot 2000: 88). This difference between the Black's relationship to structural violence and Lacan's unraced subject's relationship to structural violence blows the lid off the first element that constitutes the psychic commons known as the unconscious.

Lacan's second element of the unconscious consists of 'archival documents: these are my childhood memories, just as impenetrable as are such documents when I do not know their provenance' (Lacan 1966: 50). Even though the 'provenance' of the subject's childhood archives is too buried to be known, this does not disturb the genealogical integrity of the archive. The child of those memories is, and forever will be, *somebody's* child. This is not the *absence* of an archive; Lacan's analysand is not a 'genealogical isolate' (Patterson 1982: 15). Even if she never comes to know the provenance of her archive, the memories are still safely cradled, *rendered coherent*, by heritage and presumed inheritance; not this heritage or that heritage, but heritage as Human capacity. The *content* of childhood memories may not be what lends coherence, but the *form* of childhood temporality can never be destroyed – unless, of course, the absence of this temporal form is what constitutes your (non)being, as is the case with the Slave, the Black.

Lacan describes two of the three remaining elements of the unconscious as follows: 'Semantic evolution: this corresponds to the stock of words and acceptations of my own particular vocabulary, as it does to my style of life and to my character . . . Traditions, too, and even in the legends which, in a heroicized form, bear my history' (Lacan 1966: 50). In a direct repudiation of these last three points Fanon writes: 'An Antillean is white through the collective unconscious, through a large part of the personal unconscious, and through virtually the entire process of individuation' (Fanon 1968: 167). Marriott puts a finer point on it: 'There is no place here for what the black man [or woman] wants, or for a black unconscious driven by its own desire and aggression. On the contrary. The unconscious (*if that is what it is*) is taken over, usurped by the work of identifying (with) what the white man wants' (Marriot 2000: 12).

The psychic commons of civil society, the transindividual components of Humanity's collective unconscious, is constituted by temporal episodes (Lacan's five elements of the unconscious) that gratuitous violence (Patterson) makes inaccessible to Blacks. This is why Black revolution portends the end of the world, for if it were to prevail it would not reorder global political economy, it would blow the lid off the global unconscious.

Conclusion

Justice Taney's jurisprudential dreamwork, his deployment of land and, by extension, political community as mediating objects, shows how he and the Indian are *subjects* of those objects; it reminded the lower courts of Black people's incapacity as subjects of those same (or any other) mediating objects. Black people are among the many mediating objects through which Human subjects navigate the psychic commons of subjectivity, but Blacks cannot become *subjects* of mediating objects. The terror of Black insurgency is *terrifying* because Black possession of the transindividual components of Humanity's collective unconscious would render subjectivity incoherent. The trajectory of Black insurgency, which, as we have seen, is different from the stated goals of Black insurgency, does not expropriate the mediating objects of the state and a racist civil society and wield them in a more ethical manner (as in a Gramscian War of Position or in a Lacanian analytic encounter, in which the analysand struggles through her transition from 'empty speech' to 'full speech'). The trajectory of Black insurgency threatens the generic status of mediation writ large because it seeks access, however unintentionally, to a temporality that is legible as event by way of Black exclusion. Insurgent Blackness threatens temporality in its most crystallized form, the elemental taxonomy of the unconscious.

This goes a long way to explain why captured Black Liberation Army insurgents often have time *added* to their sentences when they come up for parole, despite spotless records of good behavior, or why some are arrested, tried, convicted, sent to prison, and then, thirty years later, when they are in their sixties and seventies, re-arrested in their prison cells for unsolved 'crimes.' The state cannot afford to be too vigilant because it is guarding a possession more precious than anything Black Liberation Army insurgents imagined they were fighting for. At stake was life itself.

Notes

1 I wish to acknowledge the Alexander von Humboldt Foundation, whose funding aided my research and writing of this chapter.
2 In her autobiography, Assata Shakur emphasizes the decentralized, nonhierarchical structure of the BLA – whether by design or desperation. Marilyn Buck, one of the few White 'task force' members of the BLA, told me the same thing on one of my visits to her in Dublin Prison.
3 The number of operations acknowledged by BLA members, presumably because this number is a matter of public record.
4 For the expropriation of funds from an armored car in Nyack, New York, and the resultant deaths of police officers.
5 Anna Agathangelou, private correspondence, January 1, 2014.
6 This is different from the Gramscian subject who is killed because s/he goes on strike or lays siege to a factory.
7 The Dred Scott Decision: Opinion of Chief Justice Taney, page 4.
8 Ibid.
9 The British government embarked on a policy of 'criminalization' of the IRA, ending the Special Category Status for paramilitary prisoners in Northern Ireland.
10 The third is the naked or gratuitous violence elaborating natal alienation and general dishonor.
11 This does not mean they would be freed from every calculus of degradation; their degradation would be relative and impermanent, as say, with Palestinians, who are dishonored in a racist, Israeli context, but this dishonor is coherent temporally and does not predate Zionist incursions. It is not a 'general dishonor.'

Bibliography

Balagoon, K. (2003) *A Soldier's Story: Writings by a Revolutionary New Afrikan Anarchist*, Montreal, Canada: Kersplebedeb.
Berger, D. (2006) *Outlaws of America: The Weather Underground and the Politics of Solidarity*, Oakland, CA: A. K. Press.
Eltis, D. (1993) 'Europeans and the Rise and Fall of African Slavery in the Americas: An Interpretation,' *American Historical Review*, 98(5):1339–1423.
Fanon, F. (1968) *Black Skin, White Masks*, New York, NY: Grove.
Feldman, A. (1991) *Formations of Violence: The Narrative of the Body and Political Terror in Northern Ireland*, Chicago, IL: University of Chicago Press.
Gordon, L. (1995) *Bad Faith and Anti-black Racism*, Atlantic Highlands, NJ: Humanities Press.
Gramsci, A. (c. 1971, 1978) *Selections from the Prison Notebooks*, New York, NY: International.
Keeling, K. (2003) '"In the Interva": Frantz Fanon and the "Problems" of Visual Representation," *Qui Parle*, 13(2):91–118.
Lacan, J. (1966, 1977). *Ecrits: A Selection*, Alan Sheridan (trans.), New York, NY: W.W. Norton.
Lee, J. (1990) *Jacques Lacan*, Boston, MA: Twayne,
Marriott, D. (2000) *On Black Men*, New York, NY: Columbia University Press.
McQueen, S. (2008) *Hunger*, Film4 Productions; Channel 4; Northern Ireland Screen Broadcasting Commission of Ireland.
Muntaqim, J. A. (18 September 1979) 'On the Black Liberation Army,' pamphlet.
O'Boyle, G. (2002) 'Theories of Justification and Political Violence: Examples from Four Groups,' *Terrorism and Political Violence*, 14(2):23–46.
Patterson, O. (1982) *Slavery and Social Death*, Cambridge, MA: Harvard University Press.
Shakur, A. (1987) *Assata: An Autobiography*, Chicago, IL: Lawrence Hill.
Spillers, H. (2003) *Black, White, and in Color: Essays on American Literature and Culture*, Chicago, IL: University of Chicago Press.
Taney, C. J. *Dred Scott Decision*, Scott v. Sandford, US Law, LII/Legal Information Institute. Cornell University Law School Legal Information Institute, 6 March 1857. Online. Available HTTP: <https://www.law.cornell.edu/supremecourt/text/60/393#writing-USSC_CR_0060_0393_ZO pp. 403–404> (Accessed 23 May 2015).
Umoja, A. O. (1999) 'Repression Breeds Resistance: The Black Liberation Army and the Radical Legacy of the Black Panther Party,' *New Political Science*, 21(2):131–155.
Varon, J. (2004) *Bringing the War Home: The Weather Underground, the Red Army Faction, and Revolutionary Violence in the Sixties and Seventies*, Berkeley, CA: University of California Press.
Wilderson, F. B. III (2002) 'Gramsci's Black Marx: Whither the Slave in Civil Society,' *Social Identities*, 9(2):225–240.
———. (2010) *Red, White & Black: Cinema and the Structure of US Antagonisms*, Durham, NC: Duke University Press.
Williams, E. (1993, 2000) *Inadmissible Evidence: The Story of the African-American Trial Lawyer Who Defended the Black Liberation Army*, Lincoln: Backprint.com [Originally published by Lawrence Hill Books 1993]

6 Outside of time
Salvage ethnography, self-representation and performing culture

Wanda Nanibush

As a young Anishinaabe-kwe (Ojibway woman), I was often gifted with or purchased for myself posters, T-shirts, hats and other products with Edward S. Curtis photographs on them. Sometimes they were coupled with a quotation from a famous 'chief' on protecting the environment, the importance of animals or the evils of white man's capitalism. I saw the photos as part of my ancestral past preserved by Curtis for my generation to reacquaint itself with its pre-contact history. Curtis is one of the most popular sources of images of pre-contact Indigenous cultures both globally and locally. Even an Indigenous person with living relatives, actual ancestral knowledge and contemporary experience to help construct her cultural identity cannot avoid him. The power of his work lies in his expression of an underlying romanticism in our connection to the land; in addition, the sitters are our ancestors.

In this chapter, I analyze Curtis's film *In the Land of the Head Hunters: A Drama of Primitive Life on the Shores of the North Pacific* (1914) and its multiple reconstructions by anthropologists in the 1970s and 2000s to show shifting attitudes toward romantic representations of Indigeneity and examine Indigenous resistance to the colonial gaze. I will not treat the film as a history of the West Coast or of the Kwakwaka'wakw but as a history of an ethnographic-anthropological colonial imagination of the West Coast and the changing nature of ethnography and anthropology. The film, really many films as it became reedited and renamed in 1973 by Bill Holm and George Quimby and reconstructed by Brad Evans and Aaron Glass in 2008, is mirror to and projection of turn-of-the-twentieth-century colonial settler society and responses to the discipline of anthropology. The recent reconstructions endeavor to reverse Curtis's narrative of the 'vanishing Indian' by foregrounding the agency of Kwakwaka'wakw actors and their descendants. As the film takes on new meanings, however, it becomes a different cultural object for the Kwakwaka'wakw and its non-Indigenous interlocutors. It represents changing attitudes toward intercultural conflict and contact, with the agency of the Kwakwaka'wakw performers and their descendants becoming key to its interpretation. Yet focusing on Indigenous agency (albeit progressive and necessary) does not minimize the danger of reinvesting in the contemporary colonial desire for the authentic Indigenous person who must be a traditionalist. Anthropologists engage contemporary Kwakwaka'wakw who claim the film as part of their history and a living culture, but Indigenous people who do not want to engage in culture in this way may be seen as not Indigenous enough or have their voices delegitimized.

The desire for authentic Indigenous culture has repercussions for land claims and Indigenous rights as the 'traditional' comes to define access to hunting and fishing rights as well as rights to territory and its use. I cannot go into these connections here, but I challenge the overemphasis on tradition as the marker of who is and is not Indigenous while continuing to honor Indigenous agency in maintaining culture. Would the culture shown in Curtis's film be what would have been salvaged if the Kwakwaka'wakw had their choice and if their culture had not been banned? The real point in looking at the agency of Indigenous subjects of colonial representation is missed when the question of cultural change is not addressed. The choice to salvage or continue an aspect of a culture is the Kwakwaka'wakw people's prerogative.

Temporality and the 'object' of salvage ethnography

Edward S. Curtis was born in Wisconsin on February 16, 1868, a time when ideas of progress, an expanding colonial frontier and technological development as emblematic of civilization were widely espoused (Davis 1985: 17). As a photographer, Curtis was often hired by promoters of American Western expansion. He travelled with and worked for colonial authorities documenting future resources for exploitation (Davis 1985: 22; Lyman 1982: 25). He used colonial expansion to work on his magnum opus, *The North American Indian* (1907–1930), featuring twenty volumes of text and photographs. He became obsessed with Indigenous peoples and their ceremonies when he saw the Hopi Snake Dance in 1900. There was already a thriving tourist industry where people engaged their fears and fantasies watching what they believed to be the 'dying' or 'vanishing' race of 'Indians.' Curtis' daughter Florence recalls her father saw the Hopi Snake dance as a spiritual ritual that was being destroyed and contaminated by civilization (white, modern, industrial) (Boesen and Graybill 1986: 12).

Curtis combined his interests as a self-taught ethnographer with his desire to make artistic photographs. Photographer Alfred Stieglitz was influential on Curtis's elevation of photography from documentary to art. Photo-artists of the time were experimenting with production techniques like close-ups and lighting, use of soft focus lenses, addition and omission of props and details. They were also experimenting with post-production techniques such as scratching negatives and hand tinting. These experiments furthered the claim that the hand of the artist could be seen in the work, the definition of art. Curtis adopted Stieglitz's pictorialist aesthetic with its evocation of sentimentality and romanticism (Fleming and Luskey 1986: 214; Lyman 1982: 34), creating images of the land as untouched, thus ideologically supporting colonialism.

The commodification of Indigenous Peoples' cultural practices has been constant since the nineteenth century. Walter Benjamin says the sense of historical loss emerging in European capitalization fuelled a fetishism of the new (Buck-Morss 1989: 82). Mechanical reproduction made new things readily accessible and entailed a loss of authenticity in the old, bringing about a commodification of authenticity. For Benjamin, an object of the past or a work of art is authentic in its unique presence. In mechanical reproduction things are infinitely reproducible and, therefore, not unique. Because the art or object is no longer an original, it is no longer authentic. Yet authenticity itself is a myth; thus, seeking the original as the real object/culture/artwork is an ideological exercise, not a truth-seeking one.

The pursuit of authenticity through commodification of originary cultures led to a nostalgic longing for a simpler pre-industrial life more in touch with nature, as expressed in Curtis's Hopi Snake Dance, for example. Curtis's desire to document Indigenous cultures for posterity was also tied to the drive to *salvage*, to document Aboriginal cultures before they ended, linked to a concomitant construction of the 'Indian' as a 'Noble Savage,' possessing traits lacked by the modern subject. As an object of salvage, Indigenous connections to the spiritual and the natural became central to their construction within the ethnographic imaginary through which Curtis sought to gain legitimacy.

We Indigenous Peoples suffered major losses from colonial expansion, wars and disease; yet by the time Curtis began documentation, our numbers were on the rise. Part and parcel of his conception of our disappearance was the idea that our modernization also meant our disappearance. It was only in our untouched, pre-contact, ahistorical and unchanging state that we were authentic 'Indians..' In his travels, he met modern Indigenous people whose modernity was not to be preserved because 'Indians' having contact with whites were contaminated and ignoble. It is interesting to note that he wanted to preserve Indigenous knowledge but not necessarily Indigenous people. Our disappearance was considered inevitable, but our knowledge had a use-value for the 'new' nations to come. In the general introduction to his life-long project, *The North American Indian*, Curtis argues:

> The passing of every old man or woman means the passing of some tradition, some knowledge of sacred rites possessed by no other: consequently the information that is to be gathered, for the benefit of future generations, respecting the mode of life of one of the great races of mankind, must be collected at once or the opportunity will be lost for all time. It is this need that has inspired the present task.
>
> (Curtis 1907–1930: xvii).

Curtis's understanding of time as a linear process with a teleological end—the white man and his progress—means he must argue that the collection of information for future generations is critical.

Curtis made extensive notes on the ceremonies, dress and architecture of the Indigenous nations he photographed. Ceremony as an aspect of governance systems, political practices and economic structures challenged the authority of the new colonial society to govern or make decisions *for* Indigenous people. In articulating the vanishing Indian, Curtis's imaginary played a significant role in showing how important it was to expand and settle westward into supposedly emptying spaces. This narrative of disappearance covered the reality of colonial policy that forced Indigenous Peoples onto reservations, sent children to residential schools and banned Indigenous ceremonies. All three disciplinary measures were part of a larger colonial policy of assimilation whereby all 'Indians' were 'civilizable' in so far as they rid themselves of their cultures and languages.

By ignoring the policies of assimilation in the communities he visited, Curtis played an active part in constructing the discourse on the authentic Indian. His photos and film become how-to manuals rather than recording devices. This becomes particularly important in the conception of film (discussed later in this chapter). Curtis saw his work as a reconstruction because contact had already 'changed' the 'primitive.' The discourse on authenticity necessitates an ahistorical conceptualization of Indigenous cultures, an unchanging nature, a timeless, or, more accurately, a frozen concept of the time of the Indigenous. Curtis states: 'These pictures were to be transcriptions for future generations that they might behold the Indian as nearly lifelike as possible as he moved about before he ever saw a paleface or knew there was anything human or in nature other than what he himself had seen' (Boesen and Graybill 1986: 13).

The removal of signs of contact also meant the removal of any sign of colonial violence, thereby converting possible guilt into nostalgia. The nostalgia for the lost origins of man is a symptom of the displaced guilt over the destruction of 'primitive' cultures and, by association, the destruction wrought by colonialism, industrialization and urbanization. It marks authentic culture as 'created' at precisely the moment it was said to be vanishing. The nobility of the Indians and the tragedy of their passing created an intrinsically aesthetic and scientific generated 'subject' (read object) for photography and film. Lost in the construction of the authentic Indian was Indigenous subjectivity and the capacity for Indigenous Peoples to represent themselves. Missing also were the processes of violence making artifacts available for salvage.

Constant in all discursive constructions of the Noble Savage or the alterity of Indigenous Peoples in colonial discourse or in the salvage paradigm of ethnology is a systematic appropriation of their cultures, bodies and territories as *objects* of study. Ronald Hawker argues: 'Since colonized societies and the objects they produced were necessarily destroyed by the process of colonization, it was the duty of those at the forefront of modernity's intrusion into the societies of the "less advanced" to vigorously record what colonialism displaced' (Hawker 2003: 26). In short, modern nostalgia for the past was monitored and released through the construction of a record of the colonial 'other' and the 'facts' of its culture.

Cinema as a technology of salvage ethnography

Simply stated, Curtis's film *In the Land of the Head Hunters* illustrates attempts to contain Kwakwaka'wakw communities and their cultural expression. For one thing, the communities are restricted by the conventions of the silent film era; for another, they are rendered visible but temporally distanced and confined within the structures of a primordial past and primitivized in a narrative of war and cannibalism. Finally, the film is structurally limited by the salvage paradigm of representation.

Film inherited from photography the notion of indexicality: because the camera is really there objectively recording what's in front of it, the film is imprinted with reality. Photos and films under this model become a captured real that can be used to reconstruct reality. Yet *In the Land of the Head Hunters* is obviously an interpretation of its maker, a perspective and a frame. The text as document or testament to a past must be conceived as an assemblage with particular effects, not a reproduction of reality, thus problematizing facile notions of the archive's use for resurrecting the past.

By 1911, Hollywood cinema was producing the first wave of Westerns. A demand for representations of 'real' Indians resulted (Gidley 2000: 237; Holm and Quimby 1980: 32). An editorial in *Moving Picture World* on March 4, 1911, says: 'It is hoped that some of our Western manufacturers will yet produce a series of films of REAL Indian life, doing so with the distinct object in view that they are to be of educational value, both for present and future use' (Gidley 2000: 238). This demand for 'real' Indian life influenced Curtis; for promoters/funders of his work, it was considered important for education and national interest. For example, Dr. Walcott of the Smithsonian Institute supported Curtis's film for its recording of the facts of Indian life: 'that part of their life that has passed, is so important to education' (Gidley 2000: 238). When the film screened in Seattle at Moore Theatre in December 1914, the handbill stated: 'Every participant an Indian and Every Incident True To Native Life' (Gidley 2000: 251). *In The Land of The Head Hunters*, completed in 1914, was advertised as an ethnographic film structured around a dramatic narrative of love and war.

The film is set on Vancouver Island in 1792 with a romantic plot loosely based on Shakespeare's *Romeo and Juliet* and Longfellow's *The Song of Hiawatha* (Gidley 2000: 232). It focuses on a young Kwakwaka'wakw male, Motana, played by Stanley Hunt, who battles the natural and supernatural throughout. A love triangle centers on Motana's love for Naida, a woman from another village, promised to Yaklus. Naida marries Motana anyway. Yaklus's brother is a sorcerer who attempts to have Motana killed but is murdered by Motana's family instead. Yaklus murders others in revenge and kidnaps Naida. Motana rescues her, and the film closes with Yaklus swallowed by immense rapids.

The film recycles 'signs' of the primitive of the time. It opens with a Kwakwaka' wakw man dressed as a feathered animal standing in a massive canoe and closes with a Kwakwaka'wakw man disappearing into a massive body of water in an ultimately empty landscape. The film contains headhunting, warfare, discipline, loyalty, vision questing, sorcery, beauty and nobility – signs of the contradictory noble and ignoble savage (Pearce 1965).

Curtis uses ethnographic historical reconstruction, a kind of bringing the dead to life, but the reconstruction takes place within a melodramatic framework, a narrative allegory whose structure is one of conflict and closure. The romantic vision of 'Indians' in the film contains no ethnographic narration to explain what is taking place on screen (Geertz 1996). Curtis avoids any frontal placement of the camera, preferring to shoot from side profiles or actors' backs. This gives spectators the sense of happening upon a spontaneous event. The shots are always medium or long. Characters have no depth, and the narrative is naturalized. The Kwakwaka'wakw stand for all vanishing peoples, and for all authentic displays of ceremony, simply through the camera placements.

Rather than examining the colonial narrative of the vanishing Indian, then, the film mimics and reaffirms it. Johannes Fabian writes: 'The Other's empirical presence turns into his theoretical absence, a conjuring trick which is worked with the help of an array of devices that have the common intent and function to keep the Other outside the Time of anthropology' (Fabian 1983: xi). The act of preserving a culture disengages contemporary culture from the process of being *in* time. The salvaged objects are ruptured from their social contexts, dehistorized, objectified and reworked within Western meanings. The film places 'primitive' people within the same space as the West but in a different time; this distances the West from the 'primitive' by constructing the latter as visual proof of an earlier stage of development.

Seeking authenticity, Curtis relied on Tlingit/Scottish informant George Hunt to construct a 1792 Kwakwaka'wakw village. Hunt was the primary informant on the Kwakwaka'wakw in the late nineteenth and early twentieth centuries (Cannizzo 1983) and had worked for anthropologist Franz Boas as a photographer and informant. He gave a sense of authenticity to any project. In this case, he hired the cast and artists and served as cultural advisor. However, he ultimately criticized Curtis for focusing on spectacle over cultural context and failing to present the Kwakwaka'wakw views on the rituals and ceremonies depicted (Griffiths 2013: 247–248).

The set for *The Head Hunters*, according to Aldona Jonaitis, had a life of its own. The village house fronts were made by the Kwakwaka'wakw, with two interior posts made by famous Kwakwaka'wakw artist Charlie James (1870–1938). The wings on the house posts were made to be interchangeable to represent different family crests without building new sets. The posts eventually became part of Stanley Park in Vancouver. The communities of Alert Bay, Fort Rupert, Kingcome Inlet and others made cedar bark clothing and large cedar bark canoes. Hunt hired actors, costume designers, mask carvers, totem pole carvers, canoe builders and painters (Jonaitis 2006: 205–206). Curtis used the totem poles as inspiring backdrops rather than explanations of cultural difference. A ledger containing Curtis's expenses during the shoot lists over twenty-one masks, new and old. He paid for six large canoes, the largest being fifty feet long, adorned with elaborate carvings such as horned serpents (Holm & Quimby 1980: 52–55).

The truth value of the film as an ethnographic text nullified the subjectivity of the actors and collaborators within the film. At the time, W. Stephen Bush said:

> The Indian mind is, I believe, constitutionally incapable of acting; it cannot even grasp the meaning of acting as we understand it. Probably nobody understands this better than Mr. Curtis. The picture speaks volumes of the producers' intimacy with the Indians and his great power over them. They are natural in every move; the grace, the weirdness and the humor of their dances has never been brought home to us like this before.
>
> (Griffiths 2013: 242)

The illusion of naturalness was furthered by the removal of all signs of modernity, but this created a paradox: 'By giving more attention to topics such as war, romance, and ceremony at the expense of everyday images . . . his film did breathe life into the iconography of Kwakwaka'wakw culture as a result of his decision to commission members of the tribe to construct ornate building facades, totem poles, masks, and costumes' (ibid: 239).

A bigger irony is the temporality of imagination. Emptying Kwakwaka'wakw of its modern everyday life while using members of the tribe to construct their own no-longer-practiced past turns this into an act of 'forgetting' the contestation around the temporality of memory. The fact that the Kwakwaka'wakw form both audience and collaborators forces the film to contend with a whole new set of relations and meanings. The film can be taken up as a reminder of past traditions; for example, the large cedar bark canoes made for the set had not been used for at least a decade. The totems and house front commissioned by Curtis and contracted by Hunt allowed the community time and resources. In other words, they were paid to participate, to re-engage older, out-of-use practices. The film serves as a community document of such practices. Gloria Cranmer Webster, an influential Kwakwaka'wakw curator at the U'mista Cultural Society in Alert Bay, says the vision of those canoes in the water was enough reason to be involved in the film; the rest she calls 'hokey' (Russell 1999: 113). According to Jonaitis, 'The Kwakwaka'wakw found the project important for themselves, for the entire production allowed them to experience if only temporarily and on film, their ancestors' way of life' (Jonaitis 2006: 205).

Agency and self-representation

Curtis worked for four years among the Kwakwaka'wakw, producing one film and volume 10 of *The North American Indian*. As Anne Makepeace points out, he was influenced by the writings on the Kwakwaka'wakw by Franz Boas, one of the main interpreters of the meaning of Kwakwaka'wakw art (Makepeace 2002: 118). Brad Evans and Aaron Glass say by the time Curtis arrived, the Kwakwaka'wakw had well-cemented ways of addressing, resisting and using for their benefit the colonial desire to collect and understand their culture. The colonial desire to collect came 'even as settlers, missionaries, and government agents were committed to eradicating those same elements' (Evans and Glass 2014: 14–15). According to Catherine Russell, the mere fact that the Indigenous actors understand themselves to be performing constitutes a resistance to contemporary readings of the film:

> Instead of a 'photoplay,' [Indigenous] audiences may well see a documentary of their performance in a white man's movie. The film constitutes a living memory of both traditional practices and the colonial containment activated by the rigorous framing and 'photoplay' conventions.
>
> (Russell 1999: 112)

Indigenous Peoples performing their cultural practices for international and colonial audiences represent an important part of cinema history generally and ethnographic film specifically. But Indigenous performers known as 'Indians' faced the conundrum of maintaining their cultural practices by performing them on stage while having that performance fulfill the desires of a subjugating colonial imagery.

The colonial period of captivity, when Indigenous people were displayed as curiosities and captives, begins the history. From the 1850s to the 1920s, Canada and the United States were constructing identities via discourses of manifest destiny and the separation of savagery from civilization. Manifest destiny is an ideology whereby settlers, artists and governments see Indigenous Peoples as destined to disappear; westward colonial expansion is inevitable and civilization always displaces savagery. Entertainment helped disseminate colonial ideologies. This included world fairs and exhibitions of colonized peoples. The steamship and the railway allowed more extensive trade routes, which the exhibitions used to move peoples from the periphery to the centers of imperial power in Britain, France and Germany. The imperial centers were shown a world where savagery was inside an exhibition and had nothing to do with their own history. Indigenous Peoples were exhibited as exotic, almost disappeared examples of primitive man. The shows helped Europeans imagine Indigenous Peoples as belonging before or outside modernity and urbanization. They were often exhibited alongside technological innovations, further reinforcing the Western man as the innovator, destined for progress. The exhibitions were also used to disseminate racism, whereby another people's inferiority could be scientifically verified by types of bodies and dress (Maxwell 1999).

By the 1880s, the shows shifted direction, traveling through the colonies. In the colonies, it was much harder to keep the hybridity of the colonial world at bay. The fact that people had been intermarrying for over two hundred years was elided by the display of 'savagery' in the exhibitions. The exhibitions also allowed a dehumanization of Indigenous Peoples to help justify colonial expansion (at that time westward).

Cinema inherited this history and became an effective means of dissemination. The presence of Indigenous people in front of and behind the cameras of early cinema complicates this story. Self-representation is emblematic of the cultural moment in which Indigenous modernity seems 'unexpected.' Historian Philip Deloria points out the work of Indigenous director James Young Deer – 'an ambiguous figure, with a shape-shifter's identity and a hazy history' – and Lillian St. Cyr, a Ho-Chunk Indian who performed under the name Princess Red Wing (Deloria 2004: 94). For a time in the 1910s, Young Deer was the head of a small studio, and Red Wing was one of the most visible actresses on the screen. Together, the married couple made a series of films that 'set out to rewrite the white man-Indian narrative structure, using inversions that allowed the films to continue functioning as domestic melodramas' (Deloria 2004: 97). Deloria carefully situates their films in the context of early film history to show how skilfully Young Deer and Red Wing altered the plots of miscegenation, frontier violence and assimilation. Michelle H. Raheja, in *Reservation Reelism*, maintains Young

Deer and Red Wing were equal to Mary Pickford and Douglas Fairbanks in popularity and power. Young Deer directed for Kalem, Lubin, Biograph, Bison and Vitagraph and was Pathé Frères East Coast studio director in 1910 (Raheja 2013: 24–25). Yet they are not canonized in the same way, and no reviews or articles on *Head Hunters* mention them. They are not the only ones; hundreds of such actors worked in film during the silent era.

Young Deer's film *White Fawn's Devotion* (1910) is about miscegenation; the main family consists of a white father, an Indigenous mother and their daughter. Raheja notes: 'The film is unique in the history of visual images of miscegenation because it does not pathologize the mixed race heteronormative union' (2013: 66). The film also shows how Indigenous families are comfortable in both the urban spaces of modernity and the bastion of cultural renewal, the reservation.

The erasure of these films as Indigenous allows the ethnographic imaginary to define Indigenous cultures. By shifting the focus to the actors and directors, we glimpse the complicated negotiation of contact and the participation of Indigenous people in *shaping* modernity. Cinema as a technology of modernity became a central site for constructing the 'primitive.'[1] But Indigenous peoples are also subjects who negotiate the colonial imaginary and perform modern differently because the dichotomy of primitive and modern is not part of their identity formation or, at least, is always in question and highly visible. Ironically, the performances that perpetuated stereotypes of 'savage Indians' and 'princesses' allowed the maintenance of traditional but banned Indigenous cultural dances and practices. They used the performance of a colonial imaginary to find physical, economic and cultural mobility at the height of colonial material expansion. In the end, while *Head Hunters* opens up the question of Indigenous performers, it cannot be seen as an Indigenously produced film and belongs to ethnographic film history.

Reconstructed *Head Hunters*?

The film did not do well at the box office and would have remained obscure if Bill Holm and George Quimby had not resuscitated it in 1973, renaming it *In The Land of The War Canoes* to remove the obvious racism of its original title (Holm and Quimby 1973). Holm and Quimby worked with the descendants of the original actors to reconstruct the film using the rituals and cultural practices as centerpieces to its new organization. They used the voices of the actors and their descendants, provided more cultural context for the cultural practices and worked with the Kwakwaka' wakw to construct a soundtrack based on cultural songs and music. Pauline Wakeham says:

> By reframing Curtis's images in the context of ethnographic documentary, the 1973 version attempts to recuperate the original 1914 film as a valuable document of authentic Kwakiutl [sic] lifeways, thereby overwriting the fact that Curtis's footage is a highly manipulated Euro-American construction of otherness.
>
> (2006: 303)

In trying to regain objectivity, the reconstruction turns to the community for some semblance of truth. But the reconstruction, possibly reflecting its time, ignores the visuality of the film as always already offering truth to a spectator raised without any knowledge of Indigenous Peoples. The value of Indigeneity remains beholden to its supposedly more authentic pre-contact past. Again, the performers *as* performers are lost. The act of preserving a culture removes the Kwakwaka'wakw from modern temporality; the preserved remainders are valued only insofar as they are symbols of the distant past. The salvaged objects are torn from their social contexts, dehistorized, objectified and reworked within Western meanings.

Holm and Quimby are part of this process, but their return to the culture for verification of the objects' veracity was thought to return the 'Indian' to time. In *Woman, Native, Other*, Trinh T. Minh-ha cautions, 'One cannot seize without smothering, for the will to freeze (capture) brings about a frozen (emptied) object' (Trinh 1989: 61). *In The Land of the War Canoes* froze Kwakwaka'wakw culture in 1792 for many museum displays, including as a permanent exhibition at the Royal British Columbia Museum.

The latest reconstruction is by Aaron Glass, an anthropologist trained at the University of British Columbia whose main fieldwork has been in the Kwakwaka'wakw community in Alert Bay, and Brad Evans, associate professor of English at Rutgers University. Each had made breakthroughs in archival research that allowed them to reconstruct *Head Hunters* with its original musical score, inter-titles and newly discovered scenes. The reconstruction is incomplete because some scenes are lost, but in a radical move, they add production stills so the score can be heard in its entirety and the original narrative structure experienced. Like Holms and Quimby, they worked closely with Kwakwaka'wakw communities. Each screening includes live performances and commentary from the Gwa'wina Dancers considered the best at representing the songs and dances that continue to play a big part of contemporary Kwakwaka'wakw communities. The dancers give context to the film by providing stories of the experience of modernity, assimilation policies and colonization.

Two criticisms of the Holm and Quimby version and the original Curtis versions are rectified: the characters are attributed to the original Kwakwaka'wakw who played the roles, and the film is given cultural context from a Kwakwaka'wakw point of view and academic/institutional context in symposia accompanying screenings. The writing produced for the film highlights the politics of the time, specifically the banning of Indigenous ceremonies and practices. Glass and Evans argue this must have influenced Kwakwaka'wakw participation: they could partake in banned practices for the camera. They also say the 'ethnographic' truth value of the film is unimportant and the film as collaboration is not just a reconstruction of the vanishing Indian:

> The film was a joint project from the beginning, a meeting of Edward Curtis and the Kwakwaka'wakw in the shared enterprise of making a motion picture. As such, *Head Hunters* not only throws new light on the development of the motion picture industry. It also documents the extensive and

complex engagement of the Kwakwaka'wakw – and by implication other First Nations – with the most modern of twentieth-century representational forms: the movies.

(Glass, Evans and Sanborn 2015)

For Evans and Glass, *Head Hunters* has documentary aspects in its reconstruction and use of pre-contact Kwakwaka'wakw culture, including 'the handling of the magnificent canoes, the staging of dramatic ceremonials, the reconstructed dress and architecture of daily life in the eighteenth and nineteenth centuries' (Evans and Glass 2014: 12). Kwakwaka'wakw ceremonies are dramatic and well suited for filmmaking. Even so:

> The very fact that *Head Hunters* was made at all, not to mention that its production involved the self-conscious performance of indigenous past-ness, is an index of an emergent Native modernity at the time, regardless of the fact that its pictorial and narrative content—its staged ethnographic fantasy—erased the visible signs of modern life in the early twentieth century.
>
> (Evans and Glass 2014: 13)

Their intervention accounts for the entanglements of Curtis with the community and shows the latter to have been active participants in the formation of the film's history and the history of film.

The film is not just a colonial document; it also belongs to the history of the Kwakwaka'wakw. It engages multiple histories: one is the Kwakwaka'wakw; another is the history of desire for authentic 'Indians.' Griffiths summarizes: 'Like the operators of natural history museums and world's fair attractions, early commercial filmmakers invited audience members to take up the role of virtual ethnographers' (Griffiths 2013: 172).

Dance and ceremony have always had a privileged spot in the colonial desire to consume the 'other's' difference: 'Because of its kineticism and visual appeal, dance offered a raw, almost tactile representation of 'Indianness' for many turn of the century spectators' (Griffiths 2013: 177). While the film's production may have been collaborative, its spectators had developed a well-honed language for consuming Indigenous alterity, especially through performance, ceremony and dance within a neo-colonial context. This continues today. The context of cultural continuity for traditional art forms whereby they are re-conceived as not past but present, such as the Gwa'wina Dancers' stage performances, does not negate spectators' expectations of Indigenous authenticity as contained within ceremony and dance.

Anne Makepeace's documentary *Coming to Light: Edward S. Curtis and the North American Indians* showcases her research among Indigenous Peoples photographed by Curtis (Makepeace 2000). She wanted to see what they would say about Curtis. In her section on filming *In the Land of the Head Hunters*, the laughter and antics of the cast and crew at Curtis's expense are beautiful moments of agency. For example, Curtis was trying to get a shot of the fifty-foot canoes coming toward him. He wanted them to paddle to the right, but no one listened. He yelled at them to paddle right, and they did, but one man's boat crashed into a rock. The actors laughed long enough for Curtis to throw the reel of film in the water. Their knowledge of the waterways outweighed his knowledge of shot composition, but they did follow his orders, showing him to be a fool. The cast is said to have had fun on the shoot. Getting paid to perform in lean times and being able to dance and wear ceremonial dress were welcomed.

Shooting Indians: A Journey with Jeff Thomas, a documentary by Ali Kazimi, corroborates this assessment in interviews with the actress who played Naida (Kazimi 1997). It is striking how well the Kwakwaka'wakw could navigate and use to their advantage the trope of the vanishing Indian. Instead of saying it is a collaboration, I argue it is a discursive field; the Kwakwaka'wakw were sophisticated and strategic in harnessing the cultural, economic or political for their own purposes. The need to reinforce that 'Indians' do not have to choose between pre-contact culture and contemporary culture, or to say they were part of modernity or are modern, is a sign of continued acceptance of Western ideas of progress and time. If Curtis was not the reference point, but we had focused on a Kwakwaka'wakw artist's work, we would be able to speak to Indigenous conceptions of geological and circular time, as well as culture as something that continually changes.

From the Kwakwaka'wakw performers' point of view, the fact that the actors are their family members introduces time into a static stereotypic image; they are allowed to exist in time, not outside it in some primordial past. The film exists as both colonial self-realization and Indigenous community history. Even as community history, only one aspect of the community is documented and deemed valuable for salvage, however, and Kazimi (1997) elicits a story from Gloria Cranmer Webster about her uncle, who was unable to participate in Curtis's film because he failed to look like the Indian of Curtis's imaginary.

Conclusions

In this chapter, I have not used the 'real' to critique representation. Rather, different histories, including Curtis and the Kwakwaka'wakw performers, nineteenth-century ethnography and popular culture and twenty-first-century Kwakwaka'wakw communities, become part of a longer neo-colonial discursive formation. But how are some of these histories legitimated while others are silenced or erased? There is authority and power in what is allowed to be said, filmed or written for any time period. The legitimacy of certain knowledges and histories is always a site of conflict within the colonial situation and implies a delegitimization of other forms of knowledge. Today, Indigenous artists are accepted as artists in the mainstream art world, yet there is still much negotiating of how they are seen by non-Indigenous peoples. Marianne Nicolson, a contemporary Kwakwaka'wakw artist, speaks to the necessity of maintaining complexity:

> I engage in the exploration of traditional concepts and incorporate contemporary media into the visual presentation of these concepts. While I consider

that the material component of Northwest Coast cultural production is well represented in museums and commercial galleries, I fear that the conceptual foundations of this work are endangered owing to radical acculturation and language loss.

(Nicolson 2015)

For Nicolson, what is 'endangered' is located in the silences and absences of legitimate institutional spaces that her work makes present. She wants to maintain the complexity of Indigenous philosophies and practices to avoid the creation of stereotypes or clichés.

We make choices about what cultural practices to continue, but the colonial imaginary interferes with our sovereignty in making those choices. *In the Land of the Head Hunters* illustrates how an art object as an artifact of culture or an archival document is more than one object; it takes on different meanings and serves different interests depending on how it becomes assembled and appropriated. It illustrates the ways knowledge of an art practice or cultural form, down to its most basic description, is and should be contested in meaning.

That a colonial archive like 'Curtis' – the man, his products and the events spun from them – is recuperated as *Indigenous* history by some communities does not alter other histories of contemporary neo-colonial and capitalist projects. The film still participates in the commodification of all things Indigenous; it is a cultural storehouse for the ills of modernity and postmodernity. The desire for the 'primitive' is alive and well, and the inclusion of Indigenous voices in the film may not be enough; we may also need an accompanying critique of the commodity fetish that is the 'performing Indian,' alive, dying or resurrected. Anthropological collaborations may require a concomitant understanding of the diversity of any Kwakwaka'wakw community and a critique of the roles of informants.

Nicolson highlights my anxiety about how we reread the colonial archive by asking *what* differences make a difference (2015). In focusing on conceptualization as a way of returning depth to cultural difference, she questions how our differences have been framed by museums and art galleries, filmmakers and photographers, anthropologists and ethnographers. If the object itself or its record does not hold a definite truth within itself, as I suggest with Curtis, we cannot ask the object to hold a definitive truth about our cultural past. Yet the multitude of engagements communities are making with institutions and our institutionalization of ourselves with our own museology is not simply nostalgia for a lost authenticity. In the conceptualizations by artists like Nicolson or the Gwa'wina Dancers, we are not saying the same things as the colonial archive even though we use the same words. Cultures, even across the same language, are undergoing a process of translation and, therefore, a process of dispersion, deferral and dissemination.

Even a single space can evoke or carry different memories and, it *isn't the same space* for everyone. For the Kwakwaka'wakw, the film enacts the cultural imaginary of their ancestors, for Hunt's descendants the film is a home movie, for Curtis it is the primordial past, for Holm it was an ethnographic truth and for

Glass it is a space of collaboration and rethinking modernity. Meanwhile, the Kwakwaka'wakw nations keep living, dancing and being Kwakwaka'wakw in their own lands, something excluded from Curtis's vision.

Note

1 D.W. Griffith made at least eighteen films featuring Indians played by white actors. See Eileen Bowser (1990, 173–177). See also the Library of Congress Paper and Print Collections for a plot description of Indian pictures.

Bibliography

Benjamin, W. (1996) *Selected Writings, Volume 1:1913–1926*, M. Bullock and M. W. Jennings (eds.), Cambridge, MA: Belknap Press of Harvard University Press.
———. (1999) *Selected Writings, Volume 2: 1927–1934*, M. W. Jennings (ed.), Cambridge: Harvard University Press.
Boesen, V., F. Graybill and H. Curtis (1986) *Edward Sheriff Curtis: Visions of a Vanishing Race*, Albuquerque, NM, South America: University of New Mexico Press.
Bowser, Eileen (1990) *The Transformation of Cinema 1907–1915*. Berkeley, CA: University of California Press.
Buck-Morss, S. (1989) *The Dialectics of Seeing: Walter Benjamin and the Arcades Project*, Cambridge, MA: MIT Press.
Cannizzo, J. (1983) 'George Hunt and the Invention of Kwakiutl Culture,' *Canadian Review of Sociology and Anthropology*, 20:44–58.
Clifford, J. (1988) *The Predicament of Culture*, Cambridge, MA: Harvard University Press.
Curtis, E. S. (1907–1930) *The North American Indian*, 20 volumes, 20 portfolios, F. W. Hodge (ed.), Cambridge, UK: Cambridge University Press.
———. (1914/2008) *In the Land of the Head Hunters*, Milestone Films.
Davis, B. A. (1985) *Edward S. Curtis: The Life and Times of a Shadow Catcher*, SanFrancisco, CA: Chronicle Books.
Deloria, P. J. (2004) *Indians in Unexpected Places*, Lawrence, KS: University of Kansas.
Dubin, M. (2001) *Native America Collected: The Culture of an Art World*, Albuquerque, New Mexico, South America: University of New Mexico Press.
Evans, B. and A. Glass (eds.) (2014) *Return to the Land of the Head Hunters: Edward S. Curtis. The Kwakwaka'wakw and the Making of Modern Cinema*, Seattle, WA, USA: University of Washington Press.
Fabian, J. (1983) *Time and the Other: How Anthropology Makes Its Object*, New York, NY: Columbia University Press.
Fleming, P. R., and J. Luskey (1986) *North American Indians in Early Photographs*, New-York, NY: Harper and Row.
Geertz, C. (1996). *After the Fact: Two Countries, Four Decades, One Anthropologist*, Cambridge, MA: Harvard University Press.
Gidley, M. (2000) *Edward S. Curtis and the North American Indian*, Boston, MA: Cambridge University Press.
Glass, A., B. Evans and A. Sanborn (2015) 'The Kwakwaka'wakw, Curtis, and the Making of Head Hunters,' *Edward Curtis Meets The Kwakwaka'wakw 'In the Land of the Head Hunters'*. Online. Available HTTP: <http://www.curtisfilm.rutgers.edu/film/making-of-head-hunters-mainmenu-34> (Accessed 13 May 2015).

Griffiths, A. (2013) *Wondrous Difference: Cinema, Anthropology and Turn-of-the-Century-Visual Culture*, New York, NY: Columbia University Press.

Hawker, R. (2003) *Tales of Ghosts: First Nations Art in British Columbia, 1922–61*, Seattle, WA, USA: University of Washington Press.

Holm, B. and G. I. Quimby (eds.) (1973) *In the Land of the War Canoes*, Milestone Films.

———. (1980) *Edward S. Curtis in the Land of the War Canoes: A Pioneer Cinematographer in the Pacific Northwest*, Seattle, WA, USA: University of Washington Press.

Johnson, T. (ed.) (1998) *Spirit Capture: Photographs from the National Museum of the American Indian*, Washington and London: Smithsonian Institution.

Jonaitis, A. (2006) *Art of the Northwest Coast*, Seattle, WA, USA: University of Washington Press.

Kazimi, A. (1997) *Shooting Indians: A Journey with Jeff Thomas*, Vtape Distribution.

Lyman, C. M. (1982) *The Vanishing Race and Other Illusions: Photographs by Edward S. Curtis*, New York, NY: Pantheon.

Makepeace, A. (2000) *Coming To Light: Edward S. Curtis and The North American Indians*, Makepeace Films.

———. (2002) *Edward S. Curtis: Coming to Light*, Washington, DC: National Geographic Society.

Maxwell, A. (1999) *Colonial Photography & Exhibitions: Representations of the 'Native' and the Making of European Identities*, London and New York: Leicester University Press.

Nicolson, M. (2015) 'Artist Statement,' *The Medicine Project*. Available HTTP: < www.themedicineproject.com/marianne-nicolson.html> (Accessed 13 May 2015).

Pearce, R. H.. (1965) *Savagism and Civilization: A Study of the Indian and the American Mind*, Berkeley, CA: University of California Press.

Raheja, M. (2013) *Reservation Reelism: Redfacing, Visual Sovereignty, and Representations of Native Americans in Film*, Lincoln, NE, USA: University of Nebraska Press.

Russell, C. (1999) *Experimental Ethnography: The Work of Film in the Age of Video*, Durham, NC: Duke University Press.

Trinh, T. Minh-Ha. (1989) *Woman, Native, Other: Writing Postcoloniality and Feminism*, Bloomington, IN, USA: Indiana University Press.

Wakeham, P. (2006) 'Becoming Documentary: Edward Curtis's In the Land of the Head Hunters and the Politics of Archival Reconstruction,' *Canadian Review of American Studies*, 36(3):293–309.

7 Impolitical mandate
De-fatalizing a port city

Suvendrini Perera and Annette Seeman

Figure 7.1 Annette Seeman, *Impolitical Mandate*, 2012

Responding to the call for a new writing that is neither about redemption or erasure, visual and verbal fragments, scraps of autobiographical and historical stories, images and narratives fleetingly cohere and diverge in this collaboration. Temporalities layer upon, transect and inscribe one another along a coastline that is no timeless landscape, but an ecology that is, precisely, *in and of time*: a portscape of human, animal and mineral freights, of multiple occupations and arrivals; of natural and unnatural excrescences; historical and asynchronous, living and dead.

Drawing on Giorgio Agamben's meditation on the eclipse of the political, what is essayed here is a de-fatalization of the united faces that comprise the 'impolitical mandate' of the present:

> The traditional historical potentialities – poetry, religion, philosophy – which from both the Hegelo-Kojevian and Heideggerian perspectives kept the historic-political destiny of peoples awake, have long since been transformed into cultural spectacles and private experiences, and have lost all historical efficacy. Faced with this eclipse, the only task that still seems to retain some seriousness is the assumption of the burden – and the 'total management' – of biological life, that is, of the very animality of man. Genome, global

economy, and humanitarian ideology are the three united faces of this process in which posthistorical humanity seems to take its own physiology as it last, impolitical mandate.

(Agamben 2004: 77)

Like a nemesis from the sea, the interrogative presence of the migrant, who announces planetary processes that are not ours to manage and define ...
(Chambers 2010: 678)

A working port

Fremantle, Australia's the nearest port to the coasts of Asia, was the first stop for migrant ships up until the 1960s. These days, it's more tourists on cruise ships. The refugees come on broken, stinking boats, under interception, or are found famished and bleeding in bushland.

> They were all very polite, and each of them shook my hand and told me they were Sri Lankan ... You could tell that they didn't fit in, and they looked like they were dressed in their Sunday best ... they were really weak when they shook my hand ... Once we had managed to make sense of each other's English I told them there was a bus coming to pick them up ... the cops' bus.
> (*Sydney Morning Herald* 2001)

Minerals and metals, swathed in heavy thicknesses of plastic intended to reassure the squeamish or fearful, are carried through the city of Fremantle on their way to the sea. In their wake, birds dropped dead from the sky and children still carry poison traces in their blood in a port not far from here. An invisible toxic trail links this city to far-away red slashes, named for dragons and dead explorers,

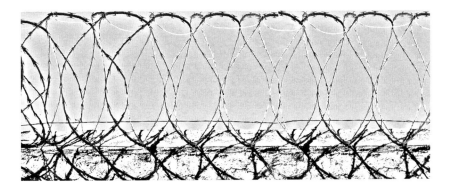

Figure 7.2 Annette Seeman, *A Working Port 1*, 2012

Figure 7.3 Annette Seeman, *A Working Port 2*, 2012

Figure 7.4 Annette Seeman, *A Working Port 3*, 2012

Figure 7.5 Annette Seeman, *A Working Port 4*, 2012

blasted into Aboriginal earth. No wild boomtowns here; instead the serviceable order of a fly-in fly-out occupation.

Several jails, a cantonment and an asylum, in addition to the port, orient this city, reminders of an earlier occupation, no more benign for their present transmutation into quaint landmarks.

Naked Noongar and Yamadji prisoners in chains were walked along these raddled limestone cliffs, through the gates of the roundhouse to the island prison of Rottnest.

And these cliffs, too, have overseen ships sailing in through the brilliant, dolphin-plied waters, stacked with hopeful comers, with papers and without, bodies redolent with unspeakable pasts.

Another's telling

What can be found of ourselves in another history and place?
What can we find of ourselves through another's telling?
How to become the rememberer of another remembering?

Mum and Pop both moved to the West Coast of Australia in the early 1980s; lots of people were moving to the West from the East.

Pop came first to Fremantle Port in 1951, same port that the *Tampa* still docks at, that ship with its cargo of rescued would-be refugees, the people, the one the prime minister declared would never set foot in Australia. Fifty years before that, Pop came in a boat from Indonesia; boat arrivals are less frequent these days. He was lucky to be here.

He was Indies or Indo, a mix. His family had lived in Indonesia since the 1500s, an old trade family of opportunistic, mixed marriages, neither one thing nor the other . . . maybe all?

His name was Earnest, but he called himself Tom. Tom was an easier fit, Tom was *friendlier*, he told the child, when she asked why he didn't use his real name.

On his arrival in 1951 to meet his white Australian wife he needed to pick the best of his mixed identities; given that he was 'coloured' and the White Australia policy was in force, he chose to be 'Dutch Indies,' with an emphasis on the Dutch. He could be, and he would be, European.

Triumphantly he tells his child we are *Europeans*. You can be proud.

Like a coconut white on the inside and brown on the outside; white like his wife, their children, her family, their neighbours. He would be white from the inside out.

They were white inside and out, except for one child, she was brown on the inside.

The mother said how people were very good to your father when he arrived, the men in the family were really very *accepting* of him.

Figure 7.6 Annette Seeman, *Another's Telling*, 2012

Much the same as the slightly darker-skinned foster girl who would appear at the aunts' house every Christmas holidays; a new one each year, only to disappear when the holidays ended. After the girls left the aunts said they were always ungrateful.

Pop said it was wrong to give false hope to children.

The jokes about sending *him* back continued after the White Australia policy was discarded in the 1970s; twenty years of jokes, all meant in good humour.

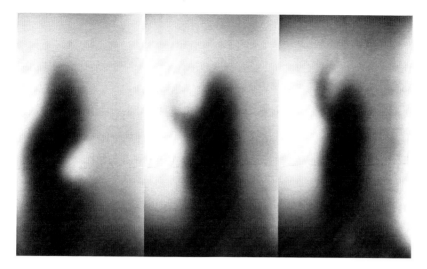

Figure 7.7 Annette Seeman, *Another's Telling 2*, 2012

Figure 7.8 John Teschendorff, *Ship of Fools (Tampa Drawing)*, 2010, Perth, WA, Australia: Galerie Dusselsorf and Curtin University; reproduced with the kind permission of the artist

A dead garden

Like growing a dead garden, things didn't die in the garden.
They were never alive in first place.

A garden of lead and rubber speaks the unspoken histories of a working port: Lead, bright and silvery, reflects the sea on a melancholy day, reminds of the ballast and bullets that carried the first ships to this harbour. Dense and ductile, lead changes like the sea; both malefic and a purifier. An element of unseen depths, it holds toxicities in suspension, impervious to light, yet, like skin, tarnishes with age. Rubber, the indestructible product of repetitive wounding, is a malleable as skin, yet quite as deadly as lead.

Like growing a dead garden, things didn't die in the garden.
They were never alive in first place.

Figure 7.9 Annette Seeman, *Dead Garden 1*, 2012

Figure 7.10 Annette Seeman, *Dead Garden 2*, 2012

Bibliography

Agamben, G. (2004) *The Open*, Kevin Attell (trans.), Stanford, CA: Stanford University Press.
Chambers, I. (2010) 'Maritime Criticism and Theoretical Shipwrecks,' *PMLA* 125(3): 678.
Sydney Morning Herald. (2001) *'Where's the bus? Ask illegal Sri Lankans'*, 20 April.

8 The productive ambivalences of post-revolutionary time

Discourse, aesthetics, and the political subject of the Palestinian present

Nasser Abourahme

> Revolutions are consummately about time. So too, perhaps, are their collapse and destruction.
>
> (Scott 2014: 15)

In 2011, as revolts in the Arab world spread at breakneck speed, in a strangely subdued Palestinian street there was a running joke: 'The Arab Spring was on its way to Palestine but got held up at a checkpoint'. Humour – with a tinge of cynicism – seemed one way to deal with the curious passivity marking the Palestinian scene amid the dizzying pace of uprising shifting the ground of politics and life so close by. That the place that for so long represented the vanguard of the region's popular-revolutionary movements would be so still, and seemingly so insulated, appeared as a mystery to many – comedy, in this case, the last refuge of the perplexed. Yet the joke also signalled a need to explain, to give account. The joke, in this sense, recognized a certain *in*capacity, one that could be deferred back to the strictures of colonial power only through humour. As such, we can read the joke as a way of asking, Why not? Why *has* nothing happened?

In every conversation one observation persistently arises: people in the West Bank don't really know what to demonstrate for (or against). This beguiling explanatory simplicity captures something of current shared sentiments – confusion, fatigue, scepticism – but obscures the full profundity of the disjuncture. The sense that political arrangements have become so mixed up and objects of protest so unclear as to be incapacitating, that people cannot locate a discursive frame in which to act politically, might signal a crisis in the relationship between the political subject and discourse. My aim is not to account for inaction per se; it is to posit a specific relationship between subjects and power as a way of thinking through the particularity of a political disjuncture that is acutely felt without being entirely apprehended. It is to ask a question not simply about stillness or torpor but about *the sharp dissonance between subjective experience and the world of meanings available to make sense of it*. It is at the same time to insist that a reckoning with this dissonance is a requirement for those committed to a politics and ethics of the anti-colonial. Coming to terms with this impasse means thinking specifically about the political and temporal effects of state-building under and *through* occupation. It also requires a political-theoretical move towards thinking through, if also beyond, a critical notion of *the political subject*.

Subjects to or subjects of?

In the study of the Arab world, the problematic of the political subject and the question of its formation are rarely taken up – theoretically or methodologically (see Mitchell 2009). The study of politics is dominated by positivist Weberian state theory and 'state-society relations' as the privileged means of explaining an enduring authoritarianism.[1] Invariably the absence or weakness of 'civil society' was trotted out to explain the 'democracy deficit'; tribes, clans, the patriarchal family, rentier economies, the weakness of the local bourgeoisie, and, of course, something called 'Islam' in its multiple variants were some of the usual impediments to the emergence of this crucial rights-based, contractual space. This has, in obvious ways, precluded a different set of theoretical questions. Scholarship on Palestine, while marked by another set of concerns, has not been immune from this omission.

As always, the exceptions are where it gets interesting. Those accounts that have begun to move away from rule-based, liberal normativism to pose questions about the *mechanisms* of political power beyond a meta-notion of the state in the Arab world can be split into two broad camps – on the one hand, those that would extend a broadly Foucauldian paradigm and at least implicitly question the absolute typological difference between (western) liberal democracy and (eastern) despotic authoritarianism on the one hand and, on the other, those that might insist on the specificity of non-western mechanisms of power – in something like 'elementary forms of domination' (Bourdieu 1997: 171) – to emphasize a symbolic economy of subjection. In a sense, this split is itself part of the split or aporia inherent to our concept of the subject. 'Why is it', asks Étienne Balibar, 'that the very *name* which allows modern philosophy to think and designate the *originary freedom* of the human being – the name of the "subject" – is precisely the name which *historically* meant the suppression, or at least an intrinsic limitation, of that freedom – i.e. *subjection*?' (Balibar 1996: 8; emphasis in original). The debate takes shape around this double bind, around the split between being *subject to* and *subject of*. Those deploying a Foucauldian toolkit take seriously the issue of interpellation and the productive nature of modern power. They operate within the veridiction-governmentality-subjectification triumvirate in which power is constitutive of subjects that self-govern (Mahmood 2011; Massad 2000). *Here structure is never an external limiting force in the face of internal human agency but always already 'inside'*. This literature comes up against those accounts arguing power in the postcolonial Arab world has never achieved hegemony and dominant discourse never operates as an effective regime of veridiction. What is at work is the stuff of obedience and not persuasion, compliance and not conviction, dissimulation and not identification – a politics of 'as if' in which *internal* belief remains untouched by *external* domination (Wedeen 1999). What we have, in short, is *authority without truth*.

In what follows, I work out a generative space between these two poles by thinking through a concept of *entanglement* borrowed, in part, from Achille Mbembe. Mbembe gives us the conceptual vocabulary for thinking about an official order of meaning operating on subjects beyond a kind of self-conscious (external/public) submission but short of a fully internalized norm or belief; a political subjectivity that is neither a discrete internality distinct from the outward rituals of *dominated* bodies nor the *constituted* effect of liberal, truth-producing instruments of rule. His insistence that a 'regime of unreality' gets entangled in people's political vernacular, that what is at work is a kind of *conviviality* or *domesticity* in which 'intimate tyrannies link the ruler with the ruled' (Mbembe 2001: 128), speaks to the state of Palestinian politics. But where Mbembe is concerned with the semiotics of the commandment's libidinal economy of signs, I try to think in wider aesthetic terms about the mediation of the state-building project in the West Bank.

This paper intervenes in this emergent debate to push forward a simple central argument: coming to terms with the current disjuncture in Palestinian politics requires a political-theoretical move that begins to take seriously the question of *the subject*. What can be gleaned from the more interesting recent literature on the Israeli occupation (Gordon 2008; Ophir, Givoni and Hanafi 2009) is that the failure of the direct occupation regime and its impetus to reorganize itself through the Oslo Accords (1993) stemmed from its failure to produce docile, self-regulating subjects *of* Israeli power. The installation of the Palestinian National Authority (PNA) was designed to move Palestinians from being the mere *objects* of military force to being the *subjects* of another power (Weizman 2007). How this was to be achieved under the aegis of a local authority with a clearly *derivative* source of power is one of the central questions taken up here. How does Palestinian political order, described as 'prosthetic power' (ibid), 'void sovereignty' (Amir 2013), or a 'subcontractor' (Gordon 2008), solicit obedience or self-aware submission (let alone conviction) beyond coercive threat? We need to think, I argue, about how a normative world, organized around a certain *impossible political fiction* (statehood/independence), is nonetheless made operative as a world of practice and meaning through a kind of aesthetico-discursive *entanglement*. Rather than think in ruptural terms about the long shift in Palestinian politics from a 'revolutionary-liberationist' to a 'statist-territorial' political order, politics here works in part through a constant slippage or inter-articulation in which the 'new' continues to partially inhabit the forms and valences of the 'old', working not strictly on linguistic-cognitive faculties but addressing a range of sensory perceptions, and here appealing to a certain *visual memory*. Indeed, what lies beneath the 'neoliberalization', 'securitization', and 'technocratization' many have rightly picked up on is the aesthetically mediated relationship between authority and its subject. We might think of this as a 'distribution of sensibility' (Rancière 2008). However, while operating as a form of *figuration* that both enables and compels behaviour, rather than creating a stable mechanism for subjectification as understood in a broadly Foucauldian sense, it works to ensnare ruler and ruled in a mutual world of signification that de-mobilizes a still-common set of aesthetic and discursive tools. This power may not produce strong identification in its subjects, it may not solicit their 'passionate attachments' (Butler 1997: 6), but it produces something much more than feigned public obedience: it saturates their political vernacular in ways that not only delimit the capacity to act but also shape a kind of self-awareness.

This chapter takes up the contemporary use of the image in the West Bank in its most ubiquitous media – posters, advertising – and 'reads' it against the past visual forms it re-stages – mainly those of the revolutionary political posters of the 1970s and 1980s. Read as such, the image appears not only as a visual formalization of emergent political order but as an unstable way of managing the foundational paradox of an authority derivative of the power it is meant to be fighting. *What marks this present is the temporality of entanglement.*

Emergent political order: Statements and visibilities

Defeat is always a moment of renewal. It 'cleans the slate' and sets in motion new political vectors. It was atop the debris of a popular uprising – the Second Intifada's military suppression but also its internal political outmanoeuvring – that the work of putting together a new, more pliant political order in the West Bank and Gaza took shape. This reading begins where that uprising ended, in 2007 and the beginning of the 'post-Oslo era'. Of course, the lineages of the political changes start much earlier, in the 'pragmatic' turn of the mid-1970s, with watershed moments along the way: the granting of UN observer status to the Palestinian Liberation Organization (PLO) in 1974, the Declaration of Independence in 1988, and the Oslo Peace Process that began in 1993. These begin to move discourse and politics away from what we can define as a 'liberationist' formation (typified in foundational texts like the Palestinian National Charter) towards the pragmatism or realpolitik of 'statist' formations. This intersects with wider changes, including the end of an era associated with third world anti-colonial nationalism, the unravelling of the Bandung moment, and the collapse of the Soviet Union. These historical points chart a process of 'statifcation' (Jayyusi 2004) in which the state-building project, as a gradual but violent closure of the 'time' of liberation, becomes not the means to an end larger than itself, but both means and end as a normative value that dominates the political imaginary. With the establishment of the PNA under the auspices of the Oslo Accords, what Ismail Nashef calls the 'instruments of statist discursive production' (*aliat intaj khitabiya nizamiya*) (Nashef 2012) were pegged to the institutional imperatives of a highly particular experiment in native authority (Mamdani 1996). The discursive field and the possibilities of framing (*ta'teer*) were tied to the conditionalities of the Oslo arrangement and to derivative and dependent (*taba'iya*) sources of authority, tethering knowledge production to colonial epistemological categories (Nashef 2012). This has been an escalating process for some time, but after 2007 we begin to see the emergence of new constituent elements in discourse along with a moment of active *inversion* in the discursive field – turning key norms on their head. This is the point at which time is indelibly marked as 'post-revolutionary', defined not

Figure 8.1 Advertising billboard, Nablus, in front of a building partially destroyed during the suppression of the 2000 Second Intifada uprising, 2011

Source: Author

Figure 8.2 A purpose-built suburban neighbourhood on the northern fringes of Ramallah

Source: Author

Figure 8.3 Police publicity images cover part of a street in Ramallah
Source: Author

Figure 8.4 Police publicity images cover part of a street in Ramallah
Source: Author

only by its distance from that which is rendered past ('the revolutionary') but also by its violent and inversive appropriation of the language and imagery of that past.

If one moment marks the shift, it is the violent split in 2007 between the West Bank and Gaza. The split (*al-inqisam*) marks a closing of a horizon in Palestinian national politics; Hamas eventually settled for a besieged and ostracized fiefdom in Gaza, and a self-disciplining Fatah in the West Bank re-integrated into the global-imperial political order. Priorities shifted, and the national lost further traction in the face of renewed factionalism and the engineering of an internal enemy. This was accompanied by spatial and juridical changes in the West Bank: the suspension of the legislature within a permanent state of emergency; class differentiation and increased purchasing power and lifestyle capacities for an emergent middle class (Taraki 2008); new opportunities for the creation of wealth, both licit and illicit but almost all tied into a wider Israeli transactional space; new suburban housing and urban development projects; the restored and expanded flows of aid and funding allowing authority to establish networks of patronage and resource allocation. In particular, in a process that harks back to the postcolonial state of the 1970s (before deregulation and structural adjustment), the state-administered salary became a resource through which the state or central authority buys obedience and gratitude, what Mbembe calls 'a relation of subjection through redistribution' (2001: 45). This was accompanied by the deployment of a host of new metrics and instruments that re-defined government: GDP and growth rate measurement, public debt management, credit and mortgage schemes, micro-finance initiatives, public/private financialization instruments, the organizational workshop, and an endless coterie of consultant experts to work the levers. These go some way toward producing both new political rationalities and knowledge and new interfaces between local authority and its subjects. Political effects take hold in this combination of emergent discourse and institutional-material restructuring.

The discursive shift has been dealt with sufficiently (Khalidi and Samour 2011; Massad 2006), but for now consider the titles of the governmental programs: 'Palestinian Reform and Development Plan' (Palestinian National Authority 2008), 'Ending the Occupation, Establishing the State' (Palestinian National Authority 2009), 'Establishing the State, Building Our Future' (Palestinian National Authority 2011), 'State Building to Sovereignty' (Palestinian National Authority 2014). A new vocabulary, organized around 'rule of law' and 'private economic growth', takes hold in these documents: 'security', 'good governance' (*al-hukm al-salih*), 'free enterprise', 'the national economy'. The language of foreign aid donors becomes the constituent vocabulary of most 'sites of discourse', from non-governmental organizations to news and print media; it provides a set of 'statements' that determine the 'limits and forms of the sayable' (Foucault 1980: 59) or the limits of political intelligibility.

This emergent discourse is *mediated* in extra-discursive ways that shape behaviour despite its otherwise unconvincing claims. In the West Bank, a kind of consumerism percolates across images circulating new markers of self: suburbanization, access to elite pedagogic and cultural institutions, movement in luxury automobiles (Figures 8.1–8.4). Likewise, the common sense of the 'rule of law' circulates visually through media like the public relations campaigns of the civil police (Figures 8.5 and 8.6) or the constant armoured convoys and motorcades and in the rising frequency of the now ubiquitous picture of *the* leader – this most generic of postcolonial power's aesthetics – replacing what used to be the most visible visual figuration – the picture of the fallen martyr. These mediations have a specific subjective valence: they appeal to a sense of normality denied by the arbitrariness and unpredictability of colonial domination or (in the case of consumption) to a sense of agency, autonomy, mobility in a society defined and beset by spatial containment and encampment. This is especially the case with technological objects (mobile phones, cars) that can compress time-space with speed; indicatively, the main cellular phone service provider has a slogan, 'We bring together what borders have separated', adding its service 'contracts distances and abolishes borders (*talghi al-hudud*)'.

Discourse, in its mediation through visibilities, can compel *and* enable; it can 'hail' *the consumer-citizen of the state-to-be* through the visible positing of a set of new ideal-type subject-positions: the technocrat, the businessman, the head of the nuclear family, the consumer. After a popular uprising characterized by affective notions of sacrifice and the bearing of public witness to shared existential experiences, there is a clear diffusion in lines of individuation, as class, professional status, lifestyle, proximity to power, and deference not just to authority but to office become prime signifiers of new inside/outside demarcations. The catch is that these norms circulate in a context far from the liberal civil society and the independent-sovereign state they are abstractly premised on. They come up

Figure 8.5 Advertising billboard, Nablus, 2011

Source: Ruanne Abou-Rahme and Basel Abbas

Figure 8.6 Advertising billboard, Ramallah, 2010
Source: Ruanne Abou-Rahme and Basel Abbas

against the totality of colonial power, and so emergent discourse and aesthetics require an inter-articulation with an order they are, in part, attempting to supplant.

The dilemmas of derivative authority: Sovereignty and other impossible political fictions

One might counter that sovereignty has always and everywhere been a kind of fiction – a theological trope, a story power recounts about itself. This may be true, but we might just as well point out 'not all fictions are born equal'. State-building discourse in Palestine appears at the point of an insurmountable lack, exactly in the temporal gap between this order's pretensions to sovereignty and its limits as derivative authority, that is, in the relatively much wider gap between the story this power tells about itself and its actual capacities. Palestinian authority both aspires and is compelled to 'behave' like an indivisible sovereign state before being anything such, but its irony is in the fact that the more it attempts to do so – with a monopoly on coercive means, demarcated jurisdictional space, control of borders, and independent decision-making – the more it exposes its derivative status. This is acutely manifest in security and the PNA's claims to a monopoly of legitimate violence. There are two issues here. First, securitization is the point at which its 'split' mandate as 'native authority' is most clear – colluding with and defending the very entity the national movement is supposed to combat.[2] Second, security is the point where the claim to a monopoly of coercive means is constantly undermined, even ridiculed. The security drive post-2007[3] is both the attempted embodiment of the state-in-making's monopoly on coercive means, an affirmation of its 'stateness', and the point at which its derivative and contingent status to colonial power is exposed, in other words, the limit of its pretension to statehood – its 'non-stateness'.

A story repeated, usually with some relish, by people in the West Bank illustrates this. It is unclear whether it is apocryphal or genuine, but this is of secondary importance; it is wholly plausible and circulates with energy because it cuts incisively through the absurdities of local power. It is a story about a group of car thieves (for which the West Bank is famous) and a wealthy suburb of Ramallah (the de facto capital of the PNA). In this wealthy suburb, a high-end apartment building on the main road leading out of the city housed some of the PNA's chiefs of security. As with other buildings housing prominent regime figures, it had its own set of armed security personnel. This building also happened to be on a road through which Israeli military patrols made regular and irregular incursions into the city. The thieves realized when Israeli military patrols entered through this main road, a central liaison office, as is protocol in many such buildings, activated a small alarm and flashing light that 'told' the security agents to go inside – standard practice to prevent 'accidental' encounters. The rest of the story almost tells itself. The thieves waited for the next patrol and then, in plain sight, took their time calmly breaking into and stealing the luxury automobiles and leisurely driving away. It is then usually repeated that the wealthy residents beseeched the security agents to go outside and stop them, gesticulating wildly and shouting frantically, only to be reminded 'orders are orders' (suggesting higher orders originate elsewhere). Besides the poetic justice some feel as they recite this story, with the security chiefs robbed by virtue of the security arrangements they maintain, it cuts to the heart of the derivative and contingent nature of Palestinian coercive power.

In the West Bank, the Israeli army controls the types and quantity of arms and the movement of forces; all need Israeli permission to travel between cities, and all are subject to a partial night-time curfew: 'All operational aspects must be approved, including the number of officers, the kinds of weapon they carry, the number and kinds of vehicles and whether they are in uniform' (International Crisis Group 2010: 22). In addition, Palestinian security forces are subject to the possibility of public humiliation by Israeli 'counterparts' at any moment. Palestinian security agents are routinely checked and searched very publicly at checkpoints, often made to get out of the car and place their hands in the air. One Palestinian security official recounts an Israeli incursion:

> This was both dangerous and humiliating for the Palestinian forces. During an uncoordinated IDF incursion into Nablus in the beginning of 2006, the Palestinian officers panicked, as they feared being the target of Israeli fire. *Some threw away their weapons and stripped off their uniforms in the middle of the street.*
> (International Crisis Group 2010: 22; emphasis added)

How does Palestinian political order in this context, with its official fictions so routinely ridiculed, impose its truisms and symbolic order on people? Leaving aside issues of conviction or constitution, how does it solicit obedience or self-aware submission beyond coercive threat? Perceived as treacherous and complicit on the one hand and subservient and ridiculous on the other, what do people make of agents of authority who can neither determine the uniforms they wear nor risk being seen in them by higher sovereign power? Indeed if the donning of the uniform is *the* interpellating moment producing the agent of authority, what kind of officers are these? What is an authority routinely recognized by its subjects not just as corrupt but as *helpless*?

What sutures this relation between 'fiction' and 'reality' (and between governed and governing) is a kind of a double-speak, a movement across lines, or the entanglement of a passing but still resonant 'old' and an emergent but not completely consolidated 'new'. This requires some unpacking. The older set of common terms (liberation, return, armed struggle) were historically in the Palestinian case, at least in the political sphere, codified in the word *al-thawabit* (the constants) and can be thought of as the collective 'red-lines' mediating interaction with colonial/occupying power and maintaining the symbolic reproduction of collective national identity (Shafiq 2010). They were the unspoken common reference points for all public or political communication – for discourse itself – so their relation to an emergent set of terms (good governance, rule of law, institution-building) was always going to be more complex than simple substitution.

When technologies of power are still in the process of being elaborated, they do not totally replace those already present: 'Sometimes they draw inspiration from the old forms, retain traces of them, or even operate behind their façade' (Mbembe 2001: 67). The emergent discursive formation works less as a coherent ideological vision and more as constant slippage between a 'statist-territorial' and a 'revolutionary-liberationist' order – an active blurring of and movement across the boundaries. To take one example, the PNA can criminalize and imprison those involved in armed struggle while paying homage to hunger-striking prisoners in Israeli jails. Authority all but officially relinquishes any demands for the return of refugees but continues to expound the sanctity of the 'right of return' in posters across cities or in statements by countless officials. Activists from Fatah (the ruling party) will lead a demonstration against the siege and bombardment of Gaza and, at the same time, arrest scores of its participants. A notion of 'resistance' is an active category, but its meaning is reworked. A senior official commented: 'Today, good governance is the highest form of resistance' (cited in Blecher 2009: 69), a telling inversion of the original revolutionary slogan: 'Armed struggle is the highest form of resistance'. It is not simply that the content of resistance shifts but that it is welded to a significational concept and practice (good governance) almost and by definition at complete odds with its previous register (armed struggle).

There is in all this a startling movement in politico-ethical categories; the marks of entry into the national body politic, the sources of legitimacy (armed struggle, civil disobedience), are rhetorically kept alive and, at the same time, inverted to become criminal and deviant. Authority tries to move between the lines as an authoritarian but self-disciplining political regime implicated in the protraction of the occupation and inserted into global order and as a besieged, mass, national-popular, ostensibly anti-colonial movement. In fact, it productively inhabits an *ambivalent* in-between space. Yet Edward Said was correct to register a deficit of meaning in all this: 'One of the things that is very interesting, I think, is the discursive environment where words like "liberation", words like "planning", words like "the common good" have all lost their meaning. They may now mean the tyranny of the state . . . So liberation has in a curious sort of way – I can't say died – but has simply gone under, gone under a sand dune' (cited in Katz and Smith 2003: 640). This entanglement – not the dying but the 'curious going under' of 'the old' – is also, as Said senses, an inversion that threatens the very shared meanings that give these 'movements' cover of legitimacy.

Revolution redux: Entanglement and the politics of visibility

It is at the level of visibilities that this entanglement exceeds the closures of discourse and mitigates some of the risks of inversion. Changes in the use of the image are not simply about a set of different representations but part of a shift in the politics of visibility – that is, changes around what is *admitted* into the field of vision. We might think of this as a Rancièrian point about aesthetics as always 'a delimitation of spaces and times, of the visible and the invisible, of speech and noise that simultaneously determines the place and the stakes of politics as a

Figure 8.7 'The land belongs to the hands that liberate it', Abed al-Rahman al-Muzayin, 1978, PLO Unified Information

Source: The Palestine Poster Project Archive, PPPA

Figure 8.8 Land Day commemoration, Abed al-Rahman al-Muzayin, 1985, PLO Unified Information

Source: The Palestine Poster Project Archive, PPPA

form of experience' (Rancière 2008: 13). To think about a 'regime of visibility' is to recognize that visibility always 'lies at the intersection of aesthetics (relations of perception) and politics (relations of power)' (Brighenti 2014: 52). Not merely a visual issue, visibility is located at the interface between the technical and the social; visibility relationships can be constituted by many 'forms of noticing, managing attention, and determining the significance of events and subjects' (ibid). The image of suburban futurity in Palestine, for example, only 'works' in and through an assemblage that includes free-market discourse, the built forms of housing projects, advertising techniques and infrastructure, the technologies of mortgage systems, road repaving, and increased rates of car ownership, as well as the potential removal of army checkpoints, statements, and even rumours, about the easing of movement restrictions and so on. Only in their interaction do these elements begin to 'appear' as visible, with a capacity to 'make sense'.

To posit this kind of material intercourse between discourse and image allows us to think about how aesthetic practices of advertising produce sensibility beyond

Figure 8.9 'Passion is not bound by tools', image of Jawwal poster advertisement, Bir Zeit, 2011

Source: Ruanne Abou-Rahme and Basel Abbas

anything internal to their visual objects. Take the mimetic way emergent consumerist aesthetics re-stage the motifs of the liberationist-revolutionary, often creating a likeness that operates through the *how* of representation – framing, pose/posture, gesture, perspective, and the device of *figuration*, as well as the techniques of image presentation—flyposting (Figure 8.9), billboards (Figure 8.16), even the use of graffiti. This activates a certain *visual memory*, not always strictly symbolic or allegorical, but often contained in *form* itself. The figure of 'the farmer' in the Jawwal advertisement (the largest cellular phone service provider) appropriates a

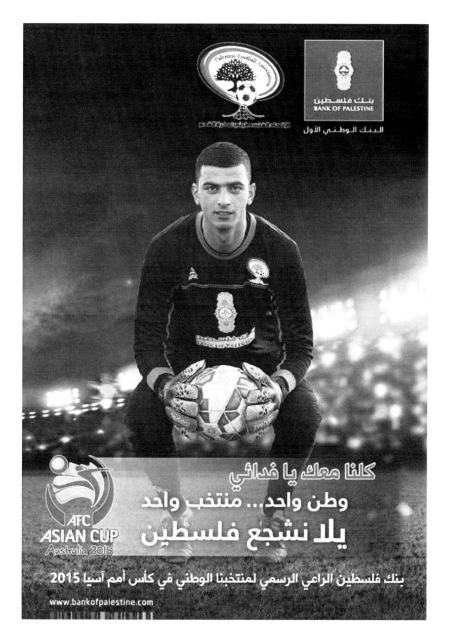

Figure 8.10 'We are all with you oh fida'i', advertisement, Ramallah, 2014
Source: Author

series of classic tropes in the confrontation with settler-colonialism – attachment to land, the dignity of work and self-reliance – now redirected as a multivalent index of the kind of individual autonomy a mobile phone can provide; the caption reads: 'Passion is not bound by tools' (Figures 8.7–8.9). The use of the word 'bound' (*had* shares an etymology with *hudud* 'border', from the root verb *hadda* 'to delimit') indexes the ongoing preoccupations with confinement and appeals to an older commitment to overcoming that confinement. Whereas the figure of the farmer previously merged into that of the militant, as in Abd al-Rahman al-Muzayin's expressionist 1978 poster, with its characteristic deep-red tones and undulating, hypnotic lines, in which the pick-axe is also a rifle, today's advertisements empty this form of figuration from its previous political vocation.

Something similar is at play in how the word and figuration *fida'i* (guerrilla/militant, lit. 'he who sacrifices') is now so disconnected from its previous referent

Figure 8.11 'We are all fida'iyun', Emile Menhem, 1977, Palestinian National Liberation Movement (FATAH)

Source: The Palestine Poster Project Archive, PPPA

that it can even refer to a football player in an advertisement sponsored by a bank (Figures 8.10 and 8.11). The 'new' inhabits the 'old', hiding behind its *imprint*. But beneath the figurative reverb, the shift is legible; the structure of slogans shift from 'we are all *fida'yun*' (*kulna fida'yun*) to 'we are all *with* you oh *fida'i*' (*kulna m'ak ya fida'i*), underscoring the collapse of political-aesthetic consensus in the vertical diffusion of subjectivities. Where previously everyone was *internal* to the generic and anonymous figuration of 'the militant', today this figure acts as a metaphoric expression of an *external* solidarity with specific individuals. This fraught reanimation is seen in the corporality of certain visual forms: the hands from which organic life springs on the cover of a governmental program or billboard appropriate the visual motifs of political posters with their intertwining of the feminine-maternal and the pastoral or land itself (Figures 8.12–8.15).

Figure 8.12 Marc Rudin, 1984, Joint Leadership PFLP and DFLP

Source: The Palestine Poster Project Archive, PPPA

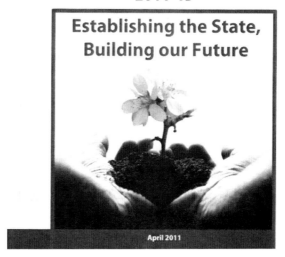

Figure 8.13 The 2011–2013 National Development Plan, Palestinian National Authority (PNA)

Source: Palestinian National Authority

The movement in figurations of the feminine is captured in the image in Figure 8.17. The two female figures mirror each other; both strike bold dynamic poses with arms open in expansive and expressive gesture; yet they sit uneasily alongside one another. The first, in traditional garb surrounded by clay jugs and an olive tree, carries a Palestinian flag and stands almost level with the village. She is rooted in land as strongly as the trees framing her and reproduces classic motifs of femininity in Palestinian nationalist discourse – the maternal, protective, supportive figure of national struggle. The second female figure strikes a very different chord; she is unmoored and de-territorialized – floating in an amorphous and abstract white space. Like the radio frequencies on either side of her, she has achieved a kind of virtual mobility; the caption above her reads: 'She has no borders'; she is mobile, fluid, independent, free. The quaint, stable village – its reproduction no longer plausible – is supplanted but not entirely negated by

The productive ambivalences 147

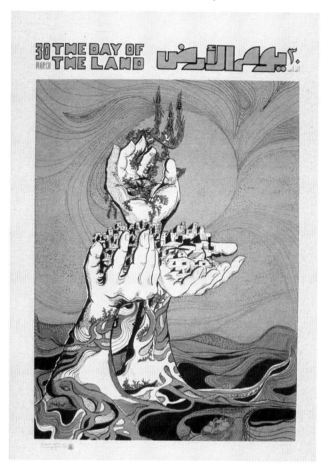

Figure 8.14 Land Day commemoration, Jamal al-Afghani, 1985, PLO Unified Information
Source: The Palestine Poster Project Archive, PPPA

the virtual space of networked communication and movement. Nonetheless, the pathos and sadness of the first foregrounded female figure are not there in the second. The moment has been resolved (or dissolved?). The trauma of statelessness, confinement, exile is seemingly transcended through the technophilic promise of consumerist utopia ('she has no borders'). The framing of the photograph renders these two significational layers into one composition, bringing into relief a mixture of mimicry and substitution, resonance and erasure. We have a salient attachment to land, the claims of memory, the sanctity of return, but this is increasingly entangled with and re-directed by new value systems of conspicuous consumption, suburbanization, law and order.[4]

Figure 8.15 Billboard advertising for cellular phone corporation, Ramallah, 2011
Source: Ruanne Abou-Rahme and Basel Abbas

This aesthetic distribution is not effective as an ideological tool of persuasion. The political effect it produces is in de-mobilizing a set of common terms/images. Keeping still-resonant figurations and terms in circulation but unhooking them from their previous political life-worlds allows authority to appropriate vocabulary or, to lean on Mbembe again, entangles ruler and ruled in a logic of conviviality or connivance. The aesthetic forms of revolutionary anti-colonialism are instrumentalized and simultaneously de-natured, as the 'new' mimics the 'old' but de-fangs its challenge. It is not simply that people cannot find the aesthetic or discursive 'language' for oppositional discourse, but that *this language itself becomes self-parodying*. 'Resistance', 'return', *sumud* all bespeak ambivalence. The figure of the guerrilla/*fida'i* cannot be used to re-formulate a subjectivity of militance because it is now conscripted as content-less metaphor. *The present forecloses 'the revolutionary' as a source of renewal by keeping it symbolically, but emptily, alive.* Mbembe talks of an equivocal vocabulary parallel to official discourse in the subaltern 're-appropriation' of hegemonic cultural form, yet here is authority itself is the appropriative agent of subversion – re-directing and banalizing shared meaning. It is in this 'domesticity' of the relationship between authority and subject that we must locate the inconsistency in popular attitudes towards the PNA, often at once rejecting and ratifying its legitimacy as political power.

Figure 8.16 Billboard of Yasser Arafat echoed by Bank of Palestine advertisement, Ramallah, 2012; the aesthetic reverb is again striking – the outward, horizon-seeking gaze, the determined posture are repeated in a kind of slippage between the two images

Source: Ruanne Abou-Rahme and Basel Abbas

Figure 8.17 Shifting forms of the feminine: New advertising and old mural juxtaposed in downtown Ramallah, 2009

Source: Ruanne Abou-Rahme

Indefinite finality: The present and its absences

If Mbembe is correct to say that what is distinctive and particular about an age – its spirit – is constituted by the material practices, signs, figures, and images that are available and actually experienced (Mbembe 2001: 15), this drawn-out sketch raises obvious questions. What *kind* of time is this? *When* is the Palestine of good governance? We might reply with the observation that in the post-revolutionary era, time as it is subjectively lived begins to fracture; it's multiple, jagged, uneven, out of sync. I don't mean this only with respect to the proliferation of differential mobilities *within* Palestinian society. Think of time as a specific and visibly mediated configuration of relations between past and future. Statist discursive formations in a Palestine still under occupation usher in a temporality that must sever its connections to the past; it must do so because 'statification' is the formalization of an endgame with no redress for the historical dispossession hitherto the starting point and line of flight for Palestinian politics. Whereas previously the future was 'telescoped' as a kind of redress of the past, the current image of the future makes reference to this past only as a floating, ahistorical figuration – as pure form. This is an image of the future with no need to respond to the historical imperative that previously defined revolutionary discourse and aesthetics. Rarely is there a sense that the future necessarily has to correct or rectify the originary 'sins' of the constitutive acts of the *Nakba*. Rather, this seemingly imminent future seeks to sublate what is now rendered a finished past, to close the openness of the historical circuit between past and future through the petrification of state-building. Statist discourse and its aesthetics, then, overwrite the geographies of 'liberation' (the expansive, originary notion of Palestine that is gradually replaced by the West Bank and Gaza, then only the West Bank, and eventually only fragments of that) and also their temporalities (return and recoverability).

Between emergent official discourse and its sublated 'old' antecedent are two incongruent relationships to the past and history. This was made clear to me watching a recent documentary film about Qalandiya Refugee Camp and listening to a remarkable statement by one young West Bank refugee: 'He who has no history should go home. There is no present without history. If you want to make a present-future than you have to know your history' (Coulter 2014). This 'history' directly overlaps with inherited memory and is the condition of making sense of a present that only by virtue of its relationship to the past opens out into a future. The past – in its incompleteness or its redeemability – still marks the trajectory of liberation; without an appreciation of it, he is saying, 'we' as political collective are finished – we 'should go home' (*rawih ala baytu*), that is, give up. There is a striking double entendre here because he is also saying that without 'history' we cannot go 'home' (with 'home' as site of past rupture and future restitution). The statist turn ushers in History proper, which must, as Pierre Nora would argue, 'divest the lived past of its legitimacy' and 'reduce memory to relic' (1996: 3). For Nora, this is inseparable from the consolidation of the national form: when 'the nation ceased to be a cause and became a given', then 'history became a social science; and memory became a purely private phenomenon' (ibid: 6). It is not simply that those who correspond to the originary figures of Palestinian nationalism (*actual* refugees, exiles, militants, prisoners) experience 'the time/age' differently, but that they are 'out of time', not part of the official flow of time or its linear progress – moored in memory that refuses to be divested from history and unable to accept a History that barters with memory only as symbol.

Of course this can be read differently, not as the point at which the nation 'becomes a given', but as the point at which it ceases to be taken for granted. Is there not something here of an undoing of what Benedict Anderson (1991), echoing Walter Benjamin, describes as 'simultaneity across homogenous, empty time' that is the time of the nation? Can we say 'homogenous empty time' is premised not only on a certain ontology of History but in equal measure on a 'smooth' territorialization at odds with the *differentially* striated geography and jagged surface of Palestine? Is there something, at least in spatio-temporal terms, that suggests that in Palestine the consolidation of proto-statist form comes precisely at the cost of the national imaginary it appeals to?[5]

In this receding of the past as reference point, we see the closure of the future as a horizon. 'Statism' here does not simply signal Palestine's entry into the community of civilized nation-states, however partial, but also the suspension of its politics in an indefinite and indeterminate form. Another way to put this would be to say the temporality of 'statism' short-circuits the political process of emancipation itself. Rather than signal a transition to a postcolonial temporality, the state-building project ensures the bypassing of decolonization, the coexistence of occupation and 'freedom', or the conjugation of colonialism with its past, the collapsing of seemingly diachronic, sequential stages into a synchronous, if incoherent, whole. We might think of this Palestine as *the tragedy of the postcolonial without the triumph, however pyrrhic, of the anti-colonial*. Elsewhere I call this the 'perpetual, suspended present' of Palestinian state-building (Abourahme 2011: 455), trapped, seemingly perpetually, between the (endless) colonial present and the (deferred) postcolonial future. In similar terms, legal theorist Samera Esmeir calls this temporality a 'lingering present' (Esmeir 2010).[6] The state, here, is both promise and premise, both *telos* and *techne*. *Statehood becomes not a vanishing point but a repetitive false threshold.* Think of the declaration of statehood in 2011 and the UN membership bid that came and went, consider the touted 'rebirth' of Palestine (Figure 8.18), or listen to an official discourse obsessively concerned with a seemingly imminent but never realized future. 'Homestretch to Freedom' was the name of the government's second program in 2009, as if the future is just (and always) around the corner, a short leap into the 'future state of Palestine' and its 'future capital of Jerusalem'. This is a futurity that is already present; all it requires is the messianic belief in the cosmological effects of 'statification'. The point is not simply the exclusion of those (refugees, militants, the poor) who cannot belong to the projected futurity of the emergent Palestinian image, but the suspension of futurity itself. It is hard to overestimate the violent closure this enacts on the temporal horizon that revolutionary Palestinian thought and praxis had – despite multiple and heavy failures – succeeded in opening in the three decades of its existence before the Oslo process. Fawaz Turki once said, 'If the Palestinian revolution is armed with a philosophy at all, it is armed with the anti-determinist vision of the

Figure 8.18 Billboard heralding Palestine's rebirth at the United Nations, Ramallah
Source: Ruanne Abou-Rahme and Basel Abbas

open-endedness of the future' (1981: 375). It is precisely this open-endedness that is at stake in the *indefinite finality* of state-building.

What forms of solidarity are workable without shared historical reference? What kind of politics is possible without futurity? What kind of effective, political logics of action are deployable outside the temporal frame of anticipation? What happens when the history of a people's revolutionary experience is foreclosed as a source of critical renewal? When the taking stock of political defeat is indefinitely deferred? What is the political subject that is neither fully 'subject of' nor 'subject to' the political order(s) it inhabits? These are some of the questions we must consider if we want to come to grips with the current disjuncture in Palestine and some of the wider temporal impasses of political action in the postcolonial and post-socialist world. What Palestinian subjects are able to fashion without the register and utopic horizon of the anti-colonial – that is, with the passing of revolutionary futurity – is germane beyond its immediate context. If the neoliberal age and the collapse of anti-colonial or socialist counter-universality means the *subjective negotiation of suspended time*, perhaps Palestine has something to teach us all. The perpetual present is not Palestine's alone. Much of David Scott's work is an urgent grappling with a distinct sense of stalled present; the opening pages of his recent book strike a sharply resonant note as he writes of postcolonial temporality: 'A certain experience of temporal afterness prevails in which the trace of futures past hangs like the remnants of a voile curtain over what feels uncannily like an endlessly extending present' (Scott 2014: 6). For Scott, this is all the more acute in the aftermath of failed revolution, not only because revolutionary action always contains the ever-lurking potential of tragedy but also because failed modern revolutions underline the growing divergence of time and history.

Palestine offers a productive vantage point from which to think through this, partly because the terms of the failure of its revolution keep installed the colonial contradiction that conversely means this failure cannot be complete and partly because its post-defeat age is defined by a constitutive blurring of temporal markers – between the revolutionary and the statist, between the colonial and the post-colonial – in which past and future are closed and at the same time made more acute, more insurmountable, more *present* even: 'as though the ends of history somehow marked the beginnings of time' (Scott 2014: 12). As though the cleft between official meaning and shared experience might offer us futurities of return and recovery free from the bucolic nostalgia and stagist development that marked their codification into politically expedient discourse. The current disjuncture may not readily provide the ethical and political resources for collective action, but in its necessarily entangled temporality, it keeps Palestinian political subjectivity indeterminate – an indeterminacy not adequately captured by notions of domination or constitution but requiring a separate theorization, not least because it might just be the very ground of political action.

Notes

1 Even Marxist accounts of Arab politics, while differing sharply from liberal or constitutionalist treatments in their causal emphasis, remain mired in a paradigm of the 'deep structure' of 'the state' (Abed-Malek 1968; Amin 1978). While Nazih Ayubi tried to redress the inflation of the state, his move to substitute hegemony for legitimacy (and Gramsci for Weber) as the central conceptual nodal point hardly mitigated the problem (Ayubi 1995).
2 'Security coordination' (tansiq amni) remains the pillar of the Oslo Peace process (despite breaking down during the Second Intifada [2000–2006]) and is where the lines of collusion are most clear: the vetting of potential security agents by Israeli and American intelligence services; the sharing of suspect lists and the 'revolving doors' of arrest; the joint patrols and so on.
3 Between 2007 and 2011 the US and EU poured 450 million dollars into the Palestinian Security Forces (PSF), creating one of the highest proportions of security officers to civilians anywhere in the world.
4 An art-research project, The Zone by Basel Abbas and Ruanne Abou-Rahme, works with the connections between political posters and the contemporary visual landscape in Palestine. My analysis stems from ongoing collaboration on a project with these artists, and many of the photographs are drawn from their collection.
5 May Jayyusi pointed this other reading out to me.
6 Esmeir describes this process as a kind of self-disciplining, the latest chapter of which is the capture of Palestinian politics by 'international strategies of rule put forward by the UN and international law' (Esmeir 2010).

Bibliography

Abdel-Malek, A. (1968) *Egypt: Military Society*, New York, NY: Random House.
Abourahme, N. (2011) 'Spatial Collisions and Discordant Temporalities: Everyday life between Camp and Checkpoint,' *International Journal of Urban and Regional Research*, 1:453–461.

Amin, S. (1978) *The Arab Nation: Nationalism and Class Struggles*, London, UK: Zed Books.
Amir, M. (2013) 'The Making of a Void Sovereignty: Political Implications of the Military Checkpoints in the West Bank,' *Environment and Planning D: Space and Society*, 31:227–244.
Anderson, B. (1991) *Imagined Communities: Reflections on the Origin and Spread of Nationalism, Revised and Extended Edition*, London, UK: Verso.
Ayubi, N. (1995) *Overstating the State: Politics and Society in the Middle East*, New York, NY: IB Tauris.
al-Ayyam (2009) *'Fayyad yu'rb 'an asafahi wa y'kid tasmim al-sulta 'ala fard al-nizam wa siyadit al-qanun'*, Monday June 1, 2009.
Balibar, E. (1996) 'Subjection and Subjectivation', in J. Copjec (ed.), *Supposing the Subject*, 1–15, New York, NY: Verso.
Blecher, R. (2009) 'Operation Cast Lead in the West Bank,' *Journal of Palestine Studies*, 38(3):64–71.
Bourdieu, P. (1997) *Outline of a Theory of Practice*, Cambridge, UK: Cambridge University Press.
Brighenti, A. (2014) 'Democracy and its Visibilities,' in K. D. Haggerty and M. Samatas (eds.), *Surveillance and Democracy*, 51–68, Abingdon, UK: Routledge.
Butler, J. (1997) *The Psychic Life of Power: Theories in Subjection*, Stanford, CA: Stanford University Press.
Coulter, J. (2014) *'Searching for Saris,'* Dubai Media and Entertainment Organization in Association with Dubai film Market (Enjazz), Parallax Productions.
Deleuze, G. (1991) *Foucault*, London, UK: Althone Press.
Esmeir, S. (2010) *'On Becoming a War Criminal'*, Paper presented at Muwatin's 15th Annual Conference 'The Palestinian Present: Pessimism of the Intellect, Optimism of the Will?', Ramallah, 26–27 February.
Foucault, M. (1980) 'Politics and the Study of Discourse' in C. Gordon (ed.), *Power/Knowledge: Michel Foucault selected interviews and other writings, 1972–1977*, 109–133, New York, NY: Pantheon Books.
Gordon, N. (2008) *Israel's Occupation*, Berkeley, CA: University of California Berkeley Press.
Al-Haq (2012) *'Munahadet al-t'dhib fi al-mawathiq al-dawliya wa al-waq' al-Filastini'*, Ramallah, West Bank.
al-Hayyah al-Jadeedah (2009) *'Istishhad thalathah min quwwat al-amn wa maqtal musalahain min Hamas wa muwatin fi isthibak Qalqilya'*, Monday June 1st, 2009.
International Crisis Group (2010) *'Squaring the Circle: Palestinian Security Reform Under Occupation'*, *Middle East Report No.98*, International Crisis Group: Washington DC.
Jayyusi, M. (2004) *'Subjectivity and Public Witness: An Analysis of Islamic Militance in Palestine'*, Paper presented at the SSRC conference 'The Beirut Conference on Public Spheres', Beirut, 22–24 October.
Katz, C. and N. Smith (2003) 'An interview with Edward Said,' *Environment and Planning D: Society and Space*, 21(6):635–651.
Khalidi, R. and S. Samour (2011) 'Neoliberalism as Liberation: The Statehood Program and the Remaking of the National Movement,' *Journal of Palestine Studies*, 40(2).
Mahmood, S. (2011) *The Politics of Piety: The Islamic Revival and the Feminist Subject*, Princeton, NJ: Princeton University Press.
Mamdani, M. (1996) *Citizen and Subject*, Princeton, NJ: Princeton University Press.

Massad, J. (2000) *Colonial Effects: The Making of National Identity in Jordan*, New York, NJ: Columbia University Press.
_____. (2006) *The Persistence of the Palestinian Question*, Abingdon, UK: Routledge.
Mbembe, A. (1991) 'The Prosaics of Servitude and Authoritarian Civilities', *Public Culture*, 5(1):123–149.
_____. (2001) *On the Postcolony*, Berkeley, CA and London, UK: University of California Press.
Mitchell, T. (2009) *The Virtues of Recalcitrance: Democracy from Foucault to Latour*, delivered at UCLA's Centre for Near Eastern Studies conference, 'Foucault and Middle East Studies', April 29, 2009. Online. Available HTTP: <http://web.international.ucla.edu/cnes/podcast/107626,> (Accessed 20 May 2012).
Nashef, I. (2012) *Hawl Imkaniat Dirasit al-Nizam al-Ist'mari: Filastin Namudhajan* ('Around the Possibilities of Studying the Colonial Regime: Palestine as Model'). Online. Available HTTP: <http://www.qadita.net/2012/01/27/ismaeel/> (Accessed 30 January 2012).
Nora, P. (1996) 'General Introduction: Between Memory and History,' in P. Nora (ed.), *Realms of Memory Vol. 1*, 1–20, New York, NY: Columbia University Press.
Ophir, A., M. Givoni and S. Hanafi (2009) *The Power of Inclusive Exclusion: Anatomy of Israeli Rule in the Occupied Palestinian Territories*, New York, NY: Zone Books.
Palestinian National Authority (2008) *Palestinian National Development Plan*, Online. Available HTTP: <mdtf.undp.org/document/download/4655> (Accessed 13 May 2015).
Palestinian National Authority (2009) *Ending the Occupation, Establishing the State*, Online. Available HTTP: <http://unispal.un.org/UNISPAL.NSF/0/A013B65A5984E671852576B800581931> (Accessed 13 May 2015).
Palestinian National Authority (2011) *Establishing the State, Building Our Future*. Online. Available HTTP: <http://mopad.pna.ps/enp.pdf> (Accessed 13 May 2015).
Palestinian National Authority (2014) *State Building to Sovereignty*. Online. Available HTTP: <http://www.mopad.pna.ps/en/images/PDFs/Palestine%20State_final.pdf> (Accessed 13 May 2015).
Rancière, J. (2008) *The Politics of Aesthetics*, New York, NY: Continuum.
Said, E. (1992) *The Question of Palestine: With a New Preface and Epilogue*, New York, NY: Vintage Books.
Scott, D. (2014) *Omens of Adversity: Tragedy, Time, Memory, Justice*, Durham, NC: Duke University Press.
Shafiq, M. (2010) *Al-thawabet al-filastiniya wa al-laght hawluha* ('The Palestinian *thawabet* and the clamour around them'), Al-Jazeera. Online. Available HTTP: http://www.aljazeera.net/pointofview/pages/ff1684c4–7761–427a-999b-d4609edc49a1 (Accessed 21 June 2012).
Taraki, L. (2008) 'Enclave Micropolis: the Paradoxical Case of Ramallah/al-Bireh', *Journal of Palestine Studies*, XXXVII(4):6–20.
Turki, F. (1981) 'Meaning in Palestinian History: Text and Context', *Arab Studies Quarterly*, 3(4):371–383.
Wedeen, L. (1999) *The Ambiguities of Domination: Politics, Rhetoric and Symbols in Contemporary Syria*, Chicago, IL: University of Chicago Press.
Weizman, E. (2007) *Hollow Land: Israel's Architecture of Occupation*, London, UK: Verso.

Section II
Neoliberal temporalities

9 Migrant day laborers, the violence of work, and the politics of time

Paul Apostolidis

Introduction: Neoliberal time and violent work

The cities of the Pacific Northwest have gained well-deserved images as hot spots for the emergence of all things new in the world wrought by neoliberal capitalism, including novel patterns of everyday time. Whether Microsoft's and Intel's digi-topian reorganization of work-time according to visions of flexible specialization in non-hierarchical networks, or Amazon's and Nike's conscription of consumer-time as unpaid labor through online product-based 'communities,' it is happening in, and emanating from, Seattle and Portland. Yet the contradictions and apparent anachronisms of neoliberal society abound in this region. Global centers of trade and investment, these cities are magnets for migrants from Asia and Latin America who have lost their land and livelihood in territories inundated by neoliberal capital flows. When we consider the industrial work of migrants in sectors like food processing and construction and the peopling of the Northwest landscape with bands of itinerant laborers unable to find steady work even in 'old' industrial jobs, the notion among some critical theorists that the digital age has implanted a new paradigm for capitalism looks suspect, notwithstanding the emergence of unprecedented social configurations. Even as the software companies and online marketers transform basic temporal patterns of everyday working and consuming life, vast populations struggle to accommodate to very different rhythms of time.

Grasping the predominant social tendencies of neoliberalism and the prospects for contesting them requires us to consider neoliberal society from the margins populated by migrant workers. This intellectual task necessitates efforts to theorize their spheres of labor and daily life and the distinctive temporalities suffusing these domains that are outside the realm of the cutting-edge but no less central to the dynamics of capitalism. This chapter pursues these objectives in tandem, first revisiting selected critical-theoretical accounts of temporal mutations in advanced capitalism and then placing these analyses in dialogue with commentaries from migrant day laborers about the procession of time as they work, seek work, and wait for work. Day laborers and the sociopolitical worlds they inhabit are not just vestiges of the past but agents of an alternative future in which passages of time can be disentangled from capital's circuitry and made more amenable to human freedom.

In what follows, I focus on major writings by Moishe Postone and André Gorz, both of whom produced influential analyses of the violence wrought by new capitalist developments with an emphasis on emergent re-temporalizations of workers' daily experiences. Revisiting Gorz and Postone, I develop a framework for imagining a radical politics of time that engages workers who drift between the normally waged industrial workforce and the irregularly employed surplus labor population. On a basic level, this framework derives theoretical inspiration from both thinkers' interest in how work-related experiences of temporality can set the stage for new forms of freedom. Each theorist contributes distinctive insights into the conditions of possibility for an anti-neoliberal, temporally attuned politics. Gorz vividly conceptualizes the political-organizational prerequisites for contesting neoliberal temporalities, with an emphasis on local cooperative initiatives that take advantage of new opportunities for questioning economic rationality cropping up in the midst of increasingly discontinuous flows of work-time. Postone calls attention to the impediments to such localized political incursions that the broadly influential, normalizing temporal dynamics of large-scale industries generate, even as he finds a basis in work-based experiences of time for radical politics.

The day labor movement and the worker centers providing its organizational base illustrate the profound potential and the scalar constraints of the effort to cultivate a politics of free time within the temporal interstices of neoliberal capitalism. My analysis is based on interviews my assistants and I conducted with nearly eighty day laborers at two day labor centers, CASA Latina in Seattle and the Martin Luther King Jr. (MLK) Day Laborers Center in Portland, run by the VOZ Worker Rights and Education Project.[1] Our interviews show these migrant day laborers face perpetual and bewildering fluctuations in the movement of time, both in terms of the marked discontinuities between stints of employment and in the qualities of time-flows during work. These conditions of temporal fragmentation yield opportunities for the kinds of politicization theorized by Gorz and Postone. Worker centers energetically take advantage of these opportunities through programs in which they spend non-work-time participating in popular education, collective self-government, and political mobilization. Yet although worker centers exemplify the exciting prospects for a radical politics of time, the problem of how to transform production processes and social structurations of time on a much grander scale remains. Ultimately, this analysis points to the need to unite worker centers and industrial worker organizations in a common struggle against the violence of neoliberal capitalism in all its temporal complexity.

Postone and Gorz on labor, capital, and the politics of time

For Postone, transformational politics in capitalist society must begin by recognizing the structurally dominating character of abstract labor under capitalism and the materialization of such domination in both historical and everyday temporal formations. Following Marx, Postone categorically distinguishes concrete from abstract labor: 'On the one hand, [labor] is a specific sort of labor that produces particular goods for others, yet, on the other hand, labor, independent of its specific content, serves the producer as the means by which the products of others are acquired' (Postone 1993: 149). Under capitalism, the latter, abstract form of labor mediates social relations in general:

> *Labor itself constitutes a social mediation in lieu of overt social relations.* That is, a new form of interdependence comes into being: No one consumes what one produces, but one's own labor or labor products, nevertheless, function as the necessary means of obtaining the products of others.
>
> (ibid: 150)

Labor-generated social mediation under capitalism has three core characteristics, according to Postone. First, it comprises a 'totality' that 'has an objective character, is not overtly social, is abstracted from all particularity, and is independent of directly personal relations' (Postone 1993: 151, 154). Second, this totality exists over and against people as 'a form of *abstract, impersonal domination*' that compels all persons 'to produce and exchange commodities in order to survive' (ibid: 159). Third, abstract labor functions in everyday life, especially working life, such that individuals continually experience the *flow of time* as subjection to 'tyranny' (ibid: 214).

For Postone, temporality furnishes both effective mechanisms of capital's general social domination and an experiential domain where such domination can be immediately felt. Postone argues that within processes of industrial production, workers endure time's tyrannical character when they struggle to synch their activity to the norm that Marx calls 'socially necessary labor time.' This norm subjects workers to its effects intensively and extensively, in each passing moment of productive labor and over the course of history. Regarding the first aspect, Postone clarifies:

> The value of a single commodity is a function not of the labor time expended on that individual object but of the amount of labor time that is socially necessary for its production . . . As a category of the totality, socially necessary labor time expresses a quasi-objective social necessity with which the producers are confronted.
>
> (Postone 1993: 190–191)

Of course, the constraints placed on capitalists by dynamics of competition render socially necessary labor time historically dynamic. The establishment of any given norm of socially necessary labor time depends on changes in productivity driven by new developments in science and technology. The general pressure to diminish socially necessary labor time thus produces an expanding body of knowledge that, in turn, acquires a developmental trajectory and momentum of its own. This corpus of social knowledge becomes another key characteristic of the alien totality confronting workers under capitalism; it becomes palpably manifest in the increasingly complex technical machinery of industrialized production

(Postone 1993: 296). The accelerating technologization and intensifying division of labor that are the hallmarks of large-scale, modern industry speed up the pace of work for the producers while making this work more 'fragmented,' 'repetitive,' and 'empty,' as well as more physically damaging to workers' bodies (Postone 1993: 337–340). The violence of socially necessary labor time mounts as capitalist development careens forward.

Postone underscores a politically provocative irony of this historical mutation of socially necessary labor time: over the long run, even as capital more and more forcefully drains surplus value from workers' labor, 'the level of productivity becomes less and less dependent on the direct labor of the workers' (Postone 1993: 296). The palpable quality of this growing disjuncture between labor's temporal intensification and its diminishing contribution to material social wealth introduces the potential for radical change. It becomes possible to perceive that it is only because social wealth is measured as value and constituted through the extraction of surplus value, rather than construed in terms of material use-values, that capitalist enterprises continually strive to lower the norms of socially necessary labor time. From this 'immanent' position within the changing norms and apparatuses of production, workers can begin to understand their labor time as 'superfluous time': 'From this point of view, one can distinguish labor time necessary for capitalism from that which would be necessary for society were it not for capitalism' (Postone 1993: 374). It becomes possible to envision radically alternative and far more creative, fulfilling, and freely directed ways of using everyday time. As Postone puts it: 'The basic contradiction of capitalism, in its unfolding, allows for the judgment of the older form and the imagination of a newer one' (1993: 375).

Postone parses his terms carefully, emphasizing that a critical awareness of this temporal contradiction becomes *possible* because of immanent features in capitalism's development. He does not specify, however, the political or cultural agencies by which such a potentiality could be realized. This reticence is a serious gap, especially given that Postone deliberately de-centers class struggle from his critique of capitalism and refuses to pin revolutionary hopes on the triumphant self-assertion of the industrial proletariat. Nevertheless, his analysis identifies temporal mechanisms and contradictions operative on a general social plane that theorists must keep in mind when envisioning modes of struggle for alternative temporalities of work and daily life under capitalism.

The project of conceptualizing such a struggle and grounding it within the historically specific conditions of post-Fordism comprises Gorz's primary concern. The rise of global competition following the postwar era and a variety of technological advances, Gorz argues, has generated a segmentation and 'disintegration of the working class' (Gorz 1989: 68). This new configuration consigns most workers, who lack jobs in the 'stable core,' either to insecure 'peripheral' jobs that are vulnerable to short-term economic fluctuations or to even more contingent employment in an 'external' workforce with no sustained connections to employers (ibid: 67).

For Gorz, notwithstanding the immense human suffering that post-Fordist conditions entail, the emergence of *discontinuity* as a fundamental feature of working life has unsettled the Fordist, temporally inflected ideology of economic rationality while breaking the Fordist linkage between work and leisure. According to this ideology, 'people were to be defined as being above all *workers,* everything else being subsidiary and a matter of private life' (Gorz 1993: 116). In turn, the strategic coordination of consumer cultures and work arrangements premised on full-time, permanent employment left 'no room for authentically free time which neither produces nor consumes commercial wealth' (ibid: 115–116). Yet the post-Fordist tendency toward discontinuity, Gorz argues, has the potential to catalyze newly critical thinking about these temporal norms of work and daily life and create new material possibilities for experimenting with novel forms of temporal freedom (ibid: 196).

Gorz thus challenges 'trade unions and the Left' to 'lay hold of this tendency towards discontinuity and, by conducting negotiations and collective struggle around it, transform it from the source of insecurity which it largely is at present into a source of new freedom' (Gorz 1993: 196). For Gorz, such freedom needs organizational anchors in new forms of human society that express 'the desire for self-definition through other activities, values and relationships than those of work' (ibid: 116). In particular, Gorz advocates the cultivation of 'grassroots community' in the sense of an 'intermediate micro-social space between the private and public, macro-social spaces' (ibid: 159). Gorz describes such a domain as 'a space of common sovereignty, shielded from commodity relations, where individuals together determine for themselves their common needs, and decide the most appropriate actions for satisfying them' (ibid: 159). Within such voluntary communal spaces, people would gain an appreciation for the value of 'co-operation on the basis of solidarity' (ibid: 160). At the same time, Gorz envisions coordinated action between such micro-level innovation and larger-scale trade union and social movement organizations.

If Postone is correct that social transformation depends on workers developing a sense of superfluous time even as they face an increasingly desperate search for jobs with ever-harsher working conditions, then Gorz clarifies that gaining an awareness of the liberating possibilities of superfluous time cannot happen only or even primarily on the job. Critical consciousness depends more on creating contexts outside the time-spaces of paid labor for concrete experiences of new forms of freedom and for community activity that insulates individuals from the burgeoning violence of employment relations. The logic of Postone's theory might tempt us to believe those workers most keenly under the sway of socially necessary labor time would grasp most acutely the futility of spending time in this way, in terms of ensuring the material satisfaction of human needs. Yet Postone clearly intends to break with prior forms of Marxism that presuppose the progressive leadership of the industrial proletariat without critically interrogating the politics of challenging abstract labor. In this sense, his theory invites inquiries into the situation of workers on the contingent peripheries of the industrial manufacturing sector and the subversive uses of time that might be cultivated among them, including activities resembling the cooperative practices that Gorz theorizes.

In what quarters of contemporary neoliberal society, then, might workers not only come to understand 'superfluous time' and the senselessness of capitalism's temporal violence, but also experimentally develop more autonomous needs by spending time out of work in ways that involve 'co-operation on the basis of solidarity'? As I show in the following, a focused consideration of the self-reported experiences of migrant day laborers can clarify these emergent time-spaces of freedom.

Migrant day laborers and the temporalities of work

The stories of migrant day laborers offer convenient lenses through which to examine the politics of work, time, and organizing in the present era. From their precarious position on the edges of the labor market, these workers submit to the violence of neoliberalism and strike occasional poses of defiance. Day laborers' never-ceasing, dire need to earn wages coincides with their daily experience of chaotically disorganized flows of time, whether in the process of seeking employment or on any given job. They live – in real time – the contradiction between the general extension of socially necessary labor time's dominating force and the multiplication of experiences of discontinuous labor time, especially those in the peripheral and external workforces. In the political and cultural initiatives of their organizations, however, we see a glimmering awareness of something like the alternative, emancipated orientation to time and labor that fascinates Gorz and Postone.

In the lives of migrant day laborers, working is a matter of urgent necessity. Harrowing instability and discontinuity are hallmark features of the individual's existence because the urgency never lets up in a hemispheric economy where adequately paying jobs, or any jobs at all, are hard to find. Our informants testified to paradoxically incessant experiences of temporal disjunction when they spoke about their far-ranging migrations to find work. Many told us they moved out from the cities to the countryside to pick apples, grapes, or other crops of fruit when they were in season. Others spent winters in Los Angeles unloading truck trailers when day labor opportunities in Portland diminished because of deteriorating weather. A significant number had traveled often between the US and Mexico since their first trip across the border, sometimes in the wintertime to see family during holidays. We might imagine that such seasonal migrations had developed a certain reassuring predictability for these day laborers, but this was not the case: countless idiosyncratic factors, from erratic weather and variable harvests to the vagaries of family relationships, made their migratory excursions anything but patterned or stable.

Apart from the instabilities induced by frequent travel and relocation, a range of additional problems caused disruptions in time-flows for the day laborers we interviewed. One problem was that the jobs they found were only temporary, but this difficulty was exacerbated by the jobs' vulnerability to macroeconomic fluctuations. A number of workers had lost steady jobs when their companies foundered and closed during the 2008 crisis. In addition, job-related injuries had a major impact on the temporalities of work for these day laborers. Workers often had stints of regular employment cut short because of job-related injuries such as falling off a ladder, dropping a heavy object and breaking a bone, or suffering lacerations during food preparation. Following such misfortunes, many workers told us they had been unable to work for days, weeks, or even months.[2]

Aggravating this stop-and-start quality of time was the fact that when our informants did find work, it was often at an intensive pitch that contrasted wildly with the way time crawled during the interim periods between gigs. One worker named Edgar Medina, for instance, described how during the months of November and December he worked around the clock pruning and harvesting Christmas trees. He would catch an hour or two of sleep in a car whenever possible, but otherwise he battled the rain, snow, and cold to make as much money as he could during what others think of as the 'holiday season.'[3] At the MLK Center, however, his employment chances were as sporadic and short-term as anyone else's. By July, Medina seemed to have a lot of time on his hands, which helped explain why he was almost always in the English classes my assistant and I taught.

As day laborers who came to the MLK Center to try to get hired (sometimes daily, sometimes less regularly), these men experienced sharp discontinuities in their working lives because of the lottery system by which jobs were allocated. From day to day, or even hour to hour, they never knew if they would get a job or not. Most said they worked, on average, two or three times a week, but some reported only getting hired once a week or even more rarely – and this was in the summer, the high season for this kind of work. Some workers blamed the ailing economy or unseasonably poor weather, but most, like Horacio Jaques, said getting hired through the lottery was 'just all about luck.'[4]

Most workers found this situation extremely difficult to tolerate. Some said they were plagued by constant, pervasive anxiety. Juan Carlos Garza struggled for words to explain what prevented him from coming to English classes on days when his luck failed in the lottery even though he had nothing else to do: 'How can I put it – it's the worries. I think that if I had a job where I worked until the evening, I'd get organized enough to study, even knowing that I already had a job. [Now] I'm working but my mind doesn't rest. I'm worried, thinking about it, so my head doesn't let me rest.'[5] Garza had good reason to feel that way. He was getting little enough work that he was living on the street and eating, when he ate at all, at a church-run soup kitchen.

The distressing uncertainties associated with seeking work through the MLK Center were fairly mild compared to the situation on two nearby street corners where day laborers congregated informally and jousted for jobs. Workers headed to the corner when they were wary of the center's structured environment, disliked the lottery system, or were desperate to get hired after striking out in the lottery.[6] In a sense, the worker could control his fate more easily on the corner than at the center: instead of submitting to the play of chance in the lottery, he could negotiate directly with an employer who came by looking to hire someone. With mobs of workers running up to any car that drove along and trying to muscle one another out of the way, an atmosphere of chaotic combat characterized the scene on the corner to such a degree that only the youngest, strongest, and most doggedly self-assertive men would find better prospects there. Garza put it this way:

> Most of the time there are twenty to thirty [workers] on the corners, and . . . when an employer comes and stops, well, we all want it, and the employer comes for one or two [workers]. And everyone can go up to him, even ten to fifteen [workers] on each of the two doors, and pushing and elbowing each other, and I don't like that . . . because I might hit someone, or they might hit me, and it's going to end badly.

The physical hazards of seeking work on the corner included not only getting jabbed or trampled by fellow workers but worse dangers as well, as Manuel Vega told us: 'A few times I've seen young guys who are there and they fall down because they grab on to the car and, so, it can run them over.'[7]

The violent contingencies of daily life on the corner went significantly beyond the melees that erupted every time an employer drove by, and in this sense, our informants confirmed findings in prior research on violence in the lives of day laborers. Interviews of day laborers in Los Angeles and Orange County, California, led Abel Valenzuela Jr. to conclude: 'Almost all day laborers have either experienced violent acts against themselves or witnessed such acts against their counterparts' (Valenzuela 2006: 207). Valenzuela's interviews of forty-six workers revealed over a hundred separate incidents of 'experienced or witnessed violence in which day laborers were victims or perpetrators,' more commonly the former (Valenzuela 2006: 196–197). Nearly 80 percent of these incidents involved undocumented workers; employers committed the majority of violent acts against day laborers, although the latter also suffered violence at the hands of police officers and gangs, as well as 'random acts of hostility and violence' from passersby (Valenzuela 2006: 196, 202). Valenzuela's interviewees frequently mentioned being treated violently by robbers and human smugglers during illegal attempts to cross the US-Mexico border (ibid: 197–99). At the same time, the workers meted out a fair amount of violence toward one another as they fought, physically, to get hired when an employer cruised by the corner (ibid: 196–197, 200–201).

The day laborers at the MLK Center had almost all gained first-hand knowledge of these problems. Jesús Fernández remarked: 'Sometimes American people go by shouting from a car, on the corner – "Fucking Mexicans!" – insulting you.'[8] Other workers said that after being questioned by a police officer on the corner for no apparent reason, they never went back because they feared their undocumented status would be discovered. Carlos Avila told me how a freakishly tall, intimidating officer the workers called 'Superman' used to walk by the corner and clear everyone out when he had a mind to do so.[9] Arturo Pedroza had even been arrested and taken to jail 'for being in those places.'[10] In sum, relentless stress prevailed on the corner, stoked by anti-immigrant hatred, power trips by police officers, and frustration, exhaustion, and substance abuse among the workers themselves. There was the ever-present possibility that something ugly or dangerous could happen without warning. The flow of time between jobs was thus not only discontinuous; it was also contorted by all manner of arbitrary hazards and non-stop anxiety.

Regardless of whether day laborers sought work on the corner or through the center, the temporalities of work experiences were just as unpredictable, mutable, and irregular as those of the times in between jobs. This was, above all, because the workers were so nakedly exposed to the precocious whims of employers. Often, bosses pressured them to work fast and without pause, to the point of endangering their safety. 'They don't want you to take a break,' complained Garza. He noted, however, that sometimes employers told them to ease up; as Ernesto Sánchez put it, 'There are others who want you to do the job slowly but well done.'[11]

The uncertain availability of protective equipment for dangerous jobs contributed crucially to the haphazard quality of time-flows on the job for the day laborers we interviewed. The issue was not just employers' frequent failure to furnish protective equipment even as they pushed the workers to work hard and fast; it was the sheer unpredictability of health and safety hazards, as well as the worker's meager means of handling them. Without protective gear, the worker might insist on taking his time to avoid getting hurt if he felt capable of resisting the employer's pressure. Many offered no such resistance because they lacked self-confidence, were desperate to earn wages, or wanted to avoid trouble with employers who might retaliate by calling the immigration authorities. Fernández articulated succinctly what many of these day laborers felt: 'When you're illegal, you always accept the employer's conditions.'

Another factor causing fluctuations in the nexus of work and time for these day laborers was wage theft – a host of devices by which employers cheat employees out of full payment for their work. While the problem affects wage laborers and salaried employees throughout the labor market, day laborers are among the most vulnerable, as our interviews verified (Bobo 2009; Valenzuela et al. 2006). Often, especially when a worker had been hired off the corner, an employer withheld some or all of his wages and promised to bring the balance the next day – but never showed up. Other employers arbitrarily lowered the wage rate after a worker had already climbed into the car, or had arrived at the work site, or had begun or even completed the job. Still other employers effectively did the same thing by demanding, without notice, that the worker perform a heavier or more dangerous type of labor than he had agreed to do.[12] The routine occurrence of wage theft dramatically destabilized the relation between time and labor for these workers. How could a worker gain a consistent, reliable sense of what it meant to get the 'full value' of his labor time when that worker never knew, from job to job, what wages he could expect to receive for certain expenditures of time and effort?

In sum, just as the day laborers we interviewed never knew whether their lottery numbers would get called, and just as they faced repeated disruptions of their working lives when they moved, got hurt, or lost their jobs, so likewise, within the day labor process, they could never be sure of how time would unfold. Their situation was one of paradoxically perpetual subjection to temporal discontinuity in their daily working lives.

Toward a politics of time in a time of violence

The situation of migrant day laborers reveals the acute vulnerability to violence for those located within what Gorz calls the external workforce, as well as the temporal coordinates of that precarious condition. In part, I am speaking here of the violence wrought by economic rationality on workers' practical habits of thought, such that they tended to see work as the only truly valuable way to spend time, continually struggled to find and execute work, and thereby left undeveloped their own desires for more creative and fulfilling forms of activity. But beyond this cultural violence Gorz underscores, day labor involves the violation of the individual's basic emotional sense of security because of the perpetual indeterminacy and frequent failure of his efforts to find jobs. In addition, migrant day laborers must contend with physical violence from employers, fellow workers, and others, especially when they go to the corner, as well as corporeal violence from being hungry, homeless, and ill or injured. In other words, examining the situation of day laborers enables us to go beyond the terms of Gorz's critique and grasp just how extensive and multi-faceted are the varieties of violence involved in the daily lives of those relegated to the external workforce. This prompts an acute sense of how formidable the obstacles are to developing an alternative politics of time among such workers.

Even more daunting barriers come into view when we consider, from a perspective informed by Postone, the pressures abstract labor exerts on these workers despite their extrusion from the industrial workforce that labors under technologically advanced conditions. Insofar as day laborers try to extricate themselves from their difficult circumstances, it usually is by trying to find manufacturing work to earn a steady paycheck at a longer-term job. But this means exposure to the constraints of socially necessary labor time in industries like meatpacking and fish processing, in which workers are now more baldly exposed to these forces than at any time since the New Deal.[13] Consequently, they endure a different type of violence, as suggested by Postone: subjection to technologized labor processes that damage their bodies, generate psychological detriments, and subordinate the worker's physical, emotional, and intellectual well-being to the imperative of squeezing surplus value from a diminishing stock of direct human labor in production.

Nevertheless, although painful and self-defeating, the situation of migrant day laborers yields opportunities for cultivating a radical politics of time along the lines envisioned by Gorz and Postone. According to the logic of Gorz's argument, day laborers' discontinuities of work carry with them the potential to spark critical awareness of how human freedom is stunted when it is defined purely in terms of economic rationality. Precisely because they are not integrated into the more stable areas of the labor market with more normative temporal characteristics – that is, because neither the ideology nor the prevailing practices of post-Fordism are working for them – day laborers may be more capable than other workers of appreciating the value of temporally experimental modes of living. Meanwhile, the technologically uncomplicated nature of day labor insulates them from the tangible, irresistible force of socially necessary labor time. This marginal position, theoretically, should make them more able than other workers to discern alternatives to the given order of production and more willing to join political initiatives aimed at radically transforming labor processes.

In fact, VOZ's MLK Center is making numerous efforts to draw the practical, emancipatory consequences of day laborers' precarious position, thereby pursuing the Gorzian goal of cultivating a distinctly alternative sense of non-work-time that opens up a new range of possibilities for free human action, operating from an imminent position within the disjunctive time-flows of the workers' daily lives. To be sure, worker centers reinforce the logic of economic rationality insofar as they focus on marginally improving day laborers' job opportunities and treatment by employers. Yet rather than seeing the time workers spend waiting anxiously for their numbers to be called as time they should always devote to economically rational goals, such as job-skills training, VOZ's organizers view this as a time for self-development and solidarity-building, and they strive to get workers to understand it this way. The theory of popular education associated with Paulo Freire informs the center's program for engaging workers in these efforts, just as it powerfully influences the day labor movement in general. Popular education approaches impoverished workers as agents on equal terms with organizational leaders in the process of analyzing problems, imagining solutions, and organizing to change oppressive situations (Freire 2000 [1973]: 48, 67, 80). The ethos of popular education finds concrete expression in many mundane activities at the center such as ESL classes, assemblies through which workers govern the center, worker leadership training, and theater, music, and videography projects.

Not only through such activities focused on community life, but also through assertive political action, worker centers bend the dominant flow of workers' waiting-time, interrupting its violent trajectories and turning it toward distinctly anti-neoliberal endeavors. On the local level in Portland, day laborers have organized themselves to show up unannounced at the home of a greedy employer whom they shame into paying one of their 'compadres' his full wages. They have successfully challenged local public officials to refrain from cooperating with federal immigration authorities in detaining and deporting undocumented migrants through the Secure Communities program. On more expansive scales, VOZ has mobilized workers to advocate for legislation at the state capital, to stage annual May Day immigrant rights marches, and to protest anti-immigrant legislation in Arizona and other states. Over half of the approximately fifty workers we interviewed at the MLK Center had participated in at least one of these actions; most viewed them positively, and many expressed passionate enthusiasm for opportunities to stand up for 'la comunidad.'

When Gorz theorizes the practical conditions for mustering a new politics of time that would respond to 'the desire for self-definition through other activities, values and relationships than those of work,' he underscores the need for 'open centres' for 'workers and the unemployed' (Gorz 1989: 116, 199). In these politicized 'meeting places,' individuals would 'oppose in practical fashion the idea that outside paid work there can be only inactivity and boredom' (ibid: 199). In Gorz's vision, each center would 'become a forum where citizens can debate and decide the self-organized activities, the co-operative services and the work projects of common interest which are to be carried out by and for themselves' (ibid: 199). If we read the term 'citizen' here in a democratic-practical rather than formal-legal sense, this is precisely the kind of center that VOZ, CASA Latina, and other day laborers' organizations are trying to build. As I have shown, these worker centers do more than enable marginalized workers to adjust to the terrible and worsening circumstances they face as neoliberal transformations continue to gather momentum. They provide a wider, alternative context of everyday life that contests the neoliberal tendencies for wage-earning labor to become a totalizing endeavor and for economic rationality to colonize the heart and mind.

How deeply these efforts have taken hold, in terms of the workers' own sensibilities about the meaning and value of these innovative ways of spending their discontinuous and anxiety-laden time, is a question that requires more extensive interpretation of our interviews than I can provide here. My point is to show how the conditions and comments of workers shunted to the side of the mainstream economy can provoke insights into neoliberal time and the violence it generates, as well as the subversive forms of cooperation that become possible when gaps open up in the temporal flow of normalized work experiences. Nevertheless, even as a Gorzian perspective draws our attention to such potentialities, Postone's critique reminds us not to relinquish the grander ambition of fundamentally refashioning the temporal mainsprings of social production. Achieving such aspirations would require strengthening coalitions between worker centers and traditional unions, between peripherally situated and core-industrial workers, and between transnational-migrant and US-born workers. Such alliances would enable day laborers and other highly marginalized workers to fortify, with their experiences and experiments, the project of politicizing time in an increasingly violent neoliberal era.

Notes

1 This chapter relies on the interviews at the VOZ's Martin Luther King (MLK) Center. My assistant, Ariel Ruiz, a native Spanish speaker and summer volunteer English teacher, and I conducted fifty-two interviews with workers in June 2010. We performed the interviews individually and spoke Spanish or English (or a combination) depending on the preference of the worker; most interviews were conducted entirely in Spanish. Each interview lasted approximately one hour; we paid each worker twenty dollars per interview. Questions were structured with a common set of topics and follow-up questions for all interviewees, but we used the protocol with some flexibility depending on the individual person; we performed the interviews with a deliberate effort to encourage workers to tell stories at length about their experiences and to move the discussion to other topics they considered important. The interviews were recorded and then transcribed for analysis in this paper.
2 Employers often hire day laborers to do dangerous jobs without providing health and safety equipment. Constrained by their lack of English, their undocumented status, and their intense need to earn money, the workers usually do not ask for such protection if

employers fail to provide it. For systematic analyses of occupational safety and health hazards facing day laborers, see Valenzuela et al. (2006); Seixas et al. (2008).
3 Edgar Medina, interview by author, Portland, Oregon, June 25, 2010. Throughout this chapter I employ pseudonyms to protect the individuals we interviewed.
4 Horacio Jaques, interview by author, Portland, Oregon, June 21, 2010.
5 Juan Carlos Garza, interview by Ariel Ruiz, Portland, Oregon, June 2010. All further comments about and quotations by Garza in this chapter refer to this interview.
6 One of the two main corners in Portland where day laborers congregate is two blocks from the MLK Center; VOZ activists focused initial organizing efforts on the workers who came to that corner when they launched the center.
7 Manuel Vega, interview by author, Portland, Oregon, June 28, 2010.
8 Jesús Fernández, interview by author, Portland, Oregon, June 22, 2010. All further comments about and quotations by Jesús Fernández in this chapter refer to this interview.
9 Carlos Avila, interview by author, Portland, Oregon, June 23, 2010.
10 Arturo Pedroza, interview by Ariel Ruiz, Portland, Oregon, June 29, 2010.
11 Ernesto Sánchez, interview by Ariel Ruiz, Portland, Oregon, June 29, 2010.
12 The Interfaith Worker Justice organization in Chicago spearheaded the national campaign to raise awareness of and opposition to wage theft; it points to the failure to pay overtime wages as a prevalent tactic of wage theft (Interfaith Worker Justice 2013; also Bobo 2009: 27–28). While day laborers have no regular working day and no way of defining 'overtime,' workers at the MLK Center sometimes face the problem of an employer hiring them for a specific period of time and then insisting they stay longer and keep working for the same wage rate.
13 On the impact of mechanization and machinery speed-ups in the modern meatpacking industry with respect to workers' occupational safety and health hazards, see Apostolidis (2010: 111–160).

Bibliography

Apostolidis, P. (2010) *Breaks in the Chain: What Immigrant Workers Can Teach America about Democracy*, Minneapolis, MN: University of Minnesota Press.
Bobo, K. (2009) *Wage Theft in America: Why Millions of Americans are Not Getting Paid – And What We Can Do about It*, New York, NY: New Press.
Freire, P. (2000 [1973]) *Pedagogy of the Oppressed*, M. Bergman Ramos (trans.), New York: Continuum.
Gorz, A. (1989) *Critique of Economic Reason*, New York, NY: Verso.
Interfaith Worker Justice. (2013) *Issues: Wage Theft*, Chicago, IL: Interfaith Worker Justice. Online. Available HTTP: <http://www.iwj.org/issues/wage-theft> (Accessed February 22).
Postone, M. (1993) *Time, Labor, and Social Domination: A Reinterpretation of Marx's Critical Theory*, Cambridge, UK: Cambridge University Press.
Seixas, N. S., Blecker, H., Camp, J. and Neitzel, R. (2008) 'Occupational Health and Safety Experience of Day Laborers in Seattle, WA,' *American Journal of Industrial Medicine*, 56:399–406.
Valenzuela, A. Jr. (2006) 'New Immigrants and Day Labor: The Potential for Violence', in R. Martinez and A. Valenzuela, Jr. (eds.), *Immigration and Crime: Ethnicity, Race, and Violence*, 189–211, New York: New York University Press.
Valenzuela, A. Jr., N. Theodore, E. Meléndez and A. L. Gonzalez (2006) *'On the Corner: Day Labor in the United States,'* University of California Los Angeles, Center for the Study of Urban Poverty.

10 Atemporal dwelling

Heterotopias of homelessness in contemporary Japan[1]

Ritu Vij

This chapter examines heterotopias of homelessness in contemporary Japan as an instance of 'de-fatalizing the present.' Inverting dominant understandings of home and homelessness, community and violence, at multiple geographical and political sites, homelessness construed as a heterotopic/heterotemporal site enables a thinking of politics otherwise. Conventionally framed as a social pathology or disaster zone, homelessness is re-figured as a practice of *atemporal* dwelling that reclaims the social as a domain of empathy and care outside the disciplinary reach of a government of the social (Donzelot 1988). Against a recuperative politics oriented to folding 'the homeless' back into the care of the state or community, the practices of atemporal dwelling observed at various sites of homelessness in Japan outline an alternative conceptual architecture of politics, calling into question dominant understandings of both statist and neoliberal frameworks and their approaches to de-fatalizing the disasters produced by their respective technologies of rule.

Between December 31, 2008, and January 5, 2009, 1,700 volunteers led by the *zenkoku Komuniti Yunion Rengokai*[2] (National Federation of Community unions) created the *Toshikoshi Hakenmura* (New Year's Eve village for dispatched workers) in Hibiya Park in central Tokyo. Ministering to 500 unemployed and homeless workers – distributing food, organizing lodging, providing counseling on unemployment and welfare benefits – the heavily mediatized Hakenmura quickly assumed iconic status via consciousness raising around Japan's lost decades (*ushinatta nijugonen*) and the shift from a predominantly middle-class (*churyu*) society to a *kakusa shakai* (divided society). As the Ministry of Health Labor and Welfare moved to open the doors of its building across the park to provide temporary shelter from the winter cold, and political parties across the spectrum expressed support for the workers, the unexpected return to national prominence of the politics of labor at a point when Japan's seemingly total embrace of neoliberalism as a form of de-politicizing rule had, scholars suggested, all but foreclosed it, signaled a politics of hope in the resuscitation of Japan's post-war egalitarian social compact and the return of a temporal politics attuned to futurity and the (re)production of the social. This return to a national social imaginary was reinforced as Yukio Hatoyama, Japan's newly elected prime minister (leader of the Democratic Party of Japan), called for the renewal of *yu-ai*, a national fraternity that ensures the 'perspectives of the disadvantaged in society and minorities are respected' (Hatoyama 2009).

On another register, the emergence of new political practices symptomatic of 'representational disenchantment' (Hayashi 2011; Mori 2005) elicit claims of a shift to a post-social mode of politics. Carnivalesque sound demonstrations, street parties, and art performances associated with the youth culture are seen as consolidating a new mode of political praxis in Japan, eschewing 'collective action' and demands on the state (as in the 1960s' leftist struggles) for 'individual,' expressive, and cultural modes of political subjectivity. Anti-nuclear rallies in Hibiya Park in Tokyo in 2003, the 246 artists meeting in 2007 against the expulsion of the homeless population at Tokyo's Shibuya railway station, the rally against the privatization of Shinjuku's Miyashita *koen* (park) in 2010, and ongoing protests in smaller forums (like the music-oriented digital commune Dommune and the Free Media Lab) are repeatedly invoked as inaugurating an age of 'cultural protest' (Mori 2005) beyond traditional conservative or left politics of representation.

Insofar as both social and post-social forms of cultural politics work within temporal frames that take the reproduction of the collectivity (the 'capital-nation-state'; Kojin Karatani 2008), as the ground of political action around homelessness, they are better seen as de-politicized forms of politics that fail to question the constitutive role of notions of home, property, community, and the temporal horizon of futurity in which homelessness is produced as a social pathology. Seen from the vantage point of sites of economic abandonment (see Elizabeth Povinelli 2011; Joao Biehl 2005; Lauren Berlant 2011), the politics that materialize in what Michel Foucault calls 'heterotopic social space' exceed national and neoliberal enclosures of the political field conventionally containing marginalization (of the homeless, destitute, chronically unemployed) within the terms of an extant social order.

Heterotopias (libraries, museums, cemeteries, ruins) function as 'counter-sites,' Foucault suggests, by bringing together multiple historical periods, incompatible parts of the population, and discordant times in one geographic space. By assembling in one place things that would otherwise remain apart, heterotopic sites function as *atemporal* spaces (out of time) in which the synchronicity of the variety of historical moments they contain potentially interrupts the illusion of temporal stability and the social and political hierarchies shaped therein. While much of the scholarship on heterotopias focuses on heterotemporal elements, the atemporality of these sites proves generative here and is the focus of the discussion.

Atemporality, a time without a future or a past, 'pulls subjects from their everyday or ideological relation to time' (McGowan 2011: 119), disrupting the spatialization of time and its quantifying and stratifying effects. The link between futurity and ideology and its pacifying effects on the subject obscures the subject's 'authentic temporality,' the recognition that 'what is fundamental to subjectivity does not change' (McGowan 2011: 119), ideological mystifications that obscure the subject's being in time notwithstanding. To exist out of time, that is, beyond the reach of ideology in which time is rendered external to the subject (a series of nows), rather than seen as essential and constitutive of the subject, attached neither to nationalist pasts nor to neoliberal futures, freed from social capture by institutions (schools, churches, welfare agencies), heterotopic sites negate the narrative of progress and futurity that lies at the heart of conventional accounts of politics.

While others explore atemporality as a facet of the singularity of the structure of subjectivity and its unchanging and therefore atemporal element in psychoanalytic terms (notably McGowan 2011), I deploy the term not to signal the atemporality of being as such (an unsustainable claim) but to suggest that subjects in zones of abandonment, here 'the homeless,' insofar as they exist out of *social time*, that is, outside the temporalities of the government of the social (Donzelot 1988), inaugurate the possibility of a nascent alternative social relationality and a politics otherwise. Atemporality, as much as heterotemporality, opens up the possibility of what, consistent with Foucault, we might consider a form of temporal 'counter-conduct,' a tactical reversal of existent (future-oriented) temporal rationalities. In the context of homelessness, atemporality occasions a repetitive practice of dwelling rather than the desire for a return to normatively given notions of home and belonging shaped by expectation, futurity, desire, and temporality. As iterant homeless tirelessly hone rituals of pitching/dismantling tents in parks and pavements across cities, each move confirming both loss and gain, homelessness transforms into a practice of dwelling. In places out of time, the possibility of forging a more humane social relatedness not bound by exclusionary temporal logics (of nation, state, market, class) comes repeatedly into view.

When viewed from the vantage point of practices of atemporal dwelling, specifically the repudiation of futurity and the embrace of repetition in the everyday, homelessness as existence out of time offers a conceptual counter-point to the politics and temporality of territorialized politics. As a universal condition, the atemporal dimension of homelessness challenges narratives of the timelessness of statist politics as a mode of belonging and home-coming, entrenched in disciplinary international relations but equally in the discourses of *nihonjinron* (Japaneseness), which renders homelessness/statelessness deeply anachronistic. Atemporal modes of dwelling prone to seeking nomadic and temporary forms of shelter (tarpaulin tents, water tanks, cardboard homes, etc.) refuse a domestication of space and a terror of time (see Karsten Harries 1998).

What follows is a discussion of homelessness as a practice of atemporal dwelling that draws critical attention to the limits of the temporal horizons shaping social and post-social politics around homelessness in urban Japan. In contrast to the politics of representation that mobilize statist social imaginaries around advocacy and care for the homeless, political heterotopias of homelessness voice a critical refusal of hegemonic interpellations of home and home-coming. The politics of the homeless (in contrast to the politics *around* homelessness) repudiate the meanings of home, community, and belonging that stabilize the sociopolitical-temporal terrain of national, statist, and neoliberal imaginaries.

The discussion is organized in three sections. The first makes a theoretical case for deploying 'heterotopia' as a heuristic device for analyzing the politics of space-time within the site of homelessness in Japan. The second outlines the context within which homelessness in Japan is produced as a sociological problem;

it draws attention to the limits of the politics *around* homelessness that reproduce either a statist social narrative (of rescue, care, protection) or enact a politics of 'representational disenchantment' (Hayashi 2011) while failing to question the temporal frames that take the reproduction of the collectivity as its ground for political action. The third section offers a reading of forms of temporal counter-conduct at various urban sites of homelessness in urban Japan, unsettling received understandings of home and home-coming and the political subjectivities temporalized to these ends. Atemporality here de-fatalizes the zone of homelessness as practices of atemporal dwelling constitute a social 'otherwise.'

Temporality, subjectivity, politics

Doreen Massey (1992) makes a persuasive case for complicating binary framings of space and time that have accompanied the spatial turn in critical social theory. Against historicist narratives of temporally constructed hierarchies between spaces, Massey's critique of claims of coeval spatialities that empty space of time, inadvertently de-politicizing space, carries particular resonance in the case of Japan. Shmuel Eisenstadt's (1996, 2002) influential reading of Japan's non-axial civilizational singularity, heavily oriented to 'strongly vertical, particularistic modes' (Eisenstadt 1996: 102) where the cultural program of modernity, institutional changes notwithstanding, remains strongly oriented to the reproduction of the collectivity, virtually empties Japanese space of (historical) time. For Eisenstadt, the timelessness of the ever-present 'dominant' of vertical particularistic modes of being offers an account of Japan's distinctive modernity. Antinomies produced by the introduction of discordant capitalist temporalities (linear as opposed to cyclical) are, by definition, subsumed to its logic, rendering the site of politics, *at the limit,* de-politicized (i.e., inherently bereft of contestation). In this view, the politics around homelessness, whether social or 'post-social,' insofar as it reproduces the nation-state-capital social imaginary with its homogenizing temporalities of nation and capital time, is rightly seen as de-politicized.

Against this notion of the timelessness of 'Japanese' space (see Hasegawa 2001; Steger 2006; Tsuji 2006), Harry Harootunian's work on 'coeval temporalities' (the co-existence of multiple ways of relating to time in different historical period) and their role in structuring everyday life in modern Japan makes possible a reading of politics in the context of the workings of a 'temporal mix.' Arguing (with Reinhart Koselleck) 'everything has the measure of its own time,' Harootunian (2005: 25) posits the temporal fixity of the collectivity emphasized by Eisenstadt is punctuated by the antithetical cyclical temporality of nature, bringing 'older practices, residual mentalities, non-contemporaneous but coeval with capitalist clock time' (Harootunian 2005: 25) into play in the everyday. The site for the production of this non-contemporaneous contemporaneity is the everyday, encompassing 'material culture, gestures of labor and desire, mechanical movements both human and properly mechanic' (Lefebvre quoted in Harootunian 2005: 48–49). Within the everyday, the time of the nation and of capital may be 'resisted,' opening up a space for contestation that Eisenstadt's framework forecloses.

Harootunian's emphasis on directing analytical attention to the production of space within the context of the antinomies contained within the temporal mix that obtains at the level of the everyday gestures toward an understanding of politics that is necessarily contingent, unstable, and subject to contestation. On this account, the (re)production of the time and space of the 'social' (nation-state) entails an ongoing negotiation with/contestation of the practices and mentalities of other times and spaces remaining co-present: modern subjectivity, in other words, is structured by this (temporally constituted) tension. Claims about the necessary (because logically prior) continuity of a politics oriented to the social collectivity or about a shift from social to post-social politics induced by a new (neoliberal) modality of capitalism cannot be sustained on this view. The subject is never either fully enclosed by the 'diagram' of constituted (capitalist) social order, nor wholly the bearer of pre-modern/capitalist cultural sensibilities (assuming these pre-modern exist based on a linear reading of time); rather, the subject is the bearer of polyrhythmic sensibilities and mentalities whose political praxis attests to this temporal multiplicity. The asymmetries produced by differing and coexisting temporalities within the everyday include not only the specters of the past but also the measure of time produced by antecedent forms of state action that themselves live on, and are never fully evacuated by, changes in the state's effort to (re)produce subjects better aligned to the times and demands of capital.

Neo-Foucauldian claims about the shift from strategies of rule of the 'social' to a post-social form of self-regulation that inaugurates the 'death of the social' (Rose 1996) elide the question of the 'temporal matrix' within which subjects are constituted. Foucault's description of 'disciplinary society' as a form of social government, in which the 'production of docility' (in schools, prisons, hospitals, military barracks) through 'technologies of temporalization' (Binkley 2009: 72) draws attention to the deployment of durational (abstract, homogeneous, clock) time as a mechanism of social integration, is evident in the regulation of workers in the labor process. The (durational) temporality of the social government of disciplinary society, however, is such that risks associated with the outcome of individual actions (workplace accidents, ill health, etc.) are displaced (distanced) from the individual to institutions, to what Jacques Donzelot (1988) calls 'social government.' Within this socialized horizon of temporality, the individual is rendered 'docile,' subject to the meticulous controls of power as time (in the workplace, military barracks, prison) penetrates the body. This docility is cushioned by the protocols of social time itself, one in which 'social government' sanctions both control and care.

The shift to neoliberal forms of governmentality that take as their object the creation of self-regulating subjects better attuned to developing forms of market agency (autonomy, self-interest, entrepreneurial risk taking) depends on the creation of new temporal horizons in the inner life of the neoliberal subject, overcoming the 'residual social temporalities that persist as a trace in the dispositions of neoliberal subjects' (Binkley 2009: 60). This 'overcoming' is neither automatic nor instantaneous, a matter of immediate 'internalization' of neoliberal policies; it entails divergent and uneven measures of time in different places, given the temporal asymmetries structuring the everyday as discussed earlier. That is, claims of a shift from social to post-social forms of politics are likely to be over-drawn, as some theorists are categorically recognizing (see Povinelli 2011; Berlant 2011). The temporal mix shaping heterotopic sites offers a productive pathway into recuperating the non-linearity of this purported shift. More specifically, traces of sedimented social time come into view, albeit attuned to a politics of dwelling marked by atemporality rather a politics of a futurity and temporality of the nation-state.

Foucault suggests 'in every civilisation, real places do exist . . . that are formed in the very founding of society – which are something like counter-sites, a kind of enacted utopia in which the real sites, all the other sites that can be found within the culture, are simultaneously represented, contested, and inverted' (1984 [1967]: 24). Key to this understanding of heterotopia as a place of Otherness unsettling spatial relations is the suspension of traditional or 'collective time.' Rather than seeing heterotopia as intrinsic, Foucault insists it is through similitude (not resemblance or representation) that heterotopic space constitutes a 'bricolage effect' with an unsettling, disturbing effect. By turning back on 'collective time,' such spaces demarcate a temporally distinct form of sociality, one whose *representation, contestation, and inversion* of other sites (and times) questions the terms of an already constituted political field. More specifically, heterotopic sites, insofar as they instantiate heterotemporality, entail temporal suspension and a political shift. Abandoning attachments to (nationalist) pasts or (neoliberal) futures, emergent practices of care, empathy, and social solidarity at heterotopic sites signal the recuperation of a sedimented memory of social time, but a social released from the disabling effects of the disciplinary power of government. Refusing dominant framings of home and homelessness and the politics of shelterization they sanction, practices of atemporal dwelling are a mode of temporal counter-conduct potentially enabling an alternative thinking of the political.

Homelessness as 'social pathology' in Japan

Japan's passage from a developmental to a neoliberal state since the late 1980s is usually attributed to the Liberal Democratic Party's aggressive pursuit of deregulation (*kisei kanwa*), privatization (*minkatsu*), and marketism (*shijo-shugi*), in keeping with the 'Washington Consensus.' The rise in the numbers of economically displaced since the bursting of the economic bubble in 1991 has generated a sustained social and economic malaise, variously indexed by categories of social classification used to disaggregate the population of late capitalist Japan – *furita*[3] (flexible part-time employed between fifteen and thirty-four years of age), *hikikomori* (chronically self-isolated individuals), NEETS (neither in education, employment, nor training), and *waakingu pua* (working poor). The creation of the 'new homeless,' more than one-third of the workforce in irregular employment, and an unprecedented (5.4%) unemployment rate (Genda 2007) has put to rest claims about Japan's 'magical' prowess in sustaining the economic miracle of the 1980s, with the *precariat*[4] rather than the *sarariman* (salaryman) increasingly figuring as the central motif of late capitalism in Japan. Japan's soaring poverty rate (16% in 2009, or 20 million/one in six Japanese in poverty),[5] etches Japan's economic decline in stark terms: Japan's poverty rate, measured as less than half of mean average income, is the second highest (after the US) among Organisation for Economic Co-operation and Development (OECD) countries (Tachibanaki 2008).

The discursive rise of homelessness as a new social problem, evident in the growing use of the term *homuresu* in the 1990s typically reserved for signifying homelessness in the West rather than the more traditional *furosha* (vagabond) used in the domestic context, is notable for its elision of a prior suppressed history of poverty and homelessness in Japan. Day laboring districts in San'ya (Tokyo), Kotobuki (Yokohama), and Kamagasaki (Osaka), populated by a transient, predominantly male population with weak or non-existent family ties, were a longstanding feature of 'miracle Japan.' Resistant to the culture of rigid social and communal hierarchies and obligations, day laborers in *yoseba* (day labor market) in the heyday of the Japanese miracle economy enjoyed a relatively secure material existence due to the construction boom sustained by a buoyant construction state.

With the bursting of the economic bubble in the early 1990s, the rapid increase of the numbers of homeless (16,000 in 1998, 24,000 in 2001, around 30,000 today)[6] has brought the problem of homelessness into greater visibility; cardboard or vinyl-covered makeshift shacks have mushroomed in public parks in cities like Tokyo and Osaka. Within a burgeoning sociological literature (Aoki 2003; Dvorak 2003; Fowler 1996; Gill 2001; Guzewicz 1996, 2000; Iwata 2010; Kennett and Iwata 2003; Mizuuchi 2003), structural reasons are cited as the predominant cause of rising homelessness, including: unemployment during the Heisei recession; disemployment of casually employed unskilled workers; reorganization of sub-contracting systems in the construction industry; above all, *deyosebisation* (collapse of the day labor market) in the aftermath of the end of *doken kokka* (construction state). *Yoseba* as a clearing house for temporary workers in the steel, shipbuilding, and coal industries or construction work in the 1980s are hubs for homeless men, as gentrification of low-income housing or *doya-gai* in places like Tokyo and Osaka have rendered those in precarious work homeless. Access to public welfare subsidies are subject to strict eligibility criteria, *koseki* (registration of origin) and a residence card, impossible for a mobile population lacking a residential address, thereby rendering the homeless no recourse to public assistance.[7] Those seeking shelter through welfare centers – male, over fifty years old (Iwata 2010) – contrast sharply to the early 1990s when most people arriving at shelters needed temporary housing on release from hospital.

The growing phenomenon of refugees, those living in *kakurega* (dormitories, cheap hostels [*doya*]), comprises a much younger demographic of part-time employees (*freeters*). Lacking adequate income or long-term stable employment, they have taken to sleeping in twenty-four-hour spots such as McDonald's or Internet cafés with access to showers, food, Internet, and a place to sleep, at affordable rates. Termed the 'hidden homeless' by the media, they do not reproduce the standard imagery of the visible homeless, as they are 'neatly dressed and carrying mobile phone, sometimes PCs and portable music devices as well' (Yoshida 2012). In mid-2007, there were 5,400 'Net Café Refugees,' McRefugees, or cyber homeless (*dennou furosha*).

The New Homeless Law (2002) defines homeless as those 'who illegally live and lead daily lives in such facilities as city parks, riversides, roads, railway stations etc.'[8] The politics of rescue and care around homelessness takes as its focus the visible homeless (Hakenmura being a case in point), thus failing to make visible the invisible homeless (those living in temporary housing) and failing to disturb the categories that stabilize the socio-political field. This de-politicizes homelessness and its intimate connections to normative notions of home, community, and belonging in Japan's 'capital-nation-state.' A politics *around* homelessness, devoted to bringing in the marginal or the excluded (rough sleepers) into normalized sociality, forecloses interrogation of the very distinctions that produce the problem in the first instance.

Thus, the trope of *mai homu shugi* (also known as *mai homeism*, a 'desiring subjectivity' shaped by the regulative ideal of owning 'my home') mobilized a family- and corporate-centered social compact in post-war Japan, suturing labor to the dream of private home ownership. The gendered dimensions of the heteronormative constellation of family-*kaisha* (company)-state around which social relations of *ibasho* (belonging) were shaped during Japan's economic miracle rendered the loss of 'home' disruptive of the normative architecture of post-war Japan's 'family corporate system' as a whole. Incentives provided by the Government Housing Loan Corporation (GHLC), for instance, targeted middle-class home ownership, with comparatively little assistance for private rental housing or low-income housing. The low level of public rental housing (around 7%), the absence of a policy to develop low-income housing, and the gentrification of housing traditionally available to day laborers (*doya*) in areas has contributed significantly to the Japanese phenomenon of 'rough sleeping.'

In this context, voluntary efforts geared toward ameliorating the condition of the visible homeless, including soup kitchens, faith-based initiatives that run night patrols in winter distributing blankets and food, or large-scale events like Hakenmura and the sound demonstrations protesting the plight of rough sleepers, supplement the socio-economic disparities in contemporary Japan. Expressing either a humanitarian ethos of charity or solidarity with those marginalized and excluded from socio-economic norms, both social and post-social forms of politics around homelessness work within the limits of a political imaginary that takes as its telos the time of the nation (Japan) and the time of capital (development). The rise of a niche market for 'poverty business' (a term coined by social reformer Makoto Yuasa) referring to the extraction of a margin of the housing and livelihood protection fee from recipients, speaks to the seamless production of both advocacy and protection for the homeless and the socio-economic terrain of capital within which it is located.

Working within the temporal parameters of a developmental logic, advocacy on behalf of the homeless de-politicizes even as it mobilizes a collective identitarian horizon of a shared or normative sociality. More pointedly, the politics of shelterization, or advocacy for the homeless, is a vivid example of the link between futurity, ideology, and politics and its role in rendering subjects docile, alienated from their fundamental temporality. A claim on behalf of the homeless is a temporal claim on behalf of the state, that is, 'an inversion of the temporal axis of the [political] demand' (Foucault [1976] 1997: 222). The right of the homeless to shelter, in other words, 'is articulated in terms of a potentiality, a future . . . which is already present *in the present* because it concerns a certain function of Statist universality that is already fulfilled by a nation within the social body, and which therefore demands that its status as a single nation must be effectively recognized and recognized in the juridical form of the State' (ibid: 222). As the economically marginalized and dispossessed are folded back into extant modes of sociality and belonging with social and post-social forms of politics centered on the provision of 'shelter,'[9] the normativity of the socio-political-temporal landscape constitutive of homelessness is reinscribed rather than repudiated.

Captured by a politics of time in which temporality exists as an external field (the durational time of home and home-coming determined by state or market and a politics around homelessness), homeless subjects' intrinsic relation to time and temporality (as the necessary condition of being) is obscured, if not erased.

Homelessness as heterotopia

Repudiating an ethics of liberal empathy contained in social and post-social forms of politics around homelessness, this section offers examples of homelessness as a practice of atemporal dwelling. Atemporality functions as a form of temporal counter-conduct (in relation to statist and neoliberal futurity) as people without 'shelter' fashion a nomadic sociality borne out of repetitive loss (the continuous making and un-making of transient dwelling spaces). Freed from the cares of social government, the vignettes that follow de-fatalize homelessness as containing within it the seed of an alternative conceptual register of politics.

Across the major cities of Japan, under bridges, at train stations, public buildings, and parks, the blue tarpaulin shelters and cardboard boxes housing the homeless, Japan's constitutional guarantee of a 'minimum standard of living' to all citizens (Article 25[10]) notwithstanding, have become a familiar sight. As instances of violence against elderly homeless men steadily increase (Aoki 2003), representations of the homeless in the media offer a mix of pity and contempt. While a small percentage (20%) construe the problem of homelessness as a 'social issue' warranting the extension of social empathy and care, for a large majority, the homeless 'have come to be regarded as an eyesore by pedestrians and neighboring residents and often are violently harassed' (Aoki 2003: 364), drawing attention to the high numbers inclined to see homelessness in terms of civic beauty and annoyance at the abuse of public spaces. Violent clashes between police and the homeless (notably in Kamagasaki in 1990 and 2008) reinforce the random violence directed at the homeless by bored youth. Social time, specifically the distancing temporality constitutive of distinctions between self and other, is key to understanding the violence in this context.

Atemporal dwelling 181

The violence sharply contrasts with the low incidence of violence directed at the *non*-homeless in neighborhoods and parks where the homeless dwell. Walking alone around the streets of Kamagasaki in Japan's biggest homeless 'ghetto' is little cause for alarm, either for social workers or *gaijin* (foreign) researchers. The contrast in incidences of violence is instructive in understanding Foucault's claim that heterotopic sites entail a suspension of social time, occasioning *temporal dislocation*, and functioning as 'counter-sites' of social order. The suspension of social time at the site of homelessness erases the distinctions and the forms of violence attendant on the boundary-making practices that flow from it, rendering the site of homelessness (because atemporal) safe. In contrast, the violence directed against the homeless is anchored in modes of being shaped by social time; the normativity attached to specific modes of being (home owners, citizens, occupants of public space) depends on a framing of some modes of being as 'other' (non-citizen, homeless, public disorder), warranting the violence unleashed against these 'disposable' others.

Inverting normatively given notions of house and home as temporally and materially secure built spaces, the cardboard structures stitched together with rope and clips, reinforced with plastic and tarpaulin along Sumida-gawa and Tama-gawa in Tokyo as well as large parks (Yoyogi, Hibiya, Ueno in Tokyo, and Nagai in Osaka), draw attention to homelessness as a mode of atemporal dwelling. Using the sides of buildings, windows, and pillars under bridges as 'walls' and recycled refuse to build shelters to withstand the rain and snow (albeit poorly), and discarded cooking utensils and stoves, in some cases, books, candles, tables, and chairs, these homes function as what musician/architect Kyohei Sakaguchi evocatively calls 'Zero Yen Houses' made from 'materials that others throw away: construction site waste, disused car batteries, and solar cells that produce just enough electricity to power a stove or a television.'[11]

The 'meticulously planned huts and shacks' are documented by a growing number of international photojournalists. Ari Saarto in his project 'In Situ' sees them as creative dwelling places, not abject zones housing the 'bare life' of 'disposable' workers (see Shiho Fukada).[12] Viewed from the outside, the blue tent villages in Yoyogi, with their recycling bins and shoes placed neatly outside tents, call to mind the conventions of Japanese culture and social practices of fastidious cleanliness and clear demarcation of formal/informal places. On the inside, however, the cooking paraphernalia, radios, blankets, clothes, and furniture are arranged in no particular order, squeezed together in an area barely large enough to accommodate a single individual. These 'urban hunter-gatherers,' in Sakaguchi's evocative phrase, assemble objects whose use value far outlives their exchange value. In this alternative notion of sustainable living, recycling conjoins with community to reformulate notions of property and ownership. In most *yoseba* and homeless communities, 'thrift shops' sell recycled products, from shoes and blankets to belts and jackets, at affordable prices.

The contrast between the gendered order of idealized notions of 'home' and the freedom from the power hierarchies contained within domestic space in Zero Yen living forms the basis of Yukihiko Tsutsumi's (2012) low-budget black-and-white feature film, *My House*, about two families in Nagogya. The middle-class family of the Shotas, with the germaphobe mother obsessively cleaning her well-proportioned house, turns out to be the object of pity because of the emptiness and neurosis corroding everyday life. In contrast, the *homuresu* (homeless) family of Suzumoto, Sumi-chan and their two friends, although living a life of material hardship, live an ordinary life of shared empathy, community, and self-reliance. Freed from the compulsions of regulative ideals of Japanese society, including its gender order, and the temporal and spatial dislocation that comes with it, the social and working lives of the Suzumotos are more humane, the stigmatized temporary shelter notwithstanding. Rather than romanticizing material hardship, however, Tsutsumi cinematically (re)creates the heterotopic moment contained within the site of homelessness itself via its mode of atemporal dwelling.

On another register, public parks, occupied as privatized blocs by the cardboard boxes of the homeless, question notions of private property, ownership, and the spatialization of time underpinning notions of 'home,' community, and the social life in capitalist contexts. Sakaguchi's construction of a mobile Zero Yen house that 'leverages a loophole in Japanese construction law in which a structure on wheels does not count' as a 'house' makes it possible for mobile residences to be set up on 'public' land, undoing settled distinctions between private and public and reinterpreting the concept of property. Referring to the first such house he saw on the banks of the Tama River, Sakaguchi reflects:

> I realized this man was not 'homeless' . . . he was the only person in Tokyo who owned a house that he had made entirely himself . . . They don't have their address. But I don't call them 'homeless.' Because they have a house. I rent a house now and don't have a house. In that sense, I may be homeless.

The inversion of the meaning of ownership and property, where ownership now depends on the deployment of one's creative labor, and property signifies use rather than exchange value, repudiates profit-driven calculations on which the capitalist exchange economy in general, and the real-estate market in particular, depend.

Atemporal dwelling here calls into calls into question notions of property and labor that accord with the spatialization of time underpinning Japan's 'capital-nation-state' order, repudiating the myth of Japan and Japanese (*nihonjin*) as citizens of an unchanging community. Symptomatic of the loss of 'housing diversity' consequent on the normalization of the private ownership of a single-family home or apartment, communities forged out of atemporal dwellings in Zero Yen homes offer an oblique and sustained critique of privatization, ownership, and property in late capitalist Japan.

Finally, the idea of community itself as the locus of *ibasho* (belonging) firmly centered on the family, corporation, and state, with rigid protocols of inclusion/exclusion and social hierarchies indexed by speech, body posture, and social practices, unravels at sites of homelessness only to be re-made in more open-ended, nomadic ways by homelessness as a practice of atemporal dwelling. As Zero Yen housing communities are made and re-made on pavements and parks with the periodic dispersion of the homeless by the police, the borders of the community remain porous, as people move in and out of specific sites. While a few residents in San'ya, Kotobuki, and Kamagasaki report living in the area for as long as fifteen to twenty years, often with day laborers they have known for as long, others report a more peripatetic life. Thus, Kawaguchi san, for a time resident in Shinjuku Park, moves to Ueno Park, despite having recourse to 'shelter' in Chiba – many miles from Tokyo, to which he repeatedly returns.

Alienated from the social time of thick, settled communities of families, primordial links with *furusato* (hometowns), and the lines of distinction they delineate, social ties among residents of Zero Yen homes, if not permanent, are no less real. Recalling Tsustumi's cinematic portrayal of homelessness as a practice of atemporal dwelling, the nomadic connections forged by homeless people across the cityscapes of urban Japan appear more open-ended and hospitable, emphasizing the singularity of encounter. The durational time (of encounter) dominates consciousness and experience, generating a 'being-with' foreclosed by the workings of the temporal distinctions (between self and other) axiomatic to the 'capital-nation-state.'

In Yoyogi Park in Tokyo, a community of tent dwellers made up of a floating nomadic population of homeless men inspired 'Enoaru Café.' Here artists Misako Ichimura and Tetsuo Ogawa provide tea and an opportunity to create art. As word of the 'Homeless Café' spreads, non-resident visitors arrive daily to take part in the life of the café, abjuring the role of consumer/spectator.

In another example, repudiating statist/identitarian logics and their demarcation of public space and time, Take Junichiro's project (in the mid-1990s) of painting hundreds of corrugated cardboard houses, home to more than 300 residents in the underground passageway to the West Exit of Shinjuku station in Tokyo, sought to de-fatalize homelessness as an aberrant disaster zone of 'miracle' Japan by drawing passers-by into an ambient practice of atemporal dwelling. As others joined the project of painting cardboard houses, and thousands stopped to look at the painted cardboard facades, encounters between people otherwise separated by the space-time distinctions in social time crystallized a fluid and shifting terrain of nomadic sociality freed from attachments to temporally differentiated socio-economic identities. A suspicious fire on February 7, 1998 (killing four people) occasioned the re-assertion of statist order as all homeless occupants were removed, allowing the government to build a moving walkway preventing any reconstruction of cardboard homes.

Punctuating the social time of the 'capital-nation-state,' homelessness reconceived as a practice of atemporal dwelling provides the conceptual architecture of an alternative socio-political imaginary, de-fatalizing homelessness and overcoming the limits of the politics of inclusion detailed by social and post-social approaches to homelessness. By calling attention to the limits of the terms of home, home-coming, property, and community, homelessness as a practice of atemporal dwelling delineates a different sociality, not predicated on a progressivist narrative of futurity, home ownership, or shelterization. Rather, by drawing attention to the practices of atemporal dwelling and the modes of sociality they occasion at sites of homelessness construed as heterotopic counter-sites, the alternative order of the political that emerges here summons homelessness as a practice of dwelling, with its emphases on fluidity, open-endedness, and hospitality attesting to a conceptual/political radicality that rebukes the settlements on offer by a compromised 'capital-nation-state' in its social and post-social guises.

Notes

1 This chapter relies on research first appearing in Protosociology in 2012; I am grateful to the editor for permission to draw on sections.
2 I have elected not to use macrons or circumflex accents to write Nihongo (Japanese) terms in Romaji (English), given the more general audience.
3 A portmanteau combining 'free' and the German arbeiter for part-timer.
4 A neologism combining the terms 'precarious' and 'proletariat'; the precariat has become the centerpiece of a growing literature on insecure labor in advanced industrialized countries.
5 Japan Times Online (2011) Poverty Rate Hit Record High in '09, Japan Times Online, July 13. Also see OECD FactBook Statistics 2011–2012 at http://www.oecd-ilibrary. org/economics/oecd-factbook-2011–2012-factbook-2011-en.
6 Thirty thousand homeless may appear a small number when compared to other countries, but homelessness as a different scopic regime not simply its empirical scale is the focus of discussion; see Koseirodosho (2006).
7 The 2002 Special Law on Temporary Measures to Support the Self-Reliance of Homeless People (Homuresu no Jiritsu jino Shien nado ni kan suru Tokubetsu Sochi-ho) allowed certain shelters to be recognized as residences, making it easier to claim living expenses.
8 The 1995 Tokyo Metropolitan Government's report on the homeless uses rojo-seikatsusha meaning 'people who live on the street.' Daily workers who are rough sleepers are termed nojukusha.
9 'Shelterization' forecloses the categories (home/homelessness, inclusion/exclusion, etc.) constitutive of homelessness as political, not sociological, conditions.
10 Constitution of Japan, Article 25. Available at http://www.kantei.go.jp/foreign/constitution_and_government_of_japan_constitutione.html.
11 From 'Zero Publics–Practice for Revolution,' an exhibition of Sakaguchi's work at Haus der Berliner Festspiele, September 27, 2012. Available at http://www.berlinerfestspiele.de/en/aktuell/festivals/foreign_affairs/program_fa/pro. (accessed October 17, 2012). See 'Kyohei Sakaguchi's Zero Yen Project' at http://www.thememagazine.com/stories/kyohei-sakaguchis-zero-yen-project/ (accessed September 19, 2012). Sakaguchi's experiments with zero yen living are available at www.0yenhouse.com/en/index.html.
12 Beijing photojournalist Shiho Fukada's work is available at http://pulitizercenter.org/project/japan-disposable-worker-laborer.

Bibliography

Act to Provide Special Measures for the Support of the Self Reliance of the Homeless (*Homuresu no jiritsu shien to ni kan suru tokubetsu sochi ho*) (2002) Online. Available HTTP: <http://www.homepage3.nifty.com/shelter-less/English/eng_idx.html>.
Allison, A. (2012) 'Ordinary Refugees: Social Precarity and Soul in 21st Century Japan,' *Anthropological Quarterly*, 85(2):345–370.

Amamiya, K. (2007) *Purekariato. Dejitaru Hiyatoi Sedai no Fuan na Ikikata*, (Precariats: The Unstable Way of Life of the Digital Day Labouring Generation), Tokyo, Japan: Yosensha.

Aoki, H. (2003) 'Homelessness in Osaka: Globalisation, Yoseba and Disemployment,' *Urban Studies*, 40:361–378.

Arai, A. G. (2005) 'The Neo-liberal Subject of Lack and Potential: Developing "the Frontier Within" and Creating a Reserve Army of Labor in 21st Century Japan,' *Rhizomes*, 10. Online. Available HTTP: <http://www.rhizomes.net/issue10/arai.htm>

Azuma, H. (2009) *Otaku: Japan's Database Animals*, J. E. Abel and S. Kono (trans.), Minneapolis, MN: University of Minnesota Press.

Berlant, L. (2011) *Cruel Optimism*, Durham, NC: Duke University Press.

Biehl, J. (2005) *Vita: Life in a Zone of Social Abandonment*, Berkeley, CA and Los Angeles, CA: University of California Press.

Binkley, S. (2009) 'The Work of Neoliberal Governmentality: Temporality and Ethical Substance in the Tale of Two Dads,' *Foucault Studies*, 6:60–78.

Brasor, P. and M. Tsubuku (2010) 'New Refuse Rules Criminalize Can-Collecting,' *Japan Times*, December 2. Online. Available HTTP: <http://www.blog/japantimes.co.jp/yen-for-living/new-refuse-rules-criminalize-can-collecting/>.

Chandler, D. (2009) 'The Global Ideology: Rethinking the Politics of the 'Global Turn' in IR,' *International Relations*, 23(4):530–547.

Dehaene, M. and L. D. Cauter (eds.) (2008) *Heterotopia and the City*, London, UK and New York, NY: Routledge.

Donzelot, J (1988) 'The Promotion of the Social,' *Economy and Society*, 13(3):394–427.

Dvorak, P. (2003) 'The Homeless in Japan Find A Place in Cities' Public Parks: Long Economic Slump, Tolerance Allow Shantytowns to Take Root,' *Wall Street Journal*, June 18, 2003.

Eisenstadt, S. N. (1996) *Japanese Civilization: A Comparative View*, Chicago, IL: University of Chicago Press.

Eisenstadt, S. N. (2002) *Multiple Modernities*, Piscataway, NJ: Transaction Publishers.

Feldman, L. C. (2004) *Citizens without Shelter: Homelessness, Democracy, and Political Exclusion*, Ithaca, NY: Cornell University Press.

Foucault, M. [1967] (1984) *Of Other Spaces. Heterotopias*, J. Miskowiec (trans.), Architecture/Mouvement/Continuite. Online. Available HTTP: <http://www.foucult.info/documents/heteroTopia/foucault.heteroTopia.en.html>

———. (1991) 'Governmentality,' in C. Gordon and P. Miller (eds.), *The Foucault Effect: Studies in Governmentality*, 87–104, Chicago, IL: University of Chicago Press.

———. [1976] (1997) *Society Must be Defended: Lectures at the College de France 1975–1976*, David Macey (trans.), New York, NY: Picador.

Fowler, E. (1996) *San'ya blues: Labouring Life in Contemporary Tokyo*, New York, NY: Cornell University Press.

Fukada, S. (2012) *Japan's Disposable Workers*. Online. Available HTTP: <http://pulitizercenter.org/project/japan-disposable-worker-laborer>.

Genda, Y. (2007) 'Jobless Youths and the NEET problem in Japan,' *Social Science Japan Journal*, 10(1):23–40.

Genocchio, B. (1995) 'Discourse, Discontinuity, Difference: The Question of Other Spaces,' in S. Watson and K. Gibson (eds.), *Postmodern Cities and Spaces*, 35–46, Oxford, UK: Blackwell.

Gill, T. (2001) *Men of Uncertainty: The Social Organization of Day Labourers in Contemporary Japan*, New York, NY: State University of New York Press.

Guzewicz, T. D. (1996) 'A New Generation of Homeless Hits Tokyo's Streets,' *Japan Quarterly*, July–September, 43–53.

———. (2000) *Tokyo's Homeless: A City in Denial*, New York, NY: Nova Science Publishers, Inc.

Harootunian, H. (2000) *History's Disquiet: Modernity, Cultural Practice and the Question of Everyday Life*, New York, NY: Columbia University Press.

———. (2005) 'Some Thoughts on Comparability and the Space-Time Problem,' *Boundary 2*, 32(2):23–52.

Harries, K. (1998) *The Ethical Function of Architecture*, Cambridge, MA: MIT Press.

Hasegawa, K. (2001) *Saijiki no jikan* (Time in Saijiki). In T. Hashimoto and S. Kuriyama (eds.), *Chikoku no Tanjo: Kindai ni okeru jikan no keisei* (The Birth of Tardiness: The Formation of Time Consciousness in Modern Japan, 241–265, Tokyo, Japan: Sangensha.

Hasegawa, M. (2006) *'We Are Not Garbage!' the Homeless Movement in Tokyo,' 1994–2002*, New York, NY: Routledge.

Hasegawa, Miki (2005) 'Economic Globalization and Homelessness in Japan,' *American Behavioral Scientist*, 48(8):989–1012.

Hatoyama, Y. (2009) 'Creating a New Nation. Yukio Hatoyama's,' *Yu-Ai – message from the Prime Minister*. Hatoyama cabinet E-mail Magazine November 4.

Hayashi, S. (2011) 'Representational Discontent,' *Cultural Anthropology*, July. Online. Available HTTP: <http://www.culanth.org/fieldsights/301-representational-discontent>.

Hetherington, K. (1997) *The Badlands of Modernity: Heterotopias and Social Ordering*, London, UK: Routledge

Hirayama, Y. (2010) 'The Role of Home Ownership in Japan's Aged Society,' *Journal of Housing and the Built Environment*, 25:175–191.

Hook, G. D. and T. Hiroko. (2007) '"Self-responsibility" and the Nature of the Postwar Japanese State: Risk through the Looking Glass, *Journal of Japanese Studies*, 33(1):93–123.

Iwabuchi, K. (2008) Lost in Translation: Tokyo and the Urban Imaginary in the Era of Globalization, *Inter-Asia Cultural Studies*, 9(4):543–546.

Iwata, M. (2010) 'New Landscape of Homelessness in Japan: The role of NPOs and Landscape of the Problem,' *City, Culture and Society*, 1:127–134.

Johnson, C. (1982) *MITI and the Japanese Miracle: The Growth of Industrial Policy 1925–1975*, Stanford, CA: Stanford University Press.

Karatani, K. (2008) 'Beyond Capital-Nation-State,' *Rethinking Marxism*, 20(4):569–595.

Kennett, P. and M. Iwata. (2003) 'Precariousness in Everyday Life: Homelessness in Japan,' *International Journal of Urban and Regional Research*, 27(1):62–74.

Koseirodosho (2003) (Ministry of Health, Labor, and Welfare). *Homuresu no jittai ni kan suru zenkoku chosa hokoku cho. Homuresu no kazu no chosa kekka* (Report on the Real Situation of the Homeless Nationwide. The Results of the Census). Online. Available HTTP: <http://www.mhlw.go.jp/houdou/2003/03/h0326–5c.html>.

Koseirodosho (2006) *Koseirodosho Hakusho: Jizoku Kanou na Shakai Hoshou Seido to Sasae ai no Junkan – 'Chiiki' Heno Sanka to 'hatarakikata' no Minaoshi* (White Paper from the Ministry of Health, Labor and Welfare: Establishing and Supporting a Lasting Social Security System- Checking the 'Regional and 'Work' Support Systems] Tokyo: Kyousei (Ministry of Health, Labor and Welfare).

Kosugi, K. (2008) *Escape from Work: Freelancing Youth and the Challenge to Corporate Japan*, Melbourne, Australia: Trans Pacific Press.

Larner, W. (2000) 'Neoliberalism, Policy, Ideology, Governmentality,' *Studies in Political Economy*, 63:5–25.

Lemke, T. (2002) 'Foucault, Governmentality, and Critique,' *Rethinking Marxism*, 1:49–64.

Lo, I. M. (2010) *'Homelessness in Japan*,' Documentary. Journeyman.tv. Online. Available HTTP: <http://vod.jouneyman.tv/store?2010p=4459&s=Homeless+In+Japan>.

Massey, D. (1992) 'Politics and Space/Time,' *New Left Review* I, 196:65–84.

McGowan, T. (2011) *Out of Time: Desire in Atemporal Cinema*, Minnesota, MN: University of Minnesota Press.

Miura, M. (2008) 'Labor Politics in Japan during the Lost Fifteen Years': From the Politics of Productivity to the Politics of Consumption,' *Labor History*, 49(2):161–176.

Miyazaki, H. (2006) 'Economy of Dreams: Hope in Global Capitalism and Its Critiques,' *Cultural Anthropology*, 21(2):147–172.

Mizushima, H. (2007) *Netto Kafue Nanmin to Hinkon Nippon* (Net café refugees and poverty in Japan). Tokyo, Japan: Nihon Terebi Hoso Kabushiki Kaisha.

Mizuuchi, T. (2003) 'The Growth in the Number of People Sleeping Rough in the City of Osaka, Japan,' *Urban Culture Research*, 1:20–36.

Mori, Y. (2005) 'Culture = Politics: The Emergence of New Cultural Forms of Protest in the Age of *Freeter*,' *Inter-Asia Cultural Studies*, 6(1):17–29.

OECD FactBook Statistics 2011–2012: Economic, Environmental and Social Statistics. (2012) Paris, France: Organization for Economic Cooperation and Development. Online. Available HTTP: <http://www.oecd-ilibrary.org/economics/oecd-factbook-2011–2012-factbook-2011-en>.

Ogawa, A. (2009) *The Failure of Civil Society: The Third Sector in Contemporary Japan*, New York, NY: SUNY.

Ong, A. (2006) *Neoliberalism as Exception: Mutations in Citizenship and Sovereignty*, Durham, NC: Duke University Press.

Povinelli, E. A. (2011) *Economies of Abandonment: Social Belonging and Endurance in Late Liberalism*, Durham, NC and London, UK: Duke University Press.

Rose, N. (1996) 'Refiguring the Territory of Government,' *Economy and Society*, 25:327–356.

Sakaguchi, K. (2012) *Zero Publics- Practice for Revolution*, Exhibition, <http://www.berlinerfestspiele.de/en/aktuell/festivals/foreign_affairs/program_fa/pro>.

———. *Zero Yen Project*. Online. Available HTTP: <http://www.thememagazine.com/stories/kyohei-sakaguchis-zero-yen-project/>.

———. *Web-Site*. Online. Available HTTP: <www.0yenhouse.com/en/index.html>.

Saldanha, A. (2008) 'Heterotopia and Structuralism,' *Environment and Planning A*, 40:2080–2096.

Sand, J. (2003) *House and Home in Modern Japan*, Boston, MA: Harvard University Press.

Shinoda, T. (2009) 'Which Side Are You On? Hakenmura and the Working Poor as a Tipping Point in Japanese Labor Politics,' *The Asia-Pacific Journal*, April 4.

Soja, E. (1995) 'Heterotopologies: A Remembrance of Other Spaces in the Citadel-LA,' in S. Watson and K. Gibson (eds.), *Postmodern Cities and Spaces*, 13–34, Oxford, UK: Blackwell.

Steger, B. (2006) 'Sleeping Through Class to Success: Japanese Notions of Time and Diligence,' *Time and Society*, 15:197–214.

Tachibanaki, T. (2008) *Introdakushyon – kakusakara hinkonhe* (Introduction – from difference to poverty). In T. Makino and E. Murakami (eds.), *Kakusa to hinkon: 20 ko* (Difference and Poverty 20 cases),8–18. Tokyo, Japan: Akashi Shoten.

Tsuji, Y. (2006) 'Railway Time and Rubber Time: The Paradox in the Japanese Conception of Time,' *Time & Society*, 15:177–194.

Tsutsumi, Y. (1991) *Homuresu*, Film.

———. (2012) *My House*, Film.

Watson, S. and K. Gibson (eds.) (1995) *Postmodern Cities and Spaces*, Oxford, UK: Blackwell.

Yoda, T. (2000) 'The Rise and Fall of Maternal Society: Gender, Labor, and Capital in Contemporary Japan,' *The South Atlantic Quarterly*, 99(4):865–902.

Yoshida, M. (2012) *The 'Hidden Homeless' in Japan's Contemporary Mobile Culture*, Online. Available HTTP: <http://www.neme.org/1500/hidden-homeless> (Accessed 30 October 2014).

Yuasa, M. (2008) Hanhinkon: '*Suberridaishakkai' kara no dasshutsu* (Reverse Poverty: Escape from a Sliding Down Society'), Tokyo, Japan: Iwanami Shinsho.

11 Child's play

Temporal discourse, counterpower, and environmental politics

Andrew R. Hom and Brent J. Steele

Introduction

A 2007 United Nations report on climate change forecasted a turbulent twenty-first century of rising seas, spreading drought and disease, weather extremes, and damage to farming, forests, fisheries, and other economic areas (United Nations 2007) while reminding global leaders they must rise to the challenge of halting climate change (Associated Press 2007). Similarly, in the UN Environment Programme (UNEP)'s 2011 Annual Report, Secretary-General Ban Ki-Moon insisted:

> Addressing inequalities, overcoming poverty, maintaining peace and building prosperity for the entire *human family* depend on rejecting the old economics of heedless pollution and the excessive exploitation of the world's natural capital . . . Environmental, economic and social indicators tell us that our current *model of progress* is unsustainable.
> (UNEP 2012: 2; emphasis added)

Such straightforward exhortations, directed from an international organization to its member states, are emblematic of a discursive modality on development and its impact on the environment. But this language also invokes a vision of time important to global economic and environmental ethics issues by virtue of its historical implication in the constitution of the 'West' and the 'rest'.

This chapter examines discourses about common but differentiated responsibilities related to environmental equity and capacity as instantiations of temporality in international politics. Temporality serves as a legitimating and Othering device, quarantining the 'underdeveloped' in unique and powerful ways. However, the temporality we identify is one of the multiple sites of struggle informing this volume. It provides an opportunity to challenge Western hegemony via environmental issues – what we title, following Brent Steele's work on aesthetics and security, a form of counterpower, a challenge of the temporal discourse that demonstrates its reversibility (Steele 2010: 46).

We first discuss how three temporal aspects in a particular narrative about the unilinear-progressive march of history toward Western modernity comprised an Othering device. Next, we read environmental policy debates as a challenge to the hegemony of Western modernity from within its own temporalized discourse.

We conclude by discussing the implications of this discourse for current thinking about time and global politics. In particular, we view temporalized environmental discourse as demonstrating the *fragility* of attempts to promulgate a unified vision of global political time.

Temporal Othering

Self and Other issues are no strangers to IR. They were central to the post-WWII realism of Reinhold Niebuhr and Hans Morgenthau and enjoyed renewed attention after the Cold War, when ethnic strife and national independence movements returned to the main stage of international affairs and social constructivist and identity research made inroads in IR (Lapid and Kratochwil 1996; McSweeney 1999; Morgenthau 1948; Niebuhr 2001; Wendt 1999). In most of these works, the delineation between Self and Other proceeds along primarily spatial lines. In essence, the Self encounters the Other at the boundaries of territorial sovereignty, between national cultures, or along the edges of ideological spheres of influence.

We suggest the temporal vision of Western modernity has been crucial to industrial modernization on a global scale. Such 'progress' is responsible for the environmental issues confronting the twenty-first century and the impetus for dissident manoeuvres from less-developed, less-prosperous members of the international system. Understanding how those members have experienced a lengthy, temporalized disciplining at the hands of Western metropoles sets the stage for our subsequent discussion of environmental dissents.

Universalizing history from fragmented experience

A key concern of early modern European historians was to slip traditional forms of Papal and Imperial authority by narrating a decisive break between the Enlightenment and its past (Hindess 2007; Inayatullah and Blaney 2004). But although they inoculated the Western European present against appeals to a dominant heritage, for many Enlightenment thinkers, the future remained a repository of progressive promise. This resulted in early modern historical narratives utilizing cosmopolitical ontologies to paint a secular gloss on Christian history's path to the Rapture. To summarize, Enlightenment thinkers pursued the idea that *cosmos* and *polis* emanate from a single source and drew inspiration from the increasingly successful mechanical depiction of the physical world. Taken together, this allowed them to understand the human *polis* as developing toward a singular and holistic endpoint located on a homogenized horizon (Toulmin 1990: 107).

This unifying view conflicted with the contemporaneous discovery of the 'New World' by European explorers. How could a single linear-progressive view account for such astounding differences? The modern relationship to time and its concomitant vision of science provided the solution. Privileging the here and now allowed historical data to be 'formally' compared and fitted together without regard to chronological order so as to produce 'general categories' of social knowledge (Blaney and Inayatullah 2006: 131). The fashionable insistence on a general or universal criterion of evaluation provided a rationale for assessing a multitude of power positions using a single rubric, and the temporal break accomplished by early modern historians demanded this rubric be based on the present of early modern Western Europe, its "here and now" enjoyed priority over other cultures and alternative temporalities because Western Europe was understood to exemplify everywhere and forever.

Making a standard of their particular temporal and spatial locale allowed Western Europeans, especially Scottish Enlightenment philosophers, to manage diversity through a new scientific method (Blaney and Inayatullah 2006: 135). This method was normative inasmuch as a moral science must make practical suggestions about how and where (when) human society must *necessarily* and *appropriately* go (Blaney and Inayatullah 2006: 136–37). Taken together with the idea of a universal human nature, this moral method made possible a conjectural history of human kind with clear cosmopolitical links to the unified, mechanistic solar system, which contained within its present all the necessary clues on its future development (Blaney and Inayatullah 2006: 137; also Hindess 2007: 329, 332). Conjectural history is based on three conceptual moves: the method of systematic comparison; the assimilation of ancient peoples and contemporary indigenous cultures in a single coeval category; the equation of human infancy with savagery (Blaney and Inayatullah 2006: 139). The first principle makes possible the final two, which, in turn, facilitate a universal interpretation.

The key claim of this general evolutionary history of mankind (Hindess 2007: 328) is that all human cultures can be explained in terms of development – the workings out in time of certain known and stable characteristics of the human mind (Blaney and Inayatullah 2006: 133). Lent an air of scientific precision by early modern encounters with indigenous peoples (Blaney and Inayatullah 2006: 127), this monogenist historical view featured in the thinking of early modern Western philosophers such as Immanuel Kant and G.F.W. Hegel (Hindess 2007: 325–328). It subsumed a plethora of differences under the umbrella of temporalized Difference – in this case backwardness, primitiveness, or degeneration, all of which were tied to the Judeo-Christian account of the fall from grace. Inayatullah and Blaney sum up the Othering implications of this move:

> The dominant *aspiration* . . . was to grasp the social world as emerging from a single point of origin (the Creation) and, even if currently fallen or divided, guided by God's purposes and plan toward an ultimate redemption and unification. The commitment to a single organization and a unified teleology constructs difference not as an intrinsic and ubiquitous part of life, but as a fall from God's grace.
>
> (Inayatullah and Blaney 2004: 49)

The Time(s) of the Self and the Other

Under a conjectural history, *present* indigenous cultures and the Western European *past* are conflated as monogenistically primitive, a category claimed to have causally preceded Western, modern civilization and, thus, to have demarcated ancient and modern epochs (Hindess 2007: 332). This produces two relations of temporal Othering. First, the current Self is distinguished from contemporaneous Others. Second, the current Self is distinguished from the prior, antiquated Self, which is more akin to contemporaneous Others in its primitive, pre-modern character.

Hindess argues these are ways of understanding difference in terms of the Self in that difference is associated with geographic (spatial) distance as well as historical (temporal) distance (Hindess 2007: 333). Inayatullah and Blaney concur: the constructed temporal backwardness of the savages is equated with the imagined temporal origins of the European Self in antiquity; the spatially distinct Other is thereby converted into a temporally prior self (Inayatullah and Blaney 2004: 64). This practice buttressed colonial governance techniques by assigning conquered populations to a *different* time (Blaney and Inayatullah 2006: 142) that submerged their histories under the historical constructions of the Enlightenment scientist (Inayatullah and Blaney 2004: 58). The relationship between time and space in temporal Othering is important not only because it assigns a different development stage to spatial Others, but also because it explains temporal distance through spatial dispersion: geographic Others are understood as temporally primitive by their distribution away from the Western European core. The further from the core, the more backward they are assumed to be (Blaney and Inayatullah 2006: 129).

Three other points are worth noting. First, such a clean ontological distinction is never actually obtained in world political experience, even in the domains of dominant temporal Selves. Second, Hindess and Inayatullah and Blaney note the many internal Others (nominally included populations differentiated by their primitiveness and attachment to a set of practices from the past) attending modern, Western states and informing their colonial encounters. A corollary to the spatial aspect of temporal Othering is the question of how Western European and later North American metropoles *created* internal spaces in which to (re)locate their temporal Others. To minimize civic dissonance, modern Selves must be as homogenous as possible. This entails protecting the gates from the 'barbarians' of the hinterland and inoculating the Self time after time by placing internal Others in ancillary and invisible spaces within the territorial state. Examples include the Native American Trail of Tears, Scottish Highlanders, Irish peasants, Northern European pagans, and the institution of slavery (Blaney and Inayatullah 2006: 147; Hindess 2007: 334).

Second is the metaphor of mirrors manifested in Othering practices and what they present in terms of the possibilities for counterpower resistance. Hindess describes a dialogic mirror, through which the Old World and current indigenous populations and practices are used to explicate each other (Hindess 2007: 332). Blaney and Inayatullah turn these mirrors on the modern Self through time-shifting, when the critique of now and here shifts first to now and there, and subsequently to then and there (Blaney and Inayatullah 2006: 134). Such reflections are typically self-congratulatory. They tautologically demonstrate how far the Self has advanced to the apex of human history, shielding modern society from external critique and establishing a chronocratic elite (Blaney and Inayatullah 2006: 144–145).

Postcolonial theorists deconstruct this way of thinking about difference, but we argue since temporal Othering brings both contemporaneous indigenous and historical practices *within* a unified historical framework, no external critique is necessary if the Other can mobilize the mirror against the Self. By unifying practices within one framework, the practice of temporal Othering contains built-in quandaries (Steele 2010: 13). As we argue in due course, the environmental equity and capacity debates of the 1990s and 2000s demonstrate the use of the Self's temporal discourse as a mechanism of internal critique by an assimilating Other.

Human development as metaphor

Modern temporal discourse, which privileges the present as distinct from the past, adopts a unified historical interpretation, employs Othering moves predicated on both, and produces a vivid metaphor of civilizational development as human development. In this image, childhood provides the temporalized metaphor for Other – whether the contemporaneous indigenous practices and social relations or the historically prior versions of the Self. The metaphor relies on Adam Smith's stage theory of human history, which explains human progress as moving from hunting and gathering to shepherding, to agriculture, to commerce (Blaney and Inayatullah 2006: 125), producing a stadial temporal register of development through which all difference is understood (Blaney and Inayatullah 2006: 125).

Hindess epitomizes the metaphor of human development in a quotation from Friedrich von Schiller, who referred to the various levels of historical development in Europe's periphery as an arrangement akin to an adult surrounded by children of different ages (Hindess 2007: 325). Likewise, Smith referred to the infancy of the American Indians and compared this to the maturity of his own industrialized, commercial society (Blaney and Inayatullah 2006: 141). This metaphor comports with universal history in that it contains an aura of inclusivity, for all children have the innate potential to grow into adults (Blaney and Inayatullah 2006: 132; Hindess 2007: 326). However, equating temporal Others with children subscribes them to the entire continuum of the development metaphor, whose inclusivity also houses its disciplinary potential: children not only *can* mature, they *should* grow up.

Globalization, especially in its industrial form, is unimaginable without economic development. And economic development was achieved, in part, by the mobilization of the human development metaphor to compel indigenous and agricultural societies to transform into approximations of Western industrialized states. Both the prior development of the West and the ongoing development of the rest have produced significant environmental degradation. As we discuss in the next section, debates about how to address these hazards globally demonstrate ways developing nations are turning the temporalized developmental discourse of modernity against its champions.

(Counter)powerful possibilities: The environmental retorts of the temporal other

Steele's *Defacing Power* engages the aesthetic bases of power and how such bases can be insecuritized (Steele 2010). He suggests the concept of counterpower as a micropressure, an unlimited event that can happen at any time and from any direction that works to manipulate or problematize centralized bodies of power (Steele 2010: 28). The limited form of resistance embedded in counterpower and the discursive material it uses are the following:

> Counter-power understood in a micro-sense is displayed as moments, styles, words, or images. These manifestations are infinitely small and light – they do not contain the material or strategic force necessary to maintain influence over a body, nation, group or organization over time. Counter-power cannot itself distribute resources, taxonomize actors and actions, synthesize, coordinate or routinize. Such displays *derive their influence, alternatively, from the power which they engage.*
>
> (Steele 2010: 20; emphasis added)

Following from Foucault's aesthetics of the Self, Steele suggests one of the mechanisms for self-creation – the working of the Self *on* the Self – is a Temporal Othering of past Selves. For instance, Steele shows how the crafting of US self-identity in the 2000s was imbricated with a negative identification with a *past* US self of the Vietnam era (Steele 2010). This Temporal Othering *of* and through the Self demonstrates the existence of fissures that can be utilized and exploited by a variety of actors. Forms of counterpower, including reflexive discourse and parrhesia (truth-telling), elicit critiques internal to – *within* – the practices of the Self of a targeted actor.

A similar potential for resistance inheres to the universalizing discourses of temporal progress. While such resistance is, like countepower's potential, modest, it marks an overlooked possibility in existing work on temporality and development. For instance, most of the accounts of temporal Othering on which we build view this process as disempowering to those being Othered. But current international environmental affairs offer an alternate picture of Others, not as temporally superseded (Blaney and Inayatullah 2006) so much as politically enabled by these very discursive constraints to claim for themselves different levels of participation, commitment, and responsibility in confronting environmental problems (Blaney and Inayatullah 2006: 151). We examine two interrelated environmental debates falling under the umbrella of common but differentiated responsibility, which tries to balance the idea that 'we are all in the same boat with respect to many large-scale environmental problems, on the one hand, with an acknowledgement that the circumstances of individual countries differ markedly, on the other' (Young 2001: 168–169).

The first debate, on environmental equity, concerns the different historical contributions made by developed and developing countries to environmental degradation. The second, on capacity, has to do with the technological and economic capabilities with which countries can contribute to environmental solutions. Developing countries' elites and public commentators have re-appropriated artefacts from temporal Othering discourses to contest Western attempts to compel the developing world's participation in international environmental regimes.[1]

Environmental equity

Young says, 'The idea of environmental equity arises from the belief of developing countries . . . that it is improper for them to be asked to pitch in to solve a problem arising from the behavior of others' (Young 2001: 168). For example, negotiations in 1988 to reduce long-range transboundary air pollution failed to mandate flat-rate reductions in nitrogen emissions due to conflicts over equity. Although the mandate that all countries will achieve an equal percentage reduction of emissions had a first blush of equality, questions arose about whether it expected states with historically low emission rates to achieve the same percentage reduction as those with high ones (Soroos 1993: 200).

The influence of environmental equity concerns was demonstrated at the 1992 United Nations Conference on Environment and Development (UNCED) in Rio de Janeiro. Principle Seven of the resultant Rio Declaration states: 'In view of the different contributions to global environmental degradation, States have common but differentiated responsibilities' (United Nations 1992). By attaching historical contributions to environmental problems to the reasoning behind expectations of response, the Rio Declaration acknowledges developed nations bear greater responsibility for the existing state of environmental affairs than their developing neighbours. Accordingly, developing countries attached to the discourse of development a correlation between historical development and environmental culpability.

This sense of equity was reflected in the absence of agreement in the Rio Declaration on a time frame for greenhouse emissions reductions. Five years after UNCED, the United States was still campaigning for an emissions time frame, angering its developing counterparts and leading to public reminders about common but differentiated responsibility (Yue 1997). In 2002, a Malaysian editorial criticizing the poor performance of developed countries in the decade following Rio reminded European and North American parties that the Declaration was based on the principle of atoning for past wrongs by developed countries (Loh 2002).

At a recent UN Climate Change Working Group, developing states made similarly pointed comments. Bolivia observed that as developed countries are largely responsible for environmental degradation from before 1750, they 'owe the world an ecological debt that should be paid literally in the form of compensation to developing countries for lost opportunities to Live Well and figuratively by accepting greater responsibility for addressing the crisis and its consequences' (Bolivia, Republic of 2008: 106–107). Algeria likewise criticized an Intergovernmental Panel on Climate Change assessment report for forgiving a major environmental debt by omitting reference to developed states' historical responsibility (Algeria 2008: 7). Chinese officials similarly contended that fully industrialized states owed a carbon debt to developing states. Chinese climate change experts provided a complementary recommendation whereby 'any agreement should allocate emissions rights that ensure [China's] right to develop' (Buckley 2010). India remained chary of explicit emission-reduction commitments because 'mature economies don't seem to have made much headway on emission reductions' (Mishra 2009). In Copenhagen, developing delegates employed procedural tactics to obstruct negotiations because of their suspicions developed states would attempt to secure lower commitments and lower penalties for themselves despite their historical responsibility for degradation (Associated Press 2009).

By finding an opportunity in the constraining and disciplinary framework of development, these countries have adapted a discourse to their engagements with global environmental regimes. This adaptation has been accepted in environmental discourse by more developed states and other powerful international actors as well (Ban 2007). By internalizing the idea that certain European state histories prefigure developing states' present, such reflexive reconfiguring of the discourse re-attaches those metropoles' early 'blooming' to a lengthy and unprecedented record of environmental wrongs. This counterpower practice takes *as its basis* the materiel of developing states' presents, to render the human development metaphor Janus-faced. Such re-figuring exposes a development antithetical to the Enlightenment discourse of unilinear-progressivism.

Environmental capacity

Debates about the capacity of countries to contribute to environmental clean-up usually revolve around the argument that poor countries, which are preoccupied with domestic problems like providing for the basic needs of their own citizens, are not in a position to make large contributions to efforts to solve transboundary or global environmental problems (Young 2001: 169). The capacity gap is epitomized in a trenchant remark by a Pakistani delegate at Rio; contrary to a developed country's delegate's hope that the Declaration would be a document hanging in every child's bedroom, he said in 'my country, most children don't have bedrooms' (Fainaru 1992). Likewise, the wording and ordering of principles of the Rio Declaration speak to the tension existing in developing countries between basic subsistence and environmental sustainability. It emphasises human welfare, a global right to development, the eradication of poverty rather than environmental protection, and state-by-state variations in environmental standards (United Nations 1992). Since Rio, capacity rhetoric has become fairly commonplace, as when Costa Rica judged proposals for assisting developing countries in adapting to climate change using funds drawn solely from those same countries as morally unacceptable (Costa Rica 2008: 5).

In addition to economic disparities, capacity relates to the technological gap between developed and developing states. Some developed countries acknowledge their responsibility, directly related to their substantial economic, technological, and political resources, to participate to a greater degree in environmental protection and to assist poorer but willing countries who lack the material capabilities (Deutsche Presse-Agentur 1997). This assistance may come in the form of investment, trade, or technological exchange and is widely regarded as crucial to any chance for improving the environmental record of development in the twenty-first century. But many of these mechanisms, processes, and technologies are relatively new and conclusive results still forthcoming. An interesting discourse across states and capacities suggests both developed and developing countries' market-based and technological proposals remain in their infancy (African Development Bank Group 2011; Agence France Presse 2009; Ban 2007; Lovell 2012; Wu and Yanghong 2010).

Internalization and reconstruction of temporal discourse

A crucial feature of these debates concerns the internalization of the basic developmental language, its acceptance into the everyday parlance of those who previously identified, categorized, and governed by it. By definition, internalization indicates a 'taking in' of some idea, identity, or narrative, but since those who are internalizing possess creative and tactical capabilities of their own, a noteworthy facet of internalization is that what gets 'taken in' may not be the same when it comes 'back out' in ongoing discourse. Internalization is a process crucial to becoming a legitimate interlocutor in a given community and a source of contestation of that community's working narratives. This might suggest that the temporal discourse of development is a tactical tool and is never internalized with any sincerity. If complete acceptance were the criterion for internalization, we would agree, but discourse also possesses a power of its own that constrains and enables those who use it regardless of their sincerity. In this way, 'internalization' refers to movement in both directions: agents 'take in' the narrative of development but in doing so are 'taken in' to the world it propounds, where they can create, contest, and manoeuvre. While frustration persists about the tension between development, environmental responsibility, and the markers of both, the story of development and its embedded human development metaphor have now been internalized by all countries, signalling the normative power of these ideas and their eligibility for use in ways more transversal and subversive.

The internalization of developmental discourse initially seems to constrain developing countries by limiting the agenda of debate, as exemplified by South African president Thabo Mbeki's 1998 remarks to the Non-Aligned Movement in Durban. He first noted the vocabulary of international discourse revolves around terms such as globalization, liberalization, deregulation, and the information society. These processes originate from the developed countries of the North and are reflective of the imperatives of the economies and the levels of development of these countries. Therefore, they 'serve the purposes of our rich global neighbors' (Mbeki 1998). He subsequently said the best hope for increased agency for developing countries in international affairs is 'the development of our economies such that we *outgrow* our designations both as developing countries and emerging economies' (Mbeki 1998; emphasis added). Mbeki's statements suggest he accepted and internalized the unilinear-progressive promise of development transmitted through the human development metaphor.

Mbeki later insisted the Organization of African Unity not engage in protectionism or command economy models because these would be no better than 'King Canute wishing the waves away' (Laufer 1999). This curious reference to a medieval Norseman during a speech about the African Renaissance indicates Mbeki's familiarity with the general distinction between pre-modern European history and superstition on the one hand and modernity and rationality on the other. In effect, Mbeki mobilized the European internal Other to exhort his African colleagues to pursue Western developmental benchmarks, leading to the 'beneficial integration of the African economy into the global economy' (Laufer 1999).

Examples of internalization are found in *pro forma* prefatory remarks in elites' speeches about the environment and development. For instance, after Nelson Mandela inaugurated South Africa's independence with a poem about a child growing up in Africa who could now travel the world freely,[2] Mbeki referred to South Africa as a newborn child (Mbeki 2004) and to its first decade of independence as the dawn of a new life (Mbeki 1999) or a period of infancy (Mbeki 2001). This set the stage for later remarks characterizing the maturation process as a success so that by 2006 South Africa was no longer a child but a giant trekking 'through all Africa and the whole world, without a pass!' (Mbeki 2006). Chinese president Jiang Zemin thought more inclusively, telling the Second Assembly of the Global Environment in 2002 that all mankind remains a child of Mother Nature (Jiang 2002).

Environmental documents suggest the internalization of the idea that development is an integral aspect of a universal human history. For example, the Adaptation Fund, launched in 2007 at the Conference on Climate Change in Bali, facilitates contributions from developed countries to developing nations to fight climate change. Expected contributions are tied directly to countries' levels of development, which are assessed as falling into one of four stages – least developed, medium developing, advanced developing, and developed – only superficially removed from Smith's four stages of civilization (Ling 2007). Such stadial evaluations facilitate capacity-based assistance, however. Recent UN environmental reports regularly acknowledge both the capacity gap and the imperative of development by highlighting various programs providing support to developing countries seeking to integrate climate change responses into national development processes (UNEP 2012: 22).

While these examples demonstrate the constraining power of a hegemonic developmental discourse, challenges to this discourse – discussed earlier as correlations between extant levels of development and environmental responsibility – have mobilized the primitive-modern dichotomy as well as the child-adult metaphor to contest the dominant environmental regime. Criticizing the increasing wealth gap between the North and the South since the Rio Declaration, Mbeki remarks: 'It is as though we are determined to regress to the most primitive condition of existence in the animal world, of the survival of the fittest' (Mbeki 2002). More recently, a Malaysian editorial criticized progress since the Kyoto Protocol of 1997 as 'a result of the worst polluters . . . playing a children's game of who should go first' with regard to emissions reductions (*New Straits Times* 2007).

Dissident invocations of primitivity and childhood turn the temporal vision of modernity and its developmental metaphor back upon Western progenitors by calling such visions into question. An additional flanking manoeuvre complementing this appears in emerging contestation of the normative implications of traditional and primitive practices and concepts in indigenous societies. Such practices are increasingly characterized as *intrinsically* sustainable, as ancient wisdom rather than ignorant anachronisms (United Nations 1992 Prin. 22). This challenge insists indigenous people and their communities and other local communities have a vital role in environmental management and development because of their knowledge and traditional practices (United Nations 1992).

As remarked earlier, the temporal discourse of modernity often acts as a mirror against which the primitive Other and the modern Self are understood through rigged categories that preclude critique of modern society. Contestations of the benefits of traditional economic and developmental practices – especially those with an environmental dimension – disturb these supposedly settled dialogic categories, posing a challenge to modernity's chronocratic elite. Such contestations occur in ways which 'refract' the power of the modern Self (Steele 2010: 35), rearranging its perceived legitimacy and calling the integrity of its formative narratives into question. Extant accounts of temporal Othering convincingly explicate its historical lineage and dynamics, but in doing so, they fail to grasp the potential for *contestation* embedded within the dominant discourse. The chronocratic elite of the Enlightenment may have insulated itself against external critique, but opportunities for dissent were *intrinsic* to the discourse of temporal Othering. Practitioners of international politics have discovered this opportunity and continue to find ways to refashion the constrictive ligatures of development into lines of dissent.

Conclusion: What child is this?

By highlighting developing countries' challenges from *within* a hegemonic temporal discourse, we bring forth the fluid nature of discourse in its ability to both constrain and enable *all* speakers, albeit asymmetrically. Thus, like many cases considered in this volume, recent environmental debates suggest intriguing links in, and pose interesting questions of, IR theory. The successful counterpowerful retorts of those often understood as temporal Others speak directly to the emerging literature on time in IR and suggest at least one way to augment its burgeoning analytical power. At its best, this literature proceeds as the works reviewed in the first section do, by unpacking the many temporal approaches and strategies embedded in political theory, such as a tendency to construct world political time as 'unitary' to the exclusion of any and all alternative viewpoints (Hutchings 2008). Less convincingly, scholars uncritically oppose a plethora of phenomena imprecisely subsumed under the generic phrase 'linear time' (Adam 1990; Dörre 2011: 201; Edkins 2003; Gallagher 2012: 76, 84; Lundborg 2011: 3; Manning 2004: 72 n17).

In either case, scholars risk overplaying the enduring power of unified and/or 'linear' temporality. Kimberly Hutchings's (2008) excellent critique of various political theories concludes with a call for heterotemporality or an acknowledgment of the plurality of temporalities in international politics. We believe this call has merit, yet the case discussed earlier suggests world political time in the modern era is tenuously unified at best, and these partial and particular efforts serve (following Steele) as an aesthetic, as one way (no means the only way) to smooth over political and historical bumps in the road. Just as individuals use aesthetics to 'appear' to be something more composed or certain or in control, international actors use images and discourses for the same purpose. These discourses can be exploited for strategic and tangential purposes.

Regardless of how certain or assured these discourses when deployed seem to us, no matter what type of facade – or 'face' – they advance, they cover up a particular form of vulnerability (Steele 2010: 5). In environmental temporal discourses, the source of contestation may be found *within* the unification effort itself; attempting to locate *all* human groups and practices along a single linear axis allows some groups to claim their subordinated 'place' on that axis but does not allow the time to address purportedly current and global problems, which presume a single moment and place in which all groups are located. Facile assaults on the multitudinous dimensions of 'linear time' tend to ignore this possibility, treating whatever 'linear time' refers to as a monolithic given that neither matches the historical record nor acknowledges the monumental sociopolitical efforts required to affect such a contingent unification.

None of this is to champion unitary or 'linear' time. We merely point out that as foils they are not omnipotent, and critical IR can benefit from reflection on the implications of treating *all* the varieties of the human relationship to time as creative, intersubjective, fragile, and ever-contested projects – as instances of political power. Doing so would make life easier for critical IR, since robbing unitary or 'linear' time of a sense of immutable hegemony demotes it to just one of many ways of relating to time – a point that the retorts of temporalized 'Others' make quite well (Hom 2010).

Our point about the counterpower potential of putatively hegemonic discourse should not be conflated with a disavowal of the material dimension of international politics. Rather, we view discourse and material factors as interacting continua of change. The temporal Othering discourse changed, but its material context was also in flux. Temporal Othering was effective in a context of geographic diffusion and imperial efflorescence, much less so as a resource for developing a systemic response to emerging transnational environmental problems. Even as the discourse of temporal hierarchy achieved some hegemony, material contexts were shifting around and under it, leaving it vulnerable to rhetoric-endogenous loopholes once a unified and egalitarian approach to environmental problems became necessary. Our analysis lends support to a more materially sensitive and contingency-focused brand of social science that refuses a sharp distinction between material and social realities (Onuf 2012: 40). The material and the social contaminate each other, but variably, in recursive interactions between agents and structures (Onuf 2012: 58).

Wherever and however power goes, tragic possibilities follow. Despite empowering 'child' states and hoisting 'adult' states on their own rhetorical petard, the temporal retorts discussed here do not move us closer to a global solution to environmental degradation, as the recent litany of failed meetings, summits, and protocols makes clear. This is not to lay blame on developing states for international inaction. Rather, there is the distinct possibility that discourses manifesting myriad dimensions of power and embracing a plurality of international political times may concatenate with (and within) enfeebled hegemonic constructs, increasing the likelihood that the international community will find itself facing a time decisively unified by a dearth of inhabitable space.

Notes

1 The debates discussed in this section are drawn almost exclusively from public discourse. For academic treatments, consult (Dobson 2000; Dobson 2005; Goodin 1990; Jakobsen 1999; Shue 1999; Young 2001).
2 The poem by Ingrid Jonker, entitled 'The Child (Who Was Shot Dead by Soldiers at Nyanga)', is quoted in (Mandela 1994).

Bibliography

Adam, B. (1990) *Time and Social Theory*, Philadelphia, PA: Temple University Press.

African Development Bank Group. (2011) *AfDB to Incorporate Biomass and Bio-energy into New Energy Strategy Daily the Pak Banker*, Abidjan: African Development Bank Group. Online. Available HTTP: < http://www.afdb.org/en/news-and-events/article/afdb-to-incorporate-biomass-and-bio-energy-into-new-energy-strategy-7938/> (Accessed 25 April 2011).

Agence France Presse (2009) *'China Now Taking Climate Change Seriously: EU's Barroso'*, Brussels, France: Agence France Presse, (26 June 2009).

Algeria (2008) 'Paper 1', *Ad Hoc Working Group on Long-term Cooperative Action under the Convention*, 7. Poznan, Poland: United Nations Framework Convention on Climate Change. Online. Available HTTP: <http://unfccc.int/files/kyoto_ protocol/application/pdf/boliviabap08122008.pdf.> (Accessed 28 March 2015).

Associated Press. (2007) *New Alarms Are Rung on Perils of Global Warming*, Paris: International Herald Tribune. Online. Available HTTP: <http://www.iht.com/ articles/2007/02/27/news/climate.php.>.

———. (2009) *Climate Talks Resume after Hours-Long Boycott*, Copenhagen, Denmark: Associated Press. Online. Available HTTP: <http://www.msnbc.msn.com/id/344 12503/ns/us_news-environment/t/climate-talks-resume-after-hours-long-boycott/> (Accessed 14 October 2012).

Ban, K. -M. (2007) *'Address to the High-Level Segment of the UN Climate Change Conference'*, Bali, Indonesia: Federal News Service, (12 December 2015).

Blaney, D. L. and N. Inayatullah (2006) 'The Savage Smith and the Temporal Walls of Capitalism', in B. Jahn (ed.), *The Classics and International Relations in Context*, 123–154, Cambridge, UK: Cambridge University Press.

Buckley, C. (2010) 'China Feels Heat of Climate Change Rifts', *Reuters*. Online. Available HTTP: <http://uk.reuters.com/article/2010/11/22/uk-climate-cancun-china-preview-idUKTRE 6AL0MV20101122. (Accessed 22 November 2010).

Costa Rica. (2008) 'Paper No. 2: Costa Rica', *Item 13 of the Provisional Agenda: Second Review of the Kyoto Protocol Pursuant to Its Article 9*, 5–6. Poznan, Poland: United Nations Framework Convention on Climate Change. Online. Available HTTP: <http://unfccc.int/files/kyoto_protocol/application/pdf/boliviabap 08122008.pdf.> (Accessed 18 October 2012).

Debrix, F. (1999) *Re-Envisioning Peacekeeping: the United Nations and the Mobilization of Ideology*, Minneapolis, MN: The University of Minnesota Press.

Deutsche Presse-Agentur. (1997) *Nations from Four Continents Call for Greenhouse Gas Reductions*, New York, NY: Deutsche Presse-Agentur (23 June 1997).

Dobson, A. (2000) *Green Political Thought*, Volume 3rd., London, UK: Routledge.

———. (2005) 'Globalisation, Cosmopolitanism and the Environment', *International Relations*, 19(3):259–273.

Dörre, K. (2011) 'Capitalism, Landnahme and Social Time Régimes: An Outline', *Time & Society*, 20(1):69–93.

Edkins, J. (2003) *Trauma and the Memory of Politics*, Cambridge, UK: Cambridge University Press.

Fainaru, S. (1992) 'Down to Earth: For all the hype surrounding the Earth Summit, it is difficult to say exactly what is going on here', *The Boston Globe* (7 June 1992).

Gallagher, B. (2012) 'Coming Home: The Temporal Presence of the U.S. Soldier's Wounded Body', in S. Opondo and M. J. Shapiro (eds.), *The New Violent Cartography: Geo-Analysis after the Aesthetic Turn*, 1st ed., 69–89, New York, NY: Routledge.

Goodin, R. E. (1990) 'International Ethics and the Environmental Crisis,' *Ethics and International Affairs*, 4:91–105.

Hindess, B. (2007) 'The Past Is another Culture,' *International Political Sociology*, 1:325–338.

Hom, A. R. (2010) 'Hegemonic Metronome: The Ascendancy of Western Standard Time,' *Review of International Studies*, 36(4):1145–1170.

Hom, A. R. and Steele, B. J. (2010) 'Open Horizons: The Temporal Visions of Reflexive Realism,' *International Studies Review*, 12(2):271–300.

Hutchings, K. (2008) *Time and World Politics: Thinking the Present*, Manchester, UK: Manchester University Press.

Inayatullah, N. and D. B. Blaney (2004) *International Relations and the Problem of Difference*, London, UK: Routledge.

Jakobsen, S. (1999) 'International Relations and Global Environmental Change: Review of the Burgeoning Literature on the Environment,' *Cooperation and Conflict*, 34(2):205–236.

Jiang, Z. (2002) 'President Jiang Zemin Addresses Global Environmental Facility Meeting,' Beijing: *Xinhua General News Service* (16 October 2002). Online. Available HTTP: <http://www.nexis.com.ezproxy.lib.gla.ac.uk/results/docview/ docview.do?docLinkInd=true&risb=21_T22077215703&format=GNBFI&sort=BOOLEAN&startDocNo=1&resultsUrlKey=29_T22077215707&cisb=22_T22077215706&treeMax=true&treeWidth=0&csi=8078&docNo=1.> (Accessed 25 May 2015).

Lapid, Y. and F. Kratochwil. (1996) *The Return of Culture and Identity in International Relations Theory*, Boulder, CO: Lynne Rienner.

Laufer, S. (1999) 'Africa Must Embrace Globalisation—Mbeki,' *Johannesburg: Business Day*. Online. Available HTTP: <http://www.hartford-hwp.com/archives/30/117. html.> (Accessed 15 September 2012).

Ling, C. M. (2007) *'Bali Achieved What It Set Out to Do,'* Kuala Lumpur, Malaysia: New Straits Times (30 December 2007).

Loh, D. (2002) '*It's Not Easy, Saving the Earth*,' Kuala Lumpur, Malaysia: New Straits Times, 3, (11 August 2002).
Lovell, J. (2012) 'Clean Energy Lag Means World Is Headed for 6-Degree-Celsius Temperature Rise, Says IEA,' *Climate Wire*, April 26, sec. Technology.
Lundborg, T. (2011) *Politics of the Event: Time, Movement, Becoming*, London, UK: Routledge.
Mandela, N. (1994) *State of the Nation Address*, Republic of South Africa. Online. Available HTTP: <http://www.info.gov.za/speeches/1994/170595002.htm.> (Accessed 19 June 2008).
Manning, E. (2004) 'Time for Politics', in J. Edkins, V. Pin-Fat and M. J. Shapiro (eds.), *Sovereign Lives: Power in Global Politics*, London & New York: Routledge.
Mbeki, T. (1998, September 1). NAM: The ties that bind us, *The Sowetan*, Johannesburg, South Africa.
———. (1999) *Address at the Opening of Parliament*, Republic of South Africa. Online. Available HTTP: <http://www.info.gov.za/speeches/1999/9906281018a 1006.htm.> (Accessed 19 June 2008).
——— (2001) *State of the Nation Address*. Online. Available HTTP: <http://www.info.gov.za/speeches/2001/0102131223p1001.htm.> (Accessed 19 June 2008).
——— (2002, August 26). *Environment and Sustainable Development; Translating the Dream of Sustainable Development into Reality*, Africa News, Johannesburg, South Africa.
——— (2004) *State of the Nation Address*. Online. Available HTTP: <http://www.info.gov.za/speeches/2004/04020610561002.htm.> (Accessed 19 June 2008).
——— (2006) *State of the Nation Address*. Online. Available HTTP: <http://www.info.gov.za/speeches/2006/06020310531001.htm.> (Accessed 19 June 2008).
McSweeney, B. (1999) *Security, Identity and Interests: A Sociology of International Relations*. Cambridge, UK: Cambridge University Press.
Mishra, J. (2009) 'Gear up for Climate-Change Policy', *The Economic Times*. Online. Available HTTP: <http://articles.economictimes.indiatimes.com/2009–11–18/news/28468323_1_climate-change-energy-efficiency-emission-curbs.> (Accessed 14 October 2012).
Morgenthau, H. J. (1948) *Politics among Nations: The Struggle for Power and Peace*, New York, NY: McGraw-Hill.
New Straits Times (2007) '*What's Next after Kyoto*', Kuala Lampur, Malaysia: New Strait Times (10 December 2007). Online. Available HTTP: <http://www.nexis.com.ezproxy. lib.gla.ac.uk/results/docview/docview.do?docLinkInd=true&risb=21_T22077257605&format=GNBFI&sort=BOOLEAN&startDocNo=1&resultsUrlKey=29_T22077257609&cisb=22_T22077257608&treeMax=true&treeWidth=0&csi=151977&docNo=4>.
Niebuhr, R. (2001) *Moral Man and Immoral Society: A Study in Ethics and Politics*, Louisville, KY: Westminster John Knox Press.
Onuf, N. G. (2012) *World of Our Making: Rules and Rule in Social Theory and International Relations*, Reissue, Abingdon, UK: Routledge.
Prozorov, S. (2011) 'The Other as Past and Present: Beyond the Logic of 'temporal Othering' in IR Theory,' *Review of International Studies*, 37(3):1273–1293.
Republic of Bolivia. (2008) 'Paper 8', *Ad Hoc Working Group on Long-term Cooperative Action under the Convention*, 102–108. Poznan, Poland: United Nations Framework Convention on Climate Change. Online. Available HTTP: <http://unfccc.int/files/kyoto_protocol/application/pdf/boliviabap08122008.pdf.> (accessed 28 March 2015).

Shue, H. (1999) 'Global Environment and International Inequality,' *International Affairs*, 75(3):531–545.

Soroos, M. S. (1993) 'Arctic Haze and Transboundary Air Pollution: Conditions Governing Success and Failure,' in O. R. Yong and G. Osherenko (eds.), *Polar Politics: Creating International Environmental Regimes*, 186–222, Ithaca, NY: Cornell University Press.

Steele, B. J. (2008) *Ontological Security in International Relations*, New York, NY: Routledge, New International Relations Series.

———. (2010) *Defacing Power: The Aesthetics of Insecurity in Global Politics*, Ann Arbor, MI: University of Michigan Press.

Toulmin, S. (1990) *Cosmopolis: The Hidden Agenda of Modernity*, Chicago, IL: University of Chicago Press.

UNEP. (2012) *United Nations Environmental Program Annual Report 2011* (No. DCP/1492/NA). Online. Available HTTP: <http://www.unep.org/annualreport/ 2011/docs/UNEP_ANNUAL_REPORT_2011.pdf.> (Accessed 17 October 2012).

United Nations (1992) *Rio Declaration on Environment and Development*. Online. Available HTTP: <http://www.unep.org/Documents.multilingual/Default.asp? DocumentID=78&ArticleID=1163.> (Accessed 25 May 2015).

———. (2007) *Interlinked Issues of Energy, Pollution, Industrial Development, Climate Change at Heart of Ensuring Sustainable Development, UN Commission Told*, New York, NY: United Nations. Online. Available HTTP: <http://www.un.org/ press/en/2007/envdev928.doc.htm> (Accessed 28 March 2015).

Wendt, A. (1999) *Social Theory of International Politics*, Cambridge, UK: Cambridge University Press.

Wu, X. and Yanghong W. (2010) '*Special Report: Hopes, Regrets in Science in Past Decade*', Xinhua General News Service, December 31, sec. World News.

Young, O. R. (2001) 'Environmental Ethics in International Society,' in J. M. Coicaud and D. Warner (eds.), *Ethics and International Affairs: Extent and Limits*, 161–193, Tokyo, Japan: United Nations University Press.

Yue, P. H. (1997) '*Will It Be another Load of Hot Air?*' Kuala Lumpur, Malaysia: New Straits Times (2 December 1997).

12 Childhood, redemption and the prosaics of waiting

Sam Okoth Opondo

Waiting, rights and redemption

To write or speak about children, especially suffering children, often results in sentimental salvific narratives and interventions that seek to redeem them from the adult and politically saturated worlds they inhabit. Among other things, these narratives disavow the political and historical contexts constituting modern ideas of childhood and subject the 'adult's imagination of the child's imagination' to a humanitarian frame of recognition and its related fabulations, solicitations and prescriptions (Taussig 2003: 454).

In contrast to these redemptive narratives, E.C. Osondu's short story 'Waiting' offers a politically perspicuous account of life in a refugee camp through a provocative conjunction of children's time, suffering, satire and the sartorial (Osondu 2008). From Zaki Orlando's identificatory remarks at the beginning of the story, readers are invited to reflect on the moral fabric and fabrications privileged by the regimes of inscription sustaining the children's precarious lives:

> My name is Orlando Zaki. *Orlando* is taken from Orlando, Florida, which is what is written on the t-shirt given to me by the Red Cross. *Zaki* is the name of the town where I was found and from which I was brought to this refugee camp. My friends in the camp are known by the inscriptions written on their t-shirts. Acapulco wears a t-shirt with the inscription, *Acapulco* . . . Some people are lucky: London had a t-shirt that said *London* and is now in London. He's been adopted by a family over there. Maybe I will find a family in Orlando, Florida that will adopt me.
>
> (Osondu 2008: 1)

By articulating the entanglements between the anticipatory (proleptic) and everyday (prosaic) dynamics of childhood in the camp, Zaki's introductory remarks highlight the tension between humanitarian time, the time of suffering and survival and the narrator's own biographical time (childhood). As the story progresses, Osondu draws our attention to the micro-practices and rhythms of everyday life in the camp that disturb, produce or are produced by the humanitarian world and its vision of childhood.

Heeding the story's insights, the explorations in the following sections foreground ways of 'thinking about the everyday, the customary, and the ordinary' that have aesthetic, ethical as well as political implications for how we think and engage childhood and humanitarianism (Barnard 2004: 282; Morson and Emerson 1990: 15; Mbembe 1992: 128).[1] Rather than offer a detailed analysis of specific humanitarian institutions and their projects and projections of childhood suffering, atrocity and redemption, I juxtapose fragments from a set of child-centered short stories with historical and theoretical texts that elucidate the critical perspectives offered by fictional children. In addition to E. C. Osondu's 'Waiting' (2008), I read his 'Janjaweed Wife' (2010) and Noviolet Bulawayo's 'Hitting Budapest' (2010) to highlight how sentimentality and moral discourses on childhood disavow the violence upon which they are founded while legitimating further intervention in the name of humanity in general and children in particular. The explorations also pay attention to how these short stories use the prosaics of waiting to articulate co-presences, heterogeneous times and entanglements that reveal or interrupt the regulatory fictions underlining humanitarian action.

In Osondu's 'Waiting' in particular, the prosaics of waiting and suffering are enjoined with redemptive practices that tie the children's lives to multiple worlds within and outside the camp. These practices range from the photographic representations of children used to facilitate transnational adoption and the donation of secondhand T-shirts from which the children acquire their names, to relationships with dogs that blur and then reinforce the human/animal and friend/foe distinctions and the genres of expression that enable displaced children to deal with their trauma. Contrary to the invocations of clock-time and emergencies that must be addressed 'now', 'Waiting' instantiates an embodied and phenomenological experience of children's time where the very act of waiting reveals the religious, aesthetic, human and child-oriented moral scripts and movements underlining humanitarian action.

The textual and extra-textual forms of waiting that mediate the children's suffering and their relationship to war and humanitarian imaginaries are captured in Zaki's description of his relationship to the local nun – Sister Nora. For instance, Sister Nora encourages him to write and read texts like Samuel Beckett's absurdist play, *Waiting for Godot*, as a way of *forgetting and remembering* his traumatic life experiences. She also informs Zaki that 'the people in the book are waiting for God to come and help them', thus infusing the act of waiting with a redemptive quality that is at once future oriented, perpetual and religious (Osondu 2008: 3). The invocation of *Waiting for Godot* and its subjection to 'extra-textual realities', such as Sister Nora's religious interpretation and Zaki's survivalist desire for humanitarian redemption, offer insights into the entanglements between 'valueless' waiting (*Waiting for Godot*) and the means-ends experience of waiting for humanitarian assistance in Osondu's short story. Through satirical over-identification with Beckett's text and the everydayness of waiting characteristic of humanitarian assistance, Osondu's 'Waiting' divests the humanitarian world in which it is implicated of its moral and symbolic authority (Dovey 1996: 139; Schweizer 2008).

To appreciate the ethical and political dimensions of Osondu's weaving of salvific and sartorial practices, we can consider Jacques Rancière's critique of discourses on rights, victimhood and humanitarian intervention. Attentive to the relationship between violence and the discourse of rights today, Rancière is critical of the redemptive assumptions and the normative consensus that matches 'global democracy' to 'the global market of liberal economy' by transforming the discourse of the rights of man into a discourse on the 'rights of the rightless' (Rancière 2004: 296). According to Rancière, the transformation of human rights into the 'rights of victims who are unable to enact any rights or even any claim in their name' legitimates a new right to 'humanitarian invasion' as powerful people get to send human rights abroad the same way 'charitable persons do with their *old clothes*' (ibid: 297, 307; also Žižek 2005:127).

Rancière's turn to the 'materiality' of used clothes, much like how 'Waiting' uses T-shirts, maps the entanglements between the current humanitarian regime, neoliberalism and necropolitics. In so doing, both reveal the time-based 'ontological trap' that foregrounds the figure of an absolute victim in whose name the powerful must act 'now' as redemptive avengers/providers (Rancière 2004: 302). In a similar critique of the consensual translation of images and voices of the suffering into urgent narratives of redemption and moral certainty, Mahmood Mamdani illustrates how agencies that refuse to wait or prioritize doing over knowing transform the 'responsibility to protect into the right to punish' (Mamdani 2009:270). According to Mamdani, the Save Darfur Coalition and other human rights interventionists in Darfur 'act first and understand later' based on the notion that one 'must respond ethically and not wait', for it is while waiting that genocide occurs (ibid: 3, 6).

Rather than reading the violence in Darfur alongside the logic of the War on Terror that provided the 'coordinates, the language, the images, and the sentiment for interpreting Darfur', the moral imperative to act now is derived from the humanitarianist framing of the Darfur conflict that does not engage the conflict's historical and contemporary context (Mamdani 2009: 71). Instead, humanitarians turn to the 'lessons of Rwanda' where people 'waited to find out, to learn the difference between Tutsi and Hutu, and why one was killing the other' – in the processes, 'needing to know turned into an excuse for doing nothing' (Mamdani 2009: 3). Drawing on the moral authority of a violence of the past while remaining inattentive to the violence of the present, the Save Darfur Coalition 'calls for a military intervention in the civil war without bothering to address the likely consequences of that intervention' (Mamdani 2009: 71).

The humanitarianist mode of sensing and making sense of such conflicts is fraught with silences, erasures and elisions. With the increasing 'prolixity of the humanitarian', we witness the increasing 'silence of survivors' with the humanitarian coming to speak for survivors (Fassin 2008: 537). This substitution of the discourse of the humanitarian for the survivor exploits the politics of genre and is articulated through war-inspired autobiographies and biography-infused solicitations for donations and NGO atrocity reports and photographs. These constitute survivors as 'speechless emissaries' or victims existing in a temporal frame where they can only speak 'worldlessly' of the immediate history of the violence they experienced (Malkki 1996: 389–390).

Thus, *the time of suffering*, especially suffering children, becomes an *exceptional time* where recognized institutions, technologies and moral sentiments are authorized to suspend the norms of political engagement or forget the history of violent entanglements to mobilize exceptional *practices* in the name of suffering others. The images, technologies and narratives of humanitarian action frequently privilege the 'immediacy of the crisis frame', and the time of childhood suffering is eventually framed as part of historical time (Roitman 2012).

Attentiveness to the dynamics of waiting and slowness and the multiple ways atrocity and humanitarian action are experienced can interrupt the moral certitude and consensus in humanitarian and human rights discourses that do not consider the political contexts of children and other figures of suffering humanity they represent.

Children's time, value and the politics of the family

To amplify the worlds brought into focus by attention to children and the humanitarian demands for immediate action, we turn to Zaki Orlando's description of the multiple times and spaces of waiting in the refugee camp:

> Here in the camp, we wait and wait and then wait some more. It is the only thing we do. We wait for the food trucks to come and then we form a straight line and then we wait a few minutes for the line to scatter, then we wait for the fight to begin, and then we fight and struggle and bite and kick and curse and tear and grab and run. And then we begin to watch the road and wait to see if the water trucks are coming.
>
> (Osondu 2008: 3)

The children also wait for a photographer to take pictures that the Red Cross sends to potential adoptive parents abroad (Osondu 2008: 3). This intense waiting for the humanitarian photograph to be transformed into the family photo focuses our attention on the relationship between humanitarian action, necropolitical spaces and domestic spaces and times. The passage from the camp to the adoptive home is facilitated by the representational capacities of a larger humanitarian apparatus, the camera's aperture and an apparitional idea of man.

Unlike the humanitarian quest for adaptive/adoptive living strategies that enhance resilience, 'Waiting' over-identifies with everyday suffering and the intimacy of redemption, resisting the humanitarian frame of resilience. Through a pensive yet playful engagement with the ambiguity and everydayness of entangled lives, the story reveals humanitarianism's naturalization of a tolerance for that which would have been intolerable under different circumstances. That is, the prosaics of waiting that animates Osondu's story and the satirical form in which it is written force us to reflect on the entanglements between humanitarian hope, horror and the redemption of children in a manner that interrupts the usual 'sentiments evoked by descriptions of poverty', suffering and redemption (Barnard 2004: 300). The story's attention to the proximity and entanglement of disparate worlds simultaneously reveals and interrupts the 'homogenous empty time' of humanitarian redemption while politicizing children's time(s) and the spaces of their enactment (Benjamin 1968).

Family time

Like 'Waiting', Osondu's 'Janjaweed Wife' offers a provocative account of the hope and horror that come with waiting and their implication for the characters' conceptions of morality, family, childhood and the valuation of life-saving and life-optimizing practices. As the child narrator describes the physical and metaphysical dimensions of violence in Fur and the Zagwara refugee camp, readers are invited to interrogate the geopolitical, ontological and identity-oriented aspects of Janjaweed violence and the discourses seeking to maintain national, humanitarian and family coherence in Darfur.

The violence manifests itself in moral discourses on the family, womanhood, Arabness/blackness, camp/non-camp spaces, human/*djinn* distinctions and the possibilities or desirability of co-habitation that the children encounter. The Janjaweed are represented as Arabic-speaking *djinns* who hate dark-skinned people. The girls are threatened with 'untimely' marriage to the militia whenever they do things their mothers disapprove of, thus enabling adults to police the rhythms of children's domestic life (Osondu 2010: 143).

Tying the violence of the warfront to the camp or the homefront, Osondu makes the reader intensely aware of children's time and its intersection with other times. This enables us to question the imagined monstrosity of the Janjaweed, the 'Arabisation of the violence' and the humanitarian and military intervention obscuring the material bases of the violence in Darfur (e.g., the land question) by disavowing its historical context or making it a purely local affair (Mamdani 2009: 71).

When the girls and their mother move to the Zagrawa refugee camp, the Janjaweed threat is kept at the camp's perimeter as the precarity of camp life forces the women and children to give up some of their family values to benefit from redemptive yet exploitative forces. The quest for survival turns the camp into a site of moral tension and negotiation when the children receive much needed T-shirts from the Red Cross with inscriptions their mother identifies with 'wayward' girls. The camp's limited relief provisions force the narrator's mother to become a concubine to a rich man (El Hajj) who sexually harasses her daughters under the guise of making them better Muslims. When they flee El Hajj's home and return to the camp, the camp refugees valorize the 'good children's' suffering; they would rather live in poverty and keep their dignity instead of being 'kept women' (Osondu 2010: 151). By treating children's time and the politics of the family, 'Janjaweed Wife' highlights the tensions between economic value, family values and survival in times of war and humanitarianism.

There is a similar interplay of camp-time, family time, children's time and wartime in 'Waiting'. Consider Acapulco's anxiety about the increasing difficulty of finding an American family to adopt him due to his advanced age, nocturnal bedwetting and orientation toward non-human animals. In a remark exemplifying his anxiety about the child-oriented apportionment of sympathy, Acapulco asks Zaki if his biological parents will join his new family in America when the war ends. As the conversation proceeds, we learn that the possibility of finding new parents to adopt Acapulco is contingent on his chronological age and his posing for pictures with a dog (white people like dogs and people who like dogs) while the possibility of being found by his biological parents is contingent on his not being adopted and the temporality and duration of war.

Acapulco's affective attachment and desire for more than one genealogical family line/time interrupts the transnational adoption narrative by bringing precarious adult lives into an order that privileges the rescue, movement and material betterment of children. As the conversation shifts from the temporality of war and humanitarianism to the temporality of generic childhood, Zaki and Acapulco draw our attention to the relationship between humanitarian concern for suffering children, the politics of the family and the modern 'valuation of childhood as a global cultural good' with moral and pedagogical imperatives (Nieuwenhuys 1998: 270). The Red Cross's involvement in the adoption and education of war children is as much a humanitarian effort as it is an attempt to realize a sentimental idea of childhood; they do not want the children to 'join the Youth Brigade' where they would 'shoot and kill and rape and loot and burn and steal and destroy . . . and die and *not go to school*' (Osondu 2008: 3).

This raises questions about the ideals/idea of childhood underlining foundational scripts such as the Convention on the Rights of the Child adopted by the UN General Assembly in 1989, programs displacing the political and cultural landscapes and the ontological significance of the discourse of universal childhood. In addition to a critique of the limited idea of childhood informing institutional and legal interventions, we can extend our critique to novels and other genres of expression articulating child-based conflict narratives amenable to humanitarian and self-help initiatives. African child soldier narratives like Ishmael Beah's memoir *A Long Way Gone: Memoirs of a Boy Soldier* and Uzodinma Iweala's *Beast of No Nation* have been inserted into humanitarian regimes that represent child soldiers as victims to be rehabilitated from war-inflicted trauma and drug addiction (Coundouriotis 2010: 192). The redemptive discourses on childhood and the genres through which the narrative of suffering children is articulated authorize state intervention through warfare and welfare and the humanitarian imperative to save, adopt and protect vulnerable children where states and, by extension, families have failed. The 'ideological confluence' and shared vision of humanity underlining these legal, literary and humanitarian projects 'create mutually enabling fictions' about children, humans and the accompanying sentiments and moral judgments (Slaughter 2007: 4).

A more critical mode of engaging the suffering of distant others and a recognition of their political agency can be realized through modalities of writing, imaging and imagining that challenge the nation-state's and humanitarian agencies' will to impose a coherent narrative of childhood suffering and redemption.

While 'Waiting' suggests the need for more effective humanitarian intervention to aid the suffering children, the laughter and tactics of delay punctuating the children's dialogue point to 'varying temporal trajectories' that enable us to stage an encounter between what Michael J. Shapiro calls 'disjunctive temporal presences' (Shapiro 2001: 124).

More specifically, the children's dialogue and descriptions of rhythms of life in 'Waiting' and 'Janjaweed Wife' articulate the intersections between 'genealogical' family time, national time, humanitarian time and chronological time in a manner that allows the 'emergence of diverse presences' while highlighting the children's precarious lives and their will to survive in the midst of adversity (Shapiro 2001: 130). These disjunctive temporalities and co-presences do not comport with national or humanitarian visions of the world and are enabled by short story 'structural ideals' such as 'brevity, brief character development, and limited temporality' that highlight the here and the now of the camp as well as the complex relationships between heterogeneous times, people, things and non-human animals (Houlihan 2010: 63). Through a subversive 'ultra-orthodoxy' enabled by the story's satirical style, the characters in 'Waiting' over-identify with humanitarianism, revealing so as to reveal its ideological formations (Žižek 2001: 123; Žižek 2006: 290). That is, by taking humanitarianism too seriously, the children reveal the disavowals characteristic of the politics of the family, the benevolence and violence underlining transnational adoption and the worlds made possible by the traffic in the images of suffering children.

Rather than encourage ironic aesthetic distancing or engaged expert testimony, the short story form compresses people in space and time allowing 'us' to laugh, cry and wait with Osondu's characters as they reflect on the sentimental discourses and uses of childhood underlining the modern will to save suffering children wherever they are found.

Sentimentality, innocence and the uses of children

Philippe Ariès's *Centuries of Childhood* explains how the idea of childhood and the corresponding universalization of the concept of humanity shifted as western societies moved from 'ignorance of childhood to the centering of the family around the child in the nineteenth century' (Ariès 1962: 10). Today, the sentimental orientation toward childhood is part of a humanitarian imaginary where transnational adoption practices enable parents from more affluent societies to rescue children from necropolitical or 'emotionally and financially bankrupt existence' as illustrated by Madonna's adoption of the Malawian boy David Banda (2006) and the Malawian girl Chifundo 'Mercy' James (2009) or earlier adoptions of Korean war orphans by US citizens (Brystom 2011: 216). Such adoptions are directly related to global inequities and structural violence that affect the well-being of women and children in some parts of the world while cultivating philanthropic and humanitarian sensibilities in others.

Riitta Högbacka attributes the increase in transnational adoption to four factors: 'war, imbalance in socioeconomic conditions between sending and receiving countries, organizational linkages between them, and a political decision in the sending country to allow inter-country adoptions' (Högbacka 2008: 313). These macropolitical factors make children and children's concerns central to the humanitarian imaginary. They are buttressed by the sentimentalization of childhood and the enactment and institutionalization of historically and culturally specific moral, legal and economic codes facilitating the inequitable distribution of precarity and charity on a global scale.

These histories of the invention and uses of childhood are central to the moral assumptions underlining the humanitarian concern for the pain of innocent children. While often disavowed, the concern over suffering children today points us to developmental and colonial concerns over children's health, education and hygiene reflected in the Christian will-to-convert and its related educational and eschatological apparatus to guide and protect children from 'destructive' aspects of the societies from which they originate. In short, the protection of children is often coterminous with a larger responsibility to protect or proliferate a desirable way of being in time, defined in terms of peace, religion, race, education, economic well-being, sexuality, modernity or citizenship.

To make child-oriented interventions in other societies effective and/or legitimate, humanitarians often turn to the iconography of childhood to elicit the feelings necessary to mobilize humanitarian action. Feelings for suffering children have not been extended to all children in the same way due, in part, to a moral valuation whereby certain children are considered innocent while others embody moral decay and decadence. Related to the moralization and sentimentality of childhood is the transformation in the meaning, value and uses of children. This shift in the value of children corresponds with race- and labor-mediated transformations in human values, market value and the valuation of life.

With the turn to sentimentality evidenced in the nineteenth century, the birth of a child was no longer considered the addition of a future laborer to the family (Zelizer 1981: 1038). Similarly, the death of a child was considered more than an economic loss as children shifted from being objects of 'utility to being objects of sentiment and from being a producer asset to a consumer good' (Zelizer 1981: 1038). As Viviana Zelizer illustrates in her study of the development of children's insurance in the US between 1875 and the early 1900s, life insurance and the related monetary evaluation of death further severed children from the labor market while simultaneously transforming their value through the emergence of the 'economically worthless but emotionally priceless child' (Ariès 1962; also Zelizer 1981: 1035).

Of course, children have never participated in the labor market in the same way across the globe. The sacralization of childhood and the removal of children from the labor market is not devoid of racial and geographically inflected partialities as illustrated by the experience of African child slaves in the Jamaica of the eighteenth and nineteenth centuries (Diptee 2007). Despite the contemporaneity of children's worlds and the imperial-colonial linkages between Britain and Jamaica, metropolitan ideals about child labor were not reproduced in the plantation colony where large numbers of African children were inserted into the 'agro-industrial' complex that transformed child laborers in Jamaica into the 'property of the subjects of the crown' (Diptee 2007: 53–55). The prevailing colonial/slave economies and legal apparatus denied the children a 'right to wages' while their parents were denied 'any legal right to the fruits of their labor', as the 'parent-child relationship' was always 'secondary to that of the slave owner and slave child' (Diptee 2007: 53–55).

Subsequent shifts in conceptions of humanity and the emergence of new forms of governments of people and things created new fields of meaning and affect that moved children deeper into the realm of sentimentality. The newfound concern over child labor, adoption and foster care, conversion, education and welfare manifested itself in transnational and transcultural moral discourses that considered children a problem for governance and a means of creating reliable and coherent 'citizens, governmental subjects, and modern nation-sates' (Gordon 2008; Stoler 2002: 19). The violence that makes possible this politics of compassion is evident in humanitarian and settler colonial projects where concern for children contributed to the removal of indigenous children in the American West and Australia as well as discriminatory education, health, sporting or religious practices in South Africa and 'South Rhodesia' based on the desire to produce viable generations of settlers and natives (Jacobs 2011; Summers 2011). The production and management of children's time as a way of managing life in general was generationally biased, as it considered the innocent native child redeemable while native mothers were 'beyond redemption', thus legitimizing the removal of native children from the care of their parents (Stoler 2002: 121).

This history of childhood purity and innocence is not so innocent. In glorifying the 'vulnerable and pure child as a repository of utopian hopes of altruism, redistribution, generosity and disinterested care', the discourse justifies 'the human rights protections we seek to accord' children without questioning the discourses on childhood, those of rights or those on humanitarianism (Bhabha 2006: 1533–1534). In disavowing the long history of violence and new forms of violence committed in the name of children against other children or 'child-like' adults, humanitarians carry out a critique of violence akin to the one carried out by the Congo Reform Association in their critique of Belgium's King Leopold II's violence against the indigenous inhabitants of the Congo Free State. In writings considered the forerunners of today's human rights campaigns, E.D. Morel (*King Leopold's Rule in Africa*), Roger Casement's damning *Congo Report* (1904–1905), Arthur Conan Doyle (*The Crime of the Congo*) and Joseph Conrad, we see a critical awareness, but as 'creatures of their time', the reformers remain limited in their orientation toward colonized others, unable to 'conclude that imperialism had to end so that natives could lead a life free of European domination' (Said 1993: 29–30). The reformers represent Africans as dependent victims in need of redemption through initiatives that are critical of horrific violence while remaining silent about the larger colonial structure and the paternalistic orientation toward Africans.

Like present-day human rights and humanitarian agencies, these reformers use visual evidence of atrocities in the Congo to create a temporality and visual imaginary of the violence, at once aesthetic, moral and forensic (Sliwinski 2006: 334).

These include photographs of Congolese children (Mola and Yoka), who, in their respective photographs, hold their mutilated limbs in a manner suggesting their redemption is 'in the hands of distant spectators' (Sliwinski 2006: 340, 356; also Thompson 2012: 197).

The recent explosion of humanitarianism in the age of neoliberalism privileges childhood innocence and dependence; this, in turn, contributes to a sentimental rather than ethico-political orientation toward the suffering of distant peoples. Such moral identification with suffering children enables a 'political consensus' about pain and trauma and endorses forms of sentimentality that confuse the 'eradication of pain with the achievement of justice' or the improvement of children's welfare with the improvement in political life, making the violences of everyday life credible and bearable (Berlant 2000: 45).

Everyday rhythms and the de-infantalizing of the present

The concern for innocent and often nameless children contributes to the proliferation of images of allochronic and timeless children (Malkki 2010: 63) wherein the suffering child is a subject with a 'known' horrific past, a hopeless yet innocent present and a promising future to be secured through timely interventions. These temporalizations of children and cultures are often considered synonymous with 'knowing' a given culture, as in Mike Moore's photographs of Luke Piri during the 2002 famine in Malawi and their re-use to dramatize the plight of Africans at large (Campbell 2011; Fabian 1983: 106). With images like Piri's, the time of African childhood becomes synonymous with the time of unhappiness and the time of Africanness, allowing the photographer, the NGO agent or the state representative to invoke children's voices and bodies in a manner that perpetuates humanitarian values, the temporality of emergency and the ideological projects they privilege (Campbell 2011; Manzo 2008).

The invocation of childhood as a site of innocence and morality contributes to calls for justice on a global scale, but childhood is also the locus of racial or class discourses. In nineteenth-century US, the discourses of childhood innocence contributed to the moral segregation of childhood through images, objects and narratives presenting a white child as fragile and innocent and a black child as an immoral 'non-child – a pickaninny' impervious to pain (Bernstein 2011: 34). In colonial Zimbabwe, a similar discourse of the black child as a 'piccanin' facilitated the employment of native children in white-owned mining compounds, farms and missionary households, providing the labor for and justification of disciplinary practices deemed necessary for the settler colonial project (Grier 1994: 27).

In contrast with moral discourses presenting the black child as a non-child or as an essentially innocent or incomplete human in need of redemption, Noviolet Bulawayo's short story 'Hitting Budapest' provides a window into the meaning-making and world-making practices of six children in postcolonial Zimbabwe. Through narratives of estrangement, suffering, play, friendship and aspiration, Darling, the protagonist and narrator of Bulawayo's short story, takes us through the rhythms of life in a slum (ironically but purposefully named Paradise) and the more affluent neighborhood known as Budapest where the children go to steal guavas. Darling and her friends, Bastard, Chipo, God-knows, Sibho and Stina, use multiple tactics to navigate everyday life between Paradise and Budapest while the polyphony of their voices reveals the entanglement and disjuncture between the children's lived experience and their dreams/aspirations, which are to be realized in another time or other places like Budapest, which Darling tells us 'is like a different country . . . where people who are not like us live' (Bulawayo 2010: 44).

As truth-tellers, holders of painful secrets, aspirations and lies, Darling and her friends highlight the ideological capture in Budapest and Paradise. They point to forms of intimacy and the hope and horror that mark their lives in Paradise and beyond; they also serve as sites of critique and ethical encounter that disrupt crisis management and moralizing narratives. Darling's narration of ten-year-old Chipo's pregnancy reveals the sexual violence in the home and the children's anxieties about possible futures given the pregnancy's disruption of the rhythms of play cementing their friendship:

> There are guavas to steal in Budapest, and right now I'd die for guavas, or anything for that matter. My stomach feels like somebody just took a shovel and dug everything out . . . We are running when we hit the bush; Bastard at the front . . . and then me and God knows, Stina, and *finally Chipo, who used to outrun everybody in Paradise but not anymore because her grandfather made her pregnant* . . . we slither through another bush, gallop along Hope Street past the big stadium with the glimmering benches we'll never sit on. Finally we hit Budapest. We have to stop once for Chipo to rest.
>
> (Bulawayo 2010: 43)

The pregnancy-induced slowness makes this child who is 'with child' a kind of 'non-child'. The pregnancy alienates her from her own body's 'developments' and from her friends and serves as evidence of the violence of the family that forcefully inserts her body into adult time.

Even though Chipo is socially embedded in the time of childhood play and its economy of survival characterized by guava-stealing escapades, the violent superimposition of adult time on Chipo's childhood and her continued engagement in child's play become a more nuanced critique of class dynamics, compassion and care. When the children hit Budapest, they meet a thirty-three-year-old woman in a 'Save Darfur' T-shirt (who is visiting her 'father's country' from London 'for the first time') whose bodily comportment and ethical orientation is called into question in her encounter with the children (Bulawayo 2010: 44). In a remark exemplifying the tensions and entanglements between the woman's world and her own, Darling notes the woman's clean and pretty feet that look 'like a baby's'. She questions the woman's interest in taking pictures of the children and her concern with Chipo's age and her stomach 'like she has never seen anybody pregnant' (Bulawayo 2010). By shifting the focus from the woman's moralistic gaze that emphasizes Chipo's pregnancy to the children's focus on the hunger and emptiness of Chipo's stomach, Darling calls our attention to the fact that this 'caring' woman has just thrown away some food without offering anything to the children (Bulawayo 2010: 43). The incommensurability of bodies, relations and times in this encounter highlights the class- and humanitarian-based disavowals that contribute to the inattention to aspects of the lives of proximate others while privileging sympathy for distant or abstract others.

Unlike the salvific narratives that focus on programmatic interventions into the children's lives, the heterogeneous narratives of hope outlined by the children focus on multiple exit and survival strategies that interrupt programmatic assumptions about children's desires, hopes and aspirations. Sibho hopes to marry a man from Budapest who will take her 'away from Paradise, away from the shacks', while Bastard plans to 'stop stealing guavas and move to bigger things inside the houses' when he grows up (Bulawayo 2010: 45). He also hopes to move to South Africa or Botswana where he can make a lot of money to buy a house in Budapest, Paris or Los Angeles. Like Bastard, Darling plans to leave the country. She hopes to go to America to live with her Aunt Fostalina, but Bastard and Chipo (who doesn't want a child, just guavas) remind her America is far away; she could get stuck 'working in nursing homes and clean[ing] poop' (Bulawayo 2010: 46).

Conclusion /evacuations

The economy of 'shortage and scarcity' within which the children operate makes 'the acquisition of things ... a goal in itself' while causing the children to resort to everyday strategies and tactics of survival and aspirational narratives that point to a time yet-to-come where things might be otherwise (Mbembe 2002: 271). Unlike the wholesale criminalization of adults operating in these survival economies, the suffering children are treated as objects of pity and deserving of charitable engagement if not removal from the milieu of suffering that includes their family members and friends.

Overlooked in the sentimental and future-oriented engagement with children striving to survive are the improved life chances and prosaic short-term calculations that make the children's lives possible. These range from stealing guavas in Budapest to migrant hustles intricately intertwined with excremental practices like synchronized public defecation where the painful and time-consuming guava-induced constipation makes the children feel they are 'trying to give birth to a country' (Bulawayo 2010: 46). The prosaics of survival and the children's implication in this milieu are captured in Darling's account of the events following the children's discovery of a woman's dead body dangling from a tree during one of their collective defecation sessions. Noting the woman's 'almost new shoes', the children agree to trade the shoes for a loaf of bread for their next meal (Bulawayo 2010: 47).

The children's faecal habitus and its related economy of survival point to the everyday experiments, tactics and excretions through which abjected people make do in cities, camps or camp-cities. We cannot overlook the humanitarian or developmentalist imaginaries that immediately subject the publicness of the children's defecation to refuse, life-managing and life-enhancing practices that make the lives of poor and vulnerable populations amenable to logics of the state, ethical corporate culture or corporate humanitarianism (Redfield 2012: 158). Nowhere is this clearer than in Peepoople's peepoo technology where a 'better plastic bag' acts as an alternative to the 'flying toilets' used to dispose of human waste by urban slum dwellers. This bag and other life technologies and/or humanitarian goods create a 'landscape of humanitarian imagination' characterized by material artifacts and objects whose design and purpose 'reflect doubts about state capacity to safeguard populations' (Redfield 2012: 158, 175).[2]

While Peepoople's focus on the excremental reinforces a humanitarian and developmentalist vision without questioning the idea of man upon which it is predicated, the excremental imagery in short stories like 'Hitting Budapest' and 'Waiting' questions the idea of man and the distinctions between the human and the animal, the living and the dead and children and adults underlining modern political imaginaries and the humanitarian ethos. In 'Waiting', in particular, the special meaning of the human/animal distinction in the humanitarian imaginary is revealed when the children discuss the ways war and the scarcity it creates have affected the relationship between children and dogs. Commenting on the absence of dogs in the refugee camp and the significance for possible adoption, as well as the excremental ecology of war in which children and dogs are implicated, Acapulco recalls a time when there were 'lots of black dogs' who acted as the children's friends and protectors in the camp (Osondu 2008: 5). A transformation in the war and humanitarian *dispositif* upset the friendly children-dog relationship by solidifying the human-animal distinction:

> Even though food was scarce, the dogs never went hungry. The women would call them whenever a child squatted down to shit and the dogs would come running. They would wait for the child to finish and lick the child's buttocks clean before they ate the shit. People threw them scraps of food. The dogs were useful in other ways too. In those days, the enemy still used to raid the camp frequently. We would bury ourselves in a hole and the dogs would gather leaves and other stuff and spread it atop the hole where we hid. The enemy would pass by the hole and not know we were hiding there.
>
> (Osondu 2008: 5)

The excremental collaboration and co-habitation disturbs the human-animal distinction and reveals the forms of life that are privileged or abjected in the process of humanity becoming human and the mediating function of excrementalism and the category of childhood.

The presence/absence of dogs in the camp reveals how humanitarian projects, in their programmatic focus on human beings, are ontological projects where the question of being is taken as settled, enabling the agents to move quickly into action rather than questioning their modalities of engagement. This is captured in Acapulco's narration of the entanglements of humanitarianism, war and the children-dog relationship in times of scarcity:

> There was a time the Red Cross people could not bring food to the camp for two weeks because the enemy would not let their plane land. We were so hungry we

killed a few of the dogs and used them to make pepper-soup . . . After that we did not see the dogs again . . . One day, a little child was squatting and having a shit. When the mother looked up, half a dozen of the dogs that had disappeared emerged from nowhere and attacked the little child . . . Some of the men began to lay ambush for the dogs and killed a few of them. They say the dogs had become as tough as lions. We don't see the dogs anymore. *People say it is the war.*
(Osondu 2008: 5)

Necropolitical and humanitarian practices do not impact on human beings alone but are implicated in the question of being. That is, attentiveness to the multiple dimensions of humanitarian action and the practices with which it is entangled reveals how the construction of the human as human and therefore an object of humanitarian action depends on the opposition between man and animal or the human and the inhuman against which various forms of life are defined as worthless and eliminable or worth saving (Agamben 2004: 33). As a 'companion species', the dogs in 'Waiting' share in the suffering and survival of the children and, as Donna Haraway puts it, illustrate that 'ways of living and dying matter' (Haraway 2008: 88). Accordingly, the dynamics of co-habiting and co-dying that emerge at the intersection of humanitarian and necropolitical practices illustrate the inadequacies and violence of taking human and generic childhood suffering as the absolute referent for moral and political action.

The children in the short stories discussed here interrupt the dominant humanitarian and developmentalist imaginaries that see childhood as an apolitical time of innocence or 'the time-space in which the human begins as an unfinished entity that undergoes a specifically developmental and so also normatively progressive trajectory' (Casteñada 2014: 59). Rather than offer explicit counter-discourses to the humanitarian conception of redemption, the stories' over-identification with the practices and narratives of suffering, redemption and enmity draws attention to everyday life or future aspirations that provoke deeper reflection on the times and uses of childhood and the violent mobilization and stasis that produce suffering or intervene in the name of suffering children. In these times of suffering and crisis, the short story form presents us with the strange figure of the 'laughing subject' or the subject of laughter who becomes an appropriate means of interrupting the perceptual, moral and temporal coordinates of the humanitarian regime of recognition and the child-oriented apparatus sustaining it.

Notes

1 While drawing upon Morson and Emerson's (1990) reading of the relationship between prosaics and the everyday, I depart from their conception of prosaics that 'designates a theory of literature that privileges prose in general and the novel in particular over the poetic genres'. Ultimately, my use of prosaics as counterpart rather than something opposed to poetics seeks to designate a form of thinking that presumes the importance of the literary, the everyday, the ordinary – the 'prosaic'. See Morson and Emerson (1990).
2 See Peepoople, http://www.peepoople.com/information/about-peepoople/

Bibliography

Agamben, G. (2004) *The Open: Man and Animal*, K. Attell (trans.), Stanford, CA: Stanford University Press.
Ariès, P. (1962) *Centuries of Childhood*, R. Baldick (trans.), New York, NY: Alfred Knopf.
Bhabha, J. (2006) 'The Child: What Sort of Human?' *PMLA*, 121(5):1526–1535.
Barnard, R. (2004) 'On Laughter, the Grotesque, and the South African Transition: Zakes Mda's Ways of Dying', *NOVEL: A Forum on Fiction*, 37(3):77–302.
Benjamin, W. (1968) 'Theses on the Philosophy of History', *Illuminations*, H. Arendt (ed.), New York, NY: Schocken.
Berlant, L. (2000) 'The Subject of True Feeling: Pain, Privacy, and Politics', in J. Dean (ed.), *Cultural Studies and Political Theory*, 42–62, Ithaca and London: Cornell University Press.
Bernstein, R. (2011) *Racial Innocence: Performing American Childhood from Slavery to Civil Rights*, New York, NY: New York University Press.
Brystom, K. (2011) 'On 'Humanitarian' Adoption (Madonna in Malawi),' *Humanity*, 2(2):213–231.
Bulawayo, N. (2010) 'Hitting Budapest,' *Boston Review*, November/December. Online. Available HTTP: <http://new.bostonreview.net/BR35.6/bulawayo.php>
Campbell, D. (2011) 'The Iconography of Famine,' in G. Batchen, M. Gidley, M. Gidley, N. K. Miller and J. Prosser (eds.), Picturing Atrocity: Reading Photographs in Crisis, 79–91, London, UK: Reaktion.
Casteñada, C. (2014) Childhood, *TSQ*, 1(1–2):59–61.
Coundouriotis, E. (2010) 'The Child Soldier Narrative and the Problem of Arrested Historicization,' *Journal of Human Rights*, (9)2:191–206.
Diptee, A. (2007) 'Imperial Ideas, Colonial Realities: Enslaved Children in Jamaica, 1775–1834,' J. Marten (ed.), *Children in Colonial America*, 48–60, New York, NY: New York University Press.
Dovy, T. (1996) 'Waiting for the Barbarians: Allegory of Allegories,' in G. Huggan and S. Watson (eds.), *Critical Perspectives on J.M. Coetzee*, 138–151, London, UK: Macmillan.
Fabian, J. (1983) *Time and the Other: How Anthropology Makes its Object*, New York, NY: Columbia University Press.
Fassin, D. (2008) 'The Humanitarian Politics of Testimony: Subjectification through Trauma in the Israeli-Palestinian Conflict,' *Cultural Anthropology*, 23(3):531–558.
Gordon, L. (2008) 'The Perils of Innocence, or What is Wrong with Putting Children First,' *The Journal of the History of Childhood and Youth*, 1(3):331–350.
Grier, B. (1994) 'Invisible Hands: The Political Economy of Child Labour in Colonial Zimbabwe, 1890–1930,' *Journal of Southern African Studies*, 20(1):27–52.
Haraway, D. J. (2008) *When Species Meet*, Minneapolis, MN: University of Minnesota Press,
Högbacka, R. (2008) 'The Quest for a Child of One's Own: Parents, Markets and Transnational Adoption,' *Journal of Comparative Family Studies*, 39(3):311–330.
Houlihan, E. (2010) 'The Ethics of Reading the Short Story: Literary Humanitarianism in 'The Gold Vanity Set,' *College Literature*, 37(3):62–83.
Jacobs, M. D. (2011) *White Mother to a Dark Race: Settler Colonialism, Maternalism, and the Removal of Indigenous Children in the American West and Australia, 1880–1940*, Lincoln, NE, South Africa: University of Nebraska Press.
Malkki, L. H. (1996) 'Speechless Emissaries: Refugees, Humanitarianism, and Dehistoricization,' *Cultural Anthropology*, 11(3):377–404.

———. (2010) 'Children, Humanity, and the Infantilization of Peace,' in I. Feldman and M. I. Ticktin (eds.), *In the Name of Humanity: The Government of Threat and Care*, Durham, NC: Duke University Press.

Mamdani, M. (2009) *Saviors and Survivors: Darfur, Politics and the War on Terror*, New York, NY: Pantheon.

Manzo, K. (2008) 'Imaging Humanitarianism: NGO Identity and the Iconography of Childhood,' Antipode, 40(4):632–657.

Mbembe, A. (1992) 'Prosaics of Servitude and Authoritarian Civilities, J. Roitman (trans.),' *Public Culture*, 5(1):123–145.

———. (2002.) 'African Modes of Self-Writing', Steven Rendall, *Public Culture*, 14(1):239–273.

Mbembe, A. and J. Roitman (1995) 'Figures of the Subject in Times of Crisis,' *Public Culture*, 7:323–352.

Nieuwenhuys, O. (1998) 'Global Childhood and the Politics of Contempt,' *Alternatives: Global, Local, Political*, 23(3):267–289.

Osondu, E. C. (2008) *Waiting*, New York, NY: Guernica/A Magazine of Art & Politics. Online. Available HTTP: <http://www.guernicamag.com/fiction/waiting/> (Accessed 1 October 2008).

———. (2010) 'Janjaweed Wife,' *The Kenyon Review New Series*, 32(2):143–152.

Rancière, J. (2004) 'Who Is the Subject of the Rights of Man?' *South Atlantic Quarterly*, 103(2/3):297–310.

Redfield, P. (2012) 'Bioexpectations: Life Technologies as Humanitarian Goods,' *Public Culture*, 24(1):157–183.

Roitman, J. (2012) *Africa, Otherwise*, New Haven, CT: Yale Agrarian Studies Colloquium. Online. Available HTTP: <http://www.yale.edu/agrarianstudies/colloqpapers/13roitman.pdf> (Accessed 1 February 2013).

Said, E. W. (1993) *Culture and Imperialism*, New York, NY: Vintage Books.

Schweizer, H. (2008) *On Waiting*, London, UK: Routledge.

Shapiro, M. J. (2001) *For Moral Ambiguity: National Culture and the Politics of the Family*, Minneapolis, MN: Minnesota University Press.

Slaughter, J. R. (2007) *Human Rights, Inc.: The World Novel, Narrative Form, and International Law*, New York, NY: Fordham University Press.

Sliwinski, S. (2006) 'The Childhood of Human Rights: The Kodak on the Congo,' *Journal of Visual Culture*, 5(3):333–363.

Stoler, A. L. (2002) *Carnal Knowledge and Imperial Power: Race and the Intimate in Colonial Rule*, Berkeley, CA, Los Angeles, CA and London, UK: University of California Press.

Summers, C. (2011) 'Boys, Brats and Education: Reproducing White Maturity in Colonial Zimbabwe, 1915–1935,' *Settler Colonial Studies*, 1, 132–152.

Taussig, M. (2003) 'The Adult's Imagination of the Child's Imagination,' in P. R. Matthews and D. McWhiter (eds.), *Aesthetic Subjects*, 449–468, Minneapolis, MN: University of Minnesota Press.

Thompson, J. (2012) *Light on Darkness? Missionary Photography of Africa in the Nineteenth and Early Twentieth Centuries*, Grand Rapids, MI: Eerdmans.

Zelizer, V. A. (1981) 'The Price and Value of Children: The Case of Children's Insurance,' *American Journal of Sociology*, 86(5):1036–1056.

Žižek, S. (2001) *On Belief*, London, UK and New York, NY: Routledge.

———. (2005) 'Against Human Rights,' *New Left Review*, 34:115–131.

———. (2006) '*The Parallax View*,' Cambridge, MA: MIT Press.

13 Temporalizing security

Securing the citizen, insecuring the immigrant in the Mediterranean

Pinar Bilgin

The tradition in Western social thought of treating one's contemporaries as belonging to the past, argues Hindess, has produced a double discourse comprising treatment of one's own past as constituting 'a kind of moral and intellectual failure' and relegating one's contemporaries to that past world (Hindess 2007: 328). This chapter focuses on the ways in such a double discourse is mobilized in in/securing *some* peoples. I offer the concept of 'temporalizing security' to capture those dynamics unleashed by the temporalization of difference and the spatializing of time, whereby insecurities of some people in some other parts of the world are portrayed as a passing phase and violent practices toward them are warranted as the only available remedy.

For purposes of illustration, the chapter looks at European security practices and policies in the Mediterranean.[1] With unfolding security co-operations between the North and South (Bensaad 2007; Jünemann 2003; Wolff 2008), the Southern Mediterranean countries are becoming enforcers of European security policies vis-à-vis their own citizens and other immigrants in transit to the EU (Galli 2008; Gammeltoft-Hansen 2008; Hejl 2007; Holm 2004; Lutterbeck 2006). South Mediterranean leaders have also made use of the context of the 'global war on terror' to pursue their own security agendas at the expense of their citizens' security.

Assumptions shaped by the temporalization of difference (i.e., relegating one's contemporaries to the past by virtue of their 'difference' in outlook or behavior) would lead us to expect people in some parts of the world to *follow* others' example and adopt citizenship regimes in view of the apparently universal and timeless benefits of citizenship for security, whereas in those parts of the world where immigrants are coming from (outside Western Europe and North America), dynamics of citizenship and security have played out differently. Actors in other parts of the world have their own agendas in adopting citizenship regimes (Mamdani 1996). In addition, historical governance of citizenship has allowed practices designed to secure one's own citizens to the detriment of other countries' citizens. In some cases, this means the adoption of violent practices directed against peoples – practices not deemed acceptable when directed at one's own citizens. In other cases, it allows unfair trade and employment practices toward other countries' citizens in view of their portrayal as belonging to another time or place. Coupled with postcolonial practices prioritizing the stability and longevity of their regime at the expense of their citizens' well-being, peoples have often found themselves between a rock and a hard place.

In the context of EU-Mediterranean dynamics, temporalizing in/security involves explaining away global structural causes of immigration ('they' are lagging behind 'us' and want to come 'here' to make use of the benefits 'we' extend to 'our' citizens'), warranting violent practices toward non-citizens who are immigrants or asylum-seekers and turning a blind eye to human rights violations by Southern Mediterranean regimes of their own citizens – all undertaken in the name of Euro-Mediterranean security cooperation.

'Temporalizing security' refers to insidious dynamics unleashed by the aforementioned double discourse, whereby one's own contemporaries in other parts of the world are relegated to a past where security dynamics work differently. Temporalizing security as such allows portraying insecurities of some people in some other parts of the world as a passing phase in search for security and overlooks the need for investigating alternative presents and futures. Insecurities experienced in the periphery are rendered explicable as trials and travails of shaking off ideas and institutions of that past world (see Goldgeier and McFaul 1992). Interventions of various kinds are, in turn, warranted as the only available remedy (see Jabri 2013). What makes temporalizing security possible is a non-reflexive notion of security, one that fails to see how our security practices produce insecurity as well as security, for ourselves and others (Bigo 2002; Booth 1997; Burgess 2011).

The first section of the chapter elucidates the meaning of temporalization of difference; the second section illustrates the implications of temporalizing difference and spatializing time by focusing on the relationship between citizenship and security. The third highlights how these processes have played out differently in some parts of the world. Section four looks at European security practices in the Mediterranean in the 9/11 era as an instance of 'temporalizing in/security'.

Temporalizing difference

'The relegation of peoples and ways of life to the status of anachronisms', writes Hindess, 'continues to be influential in Western social and political thought' (2007: 326). Whereas Hindess traces to classical antiquity the ideas and categories behind the 'temporal ordering of humanity' (Hindess 2007: 333), Grovogui emphasizes the significance of the encounter with the Americas (Grovogui 1996). According to Grovogui, the relationship between the world's peoples began to change in the aftermath of 'the discovery'; 1492 was a critical turning point in 'alterity and the ordering of the universe' in two ways: the 'discovery' of America and Americans, and Spain's defeat of African Moors, emboldened European actors toward envisioning a hierarchical universe on top of which they placed themselves (Grovogui 1996: 7).

Hindess, in turn, underscores the role played by categories and modes of thought already available to European thinkers of the time: an 'interpretative schema' received from classical antiquity (Hindess 2007: 333). One aspect of this schema was about viewing difference to be 'increasing roughly with distance'; another was 'inversion, in which case others are seen as being what one is not' (Hindess 2007: 333). Through making use of such interpretative schema inherited from classical antiquity, America and the Americans were relegated to the past of Europe and Europeans. While the Americas were labeled 'New World' in contrast to Europe's 'Old World', in European thinking the 'New World' belonged to the past. In time, non-Europeans of the 'Old World' also found themselves relegated to the past (Hindess 2007: 333).

Temporalizing difference went hand in hand with a moralizing attitude toward the past – including one's own – resulting in what Hindess calls the emergence of the 'disparaging temporalization of difference' (Hindess 2007: 331). This moralizing attitude was based on a linkage between peoples' institutional development and their moral and intellectual development: 'Peoples who are some way behind the West in their institutional development will also be behind its inhabitants in their moral and intellectual capacities' (Hindess 2007: 335). As such, the past was 'another culture', a culture that needs shaking off (Hindess 2007: 328).

Hindess reminds us the past is better thought of as 'a whole continent of different countries', not just one (Hindess 2007: 328). Put differently, portrayals of the past as 'another culture' render opaque the relationship between past and present (Hindess 2007: 328). This is important for understanding the global structural roots of postcolonial insecurities and how different ways of understanding the past are utilized in making sense of and designing security policies for one's own (postcolonial) contemporaries. The past is not unchanging, as references to 'another culture' might suggest; our understanding of the past is shaped by our view of the present and aspirations for the future. Nor can it be thought in the singular as if experienced by all in a unified fashion.

The European past with which the postcolonial present is compared is a story about the past that is a product of the present – (re)written at a particular time and place, in response to particular dynamics (Halperin 1997). What is at stake is not only understanding Europe's pasts better but also designing better policies for Europe's and others' presents.

Temporalizing difference, in/securing peoples as citizens

Not necessarily more oppressive than other forms of difference, temporalizing difference has shaped postcolonial imaginary in ways productive of inter-societal tensions and other insecurities (Grovogui 1996; Krishna 1999; Mamdani 1996). European originating notions and practices of citizenship were adopted and adapted in different parts of the world, not as part of a developmental continuum but as part of struggles for and against modern imperialism. In response to agents of modern imperialism who portrayed the absence of notions and institutions of citizenship in some societies as a moral, intellectual and institutional failure, postcolonial peoples struggled to establish their own citizenship regimes. Postimperial and/or postcolonial transition from subjects to citizens has been one of in/securing whereby security guarantees introduced by new regimes of citizenship rights have coexisted with insecurities generated as part of the dynamics of the transition process.

Much scholarship on the international politics of the postcolonial remains embedded in assumptions of temporalizing difference, oblivious to contingencies of citizenship and security. Indeed, in response to the 'citizenship and security' special issue of *Citizenship Studies*, Hindess observes: 'Citizenship tends to be represented . . . as a desirable condition for all of humanity, in principle if not always just yet in practice, and also to be associated with civilization and improvement' (Hindess 2004: 308). Contra the 'celebratory' (Hindess 2002) view of the relationship between security and citizenship that views it as a security solution regardless of time and place, paying attention to the historical and geo-cultural context allows us to see how citizenship has historically been a 'conspiracy against the rest of the world' (Hindess 2000: 1496). This conspiracy brings together 'members of particular subpopulations and [promotes] some of their interests, but also [renders] the larger population governable by dividing it into subpopulations consisting of the citizens of discrete, politically independent and competing states' (Hindess 2000: 1488). In Western Europe and North America, this conspiracy takes the form of an 'international system of population management', providing states with 'an internationally acceptable rationale for regulating the movements of those who appear (or threaten to appear) on or within their borders' (Hindess 2000: 1496).

In the world beyond these two geo-cultural contexts, the conspiracy has unfolded differently; citizenship has served to incorporate the postcolonial into international society and warranted security practices considered 'appropriate' for the postcolonial.

Contingencies of citizenship and in/securing in postcolonial locales

Different implications for the security of individuals of the adoption of citizenship regimes in myriad parts of the world are not always accounted for in international relations literature (but see Işın 2002, 2005; Mamdani 1973, 1996). Of particular interest are the implications for the colonized (say, in Africa or India) not considered worthy of governing themselves. Even as citizenship became a 'universal human condition' (Hindess 2002: 132) following decolonization, with the newly founded states adopting Western-originated notions and institutions of governance, citizenship practices had contingent implications for the security of subjects in different parts of the world.

One such contingency is *historical*: citizenship has not always been considered as constituting an improvement upon one's status. Hindess uses two examples:

> As Hobbes (1969: 266) reminds us, there is no reason to suppose that the citizens of Luca, an Italian city which had LIBERTAS emblazoned above its gates, found rule by their fellow citizens any less intrusive than the authoritarian rule which prevailed in Constantinople. The implication is that some

might have preferred the security of the latter condition to the dubious advantages of active citizenship.

(Hindess 2004: 307)

The second example is more recent:

> Throughout the history of the modern European empires there were persistent reports of Europeans who deserted their own side and chose to live with the natives. These continued well after the Europeans had begun to think of themselves as citizens and the distinction between citizen and non-citizen subject had become an important aspect of imperial government. In these cases, individuals appear to have forsaken the joys of citizenship in favour of ways of life in which the concept and practice of citizenship had no place.

(Hindess 2004: 307)

Both examples highlight the ways some individuals historically have sought security outside of the 'benefits' offered by citizenship regimes.

This is not to deny claims to citizenship rights have been an important part of struggles across the world. Nor is it to forget such struggles have introduced relative improvements in the lives of those who claimed and gained rights. Rather, the substance of the various claims need not be assumed uniform even if phrased in the familiar lexicon of citizenship rights (Grovogui 2006: 125).

Herein lies the second contingency, *geo-cultural*. For the context in which such claims to citizenship were made deserves scrutiny, as opposed to, that is, starting from the teleology that peoples in different parts of the world would inevitably be drawn to the 'benefits' of citizenship. The period from the mid-nineteenth century to the mid-twentieth century when actors in newly founded states made claims to citizenship rights was characterized by imperialism, direct and indirect rule and, later, decolonization. Citizenship practices of European states at home did not extend to peoples they did not recognize as citizens. Nor did these practices extend to peoples in the colonies, whom they did not consider to be capable of being governed through citizenship regimes. Following decolonization, citizenship regimes set up in diverse settings (including India and parts of Africa) had consequences that did not always involve the kinds of 'benefits' presumed by the universalist view (compare Krishna 1999 and Mamdani 1996). The newly founded states responded to internal demands and international dynamics as they sought to introduce citizenship regimes. In some contexts, 'citizenship became a platform for racial exclusion and a foundation for "national manhood"' (Işın and Turner 2002: 6). In the process, some postcolonial actors have adopted the liberal notion of citizenship while leaving its characteristic orientalism and synoecism unchallenged.

Throughout this period, orientalist notions of citizenship prevailed; in this view, the world comprises those who have developed a notion of liberty and can be trusted to govern themselves and those who have not. Helliwell and Hindess (2002) trace the origins of such ideas to the canons of liberalism, as in Mill and Kant, arguing a hierarchical division of the world is integral to the liberal view of citizenship as opposed to constituting an aberration from it (also see Helliwell and Hindess 2005; Hindess 2004). From this perspective, the world was populated by three categories of people: 'citizens of Western states; non-citizen subjects of Western states; and various residual populations, consisting of the subjects of states that were independent but not fully accepted as part of the states system' (Hindess 2002: 132). The latter two were further divided into 'races' and 'ethnicities'. However arbitrarily these categories may have been used, they had significant implications for politics, as they were utilized in designing legal and administrative systems (Krishna 1999; Mamdani 1996).

The way the (post)colonial experienced liberal practices in citizenship was not so 'progressive'. Mamdani (1996) labels this system of governance 'decentralized despotism,' referring to regimes that govern authoritatively through creating and reinforcing communal divisions:

> Europe did not bring to Africa a tropical version of the late-nineteenth century European nation-state. Instead it created a multicultural and multiethnic state. The colonial state was a two-tiered structure: peasants were governed by a constellation of ethnically defined Native Authorities in the local state, and these authorities were in turn supervised by white officials deployed by a racial pinnacle at the center.
>
> (Mamdani 1996: 287)

The dual problem for colonized peoples was the denial of citizenship by the imperial center and their problematic incorporation into the colonial administration, a hierarchical system of races and ethnicities that governed the latter through 'customs' and the former through a regime of rights (Mamdani 1996: 297).

Synoecism of the liberal notion of citizenship had equally long-lasting consequences. Portraying citizenship in the West in terms of universal benefits and the Western body of citizens as a unified whole with equal access to such benefits set an unrealistic model for the rest of the world. It explains away insecurities experienced in postcolonial contexts as a passing phase in search for security. A case in point is the neo-liberal governance of citizenship that renders citizens in/secure by allowing access to a system of rights while delimiting the conditions under which such rights are exercised (Hindess 1998, 2002). This system of governance rests on assumptions of temporalizing difference and spatializing time while warranting violent practices as the only available remedies.

European security practices in the Mediterranean[2]

Specific aspects of European security practices in the Mediterranean suggest the temporalizing of in/security, whereby Europe's external (Mediterranean) and internal others (non-European immigrants and asylum-seekers) are relegated to the past and security policies toward them designed accordingly.

Although the European Community (EC) began to formulate policies toward South Mediterranean countries in particular and the Middle East in general as early as the 1970s, in the 1990s, with the Euro-Mediterranean Partnership (EMP), the European Union took a more serious stance. At the time, concerns about increasing immigration aggravated social unrest and instability in the EU's southern neighbors, and the possible radicalization of the South Mediterranean diaspora in the EU ranked high among EU priorities. In 2004, the EU launched the European Neighborhood Policy (ENP) in a political context characterized by the failures of the EMP to meet its objectives, a heightened sense of insecurity in the EU because of irregular immigration within the context of the 'global war on terror', and global ambitions of the EU itself.

European security practices have rested on two assumptions of temporalizing difference and spatializing time. The EMP emphasized political and social reforms as security policy, relegating the South of the Mediterranean to Europe's past, while allowing the Mediterranean to 'grow up' and become more like 'us' by following the EU example. The ENP allowed South Mediterranean states to address their own insecurities at their own pace while engaging in security cooperation with Southern regimes with worrisome human rights records. This shift in policy signaled how European actors viewed the South as belonging to the past and deserving of security policies deemed 'appropriate' for that past world. While the approaches show little reflection on the production of insecurities as such, the ENP was influential in accepting a set of violent practices that would not be considered appropriate for EU citizens but were appropriate for the citizens of Southern Mediterranean countries, immigrants-in-transit and asylum seekers.

As part of the transition to ENP, more violent instruments of security are increasingly used by the EU or member states when cooperating with Southern neighbors, including the training of military and police forces of Southern Mediterranean countries, the training of immigration officers and the transfer of surveillance and control technology.

Over the years, through a variety of policies, the EU and its member states have sought to address challenges externally through highly technologized and sometimes violent means and/or subcontracted Southern Mediterranean regimes, before those 'external' challenges became 'internal' security concerns for Europe. Implications of European security practices for citizens of Southern Mediterranean countries and immigrants-in-transit have included abuse of fundamental rights allowed by the secrecy surrounding the endemic in/security practices of some Southern Mediterranean regimes (Amnesty International 2006), irregular migrants being directed to more dangerous routes, violent treatment of immigrants by human smugglers (Monzini 2007; Spijkerboer 2007), persistently high levels of human deaths in transit (Lutterbeck 2006) and the fading of asylum-seeking as a strategy to escape repression (Mazzella 2007; Webber 2006).

A potent example of European security practices privileging the security of EU citizens to the detriment of others is the externalization of immigration control. This policy is a singular instance of temporalizing security, whereby violent practices are allowed to take place outside the EU not by ignorance or oblivion, but by design. In 2006, Amnesty International criticized what it characterized as 'the blank-cheque approach' adopted by the EU in the externalization of immigration control policies (Amnesty International 2006). In other words, as long as immigrants (especially irregular immigrants) are kept outside EU borders by the measures taken by Southern Mediterranean countries, the EU overlooks how these measures affect immigrants. Beatings and rapes in the immigrant camps in the South Mediterranean, police brutality toward immigrants, including shootings, and attacks upon sub-Saharan immigrants by South Mediterranean natives are frequently documented (Carling 2007; Collyer 2006; Human Rights Watch 2006; Médecins Sans Frontières 2006; Simon 2006). Particularly worrying are the deportations to countries where individuals face 'torture or inhuman or degrading treatment or punishment' (Webber 2006: 4). While these are prohibited by the European Convention of Human Rights, some EU member states have found ways to circumvent such bans, including 'the unlawful removal of foreign nationals to torturing states' (Webber 2006: 33–34).

Such maltreatment of immigrants on the road to the European Union, in turn, is related to endemic insecurities in the South of the Mediterranean, namely, the limits of respect for fundamental rights and freedoms. Not only immigrants and asylum-seekers but citizens of some Southern Mediterranean countries are in/secured through North-South security cooperation. As the Directorate-General for the External Policies of the European Union calls it, a 'you scratch my back and I'll scratch yours' logic (Directorate-General 2006: 21). For example, some member states cooperated with Egypt, a country engaging in practices the EU had formerly condemned. Amnesty International called the emergency law in Egypt a serious obstacle to human rights and freedoms violated by security forces and military tribunals or state security courts (Amnesty International 2010). In the run up to the Arab Spring and in spite of the European Commission's concerns, some anti-democratic practices of the Egyptian government were overlooked by the EU, including the state of emergency, which was renewed in 2006 and again in 2010. In Tunisia, torture and ill-treatment of human rights defenders, and the imprisonment and torture of Sahrawi activists in Tunisia, were overlooked (Amnesty International 2009). From Algeria there were reports of 'spectacular repressions' taking place; here, a state of emergency had been in effect since 1992 (Benantar 2006: 170).

Citizens of these countries were in/secured directly through specific security practices of European actors and their Southern Mediterranean counterparts and indirectly through destabilization of societal balances by the 'new lease on life' the latter had gained through Euro-Mediterranean security cooperation (Nicolaidis and Nicolaidis 2007). Southern Mediterranean countries became border 'policemen' for the European Union, with all its implications for regime/state security. That said, while cooperation with the EU allowed access to new technology and weakened EU criticism of acts of repression in the short-term, it alienated civil society, thus enhancing their insecurity in the long-term.

Another worrisome implication for delicate societal balances in the Southern Mediterranean countries is the (re)emergence of us/them divides. Bensaad highlights how official South Mediterranean discourse now presents local populations as victims of invasive migratory fluxes and repeats the European security argument that sees foreigners as a 'threat' (Bensaad 2007). Such attitudes to sub-Saharan immigrants are widely documented (see Holm 2008; Human Rights Watch 2006). However, the kinds of 'repressions taking place in the Maghreb' (Bensaad 2007: 59) reported by regional scholars usually remain under the legal radar while societies remain unaware.

In the EU we now see what Bigo calls 'a growing interpenetration between internal and external security' (Bigo 2001: 91), whereby 'internal' security in the EU is increasingly sought outside its boundaries in collaboration with non-EU actors; 'external' security, in turn, is pursued at home through surveillance techniques and data mining (Bigo 2000; Collyer 2008; Debenedetti 2006).

That said, while 'internal' and 'external' are increasingly difficult to distinguish, EU policies have increasingly distinguished between 'insiders' (EU citizens) and 'outsiders' (immigrants and asylum-seekers) in designing policies. Policies become embedded in assumptions of temporalizing difference (relegating to the past those considered different) and spatializing time (relegating to the past those residing to the south). Temporalizing security in Euro-Mediterranean relations has meant designing different security policies toward different 'categories' of citizens: 'our' citizens versus 'their' citizens. Whereas the former are worthy of citizenship rights, the latter deserve 'less' protection, with still others falling somewhere in between (e.g., recent immigrants).

Conclusion

As Hindess argues, governance of citizenship has rested on assumptions of temporalizing difference and spatializing time. While universal benefits of citizenship are portrayed to have become available to all as part of the process of decolonization, what often goes unnoticed is how citizenship practices designed to secure citizens frequently marginalize non-citizens. What I call *temporalizing security* leads to assumptions and practices allowing those deemed 'different' to be treated differently. Temporalizing in/security relegates some to the past, delaying security for them by representing their insecurities as a passing phase in the search for security. Temporalizing in/security warrants increasingly technologized and sometimes violent security practices against those portrayed as belonging to the past and, therefore, deserving of practices not otherwise considered 'appropriate' (i.e., if they were to be used against one's own citizens).

In Euro-Mediterranean relations, the de-differentiation is crystallized in the predicament of immigrants who have recently become citizens, who are neither 'here' nor 'there'. The very being of immigrant citizens of Southern Mediterranean origin is increasingly securitized. Scholars highlight the risks of securitizing immigration from a state-focused perspective and call for protecting the benefits of citizenship for EU citizens, where possible, expanding them to immigrants (Dobrowolsky 2007; Huysmans 2006; Huysmans et al. 2006; Nyers 2009). The experiences of those citizens who suddenly find themselves facing 'less-than-full' citizenship rights allow an entry point for rethinking 'the present' and imagining alternative futures.

Notes

1 The term 'European security policies' is inclusive of, but not limited to, EU policy-making. Insecurities frequently follow North-South security cooperation in the Mediterranean.
2 This section draws on a collaborative project (Bilgin et al. 2011).

Bibliography

Amnesty International (2006) *Closing Eyes to Human Rights Leaves Asylum-Seekers and Migrants at Risk*, Amnesty International.
———.(2009) *Amnesty International Country Report: Human Rights in People's Democratic Republic of Algeria*, Amnesty International.
———. (2010) *Amnesty International Country Report: Egypt*, Amnesty International.
Benantar, A. (2006) 'NATO, Maghreb and Europe,' *Mediterranean Politics*, 11:167–188.
Bensaad, A. (2007) 'The Mediterranean Divide and its Echo in the Sahara: New Migratory Routes and New Barriers on the Path to the Mediterranean,' in T. Fabre and P. Sant Cassia (eds.), *Between Europe and the Mediterranean: The Challenge and the Fears*, Hampshire, UK: Palgrave Macmillan.
Bigo, D. (2000) 'When Two Become One: Internal and External Securitisations in Europe,' in M. Keltsrup and M. C. Williams (eds.), *International Relations Theory and the Politics of European Integration: Power, Security, and Community*, London, New York: Routledge.
———. (2001) 'The Möbius Ribbon of Internal and External Securit(ies)' in M. Albert, D. Jacobson and Y. Lapid (eds.), *Identities Borders Orders: Rethinking International Relations Theory*, 91–116, Minneapolis, MN: University of Minnesota Press.
———. (2002) 'Security and Immigration: Toward a Critique of the Governmentality of Unease,' *Alternatives: Global, Local, Political*, 27:63–92.
Bilgin, P., E. S. Lecha and A. Bilgic (2011) *European Security Practices vis-a-vis the Mediterranean: Implications in Value Terms*, Copenhagen, Denmark: Danish Institute for International Studies.
Booth, K. (1997) 'Security and Self: Reflections of a Fallen Realist,' in K. Krause and M. C. Williams (eds.), *Critical Security Studies: Concepts and Cases*, 83–119, Minneapolis, MN: University of Minnesota Press.
Burgess, J. P. (2011) *The Ethical Subject of Security: Geopolitical Reason and the Threat Against Europe*, New York, NY: Routledge.
Carling, J. (2007) 'Migration Control and Migrant Fatalities at the Spanish-African Borders,' *International Migration Review*, 41:316–343.
Collyer, M. (2006) 'States of Insecurity: Consequences of sub-Saharan Transit Migration,' *Centre on Migration, Policy and Society Working Paper Series*, Oxford, UK: University of Oxford.
———. (2008) 'Emigration, Immigration, and Transit in the Maghreb: Externalization of EU Policy,' in Y. H. Zoubir and H. Amirah-Fernandez (eds.), *North Africa: Politics, Region and the Limits of Transformation.* London, 394, New York, NY: Routledge.
Debenedetti, S. (2006) *Externalization of European asylum and migration policies*, Florence, Italy: European University Institute.
Directorate-General, f. t. E. P. o. t. U. (2006) *'Analysis of the External Dimension of the EU's Asylum and Migration Policies,'* DGEPU, D. B., Policy Department (ed.)., Brussels, Belgium: European Parliament.

Dobrowolsky, A. (2007) '(IN)Security and Citizenship: Security, Im/migration and Shrinking Citizenship Regimes,' *Theoretical Inquiries in Law*, 8:629–661.

Galli, F. (2008) *'The Legal and Political Implications of the Securitisation of Counter-Terrorism Measures across the Mediterranean,'* Euromesco Paper, Euromesco.

Gammeltoft-Hansen, T. (2008) *The Refugee, the Sovereign and the Sea: EU Interdiction Policies in the Mediterranean*, Copenhagen, Denmark: Danish Institute for International Studies.

Goldgeier, J. M. and M. M. McFaul (1992) 'A Tale of Two Worlds: Core and Periphery in the Post-Cold War Era,' *International Organization*, 46:467–491.

Grovogui, S. N. (1996) *Sovereigns, Quasi-sovereigns and Africans: race and Self-determination in International Law*, Minneapolis, MN: University of Minnesota Press.

———. (2006) *Beyond Eurocentrism and Anarchy: Memories of International Order and Institutions*, New York, NY: Palgrave Macmillan.

Halperin, S. (1997) *In the Mirror of the Third World: Capitalist Development in Modern Europe*, Ithaca, NY: Cornell University Press.

Hejl, N. (2007) 'Between a Rock and a Hard Place: Euro-Mediterranean Security Revisited,' *Mediterranean Politics*, 12:1–16.

Helliwell, C. and B. Hindess (2002) 'The Empire of Uniformity and the Government of Subject Peoples,' *Cultural Values*, 6:139–152.

———. (2005) 'The Temporalizing of Difference,' *Ethnicities*, 5:414–418.

Hindess, B. (1998) 'Divide and Rule: The International Character of Modern Citizenship,' *European Journal of Social Theory*, 1:57–70.

———. (2000) 'Citizenship in the International Management of Populations,' *American Behavioral Scientist*, 43:1486–1497.

———. (2002) 'Neo-liberal Citizenship,' *Citizenship Studies*, 6:127–143.

———. (2004) 'Citizenship for all,' *Citizenship Studies*, 8:305–315.

———. (2007) 'The Past is Another Culture,' *International Political Sociology*, 1:325–338.

———. (2008) 'Been there, done that ...,' *Postcolonial Studies*, 11:201–213.

Holm, U. (2004) *The EU's Security Policy towards the Mediterranean: An (Im)possible Combination of Export of European Political Values and Anti-Terror Measures?* Copenhagen, Denmark: Danish Institute for International Studies.

———. (2008) *North Africa: A Security Problem for Themselves, for the EU and for the US*, Copenhagen, Denmark: Danish Institute for International Studies.

Human Rights Watch. (2006) *Stemming the Flow: Abuses Against Migrants, Asylum-Seekers and Refugees*, Human Rights Watch.

Huysmans, J. (2006) *The Politics of Insecurity: Fear, Migration, and Asylum in the EU*, Milton Park, Abingdon, Oxon, New York: Routledge.

Huysmans, J., A. Dobson and R. Prokhovnik (eds.) (2006) *The Politics of Protection: Sites of Insecurity and Political Agency*, New York, NY: Routledge.

Işın, E. F. (2002) 'Citizenship after Orientalism,' in E. F. Işın and B. S. Turner (eds.), *Handbook of Citizenship Studies*, London, UK: Sage.

———. (2005) 'Citizenship after orientalism: Ottoman citizenship,' in F. Keyman and A. İçduygu (eds.), *Citizenship in a Global World: European Questions and Turkish Experiences*, London, UK: Routledge.

Işın, E. F. and B. S. Turner (2002) 'Citizenship Studies: An Introduction,' in E. F. Işın and B. S. Turner (eds.), *Handbook of Citizenship Studies*, London, UK: Sage.

Jabri, V. (2013) *The Postcolonial Subject: Claiming Politics/Governing Others in Late Modernity*, London, UK: Routledge.

Jünemann, A. (2003) 'Security-Building in the Mediterranean After September 11,' *Mediterranean Politics*, 8:1–20.

Krishna, S. (1999) *Postcolonial Insecurities: India, Sri Lanka, and the Question of Nationhood*, Minneapolis, MN: University of Minnesota Press.

Lutterbeck, D. (2006) 'Policing Migration in the Mediterranean,' *Mediterranean Politics*, 11:59–82.

Mamdani, M. (1973) *From citizen to refugee: Uganda Asians come to Britain*, London, UK: Frances Pinter.

———. (1996) *Citizen and Subject: Contemporary Africa and the Legacy of Late Colonialism*, Princeton, NJ: Princeton University Press.

Mazzella, S. (2007) 'Putting Asylum to the Test: Between Immigration Policy and Co-Development,' in T. Fabre and S. C. Paul (eds.), *Between Europe and the Mediterranean: The Challenge and the Fears*, 41–50, Hampshire, New York: Palgrave Macmillan.

Médecins Sans Frontières (2006) *Violence and Immigration: Report on Illegal sub-Saharan Immigrants in Morocco*, Paris, France: Médecins Sans Frontières.

Monzini, P. (2007) 'Sea-Border Crossings: The Organization of Irregular Migration to Italy,' *Mediterranean Politics*, 12:163–184.

Nicolaidis, K. A. and D. Nicolaidis (2007) 'Europe in the Mirror of the Mediterranean,' in T. Fabre and S. C. Paul (eds.), *Between Europe and the Mediterranean: The Challenge and the Fears*, 162–193, New York, NY: Palgrave Macmillan.

Nyers, P. (ed.) (2009) *Securitizations of Citizenship*, London, UK: Routledge.

Simon, J. (2006) *Irregular Transit Migration in the Mediterranean: Facts, Figures and Insights*, Copenhagen, Denmark: Danish Institute for International Studies.

Spijkerboer, T. (2007) 'The Human Costs of Border Control,' *European Journal of Migration and Law*, 9:127–139.

Webber, F. (2006) *Border Wars and Asylum Crimes*, London, UK: Statewatch.

Wolff, S. (2008) 'Border Management in the Mediterranean: Internal, External and Ethical Challenges,' *Cambridge Review of International Affairs*, 21:253–271.

14 Killing time

Writing the temporality of global politics

Aslı Çalkıvik

Introduction

Contemporary developments have forced an analytical category to be reckoned with in understanding the current nature of global political life: *time*. The increasing speed of global interactions enabled by the information revolution and the digitalization of economic, social, and cultural transactions renders 'just in time' the distinctive feature of contemporary social relations of economic production and the predominant force shaping the time(s) of our globalizing lives. The pacing of the world out of breath, the dizzying speed of turnover times – from labor to news, from fashion to technology – is the order of the day, as is the changing nature of the governance of time evidenced in the shift to the logic of risk and preemption in discourses and practices of security that render reckoning with time and thinking about temporality central political questions.

The question of time and temporality of the present and the future has been making its way into the disciplinary debates within international relations. Critical scholars are taking interest in the temporal dimension of global politics and the assumptions about time informing disciplinary analyses. Studies focus on cultural politics of memory (Edkins 2003; Malksoo 2009), discursive framing and representations of time in the constitution of nation-state and citizenship (Shapiro 2000; Walker 1993), conceptions of temporality informing the discursive construction of the War on Terror (Aradau and Van Munster 2007; de Goede 2008; Jarvis 2008), and the underlying temporal logic in the constitution of identity (Prozorov 2011).

I contribute to these nascent discussions by extending a call for a politics of time that revolves around phenomenological experience of time and a politics of time figured as the de-construction of totalizing temporal narratives. Such a call is not intended to dismiss these efforts. Rather, it is a call animated by theoretical and political concerns about the way an unproblematized focus on 'the times' might in effect render us as critical scholars-cum-political-subjects out of synch with the temporal stakes of the discussion on and of the times: namely, the question of the future.

I argue for a global analytic of social time, which attends to the temporality rooted in social production and accentuating the mediations linking phenomenological experience, individual subjectivities, and the historical conditions of existence of that experience. I ground my discussion in the question of a politics of global times in order to think about how multiple temporalities are unified into a single complex system in capitalist modernity. Attending to the temporal order of capital opens the way to a different notion of a politics of time – a politics 'that takes *temporal structures* of social practices as specific objects of its transformative (or preservative) intent' (Osborne 1995: xii). Without this attunement to the structure of time and the ensuing question of historical time, what remains unexplored is the question concerning not merely the chronologically new, but the *historically* new. In other words, such a re-orientation of the discussions on time opens up the possibility to explore the idea that the future in question and the ensuing politics of time is not about what comes next, but the possibility of alternative temporal structures and struggles over 'alternative temporalizations of history' (Osborne 1995: 200).

To elaborate, I first visit the works of IR scholars who have gone against dominant disciplinary trends by making temporality of global politics central to their analyses so as to distinguish, differentiate, and clarify the politics of time I take as my focus. Their astute observations on the time(s) of global politics provide a much needed perspective in a discipline whose overwhelming focus on territory and spatial organization of power comes at the price of an ignorance of the spatio-temporal architecture that underwrites all orders (Der Derian 1990, 1992; Hutchings 2008; Shapiro 2000, 2010). The aim is to map out the predominant ways politics of time must rightfully and forcefully be reckoned with if critical thought is to provide an adequate account of contemporary times.

In the second part, I move away from the ways time has been deployed within accounts of global politics. Drawing from materialist conceptions of time, I focus on the *structure* of time that mediates social experience and the way political temporality in modernity becomes a unit measure that inserts diverse temporalities within a charted horizon of production of value; how, in capitalist modernity, time 'becomes a material force internal to the mode of production' (Castree 2009: 30). I turn to Moishe Postone, and his conception of abstract labor and abstract time (Postone 1993), in a bid to highlight the way capital casts the future as a recapitulation of the present and inserts lived time into a 'de-historicalizing' (Osborne 2008: 16) temporal form that annihilates political time as possibility and writes the future as present, thereby rendering modern temporality a fatal structure of time. Consequently, a central stake in the struggles over time is the question of the future.

Time and global politics

Privileging the spatial over the temporal in IR has left the temporal aspects of world politics neglected in most analyses (Bell 2003). This pattern is increasingly countered by critical investigations, however, that draw attention to the idea that time is central to the constitution of global politics (Hutchings 2008; Walker 1989). Making explicit the implicit temporal commitments of mainstream accounts, they expose the historically contingent, contextual nature of core concepts such as international anarchy and the ways ostensibly unalterable, undisputable 'facts' are complicit with historically constituted modes of power and authority. They expose the manifold ways world politics entail struggles over space and also time.

Politics of time operates as a bordering practice in thought and practice (Vaughan-Williams 2009; Walker 1989). State-centric narratives, which rely on spatio-temporal compartmentalization of global politics through the principle of state sovereignty, 'discipline the horizons beyond which it is dangerous to pursue any political action that aspires to the rational, the realistic, the sensible, the responsible' (Walker 1989: 6). Further, erasing the historical nature of social arrangements and asserting what exists as what is natural, traditional, and immutable help perpetuate relations of power across class, gender, racial lines, as 'any power arrangement that is imagined to be legitimate, timeless and inevitable is pretty well fortified' (Enloe 2004: 3). Universalizing the particular as the truth of the past and the future, thereby perpetuating international hierarchies and confining political possibility within the borders of the state, is one way the politics of time is revealed as a bordering practice – a way to enclose other futures, preempting efforts to realize alternatives to what exists.

As postcolonial IR scholars have made clear, politics of time becomes a bordering practice in a different but related sense. Through the universalizing gesture of modernist discourse, hegemonic conceptions of time posit a 'developmental sequence through which all cultures must pass' (Blaney and Inayatullah 2002: 104). Informed by a linear conception of time, elitist, stagist conceptions informing developmentalist visions enact borders as markers of difference between West and non-West, positing the latter as inferior, denying it political agency.

Despite the continuing hegemony of atemporal analyses within IR, the growing interest in time and global politics is a welcome development. As time and temporality become buzzwords, it becomes necessary to probe the theoretical and political stakes in discussing global politics of time. For analytical purposes, we can discern two main tendencies within which time figures in analyses of global politics: a politics of time revolving around the phenomenological experience of time as speed or tempo and a politics of time figured as the de-construction of time of History – totalizing temporal narratives.

As exemplary of the former tendency, scholars focus on the impact of globalization spurred by the transformations in technology and the accelerating speed of economic and cultural transactions and the ways these forces restructure governance, rule, and politics. These investigations echo similar concerns in political theory, where scholars explore the implications of the temporalities dictated by innovation, change, and rapid turnover for democratic life (Connolly 2002; Wolin 1997), or among sociologists who explore the cosmopolitan possibilities enabled by de-territorializing forces and the rise of global risk society (Beck and Levy 2013), whereby potential catastrophes awaiting global politics bring the question of the future to the fore and act as the premise to re-think politics in the present.

In IR, James Der Derian's investigation of politics of global security in the post–Cold War era and how novel technologies of simulation and surveillance and the discursive practices surrounding them transform the nature of international relations is exemplary in this regard (Der Derian 1990, 1992). In his engagement with the temporal dimension of world politics, he incorporates time in his analytical framework in the form of phenomenological experience of rhythm or tempo. Drawing from Michel Foucault and Paul Virilio, Der Derian premises his overall argument on the reificatory effects of technologization: contemporary realities of world politics are generated by technical means of production, and these new forces erode the traditional foreign policy tools and the culture of diplomacy to mediate relations between political communities. He places novel technologies of simulation, surveillance, and speed at the center of his analysis (Der Derian 1990). Introduction of war games and simulations, he suggests, changes the nature of representational practices; with the increasing speed of weapon systems and communications, decision-making gives way to new forms of surveillance, generating 'a post-modern problematic' that lies beyond the grasp of conventional methods of analysis (Der Derian 1990: 297).

Put otherwise, new technological practices give way to novel forms of mediation between states through the discursive power of chronopolitics and technostrategy (Der Derian 1990). Chronopolitics is used to capture the displacement of geography/spatial determination by chronology, with pace overtaking space; technostrategy refers to the ways transformations in technology configure how wars are fought and the stakes entailed in war-making. The overall implication is that wars transform from spatial to temporal and perceptual phenomena. New forms of data-gathering and surveillance enact a new regime of normalization as conflicts are consigned to the cyberspace of simulations and war games. In *Antidiplomacy*, Der Derian analyzes 'cyberwar' and 'cyberspace' within the context of the Second Gulf War. 'Cyberwar' refers to the 'technologically generated, televisually linked, and strategically gamed form of violence that dominated the formulation as well as the representation of U.S. policy in the Gulf' (Der Derian 1992: 175), whereas 'cyberspace' designates the simulational practices through which 'globally networked, computer-sustained, computer-accessed, and computer-generated, multidimensional, artificial, or "virtual reality" is created' (ibid: 119–120). This virtual reality blurs the distinction between representation and fiction. These practices, which 'are more "real" in time than space,' exercise their power through the exchange of signs, not goods, and produce effects that are 'transparent and pervasive rather than material and discreet' (Der Derian 1992: 297). Their power consists in displacing the 'reality' of international relations they purport to represent.

The account of time in Der Derian's argument is one of time understood as rhythm or tempo. Drawing on the 'dromocratic revolution'[1] thesis of Paul Virilio, Der Derian says speed constitutes the 'final battlefield' in the contemporary era (Der Derian 1990: 307). Rapid increase in weapon delivery systems, decreasing human response time, and the appearance of real-time representation alter the battlefield. Time becomes a part of this analytical framework through the accelerating pace. Speed renders space and geopolitical accounts of war and politics redundant; it dominates transactions and replaces territorial boundaries with informational nodes as the emergent sites of power politics.

Rather than taking as its departure the political governance of time under conditions of globalization, a second approach to the politics of time endows accounting for the time(s) with an epistemological and an ontological task by calling for a strategy of writing that interrupts totalizing temporal narratives of global politics (Hutchings 2008; Lundborg 2012; Shapiro 2010). At stake in this formulation of the time(s) of global politics is an ontological concern that entails a critique of narratives of history that negate difference and leave no room to affirm the diversity of temporalities. The ontological concern is compounded with an ethical concern; these critical accounts demand resisting the epistemological pull of abstract, formalized categories that mimic the violence of abstractions in modern political life. Instead, writing of/for the time(s) become an effort to capture histories of difference and reveal the multiplicity of lived temporalities, the pasts and presents that enact other ways of being in the world. Representations of global times borrowing from sociological meta-narratives with their claim to unity and universality become the target of critique.

In *Time and World Politics* Kimberly Hutchings unpacks the temporal assumptions underwriting accounts of world politics. Her analysis takes its cue from the Kantian view on time and space as transcendental conditions of sensible experience; she makes a post-Kantian turn by focusing, not on time as the condition of individual experience, but on the 'inter-subjective time of politics' (Hutchings 2008: 4). The time of politics is essentially contested since multiple conceptions of time co-exist in each society. Distinguishing two aspects of time as *chronos* (time as qualitatively measurable duration) and *kairos* (time as transformational time of action), she analyzes the ways each theoretical framework – no matter how atemporal a narrative it might seem at first glance – implicitly relies upon a specific conception of time and temporality. For instance, on the surface, Realist and Neorealist arguments seem to provide a static, timeless image by suggesting there are certain recurrent features of international politics and these features requires actors to act according to the dictates of timeless laws by learning from the wisdom of ages. As Hutchings's investigation reveals, the diagnosis extended about the nature of the present and the ensuing prescriptions about 'what is to be done' rely on assumptions about world-political temporality wherein different conceptions of chronos and kairos and the relation between them are embedded. These theories end up universalizing a particular temporal experience inherent in western modernity. By generalizing the specific as the universal, she argues, they end up subsuming multiple temporal frameworks, homogenizing the time of the present. Through a close reading of a variety of theorists of globalization (Habermas, Hardt, Negri, among others), she argues such homogenization occludes the possibility of recognizing the temporal multiplicity of global politics. Positing that 'the time of world politics is the time of liberal capitalist states and the globalisation of capitalism,' they reduce the significance of all other phenomena by subsuming them in the master temporal narrative (Hutchings 2008: 159).

Hutchings offers an alternative account of time that neither posits politics as a matter of controlling time nor casts theoretical thinking as a matter of prophecy or time traveling. She explores Chakrabarty's critique of the assumptions informing social scientific work on capitalist modernity (its conflation of the temporality of western economic and political development with world political time) and Spivak's critique of discourses of western feminism (their justification of ' "maternalist" intervention by western women in the lives of non-western women'; Hutchings 2008: 55). Synthesizing Connolly's and Deleuze's accounts of political time, she says, ' "Presentness" is always constituted by a plurality of "presents" inscribed in diverse, immanent temporalities' and there is no 'unifying temporal orientation [that] provides the master key to the meaning of "presents"' (Hutchings 2008: 172). Rather than treating world-political time as temporally unified, we need to think of 'world-political time as heterotemporality' and attend to the way 'the theorist's own complex temporal structure is implicated in and with that which he or she seeks to describe, explain, and judge' (ibid: 176).

The ontological and ethical questions at stake in the representation of diverse temporalities, without subsuming them to the logic of identity, come across in Michael Shapiro's *The Time of the City*, where he writes against the sublation of difference within the universal 'World Historical' time of Eurocentric narratives (Shapiro 2010). Hegel is the central figure whose legacy is to be repudiated; exposing 'the parody of the Hegelian supposition that there is only one significant time' (Shapiro 2010: 27) becomes the central task of critique. At stake is 'Hegel's construction of European time as exemplary of a unified World Historical time, expressive of the movement of reason through history' (Shapiro 2010: 28).

The violence of abstraction entailed by political temporality (state time) and economic temporality (capital time) turns society into abstract economic spaces regulated by legal and bureaucratic entrepreneurial codes. This abstraction finds its intellectual equivalent in the philosophical economy of Hegel (Shapiro 2010: 42). Shapiro juxtaposes the imperial vision ingrained in the abstract world historical time of geo-philosophy to the time of lived experience, to forms of being in the world that challenge the Hegelian continuous, linear version of historical time. His analysis 'draws its energy from contra-Hegel conceptual positions' such as the one provided by postcolonial critic Achille Mbembe (Shapiro 2010: 28). Resisting the ' "violence of representation" inherent in Europe's philosophico-anthropological discourses,' Shapiro maintains, entails affirming heterotemporality and attending to 'African time – time as historical lived experience rather than as abstract World Historical Time' (Shapiro 2010: 27) or moments of political action such as labor union activism in contemporary Los Angeles, which affirm contingency and the 'intersecting temporalities of the historical moment' (ibid: 40).

A similar juxtaposition of the time of statecraft and the time of global flows (of capital and people) informs Shapiro's earlier work on the fate of national citizenship in global times (Shapiro 2000). Echoing Der Derian's account of temporality as phenomenological experience of speed, he argues the accelerating pace of world politics and the increasing movement of bodies open the way to questioning the state's 'symbolic management of citizens' by imposing a temporal coherence through official historical narratives about shared ethnic and social characteristics (Der Derian 2000: 81).

There is much to be commended in these critical accounts, yet such framings of the politics of global times reproduce the binaries they seek to negate as they oppose the particular to the universal, the concrete to the abstract, and the totalizing time of History to the de-totalizing, plural temporalities. Lack of engagement with alternative framings for fear of reproducing the logic of identity leaves critical inquiry unable to account for and theorize the presupposed universal predicaments of power that form the premise of the analyses.[2] Privileging diverse temporalities and conceptualizing world political time as 'immanent, non-linear, plural "becomings"' (Hutching 2008: 4) without situating analysis within specific social formations leaves analyses vulnerable to suggestions that flux and difference themselves stand as indications of the contemporary constellations of power (Harvey 1990).

Interestingly, scholars' claims of a historical rupture, our 'postmodern problematic' of time, as Der Derian calls it (1990: 297), and their sense that the accelerating pace of world politics is challenging the state's 'symbolic management of the citizen' (Shapiro 2000: 81) are accompanied by a historicist claim: the need for a new analytics. By casting 'the new' in an ambivalent status, such framings question whether the analytical tools 'now' deemed insufficient were ever sufficient in the first place. Assertions about a new politics of time enabled by the changing tempo of global politics leaves unanswered questions about historically specific temporal forms, specifically historical relations between the past, the present, and the future.

In the next section, I elaborate a different conception of a politics of time: a politics that takes temporal structures of social practices as its objects, the way in which different senses of time and possibility are enabled or distorted, the experience of history that they make possible or impede, and the futures they ensure. What is at stake in such a re-formulation is the question of the 'future': not the 'future' as the chronologically new – that is, what comes after – but the 'future' as the *historically* new – that is, effecting changes in the dynamics of historical temporalization (Osborne 2009).

Politics of global times

Despite the centrality of time and temporality to historical materialist analyses and critiques of modernity, there is a lack of consensus among scholars about Marx's insights into the nature of time at stake and the precise ways time matters. Lack of an explicit theorization of the time of capital by Marx and ensuing difficulty faced by his interpreters is captured by Giorgio Agamben, who observes that 'historical materialism has until now neglected to elaborate a concept of time that compares with its concept of history' (Agamben 2007: 99).

As Castree rightfully points out, the challenge of elaborating a historical materialist account of time has been compounded by 'the inconsistencies in Marx's own writings' where time makes its appearance in different guises (Castree 2009: 29–30). In *The Communist Manifesto,* Marx depicts the distinctive feature of 'the bourgeoisie epoch' as the 'constant revolutionizing of production, uninterrupted disturbance of all social conditions, everlasting uncertainty and agitation' becomes the norm (Marx 1985: 83).

This discussion of capitalism 'as a force-field of relations that constantly refashions its own history' (Castree 2009: 29) is ill at ease with Marx's discussion in his *A Contribution to the Critique of Political Economy*, where emphasis shifts toward a long-term perspective and a discussion of the changing modes of production and the ways capitalist history unfolds spatially (Castree 1970). Finally, when elaborating his labor theory of value in *Grundrisse* and *Capital*, Marx takes as his analytical premise a historically specific form of time (abstract clock time) that capitalism harnesses for its own reproduction. In other words, socially constituted time is acting as a regulatory force within capitalism (Marx 1990, 1993).

Politics of time in this latter sense – namely, the ways time is a socially constituted entity with disciplinary effects – is a neglected aspect of ongoing discussions in IR about how time matters in global politics. If 'control of time and power over time are essential components in the functioning of societies'(Le Goff 1982: xiii), the new form of appropriation of time – the temporal structure internal to the mode of production – in capitalist modernity needs to be at the center of critical engagements.

Such a conceptualization of time constitutes the thematic focus of critiques of labor in capitalism as opposed to critiques of capitalism from the standpoint of labor (Postone 1993). By the latter, what is meant is a strategy of critique positing labor (physiological expansion of energy) as a trans-historical category and privileging a sovereign subject (the working class) as the agent of capitalism's transcendence (Postone 1993: 7–8). In contrast, a critique of labor in capitalism posits labor as a 'historically specific part of the essential structures of capitalist society, hence, itself as the object of the critique of that society' (ibid: 5–6). Capitalism entails a historically specific form of mediation whereby socially constituted time (commodified, abstract time of social production) acts as a quantitative, externally imposed measure, putting the totality of social relations under its command. Taking such a perspective provides a glimpse into the temporal dimension of value, as it exposes the way time plays a constitutive role in the form of abstract domination, how it becomes a force that inserts diverse temporalities under the command of capital's 'blind desire to expand' (Gidwani 2008: 184).[3] Despite their differences, Marxist scholars such as Negri, Paolo Virno, and Postone *and* postcolonial critics such as Spivak and Chakrabarty share this critical impulse. As Vinay Gidwani observes, their common ground in ontological, epistemological, and political terms is their commitment to 'pry loose "labor's" heterogeneity and creativity from [this] abstract domination by "value" *and* from the speculative philosophical economy of the dialectic which constantly negates difference in service of higher meaning/unity/profit' (Gidwani 2008: 226). They all grapple with the dynamics of modernity as a sociality produced through commodity and the rule of 'self-valorizing value' – capital.

Moishe Postone's reading of Marx critical theory provides a useful starting point to tease out the temporal dynamics constitutive of this abstract domination and the politics of time it informs. For Postone, rather than being a form of economic exploitation imprinting itself on society, capital is *constitutive* of a particular form of society – a social universe whose structuring principle is the commodity-form (Postone 1993). Capitalism is conceptualized, not merely in terms of private property and ownership of the means of production, but as 'a historically specific form of social interdependence with an impersonal and seemingly objective character' (Postone 1993: 3). It is a form of interdependence historically produced and constituted by determinate forms of social practice (labor in capitalism), wherein the latter paradoxically attains a quasi-independent status in relation to the people engaged in the concrete practices of laboring. 'The historically specific and abstract form of social domination intrinsic to capitalism's fundamental forms of social mediation,' Postone writes, 'is the domination of people by time. This form of domination is bound to a historically specific and abstract form of temporality . . . constituted with the commodity form' (2004: 60).

To elaborate how, in the social universe of capitalism constituted by the commodity-form, time 'becomes necessity,' Postone distinguishes between 'material wealth' and 'abstract value' (1993: 191). While the measure of material wealth is a function of specificity of the product, value is 'measured not in terms of the particular objectifications of various labors, but in terms of what they all have in common, regardless of their specificity' (ibid: 188–189). As the dominant form of wealth in capitalism, value is 'the objectification of labor as socially mediating activity' (Stoetzler 2004: 266).

Material wealth and abstract value are rooted in the double character of labor in capitalism as 'abstract' and 'concrete.' The common denominator of value is abstract labor, a 'qualitatively homogenous social substance' (Postone 2004: 61). It mediates between products and constitutes a general measure of wealth, an index intrinsic to the self-valorizing movement of capital. Abstract labor implies a temporal transformation of concrete labor time into abstract labor time taking as its reference the totality of social relations – hence, the historically determinate *social* nature of the labor in capitalism. The magnitude of a commodity's value is determined by the amount of labor time that is socially necessary – meaning it takes as a reference point the society as a whole – for its production. The time expended in producing a particular commodity (concrete labor time) is mediated in a socially general manner and transformed into an average that determines the magnitude of the value of the product.

The conception of socially necessary labor time and its relation to the nature of time in modern capitalist society pivots on the distinction between 'concrete' and 'abstract' time. 'Concrete time' defined as the function of events (i.e., natural cycles and the periodicities of human life) (Postone 1993: 201) is opposed to 'abstract time' or 'uniform, continuous, homogenous, "empty" time [that is] independent of events' (ibid: 202), which is the time of abstract labor. Before the rise of capitalist society, concrete time constituted the dominant conception of time (i.e., time was not an autonomous category independent of events). In capitalist modernity, the abstract form of time associated with capitalist social relations brings about a new form of domination: 'an abstract form of compulsion' (ibid: 214). Socially necessary labor time constitutes 'a general temporal norm' to which the producers must conform, compelled to produce and exchange commodities to survive and to abide by the temporal norm expressed by socially necessary labor time to obtain 'full value' of their labor time (ibid: 191). Postone writes, 'Just as labor is transformed from an action of individuals to the alienated general principle of the totality under which the individuals are subsumed, time expenditure is transformed from a result *of* activity into a normative measure *for* activity' (ibid: 214–215).

The double character of labor in capitalism as abstract and concrete gives way to the emergence of clock time (abstract, de-contextualized measure of time) as a disciplining material force. Not invented by capitalism, yet compatible with and complicit in its functioning and reproduction, 'clock time' is both a *form* of time and a way of *recording* and *organizing* the tempo of human practice (Castree 2009: 42). It allows us to measure 'difference by way of metrical unity' because of its 'qualitative homogeneity' and 'divisibility' into definite periods (Castree 2009: 41). Jason Read elaborates on the concrete, disciplining effects of this structure of time and its indifference to the heterotemporality of heterogeneous labors:

> Effectivity of the social average of all labors is that which imposes itself on this or that particular labor as norm: failure to produce according to the speed and productivity of this norm is a failure to produce value or profit. This norm makes necessary the equalization of the diverse and heterogeneous labors of diverse and distinct individuals into an average capable of being measured.
> (Read 2003: 69)

With clock time as the general measure, axioms of socially necessary labor time in a society of generalized commodity exchange renders 'each moment . . . perpetually different from every other . . . but . . . also the same' (Perry Anderson quoted in Castree 2009: 43). Forms of time other than the time of capital are sublated in the fatal structure of time of the self-referential movement of value. Capital enacts a structure of time where mobilization transfigures as immobility, change as repetition of the same, and time becomes a machine that hammers life into a mold, reducing what is beyond measure to quantitative equivalence.

As self-valorizing value, capital's future is nothing but futures of the circulation of capital. Its horizon is not a historical future, if we understand by the latter an openness to time; rather, its future is one of ' "spurious infinity" forever reproducing itself' (Žižek 2006: 51). To that extent, capital annihilates future as possibility, writing it as future-present. In a powerful formulation of the fatal structure of time in capitalist modernity, Kordela writes: 'Capitalism has already killed time; both the time in which people can kill time, and the time in which they can also kill, be killed, and die. The eternal laws of value postulate that all that remain in legitimacy are the circulation and credit-times of exchangeable and immortal values' (2006: 561).

With a plurality of temporalities synchronized through structures of time (de-historicalizing temporal form of 'immortal values') enacted by capital, politics of time entails a struggle over what comes next, but alternative temporal forms, alternative temporalizations of history.

By way of a conclusion

We need to resist the tendency to reduce discussions on time and temporality of global politics to a question of the subjective experience of time. To open up a different way to explore the theoretical and political stakes entailed in grappling with time and temporality, I argue for a different sense of a politics of time – a politics that takes as its object the structure of time mediating social experience – by drawing on materialist conceptions, which highlight the ongoing totalization of time in modernity and draw attention to the de-historicizing time of capital. I am not suggesting there is a single, homogenous global time. Rather, a structure of time imposes itself as the temporal norm under the rule of capital. The universalizing gesture implicit in such an argument about the structure of temporality rooted in social production does not dismiss the recognition that global time is uneven and heterogeneous. 'But how do you reconcile the two?' skeptical minds might wonder.

We might, for example, re-conceptualize capital. A strategy of writing capital without succumbing to homogenizing logics is offered by Gidwani, who theorizes capital as 'an ontological multiplicity' (Gidwani 2008) in line with Louis Althusser's conceptualization of capitalist social formation as a 'complex whole' that operates in heterogeneous and nonlinear time (Althusser 1969 cited in de Sutter 2013: 209). Although 'the logic of capital demands that diverse temporalities which pose potential limits to capital be sublated to . . . abstract time,' diverse temporalities co-exist, as 'production activity oriented to profit-taking for accumulation interdigitates with other value-creating practices' (Gidwani 2008: 198). Consequently, capitalism can be depicted as 'a geographically uneven social formation where heterogeneous value-creating practices ("labors") are sutured together in lesser or greater degrees of repair (but where the wounds of that suture are never completely effaced)' (ibid: 198).

If re-conceptualizing capital is one way to reply to the 'how?' the other answer passes through 'learn[ing] to think history differently' so as 'to think politics differently' (Tomba 2009: 45). It entails an effort to pair history, historical time, and universality anew beyond reigning dualisms. A few formidable efforts raise the possibility of 're-imagin[ing] universal history out of bounds of exclusionary conceptual frames' (Buck-Morss 2009: 110; see also Vazquez-Arroyo 2008; Tomba 2009). The political import of attending to historical time outside received frameworks of history stems from the attempt to unearth silenced histories and reclaim the disavowed and from the effort to 'articulate a history of possibility' (Vazquez-Arroyo 2008), a different politics of the future that reclaims 'the future' from being a dead referent as it starts to designate nothing other than the reproduction of the same, again, again, and again. Osborne says, 'If the otherwise is to proceed, possibility of the otherwise must be produced as experience' (1995: 201). Time and temporality need to be engaged with this scholarly and political concern beyond the limits of mainstream IR and beyond the critically imposed limitations on thoughts about time and temporality of global politics.

Notes

1 Arguing that 'speed is the unknown side of politics', Virilio (2008: 57) says experience of time and temporality gain meaning in relation to spatial categories of location and proximity. Speed and acceleration of temporal experience enabled by technological developments eliminate the relevance of space; instantaneity subsumes local time and leads to the disappearance of the present.
2 This charge is leveled by Eagleton against postcolonial theory for its lack of conceptual architecture to account for postcolonialism as a historical condition (Eagleton 1998).
3 In this understanding of the labor theory of 'value,' labor is not taken to be the substance of value with a view to explain 'why prices are what they are and finding that it is labor' (Elson 1979: 123). Rather, labor theory of value is an attempt to understand 'why labor takes the form it does, and what the political consequences are' (ibid: 123).

Bibliography

Agamben, G. (2007) *Infancy and History: On the Destruction of Experience*, London, UK and New York, NY: Verso.

Aradau, C. and R. Van Munste (2007) 'Governing Terrorism through Risk: Taking Precautions, (Un)Knowing the Future,' *European Journal of International Relations*, 13(1):89–115.

Beck, U. and D. Levy. (2013) 'Cosmopolitanized Nations: Re-imagining Collectivity in World Risk Society,' *Theory, Culture, and Society*, 30(2):3–31.

Bell, D. (2003) 'History and Globalization: Reflections on Temporality,' *International Affairs*,79(4):801–814.

Blaney, D. and N. Inayatullah (2002) 'Neo-Modernization? IR and the Inner Life of Modernization Theory,' *European Journal of International Relations*, 8(1):103–137.

Buck-Morss, S. (2009) *Hegel, Haiti, and Universal History*, Pittsburg, PA: University of Pittsburg Press.

Castree, N. (2009) 'The Spatio-Temporality of Capitalism,' *Time & Society*, 18(1):26–61.

Connolly, W. E. (2002) *Neuropolitics: Thinking, Culture, Speed*, Minneapolis, MN: University of Minnesota Press.

De Goede, M. (2008) 'The Politics of Preemption and the War on Terror in Europe,' *European Journal of International Relations*, 14(1):161–185.

Der Derian, J. (1990) 'The (S)Pace of International Relations: Simulation, Surveillance, and Speed,' *International Studies Quarterly*, 34(3):295–310.

———. (1992) *Antidiplomacy: Spies, Terror, Speed, and War*, Cambridge, MA: Blackwell.

De Sutter, L. (ed.) (2013) *Althusser and Law*, New York, NY: Routledge.

Eagleton, T. (1998) 'Postcolonialism and "Postcolonialism,"' *Interventions*, 1:24–26.

Edkins, J. (2003) *Trauma and the Memory of Politics*, Cambridge, UK: Cambridge University Press.

Elson, D. (1979) 'A Value Theory of Labor,' in D. Elson (ed.), *Value*, 115–180, London, UK: CSE Books.

Enloe, C. (2004) *The Curious Feminist: Searching for Women in a New Age of Empire*, Berkeley, CA: University of California Press.

Fabian, J. (1983) *Time and the Other: How Anthropology Makes Its Object*, New York, NY: Columbia University Press.

Gidwani, V. (2008) *Capital Interrupted: Agrarian Development and the Politics of Work in India*, Minneapolis, MN: University of Minnesota Press.

Harvey, D. (1990) *The Condition of Postmodernity: An Enquiry into the Origins of Cultural Change*, Malden, MA: Blackwell.
Hutchings, K. (2008) *Time and World Politics: Thinking the Present*, Manchester, UK and New York, NY: Manchester University Press.
Jarvis, L. (2008) 'Times of Terror: Writing Temporality into the War on Terror,' *Critical Studies on Terrorism*, 1(22):245–262.
Kordela, K. (2006) 'Capital: At Least It Kills Time,' *Rethinking Marxism*, 18(4):539–563.
Le Goff, J. (1982) *Time, Work, and Culture in the Middle Ages*, Chicago, IL and London, UK: University of Chicago Press.
Lundborg, T. (2012) *Politics of the Event: Time, Movement, Becoming*, New York, NY: Routledge.
Malksoo, M. (2009) 'The Memory Politics of Becoming European: The East European Subalterns and the Collective Memory of Europe,' *European Journal of International Relations*, 15(4):653–680.
Marx, K. (1985) *The Communist Manifesto*, London, UK: Penguin.
———. (1990) *Capital: A Critique of Political Economy vol.1*, London, UK: Penguin.
———. (1993) *Grundrisse: Foundations of the Critique of Political Economy*, London, UK: Penguin.
Osborne, P. (1995) *The Politics of Time: Modernity and Avant-Garde*, New York, NY: Verso.
———. (2008) 'Marx and the Philosophy of Time,' *Radical Philosophy*, 147:15–22.
———. (2009) 'Negation, Affirmation, the New,' *CRMEP Research Seminar*, London, UK: Middlesex University Press.
Postone, M. (1993) *Time, Labor, and Social Domination: A Reinterpretation of Marx's Critical Theory*, New York, NY: Cambridge University Press.
———. (2004) 'Critique and Historical Transformation,' *Historical Materialism*, 12(3):53–72.
Prozorov, S. (2011) 'The Other as Past and Present: Beyond the Logic of 'Temporal Othering' in Ir Theory,' *Review of International Studies*, 37:1273–1293.
Read, J. (2003) *The Micro-Politics of Capital: Marx and the Prehistory of the Present*, Albany, NY: State University of New York Press.
Shapiro, M. (2000) 'National Times and Other Times: Re-Thinking Citizenship,' *Cultural Studies*, 14(1):79–98.
———. (2010) *The Time of the City: Politics, Philosophy, and Genre*, New York, NY: Routledge.
Stoetzler, M. (2004) 'Postone's Marx: A Theorist of Modern Society, Its Social Movements and Its Imprisonment by Abstract Labour,' *Historical Materialism*, 12(3):261–283.
Tomba, M. (2009) 'Historical Temporalities of Capital: An Anti-Historicist Perspective,' *Historical Materialism*, 17:44–65.
Vaughan-Williams, N. (2009) *Border Politics: The Limits of Sovereign Power*, Edinburgh, Scotland, UK: Edinburgh University Press.
Vazquez-Arroyo, A. (2008) 'Universal History Disavowed: On Critical Theory and Postcolonialism,' *Postcolonial Studies*, 11(4):451–473.
Virilio, P. (2008) *Pure War: Twenty Fiver Years Later*, Los Angeles, CA: Semiotext(e).
Walker, R. B. J. (1989) 'History and Structure in the Theory of International Relations,' *Millennium: Journal of International Studies*, 18(2):163–183.
———. (1993) *Inside/Outside: International Relations as Political Theory*, Cambridge, UK: Cambridge University Press.
Wolin, S. S. (1997) 'What Time Is It?' *Theory & Event*, 1(1):1–10.
Žižek, S. (2006) *The Parallax View*, Cambridge, MA: MIT Press.

15 Hurricane Katrina and bio-temporalities

Media representations of 'environmental' disasters[1]

Michael J. Shapiro

The discourses of environmental disaster

Decades ago I was struck by a report in *Time Magazine* on December 17, 1984, on thousands of deaths from a toxic chemical release at Union Carbide's plant in Bhopal, India. The cover image, which displayed the bodies of the dead and dying, was located under a headline reading 'Environment,' thereby implying the Bhopal incident should be understood as an accident. Years later, after Hurricane Katrina hit New Orleans, I rethought Bhopal and considered how news media create the events constituted as 'disasters,' focusing on the immediacies of suffering and mortality and allocating responsibility. While the sudden violence of armed attacks tends to be located in the discursive space of politics, a political vocabulary is missing for industrial 'accidents' and the long-term conditions making them possible.

Given the temporal rhythms of news media, the Bhopal event disappeared from the news shortly after the immediate effects were recorded, but twenty years after the toxic gas leak, the *Christian Science Monitor* said in response to 'new environmental studies' that the Indian government was preparing to hold Union Carbide responsible for polluted ground water 'affecting a new generation of Bhopal citizens' (Baldauf 2004). Testifying to Union Carbide's continuing avoidance of responsibility, a 2004 article in the *Taipei Times* reported: 'Two decades after the world's worst-ever industrial accident, many of those who survived injury are still waiting for their compensation.'[2] Bhopal again made the news on the thirtieth anniversary, with media noting the corporate world's ability to thwart compensation claims, despite proliferating birth defects caused by the still-polluted soil and water supply:

> The people who suffer are successive generations, almost all poor, whose ill health now affects babies and young children of parents who may not have even been born in 1984. Recently, the Chingari Trust, which deals with handicapped children, staged a play and candlelight vigil in Bhopal's old city. They have 700 children registered with autism, behavioral problems, sensory disorders and developmental delays.
>
> (Elliot 2014)

The posture of Union Carbide (now Dow Chemical) is typical of large US corporations. Consider the 2012 factory fire in Bangladesh that killed 1,200 workers. A year later, the *New York Times* reported 'neither Walmart, Sears, Children's Place nor any of the other American companies . . . have agreed to contribute to the [compensation] efforts' (Greenhouse 2003: B1).

Incidents like Bhopal reveal a 'policy dynamic that links strong and weak states,' rendering invisible 'the cartography of occupational danger' (Shapiro 2005: 228). In this dynamic, a discourse of environmental accidents in which humans face the vagaries of the elements (fires, water surges, chemical spills, etc.) trumps a political economy discourse of inequality and structures of dominations and control. The latter discourse fails to achieve adequate traction to either protect or compensate victims. To extend the temporality of vulnerability beyond the occurrence of so-called environmental accidents, the theme of precarity must replace the concept of the accident. Neil Smith comments: 'There is no such thing as a natural disaster. In every phase and aspect of a disaster – causes, vulnerability, preparedness, results and response, and reconstruction – the contours of disaster and the difference between who lives and who dies is to a greater or lesser extent a social calculus' (Smith 2006). He adds, 'Hurricane Katrina provides the most startling confirmation of that axiom' (2006). Smith further suggests we 'put social science to work as a counterweight to official attempts to relegate Katrina to the historical dustbin of inevitable "natural" disasters' (2006). In the following discussion of Hurricane Katrina, the 'counterweights' I employ come more from popular culture than social science. They nevertheless support Smith's emphasis on 'vulnerability.'

Early Katrina

The long-term political economy in which precarious lives are shaped was not part of public discourse when Hurricane Katrina hit New Orleans. Many early frames evoked disaster insurance. The *New York Times* reported: 'Insurance companies said yesterday that damage from Hurricane Katrina could top $9 billion, making it one of the costliest storms on record' (Story and Farzad 2005). Once the levees were breached and the city was under water, another aspect of economy was evoked. Reporters for the *New York Times* offered a longer temporal trajectory, suggesting a lust for profits led to a willingness to develop enterprises in a precarious landscape: 'Although early travelers realized the irrationality of building a port on shifting mud in an area regularly ravaged by storms and disease, the opportunities to make money overrode all objections' (Dean and Revkin 2005).

Once the enormity of the devastation became evident, news reports eschewed long-term thematization and began rehearsing a racialized angle of vision with considerable historical depth. Robert Crooks suggests the violence characterizing the US's western frontier during the nineteenth century was transformed from a mobile western boundary, as Euro-American vanquished Native American nations, into a 'relatively fixed partitioning of urban space . . . a racial frontier' (1995: 68). A mobile geography pitted Euro-Americans against a racialized, nomadic Native America; in the urban case, the geographical frontier 'now denoted relatively fixed lines of defense for the purity and order of European culture [so that they associated] black urban communities with the criminal side of the urban frontier' (Crooks 1995: 71), persisting in the profiling of (and violence against) African Americans by many urban police departments.

The material geographies and imaginaries of the racial-spatial orders of major US cities were articulated by the media in the aftermath of Katrina. Abandoning its initial coverage of Katrina's 'devastating impacts,' they turned to a frame of 'civil unrest,' attributed disproportionately to young black males (Tierney, Beve, and Kuligowski 2006). Rapper Kanye West protested:

> I hate the way they portray us in the media. If you see a black family, it says they're looting, see a white family, it says they're looking for food . . . We already realize a lot of people that could help are at war right now, fighting another way, and they [the news media] have given them permission to go down and shoot us.
>
> (Goodman 2005)

On a less passionate register, media researchers reached a similar conclusion. Distinguishing 'episodic' from 'thematic' news coverage, they noted, 'The national coverage moved from one looting event to the other or from one rooftop rescue to the other, without context . . . instead of presenting "thematic" treatments of the region's poor' (Miller, Roberts, and LaPoe 2014: 75). However, the media's abstractions pale in comparison to the testimonies of African Americans. For example, Emma Dixon reports seeing 'painted signs warning that looters would be shot [and being] warned by a white neighbor not to move around too much lest I be taken as a looter' (Dixon 2005). She locates the aftermath of Katrina in the context of an 'institutionalized racism that began centuries ago':

> The unnatural disaster of racism swept away the cars with which poor black people could have escaped Katrina. Almost a third of residents of the flooded neighborhoods did not own the cars on which the evacuation plan relied. If the promise to the freed slaves of 40 acres and a mule had been kept, then six generations later, their descendants would own more assets, and the mule would now be a Buick.
>
> (Dixon 2005)

Later temporalities: Katrina in popular culture genres

(1) When the Levees Broke

Director Spike Lee's documentary, *When the Levees Broke: A Requiem in Four Parts* (2006), 'counter actualizes' how the news media racialized Katrina's aftermath and 'rendered' the city 'foreign' in relation to the rest of the US

(Hartnell 2012: 54). The window his film provides into the disproportionate suffering of New Orleans' African American population references a long historical trajectory.

Looking at the post–Civil War period is crucial if we are to understand that trajectory: 'Louisiana's business elite had two concerns regarding the labor force: Who would maintain the levees on whose safety the commercial port depended? And who would perform the agricultural labor on the sugar and cotton plantations?' (Fussell 2007).

'State agents' tried unsuccessfully to recruit agriculture labor from abroad:

> In the end, whites continued to rely on subordinated black sharecroppers and casual laborers. Lynching and intimidation, plus the lack of a free market for mobile wage labor, effectively confined black laborers to agricultural occupations in the deep South from emancipation through the beginning of the twentieth century.
>
> (Fussell 2007)

In New Orleans and throughout the Mississippi Delta, the plantation system 'maintained its control over land, financing and water, while the new African American communities [remained] trapped inside the boundaries of the plantation complex' (Woods 1998: 6).

Whereas the black population of the city was only 9 percent when the US purchased the Louisiana territory from the French, by the twentieth century, it was a 'biracial city'; its formerly 'mixed neighborhoods' were now radically segregated, a pattern created during the Jim Crow era and consummated during the New Deal, with 'housing developments' leading to 'legally enforced segregation' while white flight to the 'suburbs accelerated both residential and educational segregation' (Fussell 2007). The New Deal was a bad deal for African American agricultural workers; 'it strengthened both traditional incentives and traditional institutions [creating] a positive incentive to Southern planters to demote their workers to the status of casual labor employed only seasonally' (D. Grubbs in Woods 1998: 13).

Not surprisingly, when Katrina hit, the hollowing out of the African American labor force had produced a statistic of 24.5 percent of the city's residents living below the poverty line (in contrast to 13.3 percent for the country as a whole) (Fussell 2007). Crucially for African Americans, 'low income black neighborhoods in low-lying areas suffered a disproportionate share of the floodwater, while wealthier, whiter neighborhoods on higher land stayed dry' (Fussell 2007).

However, these are generalizations, not specific experiences (Brunsma, Overfelt, and Picou 2007). The latter are registered in the faces intermittently in focus in Lee's documentary: 'The face is a veritable megaphone' (Deleuze and Guattari 1987: 179). The faces, along with the words of the persons who experienced Hurricane Katrina, constitute the micropolitics of the Katrina event, as seen by Lee. As I note elsewhere, the macropolitics of race is articulated in policy histories with African Americans incorporated into a 'story of legal and moral ascent' and in 'simplistic accounts of moral progress.' In contrast, the micropolitics of race is articulated through practices of everyday life in the face of 'intolerance, exclusion and violence' (Shapiro 2012: 67). The blues aesthetic permeating Lee's documentary expresses such a micropolitics. Blues aesthetics are often associated with entertainment but are understood by African American assemblages as 'insurrectionary social text[s] . . . [which have the effect of] unsettling a repressive social order' (Gussow 2002: 27).

Film and video constitute 'ideal means' to encompass past, present and future, 'to anticipate historical moments, to suggest interrelationships between the present and the past, and to construct analogies between present and past' (Wahlberg 2008: 124). To appreciate the force of Lee's *Levees*, we must recognize the encounter of 'documentary time' (Wahlberg 2008) with historical time. In Lee's film, 'the constructed temporality of camera movement, editing and sound meets with that of the filmed gestures and events, which in turn are marked by the historical moment of their representation' (Wahlberg 2008: 8).

However, meeting and marking, features of documentaries, fail to register a crucial dimension of the experiences of the Katrina event for the city's residents or the viewers of the documentary. The film's temporal rhythms, conveyed by close-ups of faces and the words of a wide variety of victims, who appear, disappear and reappear on screen, punctuated by shots of the devastation of neighborhoods, all surrounded by the varying moods evoked by Terence Blanchard's musical soundtrack, create the film's affective resonances. The assemblage of sound and image, an achievement of time measurement in the film connecting with its affective impact of tempo and rhythm, constitutes the Lee/Blanchard political version of the Katrina event. As a result, an understanding of how the documentary works requires an appreciation of the interrelationship of the rhythms of Lee's cinematic montage and those of Blanchard's musical soundtrack.

Musical genres have often been the vehicles for the articulation of the history and violence of the African American experience in the US, with no composition as historically comprehensive as Duke Ellington's *Black, Brown and Beige*, 'the story of his people,' as Ellington put it (Shapiro 2006: 151). To situate the musical contribution to the temporal structure of Lee's documentary, it's instructive to review the temporal structure of Ellington's *Black, Brown and Beige* and contrast it with Blanchard's musical soundtrack.

The narrative background of Ellington's composition is supplied by his poem, in which his character Boola's personal story is interwoven with history. The musical narrative accompanying Boola is linear, beginning with the *Black* section in which Bola begins in Africa, suffers through the Middle Passage and ends up in America, where, after taking on Christianity, he approaches a church to which he is irresistibly drawn, represented in a musical composition, 'Come Sunday.' That piece, which draws from the genre of the spiritual, contains hints of the African American blues tradition: 'Short, lyrical statements by solo trombone and trumpet introduce the song' whose structure is a 'typical blues style . . . flatted fifths'' (Peress 2004: 182–183). The musical resonates with the emotional timbres of African Americans kept outside the church while they support the spirituality in progress inside: 'The music holds still, catching its breath [as] the blacks outside grunt/Subdued approval' (ibid). When the composition enters the *Brown* section, 'the rhythms and tonalities of the spiritual follows its historical and musical migration to the blues [as it] features the traditional twelve-bar blues structure' (Shapiro 2006: 152). Finally, as it moves to *Beige*, it shifts from a 'weary blues' mood to a hopeful one 'reflected in the intellectual contributions of the Harlem Renaissance and the patriotic contributions of black America's participation in the war effort' (Shapiro 2006: 152)

In contrast with Ellington's articulation of musical and black history, expressed in a more or less linear narrative as it treats a historical trajectory of the black experience, the Lee-Blanchard documentary moves back and forth in both musical and black history as it frames Katrina in the context of the political economy of the black experience in New Orleans. The two dimensions resonate, with a homology between the rhythms of the musical soundtrack and the rhythm of Lee's editing (Callenbach 2006: 6). After Blanchard talks about the silences engendered so only the wind is heard, his soundtrack reproduces a high-pitched jazz that howls like the wind.

Ultimately, Blanchard's musical enactment of the documentary's subtitle is a crucial aspect of how *Levees* thinks. It is the musical realization of a requiem mass, inflected by the history of the African American soundscape. It is partitioned, chapter by chapter, with different musical prologues from different historical moments. Among the soundtrack's musical moments are jazz funerals, which simultaneously mark deaths and celebrate lives. Yet much of the imagery is about the former. There are shots of signs on houses, 'dead body inside.' Some interviews talk about those who did not survive. As Amos Vogel notes, historically, the cinematic medium has had a 'tendency to avert its eyes before the sight of actual death' (Vogel in Sobchack 1984: 283). Sobchack explains: 'Of all the transformations of the lived-body in our culture, the event of death seems particularly privileged in its threat to representation' (Sobchack 1984: 286). Lee's documentary shows corpses (in varying states of decay) and signs referring to them. Those moments are interspersed with vibrant (albeit often suffering) life. Lee's editing, thus, provides a 'vigorous contrast between two states of the physical body: the body as lived-body, intentional and animated – and the body as corpse, as flesh unintended, inanimate, static' (Sobchack 1984: 287). Showing the two kinds of bodies is one of the film's dominant temporalities. We see bodies who *are* subjects and bodies who *were* subjects, with the latter constituting crucial moments in the visual aspect of Lee's requiem.

At the same time, the film celebrates what New Orleans has been and what remains. The overture in chapter 1 provides 'lively scenes of the reborn Mardi Gras of 2006' (Callenbach 2006: 6). While much of Blanchard's soundtrack is elegiac, much is joyous – for example, we hear Louis Armstrong singing 'Do You Know What It Means to Miss New Orleans' and Fats Domino's 'Walking to New Orleans.' Accompanying the temporal shifts, as music from different moments in New Orleans history is summoned, are sections of old film footage, with early Mardi Gras celebrations in black and white and more recent ones in color.

Although aspects of *Levees* hint at 'individual and collective rebirth' (Gebhardt 2012), the warnings to looters, coupled with the violence of vigilantes and the militarization of the police force, suggest the racial-spatial order of New Orleans retains a disturbing permanence. And the interviews with residents, many of whom were relocated to other cities, indicate the neighborhood culture, especially in the Ninth (largely black) Ward, seems unlikely to be restored. The coercive way families were broken up with dispersion to different cities harkens (as some interviewees suggest) to the slave period when plantation owners broke up families, separately selling off husbands, wives and children. At a minimum, the last chapters in *Levees* convey ambivalence. Many are striving to restore New Orleans' musical, carnival and other aspects of its life world, but many may never return.

(2) Treme

To explore what New Orleans has been and what the future may hold consider HBO's *Treme*, which explores New Orleans past, present and future in the aftermath of Katrina. Inasmuch as *Treme* is a fictional narrative rather than a documentary, its protagonists are aesthetic rather than ethnographic subjects. Nevertheless, like Lee's ethnographic subjects, writer/director (*The Wire*) David Simon's characters in *Treme* (many of whom represent actual New Orleans residents) perform both a mapping of the post-Katrina spaces and a mixing of temporalities, entangling personal biographical time and geopolitical time.

Among the diverse civic spaces within which the meaning of events are negotiated and continually reinterpreted is 'the black public sphere,' a domain of civic association articulated not in the usual white, liberal political frame of voting and attendance at Parent Teacher Association meetings, but in the diverse artistic genres foregrounded in *Treme* and in much of the critical commentary the series has attracted. The activities and interpretive dynamics add critical temporal rhythms to the Katrina event, as they summon historical moments and personages belonging to a shadow world behind the world foregrounded in mainstream civic culture.

Johari Jabir points to a glaring oversight in the Katrina event, the lack of mention of Mahalia Jackson, even though 'in the first several days following Hurricane Katrina the US media paid tribute to numerous legendary musicians – past and present – who hailed from New Orleans' (Jabir 2009: 649). In evoking Jackson, Jabir takes a Walter Benjamin–like, critical approach to history, a moment of 'Messianic time,' which has the past shine through at moments in the present (Benjamin 1968: 254–255). For Jabir, what 'flashes up' during the post-Katrina moment is Jackson's 'Didn't It Rain' (1953), which he hears as relevant to the Katrina event (Jabri 2009). The recollection of the song provides a way to '*learn* some important lessons about race, citizenship, politics, and cultural production' (Jabir 2009: 654). His evocation of Jackson's musical archive sees a 'spark of hope' that has smoldered 'at the very heart of past events' (Rancière 2014: 53). Jabir notes 'the strong sense of swing throughout [Mahalia's] musical archive' harks back to 'a rhythm . . . held on from slavery':

> [It is] anchored by a structural organization . . . [a] sense of time which, when thinking in terms of a performing ensemble, requires a communal instinct and

epistemology ... that creates the paradox of collective coherence [because it is] ... a reflection on the past and simultaneously a vision of the future; the feeling of being held and being set free in the same moment, so that several things are taking place at the same 'time.'

(Jabir 2009: 654)

The *Treme* series conjures a musical past while envisioning a restored communal future. Although *Treme's* focus on New Orleans' 'unmistakably black and hybrid' cultural practices has drawn criticism for its tendency to 'sell the city and its culture' to spur a 'tourist economy' (Gray 2012: 274), it is also seen as contributing to 'alternative and emergent possibilities' for the reinvention of the city's cultural life world (ibid: 276). And in *Treme's* first season, there is a strong critique of the tourist economy, for example, when street musician Sonny (Michiel Huisman) mocks tourists from Wisconsin for whom New Orleans music is the iconic 'When the Saints Go Marching In.' Ultimately, the show 'is an argument for the city,' not a focus on 'single issues' (Simon in Beiser 2011).

Treme's first episode is situated three months after Hurricane Katrina. It surveys the devastation of the city while following the lives of diverse residents struggling to come to terms with their losses. As the episodes and seasons progress, the *Treme* effect is constituted as an encounter between the characters' struggles to restore or reinvent their personal and communal lives and the viewers' development of a political sense of post–Hurricane Katrina problems, screened through their own political habitus. Simon comments:

> A TV show can't hold people and institutions to account like good journalism can. But if I can make you care about a character, I may make you think a little longer about certain dynamics that might cause you to reconsider your own political inertia or your own political myopia, You might be more willing to accept a critique of the prevailing political and social systems.
>
> (Simon in Beiser 2011).

Of course, *Treme* belongs to a television, not a cinema, aesthetic. In the case of a TV series, 'the primary object of aesthetic interest ... is not the individual piece, but the format' (Cavell 1982: 79). Each episode derives coherence from the formulas generating it, including the continuing participation of characters and the progression of their relationships with each other and with the spaces within which they function (ibid: 82). Unlike the typical cinematic aesthetic, much of what is offered week to week is a background of uneventfulness – the mundane moments of interaction in life worlds – against which the special events driving each episode stand out (ibid: 89).

Characters (in different vocational, ethnic and class positions) and an event (a second line parade) stand out at the beginning of the series; each provides a different temporal depth for the Katrina event. In the first 'second line' parade in post-Katrina New Orleans, we enter the parade from the point of view of two characters, Antoine Batiste (Wendell Pierce) and Davis McClary (Steve Zhan), the former a jazz trombone player who helps lead the parade and the latter a part-time disk jockey who joins the parade in progress. Their respective locations in a genealogy of musical space help situate the significance of second line parades.

Helen Regis remarks, 'death haunts the living in New Orleans,' with second line parades constituting 'a collective space for reflection on the structures that impinge in inner city lives, often shaping the circumstances in which those lives, often too early, come to an end' (2001: 754). The first post-Katrina second line parade articulates the death and destruction wrought by Katrina. As the parade reappears in subsequent *Treme* episodes, the historical depth and multiple dimensions of the practice become evident. In part through the insertion of older documentary film footage and photographs and in part through conversations about it, viewers learn to associate it with 'dance steps,' 'brass bands,' 'social clubs' or 'social and pleasure clubs' and a dynamic of joining, as watching crowds get swept up in its rhythmic motions, switching from observation to participation (Regis 2001: 755).

Inasmuch as the *Treme* series is polydiegetic, its representations of second line parades belong to one among many of its narratives. In addition to the continuing presence of New Orleans' pluralistic musical cultures, other narratives locate characters in fraught familial, social and erotic relationships, bringing them into encounters that reveal the legal worlds, policing practices and reactions to official policy at local and federal levels. All transpire in the face of enormous barriers to the city's attempt to restore civic and social life, especially the instability of the population, as many have left and those who return cannot reestablish their former life circumstances.

As *Treme* is in many ways a 'listening text,' my emphasis is on the narrative that foregrounds musical worlds (Fuqua 2012: 237). To situate conceptually *Treme's* musical narrative, I summon philosopher Edmund Husserl's analysis of the temporal structure of a melody in *Phenomenology of Internal Time Consciousness* and French cultural minister Jacques Attali's historical genealogy of musical space.

Husserl's analysis is restricted to the phenomenology of individual consciousness. He develops two aspects of that phenomenology: 'retention,' a phenomenological expansion of the present, a 'longitudinal temporality extending the 'point-like' instant of the now; and 'protention,' an extension of the melody into an anticipation of its future occurrences (Osborne 1995: 50). For Husserl, music ('melody') is an exemplary temporal object. When the sound 'dies away,' although the music is 'not actually present,' it is still sensed because it has evoked a 'retentional' consciousness reminding listeners of a 'past sound' (Husserl 1964: 53).

As their conversations reveal, the musical narrative is clearly evocative of a past for *Treme's* characters. It is also clear that their listening is done in anticipation of a future for the New Orleans soundscape. However, its temporality goes well beyond the 'just past' and the immediate future of Husserl's analysis. Crucially, a model of immanence, which presumes an abstract listener (an individual phenomenological subject) whose presence to music is purely mental, cannot capture the temporal implications of *Treme's* musical narrative. The music different characters hear evokes different pasts and different anticipations of a future musical culture. Moreover, as the scenes in second line marches, in clubs and in the street suggest, the 'listeners' are not passive modes of pure consciousness but mobilized bodies. They dance and gesture to the resonances of the music and respond to the movements of those around them. In addition, the venues of the sounds are crucial to how pasts and potential futures are evoked.

To appreciate *Treme's* musical narrative, we must heed the venues and locate them in a historical trajectory of musical space, noting the differing allegiances of the various characters to alternative musical pasts, alternative hoped-for futures and their connections with the alternative musical spaces. For that kind of appreciation, Attali's genealogy of musical space is instructive. For Attali, the temporality of music is a function of technologies of reproduction rather than simply the listening of the phenomenological subject (Attali 1985). Because of its repeatability, enabled by recording technology, music is capable of resisting 'the ravages of time' (Attali 1985: 85). Inasmuch as people can buy more recordings than they can listen to at once, repeatable music can 'stockpile time' (ibid: 101). Attali situates the historically changing temporality of music in a narrative of musical space that precedes and incorporates its contemporary repeatability. The story begins with festivals and carnivals, staged by nomadic musicians performing in the street, a musical space given over to ritual and sacrificial functions involving participatory crowds. Those functions of music were largely displaced when 'the concert hall performance replaced the popular festival, [creating] . . . a gulf between the musicians and audience' (ibid: 47). The subsequent development of recording technologies and the emergence of radio rendered the walls of the concert hall unable to contain musical space. Temporally, the repetition enabled by recording technologies has produced 'a fundamental change in the relation of man to history, because it makes the stockpiling of time possible' (ibid: 101); spatially, musical discourse has become 'nonlocalizable' (ibid: 113).

However, Attali recognizes history is 'conjunctural' (Braudel 1979). Earlier forms of exchange persist with newer ones so that 'music, like cartography records the simultaneity of conflicting orders' (Attali 1985: 45). The musical cultures of New Orleans are exemplary. *Treme's* first season introduces musician protagonists representing different moments and life imaginations in the historical spatio-temporality mapped by Attali; those differences provide a persistent theme in subsequent seasons.

As in the Lee-Blanchard documentary, New Orleans' musical history is located in the context of the political economy of the black experience. Conflicts over musical styles in the *Treme* series, beginning in season one, are located within the moral economy/political economy divide. Music is arguably *Treme's* main character. As it is articulated though various protagonists, the most temporally significant narrative thread within which it is thematized involves the relationship between Albert 'Big Chief' Lambeaux (Clark Peters) and his son Delmond (Rob Brown), with Albert positioning himself as the guardian of the moral economy of New Orleans music and Delmond associated with modern, commercially oriented jazz. For Albert, the percussive, Indian version of jazz is a treasure with ontological depth and a ritual function (performed in the street during Mardi Gras by elaborately costumed 'Indians'); in contrast, Delmond, at least at the outset, is a performer (trumpeter) of a commoditized modern jazz in concert venues (e.g., Lincoln Hall in New York). Generational time is, thus, articulated with historical time. Albert seeks to preserve a cultural past; his son is associated with a commercial present.

As *Treme's* seasons progress, the division between Albert and Delmond attenuates. Initially, in his role as a cultural icon, Albert is involved in what Igor Kopytoff calls a 'counterdrive' to the commoditization of music, resisting performing in a musical style that renders music an exchangeable good (Kopytoff 1986: 68); his preferred venue is the street, the space of festival and ritual that preceded music's migration into the confined spaces (clubs and concert halls) of musical commoditization where the ritual aspect of music had largely disappeared (Attali 1985: 21).

However, Albert begins to lose his contempt for Delmond's musical vocation and the spatial practices within which it flourishes. At the same time, Delmond develops a passion for New Orleans' musical heritage and begins working on a temporally hybrid music that incorporates his father's ethnic, percussive musical rhythms with aspects of modern jazz to preserve the embodied resonances of the former and emphasize the swing, dance-provoking aspects of the latter. By the time *Treme's* last season is underway, Albert agrees to perform in non-street venues with Delmond's ensemble.

Kopytoff suggests, 'In every society there are things that are publically precluded from being commoditized' (1986: 68), but as *Treme* makes evident, the New Orleans ethnoscape complicates the concept of the public. *Treme* dramatizes New Orleans' plurality of publics. Albert's 'public' is a marginalized counter public that resists musical commoditization. As Delmond migrates into his father's counter public, the musical collaboration between father and son draws him physically back to New Orleans, while summoning Albert into a musical modernity that honors the past, produces a present and bids to open New Orleans jazz to a future that will bring disparate publics together.

Conclusion: Katrina's will-have-been

Lee's *Levees* and Simon's *Treme* reveal the death, dislocation, trauma and precariousness visited on black lives by Katrina: 'Despite mountains of communication and surveillance devices, America was still shocked by the revelation of impoverishment, racism, brutality, corruption, and official neglect in a place it thought it knew intimately' (Woods 2009: 428). Does that shock still register with America's mediascape? Is it still present in the affective temporalities, the ongoing effects of trauma, dislocation and suffering?

The racism, brutality and official neglect evoked by representations of Katrina have been foregrounded by the popular media in response to the shooting of unarmed African Americans Michael Brown and Tony Terrell Robinson by police officers in Ferguson, Missouri, and Madison, Wisconsin, especially after grand juries failed to indict the officers involved in the Ferguson case. One Internet outlet said those protesting the shooting of Michael Brown called it 'Obama's Katrina' (Howerton 2014). Consolidating the three episodes of police violence and the media's frequent referencing of Katrina renders the latter a 'paradigmatic experience,' the kind of experience that continues to serve as a 'measuring rod for human conduct' (Mannheim 1943: 136).

As for the ethico-political questions raised by the evocation of Katrina, Judith Butler challenges a linear reading of violence by questioning how we define an injurable or precarious life, how we grieve for some rather than others and how our perceptions are, ultimately, unknowing (predicated on norms that are accepted unreflectively). As she puts it, 'The epistemological capacity to apprehend a life is partially dependent on that life being produced by norms that qualify it as a life, or, indeed, as part of life' (2010: 3). 'Apprehension' is not mere perception for Butler: 'The precarity of life imposes an obligation on us' (ibid: 2).

Heeding Butler, I return to David Simon's remark on the temporal structure of a television series and its potential for creating consciousness of political inertia and prevailing institutions and policies. Simon suggests once a life's complicated habitus is apprehended, the obligation to regard it sympathetically can follow. That surmise is validated in the case of a drone pilot, Brandon Bryant, directed to kill a young Pakistani by firing a hellfire missile from the drone, after having observed his everyday life for weeks. Bryant quit and testified in a documentary about how his developed sense of obligation trumped the demand structure of his military vocation, leaving him angry, critical and remorseful (Greenwald 2013). Albeit too late to save the victim, Bryant was able to heed what Slavoj Žižek calls 'the ethical weight' of an other (2006: 290)

Lee's *Levees* and Simon's *Treme* allow viewers to virtually live with the precarity of particular black protagonists who have endured the Katrina event. Perhaps, therefore, they aid in the recognition of the 'ethical weight' of black lives in the entanglement of our world-making, including the desire to rid it of them.

Notes

1 Delivered at Annual Meeting of the International Studies Association, New Orleans, February 18–22, 2015.
2 TaipeiTimes, http://www.taipeitimes.com/News/world/archives/2004/12/04/2003213703

Bibliography

Attali, J. (1985) *Noise: The Political Economy of Music*, Brian Massumi (trans.), Minneapolis, MN: University of Minnesota Press.

Baldauf, S. (2004) 'Bhopal Gas Tragedy Lives on, 20 Years Later,' *The Christian Science Monitor*. Available online: <http://www.csmonitor.com/2004/0504/ p07s01-wosc.html> (Accessed 11 May 2015).

Beiser, V. (2011) 'An Interview with David Simon,' *The Progressive*. Available online: <http://www.progressive.org/news/2011/02/157458/interview-david-simon> (Accessed 11 May 2015).

Benjamin, W. (1968) 'Theses on the Philosophy of History,' in H. Arendt (ed.), *Illuminations*, Harry Zone (trans.), 253–267, New York, NY: Schocken.
Braudel, F. (1979) *Afterthoughts on Material Civilization and Capitalism*, Patricia Ranum (trans.), Baltimore, MD: Johns Hopkins University Press.
Brunsma, D. L., D. Overfelt and J. S. Picou (eds.) (2007) *The Sociology of Katrina*, Lanham, MD: Roman & Littlefield.
Butler, J. (2010) *Frames of War: When is Life Grievable*, New York, NY: Verso.
Callenbach, E. (2006) 'When the Levees broke: A Requiem in Four Acts,' *Film Quarterly*, 60(2):4–10.
Cavell, S. (1982) 'The Fact of Television', *Daedalus*, 111(4):75–96.
Crooks, R. (1995) 'From the far Side of the Urban Frontier: The Detective Fiction of Chester Himes and Walter Mosley,' *College Literature*, 22(3):68.
Dean, C. and A. C. Revkin (2005) 'After Centuries of 'Controlling' Land, Gulf Learns Who's the Boss,' *New York Times*. Online. Available HTTP: <http://www.nytimes.com/2005/08/30/national/30coast.html?_r=0> (Accessed 11 May 2015).
Deleuze, G. and F. Guattari (1987) *A Thousand Plateaus*, Brian Massumi (trans.), Minneapolis, MN: University of Minnesota Press.
Dixon, E. (2005) 'New Orleans' Racial Divide: An Unnatural Disaster,' *Common Dreams*. Online. Available HTTP: <http://www/commondreams.org/views05/1116–34.htm>.
Elliot, J. (2014) 'India: After 30 Years, Bhopal Is Still Simmering,' *Newsweek*. Online. Available HTTP: <http://www.newsweek.com/india-after-30-years-bhopal-still-simmering-88144> (Accessed 11 May 2015).
Fuqua, J. V. (2012) ''In New Orleans, We Might Say It Like This…'Authenticity, Place, and HBO's Treme,' *Television New Media*, 13(3):235–242.
Fussell, E. (2007) 'Constructing New Orleans Race: A Population History of New Orleans,' *The Journal of American History*, 94(December, 2007). Online. Available HTTP: <http://www.journalofamericanhistory.org/projects/katrina. Fussell.html> (Accessed 11 May 2015).
Gebhardt, N. (2012) 'Do You Know What it Mean to Miss New Orleans? Historical Metaphors and Mythical Realities in Spike Lee's *When the Levees Broke*,' *Jazz Research Journal*, 6(2). Online. Available HTTP: <http://www.equinoxpub.com/journals/index.php/JAZZ/article/viewArticle/1752> (Accessed 11 May 2015).
Goodman, A. (2005) 'Kanye West: 'Bush Doesn't Care About Black People,'' *Democracy Now*. Online. Available HTTP: <http://www.democracynow.org/ 2005/9/5/kanye_west_bush_doesnt_care_about> (Accessed 11 May 2015).
Gray, H. (2012) 'Recovered, Reinvented, Reimagined: Treme, Television Studies and Writing New Orleans,' *Television & New Media*, 13(3):268–278.
Greenhouse, S. (2003) 'US Retailers Decline to Aid Factory Victims in Bangladesh,' *New York Times*, November 23, 2003: B1.
Greenwald, R. (2013) *Unmanned: American's Drone Wars*. Online. Available HTTP: https://archive.org/details/scm-375343-awpt-unmannedamericasdronewar (Accessed 11 May 2015).
Gussow, A. (2002) *Seems Like Murder Here: Southern Violence and the Blues Tradition*, Chicago, IL: University of Chicago Press.
Hartnell, A. (2012) 'Hurricane Katrina as Visual Spectacle: *Hurricane on the Bayou* and the Reframing of American national identity,' in T. Cusack (ed.), *Art and Identity at the Water's Edge*, 53–66, London, UK: Ashgate.
Howerton, J. (2014) 'Ferguson Protesters' Angry Message to Obama, Democrats: 'This is Obama's Katrina, and He Ain't Doing S**t!'' *The Blaze*. Online. Available HTTP:

<http://www.theblaze.com/stories/2014/11/24/ferguson-protesters-angry-message-to-obama-democrats-this-is-obamas-katrina-and-he-aint-doing-st/> (Accessed 11 May 2015).

Husserl, E. (1964) *The Phenomenology of Internal Time-Consciousness*, James S. Churchill (trans.), Bloomington, IN: Indiana University Press.

Jabir, J. (2009) 'On Conjuring Mahalia: Mahalia Jackson, New Orleans, and the Sanctified Swing,' *American Quarterly*, 61(3):649–669.

Kopytoff, I. (1986) 'The Cultural Biography of Things: Commoditization as Process,' in A. Appadurai (ed.), *The Social Life of Things*, 64–91, New York, NY: Cambridge University Press.

Lee, S. (2006) *When the Levees Broke: A Requiem In Four Acts*, New York, NY: HBO Video.

Mannheim, K. (1943) *Diagnoses of Our Time*, London, UK: Kegan Paul, Trench, Trubner & Co.

Miller, A., S. Roberts and V. LaPoe. (2014) *Oil and Water: Media Lessons from Hurricane Katrina and the Deepwater Horizon Disaster*, Jackson, MS: University of Mississippi Press.

Osborne, P. 1995. *The Politics of Time: Modernity and the Avant-Garde*, London, UK: Verso.

Peress, M. (2004) *Dvorak to Duke Ellington*, New York, NY: Oxford University Press.

Rancière, J. (2014) *Figures of History*, Julie Rose (trans.), Cambridge, Oxford: Polity.

Regis, H. A. (2001) 'Blackness and the Politics of Memory in the New Orleans Second Line,' *American Ethnologist*, 28(4):752–777.

Shapiro, M. (2005) 'The discursive space of global spaces of global politics,' *Journal of Environmental Policy & Planning*, 7(3):227–238.

———. (2005) *Studies in Trans-disciplinary Method: After the Aesthetic Turn*, New York, NY: Routledge.

———. (2006) *Deforming American Political Thought*, Lexington, KY: Kentucky University Press.

Shapiro, M. J. (2012) *Discourse, Culture, Violence*, New York, NY: Routledge.

Smith, N. (2006) 'There's No Such Thing as a Natural Disaster,' *Understanding Katrina*. Online. Available HTTP: <http://understandingkatrina.ssrc.org/Smith/> (Accessed 11 May 2015).

Sobchack, V. (1984) 'Inscribing Ethical Space: Ten Propositions on Death, Representation, and Documentary,' *Quarterly Review of Film Studies*, 9(4):283–300.

Story, L. and R. Farzad. (2005) 'Hurricane Katrina: The Cost; Insurers Estimate Damage at $9 Billion, Among Costliest US Storms on Record,' *New York Times*. Online. Available HTTP: <http://query.nytimes.com/gst/full page.html?res=9407E3DB1631F933A0575BC0A9639C8B63> (Accessed 11 May 2015).

Tierney, K., C. Beve and E. Kuligowski (2006) 'Metaphors Matter: Disaster Myths, Media Frames, and Their Consequences in Hurricane Katrina,' *American Academy of Political and Social Science*, March: 604.

Wahlberg, M. (2008) *Documentary Time: Film and Phenomenology*, Minneapolis, MN: University of Minnesota Press.

Woods, C. (1998) *Development Arrested: The Blues and Plantation Power in the Mississippi Delta*, New York, NY: Verso.

———. (2009) 'Katrina's World: Blues, Bourbon, and the Return to the Source,' *American Quarterly*, 61(3):427–453.

Žižek, S. (2006) 'Kate's Choice, or The Materialism of Henry James,' in S. Žižek (ed.), *Lacan: The Silent Partners*, 288–311, New York, NY: Verso.

16 Re-Imagining the anonymous city
Defatalizing the digital present through analog photography

Cliff Davidson

Urban centers – cities – contain more than half the people on earth. The word 'contain,' however, is used cautiously: cities are more than just ecological places boundaried and containing. Cities are vertices of spatial and temporal social practices (Castells 2009; Harvey 1990) constitutive of and constituted by the practices within (de Certeau 1984). Though mentioned dichotomously, time and space do not exist in isolation; they are inextricably interwoven and codependent (Massey 1994). This combination of spatiality (geographies) and temporality (time) – 'timespace' as Jon May and Nigel Thrift call it – is part of contemporary society, whereby the 'totalizations' of rationalized space and time control the practices (social acts) of everyday life (de Certeau 1984; Harvey 1990; May and Thrift 2001). Timespace is implicit in the fatalization of individual agency.

In a similar vein, digital photography has subsumed analog photographic practice and removed creative agency. The rationalization of spatiality and temporality that applies to the city can be applied to photography, with similar consequences. As Susan Sontag notes, cameras have become so automated that they require no skill or expert knowledge; while her comment predates the digitalization of photography, technological advancements only accentuate this point (Sontag 1973). With digital photography's continual production and erasure of images, the photograph's once temporal fluidity as superimposition of past and reality (present) (Barthes 2000:76–77) is compressed into a singular persistent present. Timespace is also implicit in the fatalization of photographic creativity.

The anonymous city – anonymous in the sense of erasure of individuality, of making generic, of universality across geographical time (Koolhaas 1995) – and digital photography fatalize general social acts and creative expression. Individual agency gets recapitulated as bureaucratic, institutionalized, sequential practice (Castells 2009). Cities fatalize agency. However, it is possible to expunge the anonymous city and digital present's anti-agentic chronology by subverting their fatalistic, restrictive nature and reintegrating individual agency through active resistance. This active resistance is the concern of this chapter.[1]

Defatalization: The reintegration of agency over fatalism

Defatalization has roots in fatalism and fate. In the context of this chapter, there are two connected but distinct interpretations of fatalism: as attitudinal (individual) and as structural (systemic). Fatalism, on the attitudinal level, is an *acceptance* of a causative chain of happenings whereas determinism, which is similar to but different from fatalism, is an *anticipation* that encourages activity – fatalistic acceptance implies passivity (Masaryk 1994:103). Thus, to the individual, fatalism conceives everything has an appointed outcome (Scott and Marshall 2009): it is a perceived lack of control over agentic abilities, an acceptance of an individual's incapacity for purposefully active decision making as influenced by external structures.

Structures (systems) can also be fatalistic. In *Suicide*, Émile Durkheim articulates fatalistic suicide as a product of cumulative excessive oppression, that is, suicide as a result of structural influences on individual choices (Durkheim 1951). Fatalistic suicide is an act undertaken when regulation of an individual's 'futures are pitilessly blocked and passions violently choked by oppressive discipline' (Harriford and Thompson 2008: 167). The amount of oppressive discipline only partially contributes to attitudinal fatalism; the experience of social constraint as *external to the individual* – structural – and *inevitable* exacerbates the sense of fatalism within the individual (Lockwood 1992). Structures can enforce fatalism on individuals, annihilating their agency and regulating their social acts in timespace.

Fatalization is a continual process of controlling structural influences over individual agency and, at the same time, the initiation of a metanarrative of acceptance within the collective conscious of individuals. Fatality – as offspring of fate – insinuates death, manifest as social death in the city and creative death in photography. As such, defatalization is a subversion of structural influence and individual acceptance of fate, whereby agency is reified at the individual level. Defatalization dismantles the metastructure of control and acceptance and engenders an individual narrative, one that invokes purposeful agency within individual social acts. If fatality is death, defatalization is bringing life back into that which was dead.

Timespace and the continual present

Temporality and spatiality are basic categories of human existence intimately intertwined and controlling. Time is the 'basic mechanism through which social acts, organizations, institutions, cultures and social structures exist and operate' (Maines 1987: 303). As such, time and space are fused into a singular timespace (Harvey 1990; May and Thrift 2001). May and Thrift contend timespace is multiple, dynamic, and highly uneven; this chapter collapses their construct into a singular timespace (May and Thrift 2001). The granularity of their division negates an overriding contemporary neoliberal metanarrative of control.

Timespace in the context of this chapter relies on timespace compression. Contemporary society is the intersection of shrinking space and shortened time horizons as a result of neoliberal capitalism's push for a world market. Harvey states, 'The incentive to create the world market, to reduce spatial barriers, and to annihilate space through time is omni-present' (1990: 232) and 'time horizons shorten to the point where the present is all there is . . . so we have [had] to learn to cope with an overwhelming sense of compression of our spatial and temporal worlds' (1990: 240). Hence, timespace compression creates a perpetual present that annihilates the past. Timespace is the spatial and temporal locus of the now, the present as it nullifies the present's transition into the past, creating a singular social temporality – the perpetual present.

The anonymous city and fatalistic timespace

Cities are unfolding stories that encompass, create, and perpetuate neoliberal ideologies through spatial constructs and temporal practices. Within the ecological confines of the urban, citizens course through the streets as blood through veins giving the body/city life. Like the body, the city is constructed to be systematic. Efficient. Predictable. This efficiency and predictability – rationalization – establishes cities as generic and universally pedestrian across geographies, whereby the individual is constrained to paths, routes, and trajectories that encase and direct the *where* and the *how* of mobility – an enforced totalizing guide. Koolhaas notes, 'The Generic City is fractal, an endless repetition of the same simple structural module' (1995: 1251). The city is at once internally and externally generic; the anonymous city can be Mumbai, London, New York, Tokyo, Mexico City, or any city in its rationalized controlled and controlling spatial form.

Connected to spatial control is the concept of social time, which Manuel Castells contends is shaped through bureaucracy and institutionalized control over sequenced practices (Castells 2009). Time, being bound with space (timespace), abides by the same neoliberal ideologies of efficiency and predictability. As the city has become more structured and constraining, time has been torn from its moorings in the biological. The city de-sequences temporal practices, annihilating the concept of past, present, and future, replacing it with a timeless time (Castells 2009). The timespace of the city has reconstructed singular linear temporality with a palimpsest of individual incongruous temporalities figured into a continual present. The city also controls the *when* of mobility. Day and night become one: as the day-worker trudges through the streets home, the night-worker pulses from home to work. Alternate temporalities of the day- and the night-worker hold the same meaning for the individual but are at once also the opposite of the other (day as night, night as day); time means everything and nothing (Harvey 1990).

In the city, individuals follow fatalistic, predetermined patterns, immersed in constrictive and oppressive timespace. These paths are processes of forgetting; the path that is 'visible, . . . has the effect of making invisible the operation that made it possible' (de Certeau 1984: 97). Cities are anonymous and anonymizing: 'Instead of specific memories, the association the Generic City mobilizes are general memories, memories of memories: if not all memories at the same time, than at least an abstract, token memory, a déjà vu that never ends, generic memory' (Koolhaas 1995: 1257). Individual identity is obliterated, and social death occurs as the city anonymizes the social acts within. The generic city is, according

Re-Imagining the anonymous city 263

to Koolhaas, 'nothing but a reflection of present need and present ability. It is a city without history' (1995: 1250). The history-less anonymous city alienates and anonymizes the individual within its totalizing fatalistic continually present timespace.

The *flâneur*/photographer: Defatalizing the where and how of the city

Social death, anonymity, and fatalism are not inevitable: the city and the singular temporality of the present timespace can be defatalized. Disrupting and annihilating the efficiency and predictability of a singular timespace are already frequent. Subversive tactics used by the *flâneur* reconfigure the oppressive city; alternate spaces of critique are created in the interstitial timespaces surrounding what was, what is, and what will be (de Certeau 1984). The *flâneur* is an urban explorer and investigator, a 'kaleidoscope gifted with consciousness... reproducing the multiplicity of life and the flickering grace of all the elements of life. He is an "I" with an insatiable appetite for the "non-I"' (Baudelaire 1995: 9). Benjamin says, 'To the *flâneur*, his city is... no longer native ground. It represents for him a theatrical display, an arena' (1999: 347). The *flâneur* uses the city, disrupts the fatalistic scene, and reconfigures it.

As a deliberately aimless pedestrian, the *flâneur* is an ambler whose attention tends toward the aesthetically pleasing. The interconnectedness of wanderer and aesthete has led to the enmeshing of the *flâneur* with the street photographer. Victor Fournel made the early connection between *flânerie* (the act of being a *flâneur*) and photography, noting the *flâneur* is a wandering and impassioned

Figure 16.1 Happy lucky chow time
Source: Author

daguerreotype (daguerreotypes are an early form of photograph) (Fournel 1867: 267). With the camera's insinuation in the act of wandering, the street photographer and *flâneur* are melded. Susan Sontag notes:

> The photographer is an armed version of the solitary walker reconnoitering, stalking, cruising the urban inferno, the voyeuristic stroller who discovers the city as a landscape of voluptuous extremes. Adept of the joys of watching, connoisseur of empathy, the *flâneur* finds the world 'picturesque'.
>
> (Sontag 1973: 55)

The photographer, through the praxis and product of photography, deconstructs the city, reconstitutes the paths and trajectories, and recontextualizes rhythms to alter timespace to his/her own needs. The photographer invades publics, disrupts scenes, and alters spatial and temporal fixities.

The camera: Defatalizing the when of the city

The camera is the modern *flâneur*'s tool of subversion. Cameras are meant to capture a moment in time, and as such, time and photography are intimately related. Roland Barthes remembers, 'I recall that at first photographic implements were related to techniques of cabinetmaking and the machinery of precision: cameras in short, were clocks for seeing' (Barthes 2000:15). Cameras were originally available only to the wealthy, but as they became less costly they became tools to democratize photography, making it easier and more efficient to capture images.

However, technology has advanced and been co-opted by neoliberal ideologies similar to those of the city: efficiency, predictability, and the generic. More specifically, digital cameras, though key in democratizing photography, have created a glut of sameness in produced images. Digital photography is generic, fatalistic, and anonymous.

Analog photography: Defatalizing the digital present

Digital and analog photography capture an image that can be reproduced relatively easily. Digital photography, however, is about efficiency and the compression of time. Press the shutter, the digital camera auto focuses, takes the image, and stores to memory. Almost instantaneously, the image is shared globally across timespace. The image is always in the present only to be annihilated in place of the next image in the present. Take, for example, SnapChat, an application that unveils an image to a viewer, only to have it eradicated within ten seconds after viewing. Digital photography lives in the continual present – a perpetual reconfiguring of the now at the cost of the erasure of historicity. Further, the digital rejects creative agency formulating an 'ideal' through computerized calculation. Auto exposure, auto focus, auto bracketing, and auto white-balance all fatalize photographic creativity; the camera 'produces' a photo, leaving the photographer in a Marxist sense as merely a worker in a simplified division of labor. Creative agency is annihilated.

Figure 16.2 Table for none
Source: Author

If the digital present fatalizes photographic creativity, then analog is the inverse, the defatalization of the digital photographic timespace. The digital present reduces photos to a matrix of ones and zeroes, amassing a volume of meaningless similarity; images blend into one, taken not by a photographer but by a box with a light sensor. Film photography reintegrates the photographer into the act of image production and annihilates the generic of the digital present. The act of using an analog device subverts the digital now, reduces efficiency, and reconfigures photographic practice. Whereas digital photography takes a continual perpetual present for granted, analog photography reifies the past and present as distinct temporalities. This reintegration of time gives life to the individual, allows creative agency, and expunges the generic. Analog photography annihilates temporal and spatial fixities inherent in the praxis of digital photography.

The photograph: Defatalizing timespace

Similar to, and as an extension of, the act of analog photography is the photographic print. Inherently, images are violent; they murder the real according to Jean Baudrillard (Baudrillard 2002). However, the violence produced from an analog negative is much more cataclysmic to the simulacra that passes itself off as reality than that of the digital image whose violence is aesthetic plainness and perpetual self-replacement in a continual present. The negative and resulting print create a tangibility that digital images cannot reproduce. This tangibility jettisons neoliberal ideals of efficiency, predictability, and the generic, leaving behind a

Figure 16.3 Worst hiding spot ever
Source: Author

Figure 16.4 Disconnected
Source: Author

Figure 16.5 Country house, city house
Source: Author

Figure 16.6 Sketchy
Source: Author

Figure 16.7 Welcome to Chinatown – keep right
Source: Author

singular unpredictable image to be interpreted by the viewer, a tangible slice of a temporal fixity that is not continually present. When catastrophe struck a home in the past, one of the first things saved was the photo album; now, the digital photo album is forgotten and discarded as insignificant. Digital photos are disposable memories.

Sontag notes, 'Photographs, which cannot themselves explain anything, are inexhaustible invitations to deduction, speculation, and fantasy' (1973: 23). A photograph freezes time and creates a timelessness – a memory anew for each successive viewer. A tangible memory reintegrates the lost historicity of the digital present; the historicity of the photograph's content is reified. The temporality of a memory as it crosses timespace instantiates the possibility of a past and creates a new memory: 'What the Photograph reproduces to infinity has occurred only once: the Photograph mechanically repeats what could never be repeated existentially' (Barthes 2000: 4). Additionally, 'to take a photograph is to participate in another person's (or thing's) mortality, vulnerability, mutability. Precisely by slicing out this moment and freezing it, all photographs testify to time's relentless melt' (Sontag 1973: 11). The photograph is a dynamic constant that is contested and contesting of the present, an exhausted, kinetic, and potential energy.

Conclusion

The city creates a timespace stuck in a continual present that controls and directs everyday rhythms and trajectories. The photographer and the praxis and product of photography re-imagine the city, break down oppressive constructs, and defatalize the urban and the systematic and generic reproduction of universal nothingness and timeless time. Analog photography is about the subversion of the everyday, the capturing of non-scenes, non-places, and non-things in a manner that blurs the line of (in)tangibility. The continual present of digital photography is reconfigured by analog photography's ability to freeze time through the tangibility of the printed photograph and through the reintegration of the photographer. Film photography defatalizes the present, the digital, and neoliberal ideology by breathing social life back into the socially dead anonymous city.

The photos capture moments of the city that are often forgotten and re-imagine the anonymous through analog photography. These images intercede and annihilate the dominant discourse of the efficient, predictable, and generic, representing the fatalistic timespace of the contemporary city. Though the city is constricting and inhospitable, this often goes unnoticed or unchallenged. Loneliness, anomie, and alienation are accepted as necessary within the neoliberal discourse. These photographs reintegrate the photographer, recapitulate the communal, and replace the fatalistic timespace of the city by de-anonymizing individuals, spaces, and objects while insinuating their beingness into their surroundings. In this re-imagining, existence is elevated out of hidden nothingness into a visible phenomenon – a defatalization of the digital present through analog photography.

Figure 16.8 The new/old tears
Source: Author

Figure 16.9 Lonely short board
Source: Author

Figure 16.10 Spadina Dundas snow smile
Source: Author

Figure 16.11 99¢ hot dogs
Source: Author

Figure 16.12 New Year's subway pigeon
Source: Author

Note

1 Some images and text in this chapter were originally used in InTensions Academic E-Journal issue 5, (De) Fatalizing the Present and Creating Radical Alternatives, available from: http://www.yorku.ca/intent/issue5/photos/cliffdavidson/cliffdavidson.php. All images were taken with 35mm analog cameras using black and white film that was hand developed and scanned by the author.

Bibliography

Barthes, R. (2000) *Camera Lucida: Reflections on Photography*, London, UK: Vintage.
Baudelaire, C. (2nd edn1995) *The Painter of Modern Life: And Other Essays*, Jonathan Mayne (trans.), London, UK: Phaidon Press.
Baudrillard, J. (2002) *The Violence of The Image*, Leuk-Stadt, Switzerland: The European Graduate School. Online. Available HTTP: <http://www.egs.edu/faculty/jean-baudrillard/articles/the-violence-of-the-image/> (Accessed 3 April 2015).
Benjamin, W. (1999) *The Arcades Project*, Rolf Tiedemann (ed.), Cambridge, MA: Harvard University Press.
Castells, M. (2009) *Communication Power*, Oxford, UK: Oxford University Press.
De Certeau, M. (1984) *The Practice of Everyday Life*, London, UK: University of California Press.
Durkheim, É. (1951) *Suicide: A Study in Sociology*, New York, NY: Free Press.
Fournel, V. (1867) *Ce Qu'on Voit Dane Les Rues de Paris*, Paris: E. Dentu.
Harriford, D. and B. Thompson (2008) *When the Center Is on Fire*, Austin, TX: University of Texas Press.
Harvey, D. (1990) *The Condition of Postmodernity: An Enquiry into the Origins of Cultural Change*, Cambridge, MA: Blackwell.
Koolhaas, R. (1995) 'The Generic City', in J. Sigler (ed.), *S,M,L,XL*, New York, NY: Monicelli Press.
Lockwood, D. (1992) *Solidarity and Schism: 'The Problem of Disorder' in Durkheimian and Marxist Sociology*, Oxford, UK: Oxford University Press.
Maines, D. R. (1987) 'The Significance of Temporality for the Development of Sociological Theory,' *The Sociological Quarterly*, 28(3):303–311.
Masaryk, T. G. (1994) *Constructive Sogiological Theory*, A. Woolfolk and J. B. Imber (eds.), New Brunswick, NJ: Transaction Publishers.
Massey, D. (1994) *Space, Place, and Gender*, Minneapolis, MN: University of Minnesota Press.
May, J. and N. Thrift (2001) *Timespace: Geographies of Temporality*, New York, NY: Routledge.
Scott, J. and G. Marshall (eds) (2009) *'Fatalism', A Dictionary of Sociology*, New York, NY: Oxford University Press.
Sontag, S. (1973) *On Photography*, London, UK: Penguin.

Section III

Poetic interventions for social transformation

17 Freedom telling on time
The Arab Revolt's poems

Nathalie Handal

Freedom

The Arab Revolt 2011

The story begins
with a song –
it's stubborn,
breaks air into history;
for a minute
it's quiet to allow everyone in,
and then it raises to celebrate voices,
clears its throat,
says:
We will bury the smoke that blinds us,
plant our soul on every page,
we will divide our pain into towers
and fill our hands with rain,
we will arrive on time every day
to chase you away,
we will no longer be afraid
of what makes us shiver under the sun
we will leave our names in every teahouse
our messages at the bottom of every cup.
Light will no longer be illegal
nor will hope –
even the guards will count
the scars on their tongue
and prepare to heal,
even the children will keep
homeland in the mirror
and prepare to see,
even the women will turn
the fire inside the door
off, and prepare to live.

We will never whisper again.
There is evidence, there is evidence,
that now we can hear
the sounds that lift freedom
across a continent,
and say, Salaam to you,
welcome to my country.

Radio Gaza

Morning in the Streets

6:21 a.m.

When will we see what the sun can be,
when will the road not be closed,
when will winter turn snow into a river on the lips,
what secrets have they hidden in the webs, what echoes
open a fragile hour?
Is this the first time
I see a ghazel
or is it my reflection dying?

7:00 a.m.

I knew I was dying
when I heard his cry –
40 years ago –
nothing has changed,
except things got worse.
Holy water on my feet,
Music unable to distract the
noise in my mind.
Maybe when we ache
shadows become a full moon.

8:17 a.m.

At the graveyard.
He was there.
But I couldn't find him,
his soul, or his tomb?
I sliced the fog
to make a river.

9:07 a.m.

I carve you inside my body,
try to tell the world
what I have seen

but all I find is what's empty,
my mouth unable to reveal the sin
you have left.

10:02 a.m.

I heard two gunshots.
A body crying.
I wanted to call for help
but my feet were under
the ruins of a building.
I shut my eyes for a second,
unable to distinguish
the pain in my body
with the guilt of not helping the baby –
you see, she was barely two, I am ten.
I closed my eyes again –
water filled my bed, and dreams too.
I didn't want to know
what was going to happen next.
I never found my house,
but home always has a way to find you,
I've learned.

10:30 a.m.

Souraya (about her husband, Kareem)

We practice war out loud.
He fights his breath,
wants it gone –
he can't stand the blood
around his bed,
the gunshots, the slamming gates.
He wants a judgment
but no one can explain
what we need –
maybe everyone's afraid.
He looks away.
I tell him anyway, *ana bahebak.*
Maybe time is to blame –
it tells us to wait
when our bodies can't.
Maybe that's why we pray.

11:04 a.m.

He thought,
since a part of him

will never be found,
why wonder
if forever is a word,
if the heart is ready for the soul,
if music without instruments
is a way to starve,
if saints disagree
when they replace
regret with pleasure,
if forgiveness is just a shadow split into two,
if being
is simply being,
believing
simply believing,
seeing
simply an illusion
to distract us from finding,
what takes history apart
to rearrange it
into myth?
Yes, that photo is graying, but it still holds
the window open.

11:59 a.m.

When we can't distinguish
the field from the sea,
our voice from that of ghosts,
war will fill our body with ash
and death will be audacious.

A drawing of breathing

I draw a mouth,
draw lips;
I draw a forehead,
draw lines;
I draw eyes last –
there was nothing to see
behind the map of the heart
but a disfigured face.
I breathe
a child moves
breathe
a child cries
breathe

a mother kneels
breathe
a father hangs
breathe
an ocean splits into death camps
breathe
a house collapses
breathe
a tree is uprooted
breathe
a field is stolen

and on my last breath, I see
an old mattress,
mold and trash,
the roof caving in,
and there you are,
sitting on a chair.
Can you still see me love,
standing by the window?
The walls have fallen between us –
singing helps me chase away
the fear that have turned
wings into broken feathers.
They parted our cities –
history will crucify that myth,
but it was too early back then
to understand the form it would take,
too early to know that
the world we were entering
was darker than what we imagined
darkness could be.
Can they heal the gods
they have offended?
As for us,
should we blame the flame
that never came to save us, or kill us?

Guide to being Palestinian

If you are darker than most,
have a beard or wear a hijab,
it's wise not to speak too loud
when you reach an airport or any exit.

If your father begged for his house,
was dragged away,
and returned the next day
without his eyes or his honor,
don't judge him.

If your mother told you to watch
his humiliation,
it wasn't to hurt you
but to help you
understand where you are from.

If you are exiled
don't expect an open field,
a smile, a new home –
most likely you will always be a stranger.
Stand close enough to see their eyes,
far enough to protect your heart.

If you think you can write
about all the days you are missing
in your town or city,
think again –
it's another's myth now,
and if you are afraid of forgetfulness,
apathy is even more dangerous.

If you take your longing
everywhere you go,
keep the keys to your old house
even if it's inhabited by others –
it's a clue you should also keep everything else:
the photos, the art, the folklore, and even the stones.

If you laugh and feel guilty,
love and feel like you shouldn't,
remember all aching begins with desire.

If your ancestors gave you a map of your country
but didn't give you one for dispossession,
weave the distances with your history.

If our father calls you father – *baba* –
when you are his son or daughter,
asks you, *you know the name of your birthplace?*

answer in
even if you are told to speak it
only at home – for your safety.
And if the day comes
while far away
you are asked,
who gave you that name?
remember what matters
is that the land knows
your face, your voice,
the origin of your silence –
and that, what's holy is alive
in who you are,
not in who
you are told you should be.

18 Tsitsi Jaji

Blunt balm[1]

    The balm
    served up
    in Gilead
    will heal
    will shrink
    will shrug
    off the
    losses. Profit
    made elsewhere
    means
    that $300 for a bottle of the pills in India/
    Less for improv. Hep cats could lay it on ya . . .
    $10 a day or less for Sovaldi.
    That's 1%. Not the.
    That's 1% of what it costs for the Balm in Gilead.
    Baby baby baby baby Babylon.
    By the river baby lay me down down Babylon chaunt.
    Gilead can blunt criticism concerning 91/half/less/millions.
    Less than. Less grumbling. Less mumbling. Less never say
    a word. A mumbling. Never said it. Never said a mumbling word.

    Left behind: China, Brazil, Turkey.
    China plate.
    Brazil nut.
    Turkey time.
    Tacky. Tactless. The tactic is
    less about money
    and more blunt.
    Less here,
    more there.
    Less is more, then.

130 million > 350 to 500 thousand.
As in: More than 130 million people are infected with the hepatitis C virus, and 350,000 to
500,000 people die from the infections each year, according to the World Health
Organization. Whoah. Ebola, lalalalala bamba. Bowling for
combined sales, lurid scenes, blood seeping.
It just doesn't make copy.

Malaria. Yawn. Hepatitis. Yawn. AIDS. Yawn.
On the other hand: STEM.
Eyes light up for math.
Eyes light up at math.
Eyes light up at the math.
Math madness.
Big Money, money:
maker: The version of hepatitis C that is most prevalent in India requires that patients take
Sovaldi for 24 weeks, meaning that they would need six bottles for a total cost of $1,800, Mr.
Alton said. Gilead will receive a royalty of 7% of sales of the generic versions. Chaching 7 per 100
for 18 of those Benjamins. All about the. 70 and 560 and chachingalingling. Dang.
630 in his head, Mr. Alton said. Babam. Kazam. Badabang badaboo. Besides. Sovaldi is on
pace to become one of the world's top-selling drugs, with more than $10 billion in sales this year.
In the U.S., a 12-week-supply costs $84,000, which
some
critics
say
is
too
high
for a lifesaving drug. Gilead has said dang, baby, it's cheaper than those
treatments you used to try, and they didn't even work, plus dang baby,
it's cheaper than a liver transplant and dang this balm is 90% guaranteed
moneyback make you feel like a million bucks. Or at least balmy in 12
weeks.
90>60. Undeniably.
There is
a balm
in Gilead.

Ain't all wounds can be made whole.
Made whole.
Made whole.

Dust to dust[2]

There are women left who have no rage in their wrists
As they slice greens or skin tomatoes towards mealtime.
Their husbands are at the beer-gardens with
Family money – what would amount to a bag of beans
Or soap bars.

There are women who keep both lips quietly touching,
Even as they gesture a fly from their brow, and
Swallow the mucus of a chilled afternoon.
They remember vaguely when love began
And the commonplace was not where they were going.

A woman is born knowing how it happens,
Her heart turning to dust as fine as cinnamon.
It has to do with disease, redder lips,
City restaurants, the cost of deodorant.

Indeed, it so happens that their men are condemned
To spend the rest of their lives staggering home
To fuck a corpse who smells of kitchen duty
And an unwillingness to preen for a wanderer.
These women wear long, brown dresses.
They rarely hurry across busy intersections,
They move as if, inside them, they carry a heavy mound.

First published in **Bitter Oleander**, *Volume 9 Number 1 (2003)*

Notes

1. Blunt Balm, copyright 2014 by Tsitsi Jaji, was published online in issue 18 of Eleven Eleven at http://elevenelevenjournal.com/2014/12/11/tsitsi-jaji/.
2. Dust to Dust, copyright 2003 by Tsitsi Jaji, was published online at http://www.poetry-internationalweb.net/pi/site/poem/item/23127.

19 *From the Bed & Breakfast Notebooks*[1]

Alexandra Handal

From the Bed & Breakfast Notebooks   289

Film transcript

Text

She walked me to the terminal
She led me to a corner room
She held open the curtain with one hand
She watched me from outside the room

Louis Safieh (audio recording)

I think it was afternoon. I don't remember exactly. But it was the moment when the Jews began
bombing Musrara from all sides, with hundreds of mortar bombs. My father and mother decided to take my sister and me quickly to the Old City.

Text

She told me to take off my coat
She told me to take off my belt
She told me to take off my shoes
She told me to take off my watch
and put it on the wooden shelf
She came inside the room
She closed the curtain behind her
She asked me to turn around
and face the wall
I heard her put on her gloves
She slowly lifted the bottom of my pants
before putting them back down
I could feel her thin rubber gloves brush my ankles

Ari (audio recording)

We left our home a few weeks before 1948. Because many people, they start running away, you
know, and we stayed the last people in here and my father told me, 'My son, we have to leave
here now. There is nobody around our neighbourhood'. We are so afraid. Because the Israeli
militia, they were entering and going on our home. So, my father was so afraid because he was
injured during the First World War, he said: 'We have to leave now'. On the last day, on the 15th
of May, I went back to the police to work and the police officer told me: 'You have to leave now,
because we are leaving Palestine in a few hours'. So I left the police station in Jerusalem, I went
to the Old City of Jerusalem and then the war broke, 1948 war.

Text

Her gloved fingers pressed firmly against the fabric of my trousers
She moved her hands along each leg

I had to slightly spread my legs open
until my upper thighs no longer touched

Ari (audio recording)

Not even one family remains here, they all left this area in 1948, I remember. Then, a
honeymooner, also part of our family, they were to get married, you know, and prepared his home
– I'll show you now – and the war broke and they left everything, new furniture and they were thinking they would come back after. They took the key of the apartment, you know, and never
came back. I'll show you the home.

Text

I remember her hands feeling my shoulders
She told me to hold my hair up
She stroked my neck with the tips of her fingers
I could not feel her skin
It was safely protected by her latex gloves

Ahmad Muna (audio recording)

On the day Israel occupied East Jerusalem, we fled to a room given to us by the church. We
stayed there for four days. After we were allowed back, we discovered that our house was
ransacked and our furniture, clothes, food everything was stolen. We asked the soldiers the
reason for all this and they said: 'This is war, be happy you're safe'. Then another soldier came in
with his gun and ordered all women to take off all their jewelry, earrings, bracelets, necklaces.
He took it all and left.

Text

She asked me to turn around and face her
Her head reached my chin, her body as round and curvaceous as mine
Her hair was wrapped in a bun, her freckled face like my cousin A'idah's
white blouse, grey pants, black boots
just like the others

George Baramki (audio recording)

Route 1 was not there, it was a little street called Shara Sa'ad wa-Sa'id. And after '67, they
removed the barbed wire. The borderline was in the road itself.

Text

She rubbed my belly with both hands in a circular-like motion
She placed her hand around my breast
She asked me if I was wearing a wired bra

May Giacaman (audio recording)

I was twelve, I was twelve, so I remember. After '67, we came into here and we visited the house
and there were Jews coming from Arab states who lived here, so we went into the house and
that's it. Of course, nobody took his house back, but people wanted to see. This is when the pain
started.

Text

I held my breath
She moved her hands along my neck
then my face then the back of my ears
Our eyes never met
She looked at me as I put back my shoes
This time we were alone in a corner room
unlike the last time when her friend watched us
unlike the last time when I had to put down my trousers
It was even scarier that time around
She walked me to the departure gate
I never got the chance to ask her how that made her feel

Ahmad Muna and an Israeli woman: (video recording)

woman: Ah, wars, wars. Ah, peace, peace.
man: Peace. What peace, when you take my home.
woman: Yes, peace.
man: Where is the peace?
woman: There is a peace.
man: Give us our home and there is a peace.

woman: It's awful that you see me now live in your house and, and it's yours, it's awful.
man: Its ache for me.
woman: It's completely awful.

Text

I wonder if she will ever remember me
I will never forget her

Note

1   Film director, writer, photographer and sound designer: Alexandra Handal; editor and sound mixer: Boris Gerrets; producer: Alexandra Handal. Supported by Chelsea College of Art and Design, The University of the Arts London, UK.

Bibliography

Abdel-Malek, A. (1968) *Egypt: Military Society*, New York, NY: Random House.
Abourahme, N. (2011) 'Spatial Collisions and Discordant Temporalities: Everyday Life between Camp and Checkpoint,' *International Journal of Urban and Regional Research*, 1:453–461.
Adam, B. (1990) *Time and Social Theory*, Philadelphia, PA: Temple University Press.
Adler, E. (2008) 'The Spread of Security Communities: Communities of Practice, Self-Restraint, and NATO's Post Cold War Transformation', *European Journal of International Relations*, 14(2):195–230.
Adler, E. and V. Pouliot (eds.) (2011a) *International Practices*, Cambridge, UK: Cambridge University Press.
———. (2011b), 'International Practices,' *International Theory*, 3(1):1–36.
African Development Bank Group. (2011) *AfDB to Incorporate Biomass and Bio-energy into New Energy Strategy Daily the Pak Banker*. Abidjan: African Development Bank Group. Online. Available HTTP: < http://www.afdb.org/en/news-and-events/article/afdb-to-incorporate-biomass-and-bio-energy-into-new-energy-strategy-7938/> (Accessed 25 April 2011).
Agamben, G. (2004) *The Open: Man and Animal*, K. Attell (trans.), Stanford, CA: Stanford University Press.
———. (2007) *Infancy and History: On the Destruction of Experience*, London, New York: Verso.
Agathangelou, A.M. (2009) 'Necro- (neo) Colonizations and Economies of Blackness: Of Slaughters, 'Accidents,' 'Disasters' and Captive Flesh', in S. Nair and S. Biswas (eds.), *International Relations and States of Exception: Margins, Peripheries and Excluded Bodies*, 186–209, New York, NY: Routledge.
———. (2011a) 'Bodies to the Slaughter: Slavery, Reconstruction, Fanon's Combat Breath, and Wrestling for Life,' *Somatechnics Journal*, 1(1):209–248.
———. (2011b) 'Making Anew an Arab Regional Order? On Poetry, Sex, and Revolution,' *Globalizations*, 8(5):581–594.
———. (2013) 'Slavery Remains in Reconstruction and Development,' in M.K. Pasha (ed.), *Globalization, Difference, and Human Security*, 156–169, New York, NY: Routledge.
———. (2014) 'Wither Anarchy?: Harvesting the 'Global' Bio-tech Body, Indian Markets and Biomedical Technologies,' in M. Mayer et al. (eds.), *The Global Politics of Science and Technology – Vol. 2, Global Power Shift*, 1–23, Berlin, HG: Springer-Verlag.
———. (2015) 'Fanon on Decolonization and Revolution: Bodies and Dialectics,' *Globalizations*, 12(4):1–19.

Bibliography

Agathangelou, A.M. and L.H.M. Ling (2009) *Transforming World Politics; From Empire to Multiple Worlds*, New York, NY: Routledge.

Agence France Presse (2009) 'China Now Taking Climate Change Seriously: EU's Barroso,' Brussels, Belgium: Agence France Presse (26 June 2009).

Agosín, M. (2003) *At the Threshold of Memory: New and Selected Poems*, Buffalo, NY: White Pine Press.

Algeria. (2008) 'Paper 1', *Ad Hoc Working Group on Long-term Cooperative Action under the Convention, 7.* Poznan, Poland: United Nations Framework Convention on Climate Change. Online. Available HTTP: <http://unfccc.int/files/kyoto_ protocol/application/pdf/boliviabap08122008.pdf.> (Accessed 28 March 2015).

Allison, A. (2009) 'The Cool Brand, Affective Activism and Japanese Youth,' *Theory Culture Society*, 26(2–3):89–111.

———. (2012) 'Ordinary Refugees: Social Precarity and Soul in 21st Century Japan,' *Anthropological Quarterly*, 85(2):345–370.

Althusser, L. (1972) 'Ideology and the Ideological State Apparatu', in L. Althusser (ed.), *Lenin and Philosophy*, 127–186, London, UK: Monthly Review Press.

Amin, S. (1978) *The Arab Nation: Nationalism and Class Struggles*, London, UK: Zed Books.

Amir, M. (2013) 'The Making of a Void Sovereignty: Political implications of the military checkpoints in the West Bank,' *Environment and Planning D: Space and Society*, 31:227–244.

Amnesty International (2006) *Closing Eyes to Human Rights Leaves Asylum-Seekers and Migrants at Risk*, Amnesty International.

———. (2009) *Amnesty International Country Report: Human Rights in People's Democratic Republic of Algeria*, Amnesty International.

———. (2010) *Amnesty International Country Report: Egypt*, Amnesty International.

Anderson, B. (1991) *Imagined Communities: Reflections on the Origin and Spread of Nationalism, Revised and Extended Edition*, London, UK: Verso.

Aoki, H. (2003) 'Homelessness in Osaka: Globalisation, Yoseba and Disemployment,' *Urban Studies*, 40:361–378.

Apostolidis, P. (2010) *Breaks in the Chain: What Immigrant Workers Can Teach America about Democracy*, Minneapolis, MN: University of Minnesota Press.

Appleby, J.O. (1978) *Economic Thought and Ideology in Seventeenth-Century England*, Princeton, NJ: Princeton University Press.

Aradau, C. and Van Munste, R. (2007) 'Governing Terrorism through Risk: Taking Precautions, (Un)Knowing the Future,' *European Journal of International Relations*, 13(1):89–115.

Arai, A.G. (2005) 'The Neo-liberal Subject of Lack and Potential: Developing "The Frontier Within" and Creating a Reserve Army of Labor in 21st century Japan', *Rhizomes*, 10. Online. Available HTTP: <http://www.rhizomes.net/issue10/ arai.htm> (Accessed 6 March 2012).

Arias A. (2013) 'Indigenous Women at War: Discourses on Revolutionary Combat,' *A Contra Corriente*, 10(3):108–140.

Ariès, P. (1962) *Centuries of Childhood*, R. Baldick (trans.), New York, NY: Alfred Knopf.

Associated Press. (2007) New Alarms Are Rung on Perils of Global Warming, *New York Times*, February 27. Online. Available HTTP: <http://www.nytimes.com/2007/02/27/health/27iht-climate.4739361.html?_r=0>.

Attali, J. (1985) *Noise: The Political Economy of Music*, Brian Massumi (trans.), Minneapolis, MN: University of Minnesota Press.

Augustine (1984) *Augustine of Hippo: Selected Writings*, Mahwah, NJ: Paulist Press.
Ayubi, N. (1995) *Overstating the State: Politics and Society in the Middle East*, New York, NY: IB Tauris.
al-*Ayyam* (2009) *'Fayyad yu'rb 'an asafahi wa y'kid tasmim al-sulta 'ala fard al-nizam wa siyadit al-qanun'*, Monday June 1st, 2009.
Azuma, H. (2009) *Otaku: Japan's Database Animals*, J. E. Abel and S. Kono (trans.), Minneapolis, MN: University of Minnesota Press.
Baker, R. K. (1983) 'Review of *Slavery and Social Death: A Comparative Study*', *Worldview Magazine,* 26(4):20–21.
Balagoon, K. (2003) *A Soldier's Story: Writings by a Revolutionary New Afrikan Anarchist*, Montreal, Canada: Kersplebedeb Publishing.
Baldauf, S. (2004) 'Bhopal gas tragedy lives on, 20 years later', *The Christian Science Monitor.* Online. Available HTTP: <http://www.csmonitor.com/2004/0504/ p07s 01-wosc.html> (Accessed 11 May 2015).
Balibar, E. (1996) 'Subjection and Subjectivation', in J. Copjec (ed.) *Supposing the Subject*, 1–15, New York, NY: Verso.
Ban, K.-M. (2007) '*Address to the High-Level Segment of the UN Climate Change Conference*,' Bali, Indonesia: Federal News Service (12 December 2015).
al-Barghouti, T. (2007) *Obvious Matter*. Online. Available HTTP: <http://www.youtube.com/watch?v=GCt0KBx-tec&feature=related>.
———. (2008) 'A Poetic Conversation between Two Generations *Hiwar Maftouh*', Al-Jazeera. Online. Available HTTP: <http://www.aljazeera.net/channel/archive/archive?ArchiveId=1102214> (Accessed 5 August 2008).
———. (2011a) 'O, Egypt! It is so Close', *PRI*. Online. Available HTTP: <http://www.pri.org/business/social-entrepreneurs/poetry-and-the-egyptian-revolution-tamim-al-barghouti2606.html> (Accessed 7 February 2011).
———. (2011b) 'A Nation of Ululation', A-Shorouk (in Arabic). Online. Available HTTP: <http://www.shorouknews.com/columns/columns.aspx?id=377684> (Accessed 7 March 2011).
Barnard R. (2004) 'On Laughter, the Grotesque, and the South African Transition: Zakes Mda's Ways of Dying', *NOVEL: A Forum on Fiction*, 37(3):277–302.
Barrett, L. (1999) *Blackness and Value: Seeing Double*, Cambridge, UK: Cambridge University Press.
Barthes, R. (2000) *Camera Lucida: Reflections on Photography*, London, UK: Vintage.
Basu, P. (2007) 'Political Economy of Land Grab,' Economic and Political Weekly, April 7:1281–1288.
Baucom, I. (2005) *Specters of the Atlantic: Finance Capital, Slavery, and the Philosophy of History*, Durham, NC: Duke University Press.
Baudelaire, C. (1995) *The Painter of Modern Life: And Other Essays*, 2nd edn., J. Mayne (trans.), London, UK: Phaidon Press.
Baudrillard, J. (2002) *The Violence of The Image*, Leuk-Stadt, Switzerland: The European Graduate School. Online. Available HTTP: <http://www.egs.edu/ faculty/jean-baudrillard/articles/the-violence-of-the-image/> (Accessed 3 April 2015).
Beck, U. and D. Levy (2013) 'Cosmopolitanized Nations: Re-imagining Collectivity in World Risk Society,' *Theory, Culture, and Society*, 30(2):3–31.
Beiser, V. (2011) 'An Interview with David Simon,' *The Progressive*. Online. Available HTTP: <http://www.progressive.org/news/2011/02/157458/interview-david- simon> (Accessed 11 May 2015).

Bell, D. (2003) 'History and Globalization: Reflections on Temporality,' *International Affairs*, 79(4):801–814.
Benantar, A. (2006) 'NATO, Maghreb and Europe,' *Mediterranean Politics*, 11:167–188.
Benjamin, W. (1968) 'Theses on the Philosophy of History', in H. Arendt (ed.), *Illuminations*, H. Zone (trans.), 253–264, New York, NY: Schocken.
———. (1996) *Selected Writings, Volume 1: 1913–1926*, M. Bullock and M. W. Jennings (eds.), Cambridge, MA: Belknap Press of Harvard University Press.
———. (1999a) *Selected Writings, Volume 2: 1927–1934*, M. W. Jennings (ed.), Cambridge, MA: Harvard University Press.
———. (1999b) *The Arcades Project*, R. Tiedemann (ed.), Cambridge, MA: Harvard University Press.
Bennhold, K. (2011) 'From Afar, Moneymaker and Mother', New York, NY: New York
Bensaad, A. (2007) 'The Mediterranean Divide and its Echo in the Sahara: New Migratory Routes and New Barriers on the Path to the Mediterranean,' in T. Fabre and P. Sant Cassia (eds.), *Between Europe and the Mediterranean: The Challenge and the Fears*, 51–70, Hampshire, UK: Palgrave Macmillan.
Berardi, F. (2009) *The Soul at Work: From Alienation to Autonomy*, F. Cadel and G. Mecchia (trans.), Los Angeles, CA: Semiotext(e).
Berger, D. (2006) *Outlaws of America: The Weather Underground and the Politics of Solidarity*, Oakland, CA: A. K. Press.
Berlant, L. (2000) 'The Subject of True Feeling: Pain, Privacy, and Politics,' in J. Dean (ed.), *Cultural Studies and Political Theory*, Ithaca and London: Cornell University Press.
———. (2011) *Cruel Optimism*, Durham, NC: Duke University Press.
Bernstein, R. (2011) *Racial Innocence: Performing American Childhood from Slavery to Civil Rights*, New York, NY: New York University Press.
Bhabha, H. (1994) *The Location of Culture*, New York, NY: Routledge.
Bhabha, J. (2006) 'The Child: What Sort of Human?' *PMLA*, 121(5):1526–1535.
Bially, Mattern J. (2011) 'A practice theory of emotion for International Relations,' in E. Adler and V. Pouliot (eds.), *International Practices*, 63–77, Cambridge, UK: Cambridge University Press.
Biehl, J. (2005) *Vita: Life in a Zone of Social Abandonment*, Berkeley and Los Angeles: University of California Press.
Bigo, D. (2000) 'When Two Become One: Internal and External Securitisations in Europe,' in M. Keltsrup and M. C. Williams (eds.), *International Relations Theory and the Politics of European Integration: Power, Security, and Community*, 171–204, London, UK: Routledge.
———. (2001) 'The Möbius Ribbon of Internal and External Securit(ies)', in M.E.A. Albert (ed.) *Identities Borders Orders: Rethinking International Relations Theory*, Minneapolis, MN: University of Minnesota Press.
———. (2002) 'Security and Immigration: Toward a Critique of the Governmentality of Unease,' *Alternatives: Global, Local, Political*, 27(1):63–92.
Bilgin, P., E. S. Lecha and A. Bilgic (2011) *European Security Practices vis-a-vis the Mediterranean: Implications in Value Terms*, Copenhagen, Denmark: Danish Institute for International Studies.
Binkley, S. (2009) 'The Work of Neoliberal Governmentality: Temporality and Ethical Substance in the Tale of Two Dads,' *Foucault Studies*, 6:60–78.
Blackburn, R. (1997) *The Making of New World Slavery: From the Baroque to the Modern, 1492–1800*, New York, NY: Verso.

Blaney, D. and N. Inayatullah (2002) 'Neo-Modernization? IR and the Inner Life of Modernization Theory,' *European Journal of International Relations*, 8(1):103–137.

———. (2006) 'The Savage Smith and the Temporal Walls of Capitalism,' B. Jahn (ed.), *The Classics and International Relations in Context*, 123–154, Cambridge, UK: Cambridge University Press.

———. (2010) 'Undressing the Wound of Wealth: Political Economy as a Cultural Project,' in J. Best and M. Patterson (eds.), *Cultural Political Economy*, 29–47, New York, NY: Routledge.

Blecher, R. (2009) 'Operation Cast Lead in the West Bank,' *Journal of Palestine Studies*, 38(3):64–71.

Bobo, K. (2009) *Wage Theft in America: Why Millions of Americans are Not Getting Paid – And What We Can Do about It*, New York, NY: New Press.

Boesen, V., F. Graybill and H. Curtis (1986) *Edward Sheriff Curtis: Visions of a Vanishing Race*, Albuquerque, Mexico, South America: University of New Mexico Press.

Republic of Bolivia (2008) 'Paper 8', *Ad Hoc Working Group on Long-term Cooperative Action Under the Convention*. Poznan, Poland: United Nations Framework Convention on Climate Change. Online. Available HTTP: <http://unfccc.int/ files/kyoto_protocol/application/pdf/boliviabap08122008.pdf.> (Accessed 28 March 2015).

Booth, K. (1997) 'Security and Self: Reflections of a Fallen Realist,' K. Krause & M.C. Williams (eds.), *Critical Security Studies: Concepts and Cases*, Minneapolis, MN: University of Minnesota Press.

Borrows, J. (2010) *Canada's Indigenous Constitution*, Toronto, Canada: University of Toronto Press.

Bourdieu, P. (1997) *Outline of a Theory of Practice*, Cambridge, UK: Cambridge University Press.

Bowie, M. (1991) *Lacan*, Cambridge, MA: Harvard University Press.

Braudel, F. (1979) *Afterthoughts on Material Civilization and Capitalis*, Patricia Ranum (trans.), Baltimore, MD: Johns Hopkins University Press.

Brighenti, A. (2014) 'Democracy and its Visibilities,' in K.D. Haggerty and M. Samatas (eds.), *Surveillance and Democracy*, Abingdon, UK: Routledge.

Brooks, D. (2006) *Bodies in Dissent: Spectacular Performances of Race and Freedom, 1850–1910*, Durham, NC: Duke University Press.

Brotherton, D.C. and P. Kretsedemas (eds.) (2008) *Keeping Out the Other: A Critical Introduction to Immigration Enforcement Today,* New York, NY: Columbia University Press.

Brown, J. (2008) *Babylon Girls: Black Women Performers and the Shaping of the Modern*, Durham, NC: Duke University Press.

Brugués, A. (2011) *Interview with Jian Ghomeshi* on *Q*, December 21. Online. Available HTTP: <www.cbc.ca/q/>.

Brunsma, D.L., D. Overfelt and J.S. Picou (eds.) (2007) *The Sociology of Katrina*, Lantham, MD: Roman & Littlefield.

Brystom, K. (2011) 'On 'Humanitarian' Adoption (Madonna in Malawi),' *Humanity* 2(2):213–231.

Buchan, B. (2001) 'Subjecting the Natives: Aborigines, Property and Possession under Early Colonial Rule,' *Social Analysis*, 45(2):143–162.

Buckley, C. (2010) '*China Feels Heat of Climate Change Rifts*,' Reuters. Online. Available HTTP: <http://uk.reuters.com/article/2010/11/22/uk-climate-cancun-china-preview-idUKTRE6AL0MV20101122> (Accessed November 22 2010).

Buck-Morss, S. (1989) *The Dialectics of Seeing: Walter Benjamin and the Arcades Project*, Cambridge, MA: The MIT Press.

Bibliography

———. (2009) *Hegel, Haiti, and Universal History*, Pittsburg: University of Pittsburg Press.
Bulawayo, N. (2010) 'Hitting Budapest,' *Boston Review*, (35)6:43–47.
Bull, H. (2002 [1977]) *The Anarchical Society: A Study of Order in World Politics*, New York, NY: Columbia University Press.
Bureau of Democracy, H.R. and Labor (2005) 'County Reports on Human Rights Practices: Morocco,' in U.S. Dept. of. State, (ed.).[full citation needed]
Burgess, J.P. (2011) *The Ethical Subject of Security : Geopolitical Reason and the Threat Against Europe*, New York, NY: Routledge.
Butler, J. (1997) *The Psychic Life of Power: Theories in Subjection*, Stanford, CA: Stanford University Press
———. (2010) *Frames of War: When is Life Grievable*, New York, NY: Verso.
Buzan, B. (1993) 'International Political Economy and Globalization,' in A.J. Bellamy (ed.), *International Society and Its Critics*, Oxford, UK: Oxford University Press.
Callenbach, E. (2006) 'When the Levees broke: A Requiem in Four Acts,' *Film Quarterly*, 60(2):4–10.
Campbell, D. (1998) *Writing Security: United States Foreign Policy and the Politics of Identity*, Revised edition, Minneapolis, MN: University of Minnesota Press.
———. (2011) 'The Iconography of Famine,' in G. Batchen, M. Gidley, M. Gidley, N.K. Miller, and J. Prosser (eds.), *Picturing Atrocity: Reading Photographs in Crisis*, 79–91, London, UK: Reaktion Books.
Cannizzo, J. (1983) 'George Hunt and the Invention of Kwakiutl Culture,' *Canadian Review of Sociology and Anthropology*, 20:44–58.
Carling, J. (2007) 'Migration Control and Migrant Fatalities at the Spanish-African Borders,' *International Migration Review*, 41:316–343.
Carr, D. (1991) *Time, Narrative and History*, Bloomington, IN: Indiana University Press.
Castells, M. (2009) *Communication Power*, Oxford, UK: Oxford University Press.
Castree, N. (2009) 'The Spatio-Temporality of Capitalism,' *Time & Society*, 18(1):26–61.
Cavell, S. (1982) 'The Fact of Television,' *Deadalus*, 111(4):75–96.
Césaire, A. (2000 [1955]) *Discourse on Colonialism*, New York, NY: Monthly Review Press.
Chakrabarty, D. (2002) *Habitations of Modernity: Essays in the Wake of Subaltern Studies*, Chicago, IL: University of Chicago Press.
———. (2004) 'Where is the Now?' *Critical Inquiry*, 30(2):458–462.
Chakravarty, P. and D.F. da Silva (2012) 'Accumulation, Dispossession, and Debt: The Racial Logic of Global Capitalism – An Introduction,' *American Quarterly*, 64(3):361–385.
Chambers, I. (2010) 'Maritime Criticism and Theoretical Shipwrecks,' *PMLA*, 125(3):678.
Chandler, D. (2009) 'The Global Ideology: Rethinking the Politics of the 'Global Turn' in IR,' *International Relations*, 23(4):530–547.
Chandler, N. (1996) 'The Economy of Desedimentation: W.E.B. Du Bois and the Discourses of the Negro,' *Callaloo*, 19(1):78–93.
———. (2000) 'Originary Displacement,' *boundary 2*, 27(3):249–286.
———. (2008) 'Of Exorbitance: The Problem of the Negro as a Problem for Thought,' *Criticism*, 50(3):345–410.
Chang, G. (2000) *Disposable Domestics: Immigrant Women Workers in the Global Economy*, Cambridge, MA: South End Press.
Clifford, J. (1988) *The Predicament of Culture*, Cambridge, MA: Harvard University Press.

Collyer, M. (2006) 'States of Insecurity: Consequences of sub-Saharan Transit Migration,' *Centre on Migration, Policy and Society Working Paper Series*, Oxford, UK: University of Oxford.

———. (2008) 'Emigration, Immigration, and Transit in the Maghreb: Externalization of EU Policy,' in Y.H. Zoubir and H. Amirah-Fernandez (eds.), *North Africa: Politics, Region and the Limits of Transformation*, London, New York: Routledge.

Connelley, F.S. (1995) *The Sleep of Reason: Primitivism in Modern European Art and Aesthetics, 1725–1907*, Pennsylvania, PA: The Pennsylvania State University Press.

Connolly, W.E. (2002) *Neuropolitics: Thinking, Culture, Speed*, Minneapolis, MN: University of Minnesota Press.

Constitution of Japan, Article 25. Online. Available HTTP: <http://www.kantei.go.jp/foreign/constitution_and_government_of_japan_constitutione.html>.

Costa Rica. (2008) 'Paper No. 2: Costa Rica', *Item 13 of the Provisional Agenda: Second Review of the Kyoto Protocol Pursuant to Its Article 9*, 5–6. Poznan, Poland: United Nations Framework Convention on Climate Change. Online. Available HTTP: <http://unfccc.int/files/kyoto_protocol/application/pdf/boliviabap 08122008.pdf>.

Coulter, J. (2014) *Searching for Saris*, Dubai Media and Entertainment Organization in Association with Dubai film Market (Enjazz), Parallax Productions.

Coundouriotis, E. (2010) 'The Child Soldier Narrative and the Problem of Arrested Historicization,' *Journal of Human Rights*, (9)2:191–206.

Crooks, R. (1995) 'From the far Side of the Urban Frontier: The Detective Fiction of Chester Himes and Walter Mosley,' *College Literature*, 22(3):68.

Curtis, E.S. (1907–1930) *The North American Indian*, 20 volumes, 20 portfolios, F.W. Hodge (ed.), Cambridge, UK: Cambridge University Press.

———. (1914 [2008]) *In the Land of the Head Hunters*, Milestone Films.

Dalby, S. (2007) 'The Pentagon's New Imperial Cartography,' in D. Gregory and A. Pred (eds.), *Violent Geographies: Fear, Terror, and Political Violence*, New York, NY: Routledge.

Daly, R.H. (2005) *Our Box Was Full: An Ethnography for the Delgamuukw Plaintiffs*, Vancouver, Canada: UBC Press.

Darwish, M. (1970) '*Passport*'. Online. Available HTTP: <http://www.festivaldepoesiademedellin.org/pub.php/en/Diario/04.html>.

———. (1980) *The Music of Human Flesh*, Denys Johnson-Davies (trans.), London, UK: Heinemann.

———. (1995) *Memory For Forgetfulness*, Ibrahim Muhawi (trans.), Los Angeles, CA: University of California Press.

———. (2007) *The Butterfly's Burden*, Fady Joudah (trans.), Port Townsend, WA: Copper Canyon Press.

———. (2009a) *A River Dies of Thirst: Journals*, C. Cobham (trans.), New York, NY: Archipelago Books.

———. (2009b) *If I Were Another*, F. Joudah (trans.), New York, NY: Farrar, Straus and Giroux.

da Silva, D.F. (1997) *Toward A Global Idea of Race*, Minneapolis, MN: University of Minnesota Press.

Davis, B.A. (1985) *Edward S. Curtis: The Life and Times of a Shadow Catcher*, San Francisco, CA: Chronicle Books.

Davis, K. (2008) *Periodization and Sovereignty: How Ideas of Feudalism and Secularization Govern the Politics of Time*, Philadelphia, PA: University of Pennsylvania Press.

Dean, C. and A.C. Revkin. (2005) 'After Centuries of 'Controlling' Land, Gulf Learns Who's the Boss,' *The New York Times*. Online. Available HTTP: <http://www.nytimes.com/2005/08/30/national/30coast.html?_r=0> (Accessed 11 May 2015).

Debenedetti, S. (2006) *Externalization of European asylum and migration policies*, Florence, Italy: European University Institute.

Debenedetti, S. (2006) *Externalization of European Asylum and Migration Policies*, Florence, Italy: European University Institute.

Debrix, F. (1999) *Re-Envisioning Peacekeeping: the United Nations and the Mobilization of Ideology*, Minneapolis, MN: The University of Minnesota Press.

De Certeau, M. (1984) *The Practice of Everyday Life*, London, UK: University of California Press.

De Goede, M. (2008) 'The Politics of Preemption and the War on Terror in Europe,' *European Journal of International Relations*, 14(1):161–185.

Dehaene, M. and L.D. Cauter (eds.) (2008) *Heterotopia and the City*, London and New York: Routledge.

Deleuze, G. (1988) *Foucault*, S. Hand (trans.), Minneapolis, MN: University of Minnesota Press.

——. (1991) *Foucault*, London, UK: Althone Press.

Deleuze, G. and F. Guattari (1987) *A Thousand Plateaus*, B. Massumi (trans.), Minneapolis, MN: University of Minnesota Press.

Deloria, P.J. (2004) *Indians in Unexpected Places*, Lawrence, KS: University of Kansas.

Der Derian, J. (1987) *On Diplomacy: A Genealogy of Western Estrangement*, Oxford, UK: Blackwell.

——. (1990) 'The (S)pace of International Relations: Simulation, Surveillance, and Speed,' *International Studies Quarterly*, 34(3):295–310.

——. (1992) *Antidiplomacy: Spies, Terror, Speed, and War*, Cambridge, MA: Blackwell.

Deutsche Presse-Agentur (1997) 'Nations from Four Continents Call for Greenhouse Gas Reductions,' New York, NY: Deutsche Presse-Agentur (23 June 1997).

Dienstag, J.F. (2006) *Pessimism: Philosophy, Ethic, Spirit*, Princeton, NJ: Princeton University Press.

Diptee, A. (2007) 'Imperial Ideas, Colonial Realities: Enslaved Children in Jamaica, 1775–1834,' in J. Marten (ed.), *Children in Colonial America*, 48–60, New York, NY: New York University Press.

Directorate-General, f. t. E.P. o. t. U. (2006) 'Analysis of the External Dimension of the EU's Asylum and Migration Policies,' *DGEPU, D.B., Policy Department* (ed.), Brussels, Belgium: European Parliament.

Dixon, E. (2005) 'Personal Voices: An Unnatural Disaster,' *Common Dreams*. Online. Available HTTP: <http://www.alternet.org/story/28431/personal_voices%3A_an_unnatural_disaster>.

Dobrowolsky, A. (2007) '(In)Security and Citizenship: Security, Im/migration and Shrinking Citizenship Regimes,' *Theoretical Inquiries in Law*, 8:629–661.

Dobson, A. (2000) *Green Political Thought*, Third Vol., London, UK: Routledge.

——. (2005) 'Globalisation, Cosmopolitanism and the Environment,' *International Relations*, 19(3):259–273.

Domestic Workers United (2011) *History & Mission*, New York, NY: Domestic Workers United. Online. Available HTTP: <http://www.domesticworkersunited.org/index.php/en/about/history-mission> (Accessed 15 Feb. 2011).

Donzelot, J. (1988) 'The Promotion of the Social,' *Economy and Society*, 17(3):395–427.

Dörre, K. (2011) 'Capitalism, Landnahme and Social Time Régimes: An Outline,' *Time & Society*, 20(1):69–93.

Doty, R. (1996) *Imperial Encounters: The Politics of Representation in North-South Relations*, Minneapolis, MN: University of Minnesota Press.

Dovey, T. (1996) 'Waiting for the Barbarians: Allegory of Allegories,' G. Huggan and S. Watson (eds.), *Critical Perspectives on J.M. Coetzee*, London, UK: Macmillan Press.

Dubin, M. (2001) *Native America Collected: The Culture of an Art World*, New Mexico, NM, South America: The University of New Mexico Press.

Du Bois, W.E.B. (1999 [1903]) 'The Souls of Black Folk,' in H.L. Gates and T.H. Oliver (eds.), *The Souls of Black Folk: Authoritative Text, Contexts, Criticism*, Norton Critical Edition edn, New York: W.W. Norton & Company.

———. (2004) *Black Reconstruction in America 1860–1880*, New York, NY: Atheneum.

Durkheim, É. (1951) *Suicide: A Study in Sociology*, New York, NY: Free Press.

Duvall, R.D. and A. Chowdhury (2011) 'Practices of Theory,' in E. Adler and V. Pouliot (eds.), *International Practices*, 335–354, Cambridge, MA: Cambridge University Press.

Dvorak, P. (2003) 'The Homeless in Japan Find A Place in Cities' Public Parks: Long Economic Slump, Tolerance Allow Shantytowns to Take Root,' *Wall Street Journal*, 18 June, 2003.

Eagleton, T. (1998) 'Postcolonialism and 'Postcolonialism,'', *Interventions*, 1:24–26.

———. ((2014) 'Time, Personhood, and Politics,' in G. Buelens, S. Durrant and R. Eaglestone (eds.), *The Future of Trauma Theory: Contemporary Literary and Cultural Criticism*, 127–140, London, UK: Routledge.

Edkins, J. (2003) *Trauma and the Memory of Politics*, Cambridge, UK: Cambridge University Press.

Eisenstadt, S.N. (1996) *Japanese Civilization: A Comparative View*, Chicago, IL: University of Chicago Press.

———. (ed.) (2002) *Multiple Modernities*, New Brunswick, NJ: Transaction Publishers.

Elias, N. (2000) *The Civilizing Process: Sociogenetic and Psychogenetic Investigations*, Revised edn, Oxford, UK: Blackwell Publishing.

Elliot, J. (2014) 'India: After 30 Years, Bhopal is Still Simmering,' *Newsweek*. Online. Available HTTP: <http://www.newsweek.com/india-after-30-years-bhopal-still simmering-288144> (Accessed 11 May 2015).

Elson, D. (1979) 'A Value Theory of Labor,' in D. Elson (ed.), *Value*, London, UK: CSE Books.

Eltit's, D. (2002) *Mano de obra*, Santiago, South America: Seix Barral.

Enloe, C (2004) *The Curious Feminist: Searching for women in a New Age of Empire*, Berkeley, CA: University of California Press.

Epstein, C. (2008) *The Power of Words in International Relations: Birth of an Anti-Whaling Discourse*, Cambridge, MA: MIT Press.

Esmeir, S. (2010) '*On Becoming a War Criminal*,' Paper presented at Muwatin's 15th Annual Conference 'The Palestinian Present: Pessimism of the Intellect, Optimism of the Will?', Ramallah, 26–27 February.

Esposito, R. (2008) *Bíos: Biopolitics and Philosophy*, T. Campbell (trans.), Minneapolis, MN: University of Minnesota Press.

Estrada, D. (2010) '*Afro-Chileans Seek Recognition in the Census*', World News. Online. Available HTTP: <http://www.finalcall.com/artman/publish/World_News_3/article_7203.shtml> (Accessed 17 August, 2010).

Evans, B. and Glass, A. (eds.) (2014) *Return to the Land of the Head Hunters: Edward S.Curtis. The Kwakwaka'wakw and the Making of Modern Cinema*, Seattle, WA: University of Washington Press.

Fabian, J. (1983) *Time and the Other: How Anthropology Makes Its Object*, New York, NY: Columbia University Press.

———. (1991) *Time and the Other: How Anthropology Makes Its Object*, New York, NY: Columbia University Press.

Fainaru, S. (1992) 'Down to Earth: For all the hype surrounding the Earth Summit, it is difficult to say exactly what is going on here,' *The Boston Globe* (7 June 1992).

Fanon, F. (1958) *Black Skin White Masks*, New York, NY: Grove Press.

———. (1964) *Toward the African Revolution,* New York, NY: Grove Press.

———. (1967a) *Black Skin, White Masks*, New York, NY: Grove Press.

———. (1967b) *The Wretched of the Earth*, New York, NY: Grove Press.

———. (1968) *Black Skin, White Masks*, New York, NY: Grove Press.

———. (2008 [1952]) *Black Skin/White Masks*, London, UK: Pluto Press.

Farley, A. (2005) 'Accumulation,' *Michigan Journal of Race and Law*, 11(51):51–73.

Fassin, D. (2008) 'The Humanitarian Politics of Testimony: Subjectification through Trauma in the Israeli-Palestinian Conflict,' *Cultural Anthropology*, 23(3):531–558.

Finnemore, M. and Sikkink, K. (1998) 'International Norm Dynamics and Political Change', *International Organization*, 52(4):887–917.

Fleming, P.R. and J. Luskey (1986) *North American Indians in Early Photographs*, New York, NY: Harper and Row Publishers.

Foucault, M. (1977) *Discipline and Punish: The Birth of the Prison*, 2nd edn, A. Sheridan (trans.), New York, NY: Pantheon Books.

———. (1984 [1967]) 'Of Other Space', *Heterotopias*, J. Miskowiec (trans.), *Architecture/Mouvement/Continuite*. Online. Available HTTP: <http://www.foucault.info/documents/heteroTopia/Foucault.heteroTopia.en.html>.

———. (1997 [1976]) *Society Must be Defended: Lectures at the College de France 1975–1976*, David Macey (trans.), New York, NY: Picador.

———. (1980) 'Politics and the Study of Discourse,' in C. Gordon (ed.), *Power/Knowledge: Michel Foucault selected interviews and other writings, 1972–1977*, New York, NY: Pantheon Books.

———. (1990) *The History of Sexuality, Volume I: An Introduction*, London, UK: Penguin.

Fournel, V. (1867) *Ce Qu'on Voit Dane Les Rues de Paris*, Paris: E. Dentu.

Fowler, E. (1996) *San'ya blues: Labouring Life in Contemporary Tokyo*, New York, NY: Cornell University Press.

Franklin, V.P. (1983) 'Reviewed Work(s): *Slavery and Social Death* by Orlando Patterson,' *Journal of Negro History*, 68(2):212–216.

Frazier, L.J. (2007) *Salt in the Sand: Memory, Violence and the Nation-State in Chile, 1980 to the Present*, Durham, NC: Duke University Press.

Freedman, A. (2011) 'The *Homeless Junior High School Student* Phenomenon: Personalising a Social Problem,' *Japanese Studies*, 31(3):387–403.

Freeman, E. (2007) 'Introduction,' *GLQ: A Journal of Lesbian and Gay Studies* 13(2–3):159–176.

Freire, P. (1973 [2000]) *Pedagogy of the Oppressed*, Revised edn, M. Bergman Ramos (trans.), New York, NY: Continuum.

Fukada, S. (2012) *Japan's Disposable Workers*. Online. Available HTTP: <http://pulitizercenter.org/project/japan-disposable-worker-laborer>.

Fuqua, J.V. (2012) "'In New Orleans, We Might Say It Like This . . . 'Authenticity, Place, and HBO's Treme,' *Television New Media*, 13(3):235–242.

Fussell, E. (2007) 'Constructing New Orleans Race: A Population History of New Orleans', *The Journal of American History*, 94(December, 2007). Online. Available HTTP:

<http://www.journalofamericanhistory.org/projects/katrina. Fussell.html> (Accessed 11 May 2015).
Gallagher, B. (2012) 'Coming Home: The Temporal Presence of the U.S. Soldier's Wounded Body,' in S. Opondo and M.J. Shapiro (eds.), *The New Violent Cartography: Geo-Analysis After the Aesthetic Turn*, first edition, New York, NY: Routledge.
Galli, F. (2008) 'The Legal and Political Implications of the Securitisation of Counter-Terrorism Measures across the Mediterranean,' *Euromesco Paper*. Euromesco.
Gammeltoft-Hansen, T. (2008) *The Refugee, the Sovereign and the Sea: EU Interdiction Policies in the Mediterranean*, Copenhagen, Denmark: Danish Institute for International Studies.
Gebhardt, N. (2012) 'Do You Know What It Mean to Miss New Orleans? Historical Metaphors and Mythical Realities in Spike Lee's *When the Levees Broke*,' *Jazz Research Journal* 6(2). Online. Available HTTP: <http://www.equinoxpub>.Com/journals/index.php/JAZZ/article/viewArticle/1752> (Accessed 11 May 2015).
Genda, Y. (2007) 'Jobless Youths and the NEET problem in Japan,' *Social ScienceJapan Journal*, 10(1):23–40.
Genocchio, B. (1995) 'Discourse, Discontinuity, Difference: The Question of Other Spaces,' in S. Watson and K. Gibson (eds.), *Postmodern Cities and Spaces*, Oxford, UK: Blackwell.
Ghosh, A. (2002) *The Imam and the Indian: Prose Pieces*, Delhi, India: Ravi Dayal Publisher.
Gidley, M (ed.) (1987) *The Vanishing Race: Selections from Edward S. Curtis's The North American Indian*, New York, NY: Taplinger Publishing.
Gidwani, V. (2008) *Capital Interrupted: Agrarian Development and the Politics of Working India*, Minneapolis, MN: University of Minnesota Press.
Gikandi, S. (2008) 'Unhappy Consciousness: The Black Atlantic and the Phenomenology of Modern Time,' Paul Gilroy Conference, Institute of Arts and Humanities, University of North Carolina at Chapel Hill, 19 January 2008.
Gill, T. (2001) *Men of Uncertainty: The Social Organization of Day Labourers in Contemporary Japan*, New York, NY: State University of New York Press.
Glass, A., B. Evans and A. Sanborn (2015) 'The Kwakwaka'wakw, Curtis, and the Making of Head Hunters,' *Edward Curtis Meets the Kwakwaka'wakw 'In the Land of the Head Hunters'*. Online. Available HTTP: <http://www.curtisfilm.rutgers.edu/film/making-of-head-hunters-mainmenu-34> (Accessed 13 May 2015).
Go, J. (2004) "'Racism' and Colonialism: Meanings of Difference and Ruling Practices in America's Pacific Empire,' *Qualitative Sociology*, 27(1):35–58.
Goldgeier, J.M. and M.M. McFaul (1992) 'A Tale of Two Worlds: Core and Periphery in the Post-Cold War Era,' *International Organization*, 46:467–491.
Goodin, R.E. (1990) 'International Ethics and the Environmental Crisis,' *Ethics and International Affairs*, 4:91–105.
Goodman, A. (2005) 'Kanye West: 'Bush Doesn't Care About Black People,' *Democracy Now*. Online. Available HTTP: <http://www.democracynow.org/ 2005/9/5/kanye_west_bush_doesnt_care_about> (Accessed 11 May 2015).
Gordon, L. (1995) *Bad Faith and Anti-black Racism*, Atlantic Highlands, NJ: Humanities Press.
———. (2000) *Existentia Africana: Understanding Africana Existential Thought*, New York, NY: Routledge.
———. (2008) 'The Perils of Innocence, or What is Wrong with Putting Children First,' *The Journey of the History of Childhood and Youth*, 1(3):331–350.

Gordon, N. (2008) *Israel's Occupation*, Berkeley, CA: University of California Berkeley Press.
Gorz, A. (1989) *Critique of Economic Reason*, New York, NY: Verso.
Gramsci, A. (c1971, 1978) *Selections from the Prison Notebooks*, New York, NY: International Publishers.
Grandin, G (2010) 'Living in Revolutionary Time: Coming to Terms with the Violence of Latin America's Long Cold War,' in G. Joseph and G. Grandin (eds.), *A Century of Revolution: Insurgent and Counterinsurgent Violence During Latin America's Cold War*, 1–45, Durham, NC: Duke University Press.
Gray, H. (2012) 'Recovered, Reinvented, Reimagined: Treme, Television Studies and Writing New Orleans,' *Television & New Media*, 13(3):268–278.
Greenhouse, S. (2003) 'U.S. Retailers Decline to Aid Factory Victims in Bangladesh,' *The New York Times*, November 23, 2003: B1.
Greenwald, R. (2013) *Unmanned: American's Drone Wars*. Online. Available HTTP: <https://archive.org/details/scm-375343-awpt-unmannedamericasdronewar> (Accessed 11 May 2015).
Grier, B. (1994) 'Invisible Hands: The Political Economy of Child Labour in Colonial Zimbabwe, 1890–1930,' *Journal of Southern African Studies*, 20(1):27–52.
Griffiths, A. (1999) *Wondrous Difference: Cinema, Anthropology and Turn-of-the-Century Visual Culture*, New York, NY: Columbia University Press.
Griffiths, M. (1995) *Realism, Idealism, and International Politics*, Abingdon, UK: Routledge.
Grosz, E. (2005) *The Nick of Time: Politics, Evolution, and the Untimely*, Durham, NC: Duke University Press.
Grovogui, S. N. (1996) *Sovereigns, Quasi-sovereigns and Africans: Race and Self-determination in International Law*, Minneapolis, MN: University of Minnesota Press.
———. (2006) *Beyond Eurocentrism and Anarchy: Memories of International Order and Institutions*, New York, NY: Palgrave Macmillan.
———. (2011) 'To the Orphaned, Dispossessed, and Illegitimate Children: Human Rights Beyond Republican and Liberal Traditions,' *Indiana Journal of Global Legal Studies*, 18(1):41–63.
Gussow, A. (2002) *Seems Like Murder Here: Southern Violence and the Blues Tradition*, Chicago, IL: University of Chicago Press.
Guzewicz, T.D. (1996) 'A New Generation of Homeless Hits Tokyo's Streets,' *Japan-Quarterly*, July-September: 43–53.
———. (2000) *Tokyo's Homeless: A City in Denial*, New York, NY: Nova Science Publishers, Inc.
Guzmán, P. (1971) *El primer año (The First Year)*.
———. (1978) *La batalla de Chile (The Battle of Chile)*.
———. (1997) *Chile: Memoria obstinada (Obstinate Memory)*.
———. (2006) *Salvador Allende*.
———. (2010) *Nostalgia por la luz (Nostalgia for/of the Light)*, United States: IcarusFilms.
Hall, S. (1992) 'The West and the Rest: Discourse and Power,' in S. Hall and B. Gieben (eds.), *Formations of Modernity: Understanding Modern Societies*, 184–227, Cambridge and Oxford: The Open University and Polity Press.
Halperin, S. (1997) *In the Mirror of the Third World: Capitalist Development in Modern Europe*, Ithaca, NY: Cornell University Press.
Hanchard, M. (1999) 'Afro-Modernity: Temporality, Politics, and the African Diaspora,' *Public Culture*, 11(1):245–268.

Hansen, L. (2006) *Security as Practice: Discourse Analysis and the Bosnian War*, New York, NY: Routledge.

———. (2011) 'Performing Practices: a poststructuralist analysis of the Muhammed cartoon crisis,' in E. Adler and V. Pouliot (eds.), *International Practices*, 280–309, Cambridge, UK: Cambridge University Press.

al-Haq (2012) '*Munahadet al-t'dhib fi al-mawathiq al-dawliya wa al-waq' al-filastini*', Ramallah, West Bank.

Haraway, D. J. (2008) *When Species Meet*, Minneapolis, MN: University of Minnesota Press.

Harney, S. and Fred M. (2013) *The Undercommons: Fugitive Planning and Black Study*, New York, NY: Minor Compositions.

Harootunian, H. (2005) 'Some Thoughts on Comparability and the Space-Time Problem,' *boundary 2*, 32(2):23–52.

Harries, K. (1998) *The Ethical Function of Architecture*, Cambridge, MA: The MIT Press.

Harriford, D. and B. Thompson (2008) *When the Center Is on Fire*, Austin, TX: University of Texas Press.

Hartman, S. (1997) *Scenes of Subjection: Terror, Slavery and Self-Making in Nineteenth-Century America*, New York, NY: Oxford University Press.

———. (2002) 'The Time of Slavery,' *The South Atlantic Quarterly*, 101(4):757–777.

———. (2007) *Lose Your Mother: A Journey along the Atlantic Slave Route*, New York, NY: Macmillan.

———. (2008) *Lose Your Mother: A Journey along the Atlantic Slave Route*, New York, NY: Farrar, Strauss and Giroux.

Hartman, S. and F. B. Wilderson III. (2003) 'The Position of the Unthought,' *Qui Parle*, 13(2):83–201.

Hartnell, A. (2012) 'Hurricane Katrina as Visual Spectacle: *Hurricane on the Bayou* and the Reframing of American national identity,' in T. Cusack (ed.), *Art and Identity at the Water's Edge*, XX–XX, London, UK: Ashgate.

Harvey, D. (1990) *The Condition of Postmodernity: An Enquiry into the Origins of Cultural Change*, Malden, MA: Blackwell.

Hasegawa, K. (2001) '*Saijiki no jikan*' (Time in Saijiki), in T. Hashimoto and S. Kuriyama (eds.), *Chikoku no Tanjo: Kindai ni okeru jikan no keisei* (The Birth of Tardiness: The Formation of Time Consciousness in Modern Japan), Tokyo, Japan: Sangensha.

Hasegawa, M. (2006) "*We Are Not Garbage!' the Homeless Movement in Tokyo,1994–2002*', New York, NY: Routledge.

Hatoyama, Y. (2009) 'Creating a New Nation. Yukio Hatoyama's *Yu-Ai* – message from the Prime Minister,' *Hatoyama cabinet E-mail Magazine*, 4. Online. Available HTTP: <https://www.mmz.kantei.go.jp/foreign/m-magazine/backnumber/2009/ 1102.html>.

Hawker, R. (2003) *Tales of Ghosts: First Nations Art in British Columbia, 1922–61*, Seattle, WA: University of Washington Press.

Hayashi, S. (2011) 'Representational Discontent,' *Cultural Anthropology*, July. Online. Available HTTP: <http://www.culanth.org/fieldsights/301-representational-discontent> (Accessed 24 May 2015).

al-Hayyah al-Jadeedah (2009) 'Istishhad thalathah min quwwat al-amn wa maqtal musalahain min Hamas wa muwatin fi isthibak Qalqilya', Monday June 1st, 2009.

Heidegger, M. (1962) *Being and Time*, J. Macquarrie and E. Robinson (trans.), New York, NY: Harper & Row Publishers.

Hejl, N. (2007) 'Between a Rock and a Hard Place: Euro-Mediterranean Security Revisited,' *Mediterranean Politics*, 12:1–16.

Helliwell, C. and B. Hindess (2002) 'The Empire of Uniformity and the Government of Subject Peoples,' *Cultural Values*, 6:139–152.

———. (2005) 'The Temporalizing of Difference,' *Ethnicities*, 5:414–418.

Hetherington, K. (1997) *The Badlands of Modernity: Heterotopias and Social Ordering*, London, UK: Routledge.

Hill, T. (2011) '*From the small zinzana to the bigger zinzana: Israeli prisons, Palestinian prisons*', unpublished paper.

Hindess, B. (1998) 'Divide and Rule: The International Character of Modern Citizenship,' *European Journal of Social Theory*, 1:57–70.

———. (2000) 'Citizenship in the International Management of Populations,' *American Behavioral Scientist*, 43:1486–1497.

———. (2002) 'Neo-liberal Citizenship,' *Citizenship Studies*, 6:127–143.

———. (2004) 'Citizenship for all,' *Citizenship Studies*, 8:305–315.

———. (2007) 'The Past is Another Culture,' *International Political Sociology*, 1:325–338.

———. (2008) 'Been there, done that . . . ', *Postcolonial Studies*, 11:201–213.

Hirayama, Y. (2010) 'The Role of Home Ownership in Japan's Aged Society,' *Journal of Housing and the Built Environment*, 25:175–191.

Hobbes, T. (1969) *The Elements of Law Natural and Politic*, 2nd edn, F. Tönnies (ed.), New York, NY: Barnes and Noble.

———. (1996 [1651]) *Leviathan*, R. Tuck (ed.), Cambridge, UK: Cambridge University Press.

———. (1998 [1642] *On the Citizen* (Originally published as *De Cive*), R. Tuck (trans.) and M. Silverthorne (eds.), Cambridge, UK: Cambridge University Press.

Högbacka, R. (2008) 'The Quest for a Child of One's Own: Parents, Markets and Transnational Adoption,' *Journal of Comparative Family Studies*, 39(3):311–330.

Holm, B. and G. I. Quimby (eds.) (1973) *In the Land of the War Canoes*. Milestone Films.

———. (1980) *Edward S. Curtis in the Land of the War Canoes: A Pioneer Cinematographer in the Pacific Northwest*, Seattle, WA: University of Washington Press.

Holm, U. (2004) *The EU's Security Policy towards the Mediterranean: An (Im)possible Combination of Export of European Political Values and Anti-Terror Measures?*, Copenhagen, Denmark: Danish Institute for International Studies.

———. (2008) *North Africa: A Security Problem for Themselves, for the EU and for the US*, Copenhagen, Denmark: Danish Institute for International Studies.

Hom, A. (2008) '*Time and International Relations Theory*,' Master of Arts Thesis, University of Kansas.

———. (2010) 'Hegemonic Metronome: The Ascendancy of Western Standard Time,' *Review of International Studies*, 36(4):1145–1170.

———. (2013) 'Reckoning Ruin: International Relations Theorising and the Problem of Time,' Ph.D. Thesis, Aberystwyth, Wales: Aberystwyth University.

Hom, A. R., and B. J. Steele (2010) 'Open Horizons: The Temporal Visions of Reflexive Realism,' *International Studies Review*, 12(2):271–300.

Homer, S. (2006) 'Narratives of History, Narratives of Time,' C. Irr and I. Buchanan (eds.), *On Jameson: From Postmodernism to Globalization*, 71–91, Albany, NY: State University of New York Press.

Homuresu. (1991) Film. Directed by Yukihiko Tsutsumi.

Hook, G. D. and T. Hiroko (2007) *'Self-responsibility' and the Nature of the Postwar*, Japanese State.

Houellebecq, M. (2011) *The Map and the Territory*, G. Bowd (trans.), London, UK: William Heinemann.

Houlihan, E. (2010) 'The Ethics of Reading the Short Story: Literary Humanitarianism in 'The Gold Vanity Set'', *College Literature*, 37(3):62–83.

Howerton, J. (2014) 'Ferguson Protesters' Angry Message to Obama, Democrats: "This is Obama's Katrina, and He Ain't Doing S**t!"', *The Blaze*. Online. Available HTTP: <http://www.theblaze.com/stories/2014/11/24/ferguson-protesters-angry-message-to-obama-democrats-this-is-obamas-katrina-and-he-aint-doing-st/> (Accessed 11 May 2015).

Hoy, D.C. (2009) *The Time of Our Lives: A Critical History of Temporality*, Cambridge, MA: MIT Press.

Hughes, L. (2001) *The Collected Works of Langston Hughes, Volume 1:ThePoems: 1921–1940*, Columbia, MI: University of Missouri Press.

Human Rights Watch. (2006) *Stemming the Flow: Abuses Against Migrants, Asylum-Seekers and Refugees*, Human Rights Watch.

Hurrell, A. (1995) 'Explaining the Resurgence of Regionalism in World Politics,' *Review of International Studies*, 21:331–388

Husserl, E. (1964) *The Phenomenology of Internal Time-Consciousness*, J.S. Churchill (trans.), Bloomington, IN: Indiana University Press.

Hutchings, K. (2007) 'Happy Anniversary! Time and Critique in International Relations Theory,' *Review of International Studies*, 33:71–89.

———. (2008) *Time and World Politics: Thinking the Present*, Manchester, UK: Manchester University Press.

Huysmans, J. (2006) *The Politics of Insecurity: Fear, Migration, and Asylum in the EU*, New York, NY: Routledge.

Huysmans, J., Dobson, A. and Prokhovnik, R. (eds) (2006) *The Politics of Protection: Sites of Insecurity and Political Agency*, New York, NY: Routledge. *In the Heat of the Night*. (1967) Film. Directed by Norman Jewison. USA: United Artists.

Inayatullah, N., and D.B. Blaney (2004) *International Relations and the Problem of Difference*, London, UK: Routledge.

Interfaith Worker Justice. (2013) '*Issues: Wage Theft*', Chicago, IL: Interfaith Worker Justice. Online. Available HTTP: <http://www.iwj.org/issues/wage-theft> (Accessed February 22).

International Crisis Group (2010) 'Squaring the Circle: Palestinian Security Reform under Occupation,' *Middle East Report No.98*, Washington, DC: International Crisis Group.

International Herald Tribune. (2007) Online. Available HTTP: <http://www.iht.com/articles/2007/02/27/news/climate.php>.

———. (2008) 'At Tax Time, Illegal Immigrants are Paying Too', New York, NY.

Ireland, C. and D. Carvounas (2008) 'Unpredictability, the Economically Secured Present, and the Open Future of Modernity: Learning from Koselleck and Extrapolating from Elias,' *Time & Society*, 17(2/3):155–178.

Işın, E.F. (2002) 'Citizenship after Orientalism,' in E.F. Işın & B.S. Turner (eds.), *Handbook of Citizenship Studies*, London, UK: Sage.

———. (2005) 'Citizenship after orientalism: Ottoman citizenship,' in F. Keyman and A. İçduygu (eds.), *Citizenship in a Global World: European Questions and Turkish Experiences*, London, UK: Routledge.

Işın, E.F. & Turner, B.S. (2002) 'Citizenship Studies: An Introduction,' in E.F. Işın and B.S. Turner (eds.), *Handbook of Citizenship Studies*, London, UK: Sage.

Issachrof, A. (2008) 'U.S. supervising training of elite PA unit in Jordan,' *Ha'aretz*, Sunday 6 April, 2008.

Iwabuchi, K. (2008) 'Lost in Translation: Tokyo and the Urban Imaginary in the Era of Globalization,' *Inter-Asia Cultural Studies*, 9(4):543–546.

Iwata, M. (2010) 'New Landscape of Homelessness in Japan: The role of NPOs and Landscape of the Problem,' *City, Culture and Society*, 1:127–134.

Jabir, J. (2009) 'On Conjuring Mahalia: Mahalia Jackson, New Orleans, and the Sanctified Swing,' *American Quarterly*, 61(3): 649–669.

———. (2013) *The Postcolonial Subject: Claiming Politics/Governing Others in Late Modernity*, London, UK: Routledge.

Jackson, R. (2005) *Writing the War on Terrorism: Language, Politics, and Counter-terrorism*, Manchester, UK: Manchester University Press.

Jacobs, M. D. (2011) *White Mother to a Dark Race: Settler Colonialism, Maternalism, and the Removal of Indigenous Children in the American West and Australia, 1880–1940*, Lincoln, NE, USA: University of Nebraska Press.

Jaji, T. (2009) 'Sound Effects: Synaesthesia as Purposeful Distortion in Keorapetse Kgositsile's Poetry,' *Comparative Literature Studies*, 46(2):287–310.

Al-Jakh, H. (2011a) *Joha*. Online. Available HTTP: <http://www.youtube.com/watch?v=hE_HNt7QwYE>.

———. (2011b) *A Panoramic View from Tahreer Square*. Online. Available HTTP:<http://www.youtube.com/watch?v=T6_dz_6lgpM&feature=related>.

Jakobsen, S. (1999) 'International Relations and Global Environmental Change: Review of the Burgeoning Literature on the Environment,' *Cooperation and Conflict*, 34(2):205–236.

Japan Times (2011) 'Poverty Rate Hit Record High in '09'. Online. 13 July 2011.

Japanese State. Risk through the Looking Glass,' *Journal of Japanese Studies*, 33(1):93–123.

Jarvis, L. (2008) 'Times of Terror: Writing Temporality into the War on Terror,' *Critical Studies on Terrorism*, 1(22):245–262.

———. (2009) *Times of Terror: Discourse, Temporality, and the War on Terror*, Basingstoke, England: Palgrave Macmillan.

Jasanoff, S. (ed.) (2004) *States of Knowledge: The Co-Production of Science and Social Order*, New York, NY: Routledge.

Jay, M. (2011) 'In the Realm of the Senses: An Introduction,' *The American Historical Review*, 116(2):307–315. doi:10.1086/ahr.116.2.307

Jayyusi, M. (2004) '*Subjectivity and Public Witness: an Analysis of Islamic Militance in Palestine*', Paper presented at the SSRC conference 'The Beirut Conference on Public Spheres', Beirut, 22–24 October.

Jiang, Z. (2002) '*President Jiang Zemin Addresses Global Environmental Facility Meeting*', Beijing: Xinhua General News Service (16 October 2002). Online. Available HTTP: <http://www.nexis.com.ezproxy.lib.gla.ac.uk/results/docview/ docview.do?docLinkInd=true&risb=21_T22077215703&format=GNBFI&sort=BOOLEAN&startDocNo=1&resultsUrlKey=29_T22077215707&cisb=22_T22077215706&treeMax=true&treeWidth=0&csi=8078&docNo=1> (Accessed 25 May 2015).

Johnson, E. P. (2003) *Appropriating Blackness: Performance and the Politics of Authenticity*, Durham, NC: Duke University Press.

Johnson, T. (ed.) (1998) *Spirit Capture: Photographs from the National Museum of the American Indian*, Washington and London: Smithsonian Institution Press.

Jonaitis, A. (2006) *Art of the Northwest Coast*, Seattle, WA: University of Washington Press.

Jones, D. V. (2010) *The Racial Discourses of Life Philosophy: Vitalism, Négritude, and Modernity*, New York: Columbia University Press.

Judy, R. (1996) 'Fanon's Body of Black Experience,' in L. R. Gordon, T. D. Sharpley-Whiting and R. T. White (eds.), *Fanon: A Critical Reader*, New York, NY: Wiley-Blackwell.

Jünemann, A. (2003) 'Security-Building in the Mediterranean After September 11,' Mediterranean Politics, 8:1–20.
Kant, I. (2008 [1755]) Critique of Pure Reason, M. Muller (ed.), New York, NY: Penguin.
Karatani, K. (2008) 'Beyond Capital-Nation-State,' Rethinking Marxism, 20(4):569–595.
Katz, C. and Smith N. (2003) 'An interview with Edward Said,' Environment and Planning D: Society and Space, 21(6):635–651.
Kazimi, A. (1997) Shooting Indians: A Journey with Jeff Thomas. Vtape Distribution.
Keeling, K. (2003) "'In The Interval': Frantz Fanon and the 'Problems' of Visual Representation', Qui Parle, 13(2):91–118.
———. (2007) The Witch's Flight: The Cinematic, the Black Femme, and the Image of Common Sense, Durham, NC: Duke University Press.
Kennett, P. and Iwata, M. (2003) International Journal of Urban and Regional Research, 27(1):62–74.
Khalidi, R. and Samour, S. (2011) 'Neoliberalism as Liberation: the Statehood Program and the Remaking of the National Movement,' Journal of Palestine Studies, 40(2).
Khayyat, E. (2014) 'How to Turn Turk?' Eurozine, September 17. Online. Available HTTP: <http://www.eurozine.com/authors/khayyat.html> (Accessed 7 January 2016).
Kilgour, D. M. and Wolinsky-Nahmias, Y. (2004) 'Game Theory and International Environmental Policy,' in D. F. Sprinz, and Y. Wolinsky-Nahmias (eds.), Models, Numbers, and Cases: Methods for Studying International Relations, Ann Arbor, MI: University of Michigan Press.
Kim, N. Y. (2007) 'A Return to More Blatant Class and 'Race' Bias in U.S. Immigration Policy?' Du Bois Review, 4(2):469–477.
Kirkwood, J. (1986) Ser política en Chile: las feministas y los partidos, Santiago-Chile: Facultad Latinoamericana de Ciencias Sociales.
Koolhaas, R. (1995) 'The Generic City,' in J. Sigler (ed.), S,M,L,XL, New York, NY: Monicelli Press.
Kopytoff, I. (1986) 'The Cultural Biography of Things: Commoditization as Process', in A. Appadurai (ed.) The Social Life of Things, New York, NY: Cambridge University Press.
Kordela, K. (2006) 'Capital: At Least It Kills Time,' Rethinking Marxism, 18(4):539–563.
Koseirodosho (Ministry of Health, Labor and Welfare) (2006) Koseirodosho Hakusho: Jizoku Kanou na Shakai Hoshou Seido to Sasae ai no Junkan – 'Chiiki' Heno Sanka to 'hatarakikata' no Minaoshi (White Paper from the Ministry of Health, Labor and Welfare: Establishing and Supporting a Lasting Social Security System- Checking the 'Regional and 'Work' Support Systems), Tokyo, Japan: Kyousei.
Krasner, S. (2001) 'Sovereignty'. Online. Available HTTP: <http://www.globalpolicy.org/nations/realism.htm> (Accessed 30 May, 2015).
Kratochwil, F. V. (1989) Rules, Norms and Decisions: On the Conditions of Practical and Legal Reasoning in International Relations and Domestic Affairs, New York, NY: Cambridge University Press.
Kremeniuk, V. A. and Sjostedt, G. (eds) (2000) International Economic Negotiation: Models vs. Reality, Cheltenham, UK: Edward Elgar Press.
Krishna, S. (1999) Postcolonial Insecurities: India, Sri Lanka, and the Question of Nationhood, Minneapolis, MN: University of Minnesota Press.
Lacan, J. (1966, 1977) Ecrits: A Selection, A. Sheridan (trans.), New York, NY: W.W. Norton & Co.
———. (2006) Ecrits, B. Fink (trans.), New York and London: W.W. Norton & Company.

Lapid, Y. and K. Friedrich (1996) *The Return of Culture and Identity in International Relations Theory*, Boulder, CO: Lynne Rienner.
Laufer, S. (1999) '*Africa Must Embrace Globalisation – Mbeki*', Johannesburg: Business Day. Online. Available HTTP: <http://www.hartford-hwp.com/archives/30/117.html.> (Accessed 15 September 2012).
Leander, A. (2011) 'The Promises, Problems, and Potentials of a Bourdieu-Inspired Staging of International Relations,' *International Political Sociology*, 5(3):294–313.
Lee, J. (1990) *Jacques Lacan*, Boston, MA: Twayne Publishers.
Lee, S. (2006) *When the Levees Broke: A Requiem In Four Acts*, New York, NY: HBO Video.
Le Goff, J. (1982) *Time, Work, and Culture in the Middle Ages*, Chicago, London: The University of Chicago Press.
Lemke, T. (2011) *Biopolitics: An Advanced Introduction*, New York, NY: NYU Press.
Levinas, E. (1987) *Time and the Other and Other Essays*, R.A. Cohen (trans.), Pittsburgh, PA: Duquesne University Press.
Levi-Strauss, C. (1966) *The Savage Mind*, Chicago, IL: Chicago University Press.
Lewis, M. (2008) *Derrida and Lacan: Another Writing*, Edinburgh, UK: Edinburgh University Press.
Ling, C.M. (2007) 'Bali Achieved What It Set Out to Do', Kuala Lumpur, Malaysia: New Straits Times (30 December 2007).
Little, R. (2007) *The Balance of Power in International Relations: Metaphors, Myths and Models*, Cambridge, UK: Cambridge University Press.
Locke, J. (1988[1690]) *Two Treatises of Government*, P. Laslett (ed.), Cambridge, UK: Cambridge University Press.
Lockwood, D. (1992) *Solidarity and Schism: 'The Problem of Disorder' in Durkheimianand Marxist Sociology*, Oxford, UK: Oxford University Press.
Loh, D. (2002) '*It's Not Easy, Saving the Earth*', Kuala Lumpur, Malaysia: New Straits Times, 3(11 August 2002).
Lovell, J. (2012) 'Clean Energy Lag Means World Is Headed for 6-Degree-Celsius Temperature Rise, Says IEA,' *Climate Wire*, April 26, sec. Technology.
Lukács, G. (1989) *The Historical Novel*, London, UK: Merlin Press.
Lundborg, T. (2011) *Politics of the Event: Time, Movement, Becoming*, New York, NY: Routledge.
———. (2012) *Politics of the Event: Time, Movement, Becoming*, New York, NY: Routledge.
Lutterbeck, D. (2006) 'Policing Migration in the Mediterranean,' *Mediterranean Politics*, 11: 9–82.
Lyman, C.M. (1982) *The Vanishing Race and Other Illusions: Photographs by Edward S. Curtis*, New York, NY: Pantheon Books.
Machiavelli, N. (2008 [1532]) *The Prince*, Oxford, UK: Oxford University Press.
Mahmood, S. (2011) *The Politics of Piety: The Islamic Revival and the Feminist Subject*,: Princeton, NJ: Princeton University Press.
Maines, D.R. (1987) 'The Significance of Temporality for the Development of Sociological Theory,' *The Sociological Quarterly*, 28(3):303–311.
Makepeace, A. (2000) *Coming To Light: Edward S. Curtis and The North American Indians*. Makepeace Films.
———. (2002) *Edward S. Curtis: Coming to Light*, Washington, DC: National Geographic Society.
Malkki, L.H. (1996) 'Speechless Emissaries: Refugees, Humanitarianism, and Dehistoricization,' *Cultural Anthropology*, 11(3):377–404.

———. (2010) 'Children, Humanity, and the Infantilization of Peace,' I. Feldman and M.I. Ticktin (eds.), *In the Name of Humanity: The Government of Threat and Care*, 58–85, Durham, NC: Duke University Press.
Malksoo, M. (2009) 'The Memory Politics of Becoming European: The East European Subalterns and the Collective Memory of Europe,' *European Journal of International Relations*, 15(4):653–680.
Mamdani, M. (1973) *From Citizen to Refugee: Uganda Asians Come to Britain*, London, UK: Frances Pinter.
———. (1996) *Citizen and Subject: Contemporary Africa and the Legacy of Late Colonialism*, Princeton, NJ: Princeton University Press.
———. (2009) *Saviors and Survivors: Darfur, Politics and the War on Terror*, New York, NY: Pantheon Books.
Mandela, N. (1994) '*State of the Nation Address*', Republic of South Africa. Online. Available HTTP: <http://www.info.gov.za/speeches/1994/170595002.htm.> (Accessed 19 June 2008).
Mannheim, K. (1943) *Diagnoses of Our Time*, London, UK: Kegan Paul, Trench, Trubner & Co.
Manning, E. (2004) 'Time for Politics,' in J. Edkins, V. Pin-Fat and M.J. Shapiro (eds.), *Sovereign Lives: Power in Global Politics*, 61–80, New York: Routledge.
Manzo, K. (2008) 'Imaging Humanitarianism: NGO Identity and the Iconography of Childhood,' *Antipode*, 40(4):632–657.
Marable, M., and Mullings, L. (eds.) (2009) *Let Nobody Turn Us Around: An African American Anthology*, 2nd edn, Lanham, MD: Rowman & Littlefield.
Marazzi, C. (2010) *The Violence of Finance Capitalism*, K. Lebedeva (trans.), Los Angeles, CA: Semiotext(e).
Marriott, D. (2000) *On Black Men*, New York, NY: Columbia University Press.
———. (2011) 'Whither Fanon?' *Textual Practices*, 25(1):33–69.
———.. (2014) 'No Lords A-Leaping: Fanon, C.L.R. James, and the Politics of Invention,' *Humanities*, 3:517–545.
Marx, K. (1970) *A Contribution to the Critique of Political Economy*, New York, NY: International Publishers.
———. (1985) *The Communist Manifesto*, London, UK: Penguin Books.
———. (1990) *Capital: A Critique of Political Economy vol.1*, London, UK: Penguin Books.
———. (1993) *Grundrisse: Foundations of the Critique of Political Economy*, London, UK: Penguin Books.
Masaryk, T.G. (1994) *Constructive Sogiological Theory*, A. Woolfolk and J.B. Imber (eds), New Brunswick, NJ: Transaction Publishers.
Massad, J. (2000) *Colonial Effects: The Making of National Identity in Jordan*, New York, NY: Columbia University Press.
———. (2006) *The Persistence of the Palestinian Question*, Abingdon, UK: Routledge.
———. (2013) 'Love, Fear and the Arab Spring,' *Public Culture*, 26(1):127–152.
Massey, D. (1992) 'Politics and Space/Time,' *New Left Review* I, 196:65–84.
———. (1994) *Space, Place, and Gender*, Minneapolis, MN: University of Minnesota Press.
Mathur, R. and J. Marsden (2004) 'Trauma and temporality: On the Origins of Post-Traumatic Stress,' *Theory and Psychology*, 14(2):205–219.

Maxwell, A. (1999) *Colonial Photography & Exhibitions: Representations of the 'Native' and the Making of European Identities*, London and New York: Leicester University Press.

May, J., and Thrift, N. (2001) *Timespace: Geographies of Temporality*, New York, NY: Routledge.

Mazzella, S. (2007) 'Putting Asylum to the Test: Between Immigration Policy and Co-Development,' in T. Fabre and S.C. Paul (eds.), *Between Europe and the Mediterranean: The Challenge and the Fears*, 41–50, New York, NY: Palgrave Macmillan.

Mbeki, T. (1998) 'NAM: The ties that bind us,' Johannesburg, South Africa: The Sowetan.

———. (1999) '*Address at the Opening of Parliament*', Republic of South Africa. Online. Available HTTP: <http://www.info.gov.za/speeches/1999/9906281018a 1006.htm.> (Accessed 19 June 2008).

———. (2001) '*State of the Nation Address*'. Online. Available HTTP:<http://www.info.gov.za/speeches/2001/0102131223p1001.htm.> (Accessed 19 June 2008).

———. (2002) '*Environment and Sustainable Development; Translating the Dream of Sustainable Development into Reality*,' Johannesburg, South Africa: Africa News.

———. (2004) *State of the Nation Address*. Online. Available HTTP: <http://www.info.gov.za/speeches/2004/04020610561002.htm.> (Accessed 19 June 2008).

———. (2006) *State of the Nation Address*. Online. Available HTTP: <http://www.info.gov.za/speeches/2006/06020310531001.htm.> (Accessed 19 June 2008).

Mbembe, A. (1992a) '*Prosaics of Servitude and Authoritarian Civilities*,' J. Roitman (trans.), *Public Culture*, 5(1):123–145.

———. (1992b) 'Provisional Notes on the Postcolony,' *Africa: Journal of the International African Institute*, 62(1):3–34.

———. (2001) *On the Postcolony*, Berkeley, CA: University of California Press.

———. (2002) 'African Modes of Self Writing,' *Public Culture*, 14(1):239–273.

———. (2003) 'Necropolitics,' L. Meintjes (trans.), *Public Culture*, 15(1):11–40.

———. (2010) 'Africa in Theory: A Conversation between Jean Comaroff and Achille Mbembe, *Anthropological Quarterly*, 83(3):653–678.

Mbembe, A. and Roitman J. (1995) 'Figures of the Subject in Times of Crisis,' *Public Culture*, 7:323–352.

McClintock, A. (1994) *Imperial Leather: Race, Gender and Sexuality in the Colonial Contest*, New York, NY: Routledge.

McGowan, T. (2011) *Out of Time: Desire in Atemporal Cinema*, Minneapolis, MN: University of Minnesota Press.

McSweeney, B. (1999) *Security, Identity and Interests: A Sociology of International Relations*, Cambridge, UK: Cambridge University Press.

Médecins Sans Frontières (2006) *Violence and Immigration: Report on Illegal sub-Saharan Immigrants in Morocco*, Paris: Médecins Sans Frontières.

Merchant, C. (2008) '"The Violence of Impediments': Francis Bacon and the Origins of Experimentation,' *History of Science Society*, 99:731–760.

Miller, A., S. Roberts and V. LaPoe. (2014) *Oil and Water: Media Lessons from Hurricane Katrina and the Deepwater Horizon Disaster*, Jackson, MS: University of Mississippi Press.

Milliken, J. (1999) 'The Study of Discourse in International Relations,' *European Journal of International Relations*, 5(2):225–254.

Mishra, J. (2009) 'Gear up for Climate-Change Policy,' *The Economic Times*. Online. Available HTTP: <http://articles.economictimes.indiatimes.com/2009-11-18/news/

28468323_1_climate-change-energy-efficiency-emission-curbs.> (Accessed 14 October 2012).

Mitchell, T. (2009) 'The Virtues of Recalcitrance: Democracy from Foucault to Latour,' delivered at UCLA's Centre for Near Eastern Studies conference, 'Foucault and Middle East Studies', April 29, 2009. Online. Available HTTP: <http://web.international.ucla.edu/cnes/podcast/107626,> (Accessed 20 May 2012).

Miura, M. (2008) "*Labor Politics in Japan during the Lost Fifteen Years': From the Politics of Productivity to the Politics of Consumption*", *Labor History*, 49(2):161–176.

Mizushima, H. (2007) *Netto Kafue Nanmin to Hinkon Nippon* (Net café refugees and poverty in Japan), Tokyo, Japan: *Nihon Terebi Hoso Kabushiki Kaisha.*

Mizuuchi, T. (2003) 'The Growth in the Number of People Sleeping Rough in the City of Osaka, Japan,' *Urban Culture Research*, 1:20–36.

MSNBC. Online. Available HTTP: <http://www.nbcnews.com/id/24054024/ns/business-personal_finance/t/tax-time-illegal-immigrants-are-paying-too/> (Accessed 10 January 2011).

———. (2009) '*Climate Talks Resume after Hours-Long Boycott*', Copenhagen, Denmark: *Associated Press*. Online. Available HTTP: <http://www.msnbc.msn.com/id/344 12503/ns/us_news-environment/t/climate-talks-resume-after-hours-long-boycott/> (Accessed 14 October 2012).

Moloney, P. (2011) 'Hobbes, Savagery, and International Anarchy,' *American Political Science Review*, 105(1):189–204.

Monzini, P. (2007) 'Sea-Border Crossings: The Organization of Irregular Migration to Italy,' *Mediterranean Politics*, 12:163–184.

Morgenthau, H. J. (1948) *Politics Among Nations: The Struggle for Power and Peace*, New York, NY: McGraw-Hill.

———. (1951) *In Defense of the National Interest: A Critical Examination of American Foreign Policy*, New York, NY: Alfred A. Knop.

Mori, Y. (2005) 'Culture = Politics: The Emergence of New Cultural Forms of Protest in the Age of *Freeter*,' *Inter-Asia Cultural Studies*, 6(1):17–29.

Moss, P. and Tilly, C. (1996) "'Soft skills' and Race: An Investigation of Black Men's Employment Problems,' *Work and Occupations*, 23(3):252–276.

Moten, F. (1994) 'Music Against the Law of Reading the Future and *Rodney King*,' *Journal of the Midwest Modern Language Association*, 27(1):51–64.

———. (2003) *In the Break: The Aesthetics of the Black Radical Tradition*, Minneapolis, MN: University of Minnesota Press.

———. (2004) 'Knowledge of Freedom,' *CR: The New Centennial Review*, 4(2):269–310.

———. (2007) '*Black Optimism/Black Operation*', unpublished paper on file with the author.

———. (2008a) 'Black Op,' *PMLA*, 123(5):1743–1747.

———. (2008b) 'The Case of Blackness,' *Criticism*, 50(2):177–218.

Muller, J. and W. Richardson. (eds.) (1988) *The Purloined Poe: Lacan, Derrida and Psychoanalytic Reading*, Baltimore, MD: Johns Hopkins University Press.

Munif, A. (1989) *Cities of Salt*, P. Theroux (trans.), New York, NY: Vintage.

Muñoz, J. E. (1999) *Disidentifications: Queers of Color and the Performance of Politics*, Minneapolis, MN: University of Minnesota Press.

Muntaqim, J. A. (18 September 1979) 'On the Black Liberation Army,' *Arm the Spirit*.

Murillo, J. III (2013) 'Black (in) Time – Untimely Blackness,' in *Quantum Blackanics* (forthcoming), Providence, Rhode Island: Brown University.

My House. (2012) Film. Directed by Yukihiko Tsutsumi.

Nhat Hanh, T. (1999) *Call Me by My True Names*, Berkeley, CA: Parallax Press.

Najm, A. F. (2011) 'I am the People', in S. Antoon (ed.), 'Singing for the Revolution', *Jadaliyya*. Online. Available HTTP: <http://www.jadaliyya.com/pages/index/508/singing-for-the-revolution>.

Nandy, A. (1988) *The Intimate Enemy: Loss and Recovery of Self Under Colonialism*, New Delhi, India: Oxford University Press.

Nashef, I. (2012) '*Hawl Imkaniat Dirasit al-Nizam al-Ist'mari: Filastin Namudhajan*' ('Around the Possibilities of Studying the Colonial Regime: Palestine as Model'). Online. Available HTTP: <http://www.qadita.net/2012/01/27/ismaeel/> (Accessed 30 January 2012).

Nassar, H. K. and N. Rahman (2008) *Mahmoud Darwish: Exile's Poet. Critical Essays*, Northampton, MA: Olive Branch Press.

Navarrette, R., Jr. (2005) '*The Wrong Color in New Orleans?*' Chicago, IL: Chicago Tribune. Online. Available HTTP: <http://articles.chicagotribune.com/2005-10-21/news/0510210277_1_nagin-big-easy-immigration-debate> (Accessed 10 January 2011).

Neckerman, K. M., and Kirschenman, J. (1991) 'Hiring Strategies, Racial Bias, and Inner-City Workers,' *Social Problems*, 38(4):433–447.

Neumann, I. (2002) 'Returning Practice to the Linguistic Turn: The Case of Diplomacy,' *Millennium*, 31(3):627–651.

New Straits Times (2007) '*What's Next after Kyoto*', Kuala Lampur, Malaysia: New Strait Times (10 December 2007). Online. Available HTTP: <http://www.nexis.com.ezproxy.lib.gla.ac.uk/results/docview/docview.do?docLinkInd=true&risb=21_T22077257605&format=GNBFI&sort=BOOLEAN&startDocNo=1&resultsUrlKey=29_T22077257609&cisb=22_T22077257608&treeMax=true&treeWidth=0&csi=151977&docNo=4>.

Nicolaidis, K. A. and Nicolaidis, D. (2007) 'Europe in the Mirror of the Mediterranean,' in T. Fabre and S.C. Paul (eds.), *Between Europe and the Mediterranean: The Challenge and the Fears*, New York, NY: Palgrave Macmillan.

Nicolson, M. (2015) 'Artist Statement,' *The Medicine Project*. Online. Available HTTP: <http://www.themedicineproject.com/marianne-nicolson.html> (Accessed 13 May 2015).

Niebuhr, R. (2001) *Moral Man and Immoral Society: A Study in Ethics and Politics*, Louisville, KY: Westminster John Knox Press.

Nieuwenhuys, O. (1998) 'Global Childhood and the Politics of Contempt,' *Alternatives: Global, Local, Political*, 23(3):267–289.

Nixon, R. (2011) *Slow Violence and the Environmentalism of the Poor*, Cambridge, MA: Harvard University Press.

Nolin, C. (2006) *Transnational Ruptures: Gender and Forced Migration*, Hampshire, UK: Ashgate.

Nora, P. (1996) 'General Introduction: Between Memory and History,' in P. Nora (ed.), *Realms of Memory Vol. 1*, 1–20, New York, NY: Columbia University Press.

Nyers, P. (ed.) (2009) *Securitizations of Citizenship*, London: Routledge.

Nyong'o, T. (2002) 'Racist Kitsch and Black Performance,' *Yale Journal of Criticism*, 15(2):371–391.

———. (2009) 'Barack Hussein Obama, Or The Name of the Father', *The Scholar & Feminist Online*, 7(2), New York: Barnard Centre for Research on Women. Online. Available HTTP: <http://sfonline.barnard.edu/africana/print_nyongo.htm> (Accessed 26 March 2015).

Nyquist, M. (2013) *Arbitrary Rule: Slavery, Tyranny, and the Power of Life and Death*, Chicago, IL: University of Chicago Press.

O'Boyle, G. (2002) 'Theories of Justification and Political Violence: Examples from Four Groups,' *Terrorism and Political Violence*, 14(2):23–46.

OECD (2012) *OECD FactBook Statistics 2011–2012: Economic, Environmental and Social Statistics*. (2012) Paris, France: Organization for Economic Cooperation and Development. Online. Available HTTP: <http://www.oecd-ilibrary.org/economics/oecd-factbook-2011–2012-factbook-2011-en>.

Ogawa, A. (2009) *The Failure of Civil Society: The Third Sector in Contemporary Japan*, New York, NY: SUNY Press.

Onuf, N.G. (2012) *World of Our Making: Rules and Rule in Social Theory and International Relations*, reissue, Abingdon, UK: Routledge.

Ophir, A., M. Givoni, and S. Hanafi (2009) *The Power of Inclusive Exclusion: Anatomy of Israeli Rule in the Occupied Palestinian Territories*, New York, NY: Zone Books.

Osborne, P. *The Politics of Time: Modernity and the Avant-Garde*, London, UK: Verso.

———. (2008) 'Marx and the Philosophy of Time,' *Radical Philosophy*, 147:15–22.

———. (2009) 'Negation, Affirmation, the New,' *CRMEP Research Seminar*, London, UK: Middlesex University Press.

Osho (1996) 'Osho on Time', *Osho Times*. Online. Available HTTP: <http://oshotimes.blog.osho.com/category/osho-on-time/>.

Osondu, E.C. (2008) *Waiting*, New York, NY: Guernica/A Magazine of Art & Politics. Online. Available HTTP: <http://www.guernicamag.com/fiction/waiting/> (Accessed 1 October 2008).

———. (2010) 'Janjaweed Wife,' *The Kenyon Review New Series*, 32(2):143–152.

Pagden, A. (1993) *European Encounters with the New World: From Renaissance to Romanticism*, New Haven, CT: Yale University Press.

Palestinian National Authority (2008) *Palestinian National Development Plan*. Online. Available HTTP: <mdtf.undp.org/document/download/4655> (Accessed 13 May 2015).

———. (2009) *Ending the Occupation, Establishing the State*. Online. Available HTTP: <http://unispal.un.org/UNISPAL.NSF/0/A013B65A5984E671852576 B800581931> (Accessed 13 May 2015).

———. (2011) *Establishing the State, Building Our Future*. Online. Available HTTP: <http://mopad.pna.ps/enp.pdf> (Accessed 13 May 2015).

———. (2014) *State Building to Sovereignty*. Online. Available HTTP: <http://www.mopad.pna.ps/en/images/PDFs/Palestine%20State_final.pdf> (Accessed 13 May 2015).

Park, E.J.W. (1999) 'Racial Ideology and Hiring Decisions in Silicon Valley,' *Qualitative Sociology*, 22(3):223–233.

Patterson, O. (1982) *Slavery and Social Death*, Cambridge, MA: Harvard University Press.

Pearce, R.H. (1965) *Savagism and Civilization: A Study of the Indian and the American Mind*, Berkeley, CA: University of California Press.

Peress, M. (2004) *Dvorak to Duke Ellington*, New York, NY: Oxford University Press.

Persaud, R. and R.B.J. Walker (2001) 'Apertura: Race in International Relations', *Alternatives: Global, Local, Political*, 26:373–376.

Pham, Q. and H. Muppidi (2012) 'Colonial Wars, Postcolonial Spectres: The Anxiety of Domination,' in T. Barkawi and K. Stanski (eds.), *Orientalism and War*, London, UK: Hurst Publishers.

Poo, A. (2007) *Unregulated Economy in NYC, Ai-jen Poo*, Labor Research Association. Online. Available HTTP: <https://www.youtube.com/watch? v=vbXl4GTH_ik> (Accessed 10 February 2011).

Postone, M. (1993) *Time, Labor, and Social Domination: A Reinterpretation of Marx's Critical Theory*, Cambridge, UK: Cambridge University Press.

———. (2004) 'Critique and Historical Transformation,' *Historical Materialism*, 12(3):53–72.

Pouliot, V. (2008) 'The Logic of Practicality: A Theory of Practice of Security Communities,' *International Organization*, 62(2):257–288.

———. (2010) *International Security in Practice*, Cambridge, UK: Cambridge University Press.

Povinelli, E.A. (2011) *Economies of Abandonment: Social Belonging and Endurance in Late Liberalism*, Durham and London: Duke University Press.

Prashad, V. (2008) *The Darker Nations: A People's History of the Third World*, New York, NY: The New Press.

Pratt, M. L. (1992) *Imperial Eyes: Travel Writing and Transculturation*, New York, London: Routledge.

Prozorov, S. (2011) 'The Other as Past and Present: Beyond the Logic of 'Temporal Othering' in IR Theory,' *Review of International Studies*, 37:1273–1293.

Purchas, S. (1906[1625]) *Hakluytus Posthumus or Purchas His Pilgrimes, Vol. XIX*, Glasgow, Scotland, UK: James MacLehose.

Putnam, R. (1988) 'Diplomacy and Domestic Politics: The Logic of Two-Level Games,' *International Organization*, 42:427–460.

Qabbani, N. (1986) 'Footnotes to the Book of Setback', in A. al-Udhari (ed) *Modern Poetry of the Arab World*, A. al-Udhari (trans.), London, UK: Puffin.

Quayson, A. (2002) 'Obverse Denominations: Africa?' *Public Culture*, 14(3):585–588.

Quijano, A. (2000) 'Coloniality of Power, Eurocentrism, and Latin America,' M. Ennis (trans.), *Nepantla: Views from the South*, 1(3):533–580.

Raheja, M. (2013) *Reservation Reelism: Redfacing, Visual Sovereignty, and Representations of Native Americans in Film*, Lincoln, NE, USA: University of Nebraska Press.

Rancière, J. (2004) 'Who Is the Subject of the Rights of Man?' *The South Atlantic Quarterly*, 103(2/3):297–310.

———. (2008) *The Politics of Aesthetics*, New York, NY: Continuum.

———. (2014) *Figures of History*, J. Rose (trans.), Cambridge, UK: Polity.

Ransby, B. (2006) 'Katrina, Black Women, and the Deadly Discourse on Black Poverty in America,' *Du Bois Review*, 3(1):215–22.

Read, J. (2003) *The Micro-Politics of Capital: Marx and the Prehistory of the Present*, Albany, NY: State University of New York Press.

Redfield, P. (2012) 'Bioexpectations: Life Technologies as Humanitarian Goods,' *Public Culture*, 24(1):157–183.

Regis, H.A. (2001) 'Blackness and the Politics of Memory in the New Orleans Second Line,' *American Ethnologist*, 28(4):752–777.

Revill, J. (1992) 'Can Rio Save Planet Earth?' *Mail on Sunday*, 8–9 (17 May 1992).

Richard, N. (2000) 'The Reconfigurations of Post-Dictatorship Critical Thought,' *Journal of Latin American Cultural Studies*, 9:273–282.

Robinson, C. (2000) *Black Marxism: The Making of the Black Radical Tradition*, Durham. NC: University of North Carolina Press.

Roitman, J. (2012) *Africa, Otherwise*, New Haven, CT: Yale Agrarian Studies Colloquium. Online. Available HTTP: <http://www.yale.edu/agrarianstudies/colloqpapers/13roitman.pdf> (Accessed 1 February 2013).

Rony, F.T. (1996) *The Third Eye: Race, Cinema, and Ethnographic Spectacle*, Durham, NC: Duke University Press.

Rose, N. (1996) 'Refiguring the Territory of Government', *Economy and Society,* 25(3):327–356.

Russ, A.R. (2013) *The Illusion of History: Time and the Radical Political Imagination,* Washington, DC: The Catholic University of America Press.

Russell, C. (1999) *Experimental Ethnography: the Work of Film in the Age of Video,* Durham, NC: Duke University Press.

Sahlins, M. (2005) 'Hierarchy, Equality, and the Sublimation of Anarchy: The Western Illusion of Human Nature,' The Tanner Lectures on Human Values, the University of Michigan, November 4.

Said, E.W. (1992) *The Question of Palestine: With a New Preface and Epilogue,* New York: Vintage Books:

Sakaguchi, K. (1993) *Culture and Imperialism,* New York, NY: Vintage Books.

———. *Zero Yen Project.* Online. Available HTTP: <http://www.thememagazine.com/stories/kyohei-sakaguchis-zero-yen-project/>.

———. (2006) *Zero Yen House.* Online. Available HTTP: <http://www.0yenhouse.com/en/index.html>.

———. (2012) *Zero Publics- Practice for Revolution.* Exhibition. Online. Available HTTP: <http://www.berlinerfestspiele.de/en/aktuell/festivals/ foreign_affairs/p rogram_fa/pro>.

Saldaña-Portillo, M.F. (2003) *The Revolutionary Imagination in the Americas and the Age of Development,* Durham, NC: Duke University Press.

Saldanha, A. (2008) 'Heterotopia and Structuralism,' *Environment and Planning A,* 40:2080–2096.

Sandoval, C. (2010) *Citizenship and the Barriers to Black and Latino Coalitions in Chicago,* New York, NY: North American Congress on Latin America. Online. Available HTTP: <https://nacla.org/article/citizenship-and-barriers-black-and-latino-coalitions-chicago> (Accessed 25 February 2011).

Sartre, J.-P. (1976 [1960]) *Critique of Dialectical Reason, Volume I: Theory of Practical Ensembles,* London, UK: NLB.

Saussure, F. (2011) *Course in General Linguistics,* W. Baskin (trans.), P. Meisel and H. Saussy (eds.), New York, NY: Columbia University Press.

Schatzki, T.R., K.K. Cetina and E. von Savigny (eds.) (2001) *The Practice Turn in Contemporary Theory,* New York, NY: Routledge.

Schweizer, H. (2008) *On Waiting,* London, UK: Routledge.

Scott, D. (2008) 'Tragedy's Time: Post Emancipation Futures Past and Present,' in R. Felski (ed.), Rethinking Tragedy, 199–218. Baltimore, MD: John Hopkins University.

———. (2014) *Omens of Adversity: Tragedy, Time, Memory, Justice,* Durham, NC: Duke University Press.

Scott, J. and G. Marshall (eds.) (2009) 'Fatalism,' *A Dictionary of Sociology,* New York, NY: Oxford University Press.

Seixas, N.S., H. Blecker, J. Camp and R. Neitzel (2008) 'Occupational Health and Safety Experience of Day Laborers in Seattle, WA', *American Journal of Industrial Medicine,* 56:399–406.

Sexton, J. (2007) 'The Obscurity of Black Suffering,' in G. Ford, J. Flaherty and b. hooks (eds.) *What Lies Beneath: Katrina, Race, and the State of the Nation,* Cambridge, MA: South End Press.

———. (2009) 'The Ruse of Engagement: Black Masculinity and the Cinema of Policing,' *American Quarterly,* 61(1): 39–63.

———. (2010a) 'African American Studies', John Carlos Rowe (ed.), *A Concise Companion to American Studies,* 210–228, Malden, MA: Wiley-Blackwell:.

——. (2010b) 'People-of-Color-Blindness: Notes on the Afterlife of Slavery,' *Social Text*, 28(2):31–56.
Sexton, J. and H. Copeland (2003) 'Raw Life: An Introduction,' *Qui Parle*, 13(2):53–62.
Al-Shabbi, A. (1955) *The Will of Life*, E. Colla (trans.). Online. Available HTTP: <http://arablit.wordpress.com/2011/01/16/two-translations-of-abu-al-qasim-al-shabis-if-the-people-wanted-life-one-day/>.
——. (1955) *To the Tyrants of the World!*, A. J. Arberry (trans.). Online. Available HTTP: <http://aasilahmad.net/abu-al-qasim-al-shabi-the-poet-of-the-tunisia-and-egyptianrevolution/>.
Shafiq, M. (2010) 'Al-thawabet al-filastiniya wa al-laght hawluha' ('The Palestinian *thawabet* and the clamour around them'), *Al-Jazeera*. Online. Available HTTP: <http://www.aljazeera.net/pointofview/pages/ff1684c4-7761-427a-999b-d4609edc49a1> (Accessed 21 June 2012).
Shakur, A. (1987) *Assata: An Autobiography*, Chicago, IL: Lawrence Hill Books.
Shapiro, M. (2000) 'National Times and Other Times: Re-Thinking Citizenship,' *Cultural Studies*, 14(1):79–98.
——. (2001) *For Moral Ambiguity: National Culture and the Politics of the Family*, Minneapolis, MN: Minnesota University Press.
——. (2005a) 'The Discursive Space of Global Spaces of Global Politics,' *Journal of Environmental Policy & Planning*, 7(3):227–238.
——. (2005b) *Studies in Trans-disciplinary Method: After the Aesthetic Turn*, 2012. New York, NY: Routledge,.
——. (2006) *Deforming American Political Thought*, Lexington, KY: Kentucky University Press.
——. (2010) *The Time of the City: Politics, Philosophy, and Genre*, New York, NY: Routledge.
Sharpe, C. (2010) *Monstrous Intimacies: Making Post-Slavery Subjects*, Durham, NC: Duke University Press.
Shilliam, R. (2004) 'Hegemony and the Unfashionable Problematic of 'Primitive Accumulation'', *Millennium: Journal of International Studies*, 33(1):59–88.
——. (2015) *The Black Pacific: Anti-Colonial Struggles and Oceanic Connections*, New York, New Delhi, Sydney and London: Bloomsbury Publishers.
Shue, H. (1999) 'Global Environment and International Inequality,' *International Affairs*, 75(3):531–545.
Simon, J. (2006) *Irregular Transit Migration in the Mediterranean: Facts, Figures and Insights*, Copenhagen, Denmark: Danish Institute for International Studies.
Singer, J. D. (1961) 'The Level of Analysis Problem,' *World Politics*, 14(1):77–92.
Slaughter, J. R. (2007) *Human Rights, Inc.: The World Novel, Narrative Form, and International Law*, New York, NY: Fordham University Press.
Sliwinski, S. (2006) 'The Childhood of Human Rights: The Kodak on the Congo,' *Journal of Visual Culture*, 5(3):333–363.
Smith, J. (1969[1612]) 'A Map of Virginia,' in P. L. Barbour (ed.) *The Jamestown Voyages under the First Charter 1606–1609, Vol. II*, Cambridge, MA: Hakluyt Society.
Smith, N. (2006) 'There's No Such Thing as a Natural Disaster,' *Understanding Katrina*. Online. Available HTTP: <http://understandingkatrina.ssrc.org/Smith/>(Accessed 11 May 2015).
Sobchack, V. (1984) 'Inscribing Ethical Space: Ten Propositions on Death, Representation, and Documentary,' *Quarterly Review of Film Studies*, 9(4):283–300.

Soja, E. (1995) 'Heterotopologies: A Remembrance of Other Spaces in the Citadel-LA,' in S. Watson and K. Gibson (eds.), *Postmodern Cities and Spaces*, Oxford, UK: Blackwell.

Solomon, T. (2013) 'Time and Subjectivity in World Politics,' *International Studies Quarterly*, 58(4):671–681.

Sontag, S. (1973) *On Photography*, London, UK: Penguin.

Soroos, M. S. (1993) 'Arctic Haze and Transboundary Air Pollution: Conditions Governing Success and Failure,' in O. R. Yong and G. Osherenko (eds.), *Polar Politics: Creating International Environmental Regimes*, Ithaca, NY: Cornell University Press.

Spijkerboer, T. (2007) 'The Human Costs of Border Control,' *European Journal of Migration and Law*, 9:127–139.

Spillers, H. (1987) "'Mama's Baby, Papa's Maybe': An American Grammar Book,' *Diacritics*, 17(2):64–81.

———. (2003) *Black, White, and in Color: Essays on American Literature and Culture*, Chicago, IL: University of Chicago Press.

Spira, T. L. (2009) '*Remembering Trauma in a Time of War: The Psycho-Affective Economies of Neoliberalism and the Radical Imagination of Dissent*', Ph.D. dissertation, University of California Santa Cruz.

———. (2011) 'Neoliberal Captivities: Pisagua Prison and the Low Intensity Form,' in M. Soderstrom, J. Stahl and H. Tinsman (eds.), *Radical History Review*, 112:127–146.

———. (2014) 'Neoliberal Transitions: The Santiago General Cemetery and the Affective Economies of Counter-Revolution,' *Identities: Global Studies in Culture and Power*, 21(4):344–363.

Starobinski, J. (1993) *Blessings in Disguise; Or, the Morality of Evil*, A. Goldhammer (trans.), Cambridge, MA: Polity.

Steele, B. J. (2008) *Ontological Security in International Relations*, New York, NY: Routledge, New International Relations Series.

———. (2010) *Defacing Power: The Aesthetics of Insecurity in Global Politics*, Ann Arbor, MI: University of Michigan Press.

———. (2012) *Alternative Accountabilities in Global Politics: The Scars of Violence*, Abingdon, UK: Routledge.

Steger, B. (2006) 'Sleeping Through Class to Success: Japanese Notions of Time and Diligence,' *Time and Society*, 15:197–214.

Stoetzler, M. (2004) 'Postone's Marx: A Theorist of Modern Society, Its Social Movements and Its Imprisonment by Abstract Labour,' *Historical Materialism*, 12(3):261–283.

Stoler, A. L. (2002) *Carnal Knowledge and Imperial Power: Race and the Intimate in Colonial Rule*, Berkeley, Los Angeles, and London: University of California Press.

Stolorow, R. D. (2003) 'Trauma and Temporality,' *Psychoanalytic Psychology*, 20(1):158–161.

Story, L. and R. Farzad. (2005) 'HURRICANE KATRINA: THE COST; Insurers Estimate Damage at $9 Billion, Among Costliest U.S. Storms on Record,' *The New York Times*. Online. Available HTTP: <http://query.nytimes.com/gst/full page.html?res=9407E3DB 1631F933A0575BC0A9639C8B63> (Accessed 11 May 2015).

Suganami, H. (1999) 'Agents, structures, narratives,' *European Journal of International Relations*, 5(3):365–386.

Summers, C. (2011) 'Boys, Brats and Education: Reproducing White Maturity in Colonial Zimbabwe, 1915–1935,' *Settler Colonial Studies*, 132–152.

Tachibanaki, T. (2008) *Introdakushyon – kakusakara hinkonhe* (Introduction – from difference to poverty), in T. Makino and E. Murakami (eds.), *Kakusa to hinkon: 20 ko* (Difference and Poverty 20 cases), Tokyo, Japan: Akashi Shoten.

Taney, R. B. (2015) *The Dred Scott Decision: Opinion of Chief Justice Taney* with an introduction by J. H. Van Evrie. Online. Available HTTP: <http://www.archive.org/stream/dredscottdecisio00unit/dredscottdecisio00unit_djvu.txt> (Accessed 26 March 2015).

Taraki, L. (2008) 'Enclave Micropolis: the Paradoxical Case of Ramallah/al-Bireh,' *Journal of Palestine Studies*, XXXVII(4):6–20.

———. (1987) *Shamanism, Colonialism and the Wild Man*, Chicago, IL: University of Chicago Press.

Taussig, M. (2003) 'The Adult's Imagination of the Child's Imagination,' in P. R. Matthews and D. McWhiter (eds.), *Aesthetic Subjects*, Minneapolis, MN: University of Minnesota Press.

The Black Public Sphere Collective (eds.) (1995) *The Black Public Sphere*, Chicago, IL: University of Chicago Press.

The New Homeless Law (2002) *Act to Provide Special Measures for the Support of the Self Reliance of the Homeless* (Homuresu no jiritsu shien to ni kan suru tokubetsu sochi ho). Online. Available HTTP: <http://www.homepage3.nifty.com/shelter-less/English/eng_idx.html>.

Thomas, W. F. (2003) 'The Meaning of Race to Employers: A Dynamic Qualitative Perspective,' *The Sociological Quarterly*, 44(2):227–242.

Thompson, J. (2012) *Light on Darkness? Missionary Photography of Africa in the Nineteenth and Early Twentieth Centuries*, Grand Rapids, MI: Eerdmans.

Tierney, K., C. Beve and E. Kuligowski (2006) 'Metaphors Matter: Disaster Myths, Media Frames, and Their Consequences in Hurricane Katrina,' *American Academy of Political and Social Science*, March: 604.

Times Online. Available HTTP: <http://www.nytimes.com/2011/03/08/world/europe/08iht-ffhelp08.html?_r=0> (7 March 2011).

Tirawi, T. (2013) *Former head of General Intelligence, speaking at the Palestinian Academy for Security Sciences*. Online. Available HTTP: <https://www.youtube.com/watch?v=n3_b8z2Em4hg&feature=c4-overview-vl&list=PLpg_UXRnIpZuyuLb8Io5S-V2Sal6XIFJlS> (Accessed 13 May 2015).

Tomba, M. (2009) 'Historical Temporalities of Capital: An Anti-Historicist Perspective,' *Historical Materialism*, 17:44–65.

Toulmin, S. (1990) *Cosmopolis: The Hidden Agenda of Modernity*, Chicago, IL: University of Chicago Press.

Trinh, T. Minh-Ha. (1989) *Woman, Native, Other: Writing Postcoloniality and Feminism*, Bloomington, IN: Indiana University Press.

Trouillot, M.-R. (1997) *Silencing the Past: Power and the Production of History*, Boston, MA: Bacon.

Tsuji, Y. (2006) 'Railway Time and Rubber Time: The Paradox in the Japanese Conception of Time,' *Time & Society*, 15:177–194.

Tuck, R. (1999) *The Rights of War and Peace: Political Thought and International Order From Grotius to Kant*, New York, NY: Oxford University Press.

Turki, F. (1981) 'Meaning in Palestinian History: Text and Context,' *Arab Studies Quarterly*, 3(4):371–383.

Umoja, A. O. (1999) 'Repression Breeds Resistance: The Black Liberation Army and the Radical Legacy of the Black Panther Party,' *New Political Science*, 21(2):131–155.

UNEP (2012) *United Nations Environmental Program Annual Report 2011*. Online. Available HTTP: <http://www.unep.org/annualreport/2011/docs/UNEP_ ANNUAL_ REPORT_2011.pdf.>.
United Nations (1992) *Rio Declaration on Environment and Development*. Online. Available HTTP: <http://www.unep.org/Documents.multilingual/Default.asp? DocumentID=78&ArticleID=1163.> (Accessed 25 May 2015).
———. (2007) *Interlinked Issues of Energy, Pollution, Industrial Development, Climate Change at Heart of ensuring Sustainable Development, UN Commission Told*, New York, NY: United Nations. Online. Available HTTP: < http://www.un.org/ press/en/2007/envdev928.doc.htm > (Accessed 28 March 2015).
Valenzuela, A. Jr. (2006) 'New Immigrants and Day Labor: The Potential for Violence,' in R. Martinez and A. Valenzuela, Jr. (eds.), *Immigration and Crime: Ethnicity, Race, and Violence*, 189–211, New York, NY: New York University Press.
Valenzuela, A. Jr., N. Theodore, E. Meléndez and A.L. Gonzalez (2006) '*On the Corner: Day Labor in the United States*,' University of California Los Angeles, Center for the Study of Urban Poverty.
van Atten, M. (2015) *Essays on Gödel's Reception of Leibniz, Husserl, and Brouwer*, New York, NY: Springer.
van Fossen, A. (1998) 'Globalisation,' in G. Dow and G. Lafferty (eds.), *Everlasting Uncertainty: Interrogating the Communist Manifesto 1848–1998*, Annandale, NSW: Pluto Press.
Varon, J. (2004) *Bringing the War Home: The Weather Underground, the Red Army Faction, and Revolutionary Violence in the Sixties and Seventies*, Berkeley, CA: University of California Press.
Vaughan-Williams, N. (2009) *Border Politics: The Limits of Sovereign Power*, Edinburgh, UK: Edinburgh University Press.
Vazquez-Arroyo, A. (2008) 'Universal History Disavowed: On Critical Theory and Postcolonialism,' *Postcolonial Studies*, 11(4):451–473.
Vij, R. (2012) 'Time, Politics and Homelessness in Contemporary Japan,' *ProtoSociology: An International Journal of Interdisciplinary Research*, 29:117–142.
Virilio, P. (2008) *Pure War: Twenty Fiver Years Later*, Los Angeles, CA: Semiotext(e).
Vitalis, R. (2010) 'The Noble American Science of Imperial Relations and its Laws of Race Development,' *Comparative Studies in Society and History*, 52(4):909–938.
Vucetic, S. (2011) *The Anglosphere: A Geneaology of a Racialized Identity in International Relations*, Stanford, CA: Stanford University Press.
Wagner, B. (2009) *Disturbing the Peace: Black Culture and the Police Power after Slavery*, Cambridge, MA: Harvard University Press.
Wahlberg, M. (2008) *Documentary Time: Film and Phenomenology*, Minneapolis, MN: University of Minnesota Press.
Wakeham, P. (2006) 'Becoming Documentary: Edward Curtis's In the Land of the Head Hunters and the politics of archival reconstruction,' *Canadian Review of American Studies*, 36(3):293–309.
Walker, R.B.J. (1989) 'History and Structure in the Theory of International Relations', *Millennium: Journal of International Studies*, 18(2):163–183.
———. (1993) *Inside/Outside: International Relations as Political Theory*, Cambridge, UK: Cambridge University Press.
———. (2010) *After the Globe/Before the World*, London, UK: Routledge.
Waltz, K. (1979) *Theory of International Politics*, Reading, MA: Addison-Wesley.

Bibliography

Walzer, M. (1977) *Just and Unjust Wars: A Moral Argument with Historical Illustrations*, New York, NY: Basic Books.

Watson, S. and Gibson, K. (eds) (1995) *Postmodern Cities and Spaces*, Oxford, UK: Blackwell.

Webber, F. (2006) *Border Wars and Asylum Crimes*, London, UK: Statewatch.

Weber, R. (2010) 'Selling City Futures: the Financialization of Urban Redevelopment Policy,' *Economic Geography*, 85(3):251–274.

Weheliye, A. (2005) *Phonographies: Grooves in Sonic Afro-Modernity*, Durham, NC: Duke University Press.

Wedeen, L. (1999) *The Ambiguities of Domination: Politics, Rhetoric and Symbols in Contemporary Syria*, Chicago, IL: University of Chicago Press:.

Weik von Mossner, A. (2011) 'Reframing Katrina: The Color of Disaster in Spike Lee's *When the Levees Broke*', *Environmental Communication*, 5(2):146–165.

Weizman, E. (2007) *Hollow Land: Israel's Architecture of Occupation*, London, UK: Verso.

Wendt, A. (1992) 'Anarchy is What States Make of it: The Social Construction of Power Politics,' *International Organization*, 46(2):391–425.

———. (1999) *Social Theory of International Politics*, Cambridge, UK: Cambridge University Press.

———. (2004) 'The State as Person in International Theory,' *Review of International Studies*, 30:289–316.

Wight, C. (2006) *Agents, Structures and International Relations: Politics as Ontology*, Cambridge, UK: Cambridge University Press.

Wilderson, F. B. III (2002) 'Gramsci's Black Marx: Whither the Slave in Civil Society,' *Social Identities*, 9(2):225–240.

———. (2003) 'Gramsci's Black Marx: Whither the Slave in Civil Society?' *Social Identities*, 9(2):225–240.

———. (2008) *Red, White and Black: Cinema and the Structure of U.S. Antagonisms*, Durham, NC: Duke University Press.

———. (2009) 'Grammar and Ghosts: The Performative Limits of African Freedom,' *Theater Survey*, 50(1):119–125.

———. (2010) *Red, White & Black: Cinema and the Structure of U.S. Antagonisms*, Durham, NC: Duke University Press.

Williams, E. (1993 [2000]) *Inadmissible Evidence: The Story of the African-American Trial Lawyer Who Defended the Black Liberation Army*, Lincoln, ND: Backprint.com [originally published by Lawrence Hill Books (1993)].

Williams, M. C. (2007) 'Morgenthau Now: Neoconservatism, National Greatness, and Realism,' in M.C. Williams (ed.), *Realism Reconsidered: The Legacy of Hans J. Morgenthau in International Relations*, Oxford, UK: Oxford University Press.

Wilson, W. J. (1996) *When Work Disappears: The World of the New Urban Poor*, New York, NY: Alfred A. Knopf.

Wolfe, G. C. (1985) *The Colored Museum: A Play*, New York, NY: Grove Press.

Wolff, S. (2008) 'Border management in the Mediterranean: internal, external and ethical challenges,' *Cambridge Review of International Affairs*, 21:253–271.

Wolin, S. S. (1997) 'What Time Is It?' *Theory & Event*, 1(1):1–10.

Woods, C. (1998) *Development Arrested: The Blues and Plantation Power in the Mississippi Delta*, New York, NY: Verso.

———. (2009) 'Katrina's World: Blues, Bourbon, and the Return to the Source,' *American Quarterly*, 61(3):427–453.

Wright, R. (1994 [1956]) *The Color Curtain: A Report on the Bandung Conference*, Jackson, MI: University of Mississippi Press.
Wu, X. and W. Yanghong (2010) '*Special Report: Hopes, Regrets in Science in Past Decade*,' Xinhua General News Service, December 31, sec. World News.
Yamanaka, L.A. (2011) '*Personal Interview with Mie Omori*', 7 January 2011.
Yoshida, M. (2012) *The 'Hidden Homeless' in Japan's Contemporary Mobile Culture.* Online. Available HTTP: <http://www.neme.org/1500/hidden-homeless> (Accessed 30 October 2014).
Young, O.R. (2001) 'Environmental Ethics in International Society', in J.M. Coicaud and D. Warner (eds) *Ethics and International Affairs: Extent and Limits*, Tokyo: United Nations University Press.
Youssef, S. (2002) *Without an Alphabet, Without a Face*, trans. K. Mattawa, Saint Paul, MI: Graywolf Press.
Yuasa, M. (2008) 'Hanhinkon: '*Suberridaishakkai' kara no dasshutsu'* (Reverse Poverty: Escape from a Sliding Down Society), Tokyo: Iwanami Shinsho.
Yue, P.H. (1997) 'Will It Be Another Load of Hot Air?', Kuala Lumpur: New Straits Times (2 December 1997).
Zaloom, C. (2009) 'How to Read the Future: The Yield Curve, Affect and Financial Prediction', *Public Culture*, 21(2): 245–268.
Zelizer, V.A. (1981) 'The Price and Value of Children: The Case of Children's Insurance', *American Journal of Sociology*, 86(5): 1036–1056.
Zibechi, R (2013) 'A Journey in Exile', *NACLA Report on the Americas* 46(3): 49–51.
Žižek, S. (1989) *The Sublime Object of Ideology*, London and New York: Verso.
———. (1993) *Tarrying with the Negative: Kant, Hegel, and the Critique of Ideology*, Durham: Duke University Press.
———. (2001) *On Belief*, London and New York: Routledge.
———. (2002) 'A Plea for Leninist Intolerance', *Critical Inquiry,* 28(2): 542–66.
———. (2005) 'Against Human Rights', *New Left Review*, 34 Jul–Aug: 115–131.
———. (2006a) 'Kate's Choice, or The Materialism of Henry James', in S. Žižek (ed.), *Lacan: The Silent Partners*, New York: Verso.
———. (2006b) *The Parallax View*, Cambridge, MA: MIT Press.

Index

Abourahme, Nasser xx, 17, 129–56
abstract labor 160–1, 234, 241–2
abstract time 234, 240, 241, 243
abstract value 26, 241
active resistance 260
Adaptation Fund 198
Adler, Emmanuel 77–8, 82–4
adoption 211–12
advertising 141–9
aesthetic experiences 56–9
affect: affective attachment 210
Africa 3, 7, 28, 30–1, 38, 94, 197–8, 213, 226, 250
African Americans 30–1, 61–73, 247, 248–51, 256–7
African black 33
African child slaves 212–13
African child soldiers 210
African Moors 222
African peoples 27, 29, 30, 33, 36, 66, 87, 197–8, 213
African time 238
afro-pessimism 67–72
Agamben, Giorgio 12, 63, 64, 119–20, 239
Agathangelou, Anna M. i, xix, 1–42
agency: afro-pessimism and 67, 73; consumerist aesthetics and 136; creative agency 260, 264–5; denial of political agency to the non-West 235; fatalization of individual agency 260; indigenous peoples 104, 105, 110–12, 114–15; *internal human agency* 130; as promised by Négritude 35; reintegration of agency over fatalism 260–1; of the slave 66
agricultural workers 249
Algeria 228
alienation 34, 36, 38, 98
alternatives: alternatives to a given order 169; alternatives to what exists 235

al-thawabit (the constants) 139
Althusser, Louis 243
ambivalent: in-between space 140
Amnesty International 227, 228
analog photography 260, 264–5, 269
anarchy 2, 24, 26, 48, 53, 235
Anderson, Benedict 151
Anderson, Perry 242
Andrew R. Hom xxi, 189–204
'angry white males' 66
Anna M. Agathangelou and Kyle D. Killian introduction 1–19; 23–42
anonymous city: fatalistic timespace and 262–3; *flâneur* 263–4; re-imagining 260–73; street photographers 263–4
anthropology 104; *see also* salvage ethnography
anti-blackness 16, 67, 68, 72, 73
Apostolidis, Paul 159–71
Arabness/blackness 209
Aradau, Claudia 233
Archives 2, 30, 101
archival documents 101
Ariès, Philippe 211
Aristotle 55
armament 49
Armstrong, Louis 251
Asad, T. 11
atemporal dwelling 172–84
atemporality 95, 173–5, 177, 180
atrocities 92, 213–14
attachments 132, 144, 147, 183, 210; nationalism 177; past 192
Attali, Jacques 254–5
Australia 120–4
authenticity 105–7, 109, 114, 116
authority: derivative authority 137–40

Index

background knowledge 76–8, 83
Baker, Ross 66–7
Balagoon, Kuwasi 90, 91–2, 94
Balibar, Étienne 130
Bali Climate Change Conference 198
Banda, David 211
Bangladesh factory fire 247
Barrett, Lindon: and value 29; value as disfiguration 29; value as violence 29
Barthes, Roland 264
Baucom, I. 26–7
Baudrillard, Jean 265
Beah, Ishmael 210
Beast of No Nation (Iweala) 210
Beckett, Samuel 206
Bed & Breakfast Notebooks, From the (Handal) 290–3
being: blackness as flesh 30; necropolitical 208, 211, 218; unfinished entity 218
belief 82–3
benefit 76, 80, 106, 110, 200, 209
Benjamin, Walter 11, 105–6, 151
Bergson, Henri 64
Bhopal disaster 246–7
Bible 7, 49
Bilgin, Pinar xx, 17, 221–32
Black, Brown and Beige (Ellington) 250–1
black children 214–16
black insurgency 87–102
Black Liberation Army's (BLA) 87–9, 90, 92–3, 95, 102
'Black Man and Language, The' (Fanon) 69
Black Men, On (Marriott) 63
blackness 39, 63–4, 65, 68, 70–3, 90
black optimism 67, 69, 71–3
Black Skin, White Masks (Fanon) 33, 35, 39
black social life 68–9, 72–3
black studies 62–3, 65, 67, 68, 71–3
Blanchard, Terence 250
Blaney, David 1, 4, 14, 26, 190–4, 235
blues aesthetics 250–1
Blunt Balm (Jaji) 284–6
Boas, Franz 109, 110
body: 7, 278, 279, 280, 292, Agathangelou and Killian 12, 19, 26, 27, 28, 29, 30, 31, 33; Grovogui 51; America as body 7; body as corpse 251; body as flesh 27; body politics 27; city/life 262; Cliff Davidson 262; colonized 19, 33; racially marked body 30
Bowie, Malcolm 82
Breathe: breathe life into 110; a drawing on breathing 280; Handal, Alexandra 293; Handal, Natalie 280–1; held my breath 293; Wanda Nanibush 110
Brent J. Steele xxii, 189–204
Brinks Trial 90
Brown, Michael 256–7
Bulawayo, NoViolet 206, 214
Bush, W. Stephen 109
Butler, Judith 257

Çalkivik, Asli xx, 17, 233–45
cameras 264
Campbell, David 83
Canada 111
capacity gap 196
capital 13, 25, 240–3
capitalism 8, 17, 23, 25–6, 29, 31, 36, 89, 104, 159–64, 176, 239–43, 261; capitalism as force-field relations 240; globalization of capitalism 237
capitalist modernity 234, 238–42
Capital (Marx) 240
cardboard houses 174, 178, 180–3
Carolus Magnus (Charlemagne) 46
CASA Latina 160, 170
Casement, Roger 213
'Case of Blackness, The' (Moten) 62, 63
Castells, Manuel 262
castles: Ghana 30–1, Hartman, Saidiya 31; slave 30–1
Castree, Noel 234, 239–40, 242
celestial time 46
Centuries of Childhood (Ariès) 211
ceremonies 106–7, 114–15
Césaire, Aimé 64
Chakrabarty, Paula 10, 237, 240
Chakrabarty, D. 10, 237, 240
change: change oppressive situations 169; climate change 189, 195–6, 198
childhood memories 101
children: African child slaves 212–13; black children 214–16; childhood innocence 214; child labor 212–13, 214; children's insurance 212; child soldiers 210; equating temporal Others with 193; human rights protections 213; in labor market 212–13, 214; production and management of children's time 213; sentimentality and moral discourses on 206; sentimentalization of childhood 211–13; suffering 205–8, 210; transnational adoption 211–12; waiting for humanitarian assistance 205–8
China 196
Chowdhury, Arjun 78–9, 83

Christian 7, 10, 12, 14, 45–7, 49, 52, 56, 190, 191, 212, 246, 250
Christian faith 49
Christian Science Monitor 246
chronopolitics 236
chronos 237
cinema: aesthetic 253; *Coming to Light* (Makepeace) 113; death 251; indigenous people in 111–12; *In the Land of the Head Hunters* (Curtis) 104–5, 107–9, 112–17; *In The Land of The War Canoes* 112–13; portrayal of homelessness 181–2, 183; *When the Levees Broke* (Lee) 248–52, 256, 257; *White Fawn's Devotion* (Young Deer) 112
cinema, as a technology of salvage ethnography 107–10; as defatalizing technology 260, 263–9
citizenship 224–6, 229, 238
civil society 6–7
Clark, Judy 90
clock time 242
coercive means 137–8
'coeval temporalities' 175–6
coherence 95, 96, 98, 100, 238
'collective time' 177
colonial 12–17, 24, 33–4, 38, 52, 64, 69, 104–7, 109–12, 114–16, 136–40, 153, 192, 212, 226
colonial archives 115–17
colonial encounters 34
colonialism 13, 14, 31, 34, 50, 105, 107, 151
colonization: concept in international relations theory 13–14, 15; Fanon's analysis of 33, 34; of indigenous peoples 52–3, 107, 113; justification of 52–3; slavery and 23–5
Coming to Light (Makepeace) 114
'commodification of humanity' 29
commodification of originary cultures 105–6
Communist Manifesto, The (Marx) 239
community: European superiority and 49; 'grassroots community' 163; homelessness and 172, 173, 179, 181–3; indigenous peoples 110, 113–15; internalization and 197; slaves 34, 89–90, 93–4, 99; subaltern political community 87–8, 95–6
community 8, 17, 34, 49, 87–90, 93–6, 99, 101, 110, 113–16, 151, 163, 181–3; Africa is void of political community 94
competency 77
'competent performances' 78
concrete labor 160, 241–2

'concrete time' 241
Congo: Congo Report 213; the Crime of the Congo 213
Congo 213–14
Congo Reform Association 213
Congo Report (Casement) 213
conjectural history 191, 255
conquest 52
Conrad, Joseph 213
consciousness 33–5, 45, 50–3, 55, 93, 97–100, 163, 172, 183, 254–5, 257, 263; of the body 33; critical consciousness 163; durational time and 183; Husserl's analysis of 254; manifestation of 51; of slaves 97; the unconscious and 98–9
consumer, citizen-of-the state-to-be 136
consumerist aesthetics 142
contingency 82
Contribution to the Critique of Political Economy, A (Marx) 240
Convention on the Rights of the Child 210
Copenhagen Summit 196
corporeal punishment 12
Costa Rica 196
counterpower resistance 192, 194
creative agency 260, 264–5
Creative Evolution (Bergson) 64
'credit' 32
Crime of the Congo, The (Doyle) 213
critical consciousness 163
Critique of Political Economy, A (Marx) 240
Critique of Pure Reason (Kant) 10
Crooks, Robert 247
cultural difference 116
culture preservation 113
Curtis, Edward S.: *In the Land of the Head Hunters* 104, 107–9, 112–15; *The North American Indian* 105–7
'cyberspace' 236
'cyberwar' 236

dance 105, 106, 114–15, 254–5
Dante Alighieri 48
Darfur 207
Darker Nations, The (Prashad) 50
Darwin, Charles 64
da Silva, Denise 24, 36
Davidson, Cliff xx, 19, 260–74
day laborers (*doya*) 179
death: acceptability/unaccesability of 12; cinematic aversion to 251; creative death 261; death as audacious 280; death as fatality 261; death camps 281;

330 *Index*

dust to dust 286; human death 96, 227; Jaji, Tsitsi 284–6; Michel Foucault and askesis 12; Michel Foucault and death 11; Handal, Natalie 280, 281; role of death in formation of the subject 96–7; thanatological death 65; Wilderson 87, 89–93, 96–7, 99–101
death of the social 176
De Cive (Hobbes) 7
decolonization 25, 39,50, 64, 151, 224, 225, 229; as a defatal alternative; as defatalization 16, 260–1, 265, 269; as tabula rasa 39; as a defatal moment i, 16
Defacing Power (Steele) 194
defatalization: Agathangelou and Killian 16; Davidson 260–1, 265, 269; of digital photography 265; of practices of power and violence 84; process of 260–1; of timespace 265, 269
de Goede, Marieke 233
Deleuze, Gilles 64
Deloria, Philip 111
Der Derian, James 79, 234–6, 238–9
determinism: Agathangelou, Anna and Killian, Kyle 261; Cliff Davidson 261
developed states 196–7
development: in evolutionary history of mankind 191; human development as metaphor 193; internalization of developmental discourse 197–9; interventions and 49; in temporal Othering 192
deyosebisation (collapse of the day labor market) 178
dialectical thought 34–5
dialectics: Anna Agathangelou and Kyle Killian 6, 24, 34; Frantz Fanon 34–6, 38, 39
diaspora 31
'Didn't It Rain' (Jackson) 252
difference: conceptualization of 116; role of dance and ceremony 114–15; subjectivity and 80–2; temporalization of 221, 222–3, 229; temporalizing difference 17, 222–4, 226, 227, 229; of white imagination and black imagination 70
digital photography 260, 264–5
discipline 12
discourses: of childhood innocence 214; of environmental disasters 246–7; environmental temporal discourses 200; internalization and reconstruction of temporal discourse 197–9; in its

mediation through visibilities, 136; material intercourse between image and 140–9; meaning-making and subjectivity 80; media representations of environmental disasters 246–57; oppositional discourse 148; philosophico-anthropological discourses 238; redemptive discourses 206–7, 210; of the rights of man 207; of 'rights of the rightless' 207; Spivak's critique of discourses of western feminism 238; as symbolic systems 80; temporal discourse 189, 193, 197–9
discursive practices 84
disjunctive temporalities 211
Dixon, Emma 248
dogs 217–18
doken kokka (construction state) 178
domesticity 131, 148
Domino, Antoine "Fats," Jr. 251
doya-gai 178
Doyle, Arthur Conan 213
'Do You Know What It Means to Miss New Orleans' (Armstrong) 251
drawing of breathing, A (Handal) 280–1
drone technology 54
Du Bois, W.E.B. 68
durational time 176, 183
Durkheim, Émile 261
Dust to Dust (Jaji) 286
Duvall, Raymond 78–9, 83
dwelling 172, 175, 180–4; pavement 174, 183

Earth: environmental politics 189–205; climate 61, 189, 195–6, 198; environmental capacity 196–7; environmental regimes 195, 196
earthly time 46
economic temporality 238
Ecrits (Lacan) 96
Edkins, Jenny 1, 199, 233
Egypt 228
Eisenstadt, Shmuel 175
Ellington, Edward Kennedy "Duke" 250–1
embodiment 31, 93, 138
emergence of discontinuity 163
emergent political order 132–7
emission-reduction commitments 196
emotion-based approach 85
Enlightenment 53, 190, 199
Enloe, Cynthia 235
'Enoaru Café' 183
entanglement 131–2, 140–8

entrepreneurial 176, 238
environmental capacity 196–7
environmental disasters: Bhopal disaster 246–7; discourses of 246–7; Hurricane Katrina 246, 247–57; media representations of 246–57
environmental equity 195–6
environmental temporal discourses 200
Esmeir, Samera 151
ethics 53–6
ethnography *see* salvage ethnography
Euro-Mediterranean Partnership (EMP), 227
European Commission 228
European Community (EC) 226
European Convention on Human Rights (ECHR) 228
European imperialism 32
European man: Europe 39; European white 33
European Neighborhood Policy (ENP) 227
European security policies/practices 221–2, 226–9
European Union (EU) 227–9
Europe: Frantz Fanon 97, 99,
Evans, Brad 110, 113–14
event 2–3, 12–14, 19, 24, 30, 36, 38–9, 45, 50, 52, 61, 90, 95, 98, 141, 194, 241, 246, 250–3, 257
event: postcolonial event 15, 16, 24, 38
external security 229

Fabian, Johannes 109
Fairbanks, Douglas 112
faith 49
fallen martyr 136
family: child 209, 210, 212, 215; child's play 189, 199, 208; politics of the family 208–11
family time 209–11
Fanon, Frantz 13, 23–4, 32–40, 63, 68, 97; 'The Black Man and Language' 69; *Black Skin, White Masks* 33, 35, 39; 'Racism and Culture' 33; *The Wretched of the Earth* 33–4, 39
fantasy 94, 105, 114, 269
Farley, Anthony 28–30
farmer: the figure of the farmer 144
fatalism: Agathangelou and Killian introduction 1; Cliff Davidson 260–1, 263
fatalistic suicide 261; attitudinal fatalism 261; Cliff Davidson 260–4, 269; as cumulative excessive oppression 261; David Lockwood 261; fatalism as paradox Agathangelou and Killian 1; fatalisms of neoliberalisms 17; 260–1; fatalistic time space 262–3, 269; Masaryk, Thomas, 1994 261; structure as fatalistic 261
fatalistic timespace 262–3
fatalization 11, 24, 119; fatalization as a continual process controlling structural influences 261; Cliff Davidson 260–1, 265, 269
'fatal leap' 32
father; baba 282; Natalie Handal 281, 282
female slaves 28–9
feminine 26, 145; female figures 146; movement of figurations 146; shifting forms of feminine 149
Ferguson case 256–7
Fiction: Anna M. Agathangelou and Kyle Killian 3, 6, 9, 16, 18, 28, 33, 38; Fanon 28, 33
Fida'i 143–5, 148; fida'iyun xvii, 144
figuration: 'distribution of sensibility' and 131; of fallen martyr 136; of the feminine 146–7; of 'the militant' 144–5; *visual memory* and 142
finance capital 26, 31, 32
financial crises 36, 38
finitude 10
flâneur 263–4
flesh 24, 27–30, 35, 97, 251; flesh of the enslaved woman 27; slave as flesh 30, 99
flesh: also body 27
Force: coercive force 131, 137–9, 252; *see also* violence
forced exclusion as violence 33
Foucault, Michel 10, 11, 12, 63, 64, 173, 177, 181, 194, 236
Fournel, Victor 263
Frank B. Wilderson III xxii, 17, 87–103
Franklin, V.P. 65–6
Freedom (Handal) 277–8
Freedom telling on time (Handal) 277–83
Fremantle, Australia 120–4
Freudian discovery of the unconscious 98
fugitives 31, 61, 62, 71; fugitive leaps 31–4
fungible: female slaves as fungible objects 28; fungible objects 28–9
furosha (vagabond) 178
furusato (hometowns) 183
future: radically indeterminate 39; as telos 70, 151, 179

garden, dead; Seeman, Annette 126–7
Garza, Juan Carlos 165–7

Gaza 55, 135
Gender: gendered 7, 24, 90, 179, 251; gendered order 181
genealogical isolate 89, 94, 100, 101
generation 8, 57, 104–7, 191, 213, 246, 248; generational time 256
Generic City 262
Genesis 8
Genovese, Eugene 66
geographic Others 192
Ghana 30–1
Gidwani, Vinay 240, 243
Gilbert, David 90
Glass, Aaron 110, 113–14, 117
globalization 193, 235, 237
global politics 234–9
global war on terror 38, 221, 227
God 3, 8, 9, 10, 12, 39, 48, 50, 52, 191
Good Friday Agreement 89
Gordon, Lewis 68–9
Gorz, André 160–4
Government Housing Loan Corporation (GHLC) 179
governmentality 12, 130, 176
Gramsci, Antonio 92
Gramscian War of Position 92, 102
'grassroots community' 163
Greece 36, 38
Grotius, Hugo 48
ground-level practices 76
Grundrisse: Marx, Karl 240
guardianship 49
Guattari, Félix 64
guerilla war 87–8
Guernica (Picasso) 55
guerrilla/*fida'i* 144–5, 148
Guide to being Palestinian (Handal) 281–3
Gwa'wina Dancers 114

Hall, Stuart. 31
Handal, Alexandra xxi, 19, 290–3
Handal, Nathalie xxi, 18, 277–83
Hansen, Lene 79
Haraway, Donna 218
Harootunian, Harry 175–6
Hartman, Saidiya 23–4, 63, 67
Hatoyama, Yukio 172
Hawker, Ronald 107
Heat of the Night, In the (Jewison) 61–2
Hegel, F.G.W. 13, 34, 35, 48, 53, 191, 238
Hegelian dialectic 34, 97
Heidegger, Martin 55
heterotemporality 238

heterotopias 173, 177
hierarchy: asymmetry 199; hierarchical divisions 225; hierarchization 26
'hidden homeless' 178–9
Hindess, Barry 190–3, 221–6, 229
historical reconstruction 108
historical time 234, 243
historicism 2, 10
historicity 5, 24, 72, 96, 264, 269
history: conjectural history 191, 255; homogeneous time and 11; as property the present inherits 27; 'unilinear' understandings of 6; universal history 193, 243
'Hitting Budapest' (Bulawayo) 206, 214–16
Hobbes, Thomas 6–7, 48; *Leviathan* 6
Holm, Bill 112–13, 116
Hom, Andrew: Anna M. Agathangelou and Kyle Killian introduction 3–5, 8–10; narrativizing activity 8, 9–10; time as narrative 4
home 173, 174–5, 179–83; durational time of home 180; Ghana 30, 31; Hartman, Saidiya 16, 23, 63, 67
homelessness: atemporality and 173–4; barracks 176; dwelling 172–5, 177–84; as heterotopia 180–4; as a practice of atemporal dwelling 172; as 'social pathology' in Japan 177–80; Ritu, Vij 172–88
'Homestretch to Freedom' 151
homogeneous time 11
'homogenous empty time' 151
homuresu (homeless) 178, 182
house 181–2; dwelling 172, 174, 175, 177, 180; home 17, 47, 67, 150; hometown*s*, *furusato* 183; *My House* 82, 279; zero-yen houses 181–3
human: humanitarian 52, 120, 179, 205–14, 216–18; speechless emissaries 207
human-animal distinction 217
human development 193, 196–8
humanitarians 207–8, 210–11, 213–14, 216–18
human rights 207, 213, 228
human, species: after species division 100
Hunt, George 109, 110, 116
Hurricane Katrina: media representations of 246, 247–8; *Treme* (Simon) 252–6; *When the Levees Broke* (Lee) 248–52
Husserl, Edmund 254
Hutchings, Kimberley 1–4, 10, 199–200, 234, 237–9
Huysmas, Andreas 229

ibasho (belonging) 182–3
Ichimura, Misako 183
immanence 35, 64, 73, 254
Immanent 7, 35; immanent features 162; immanent non-linear plural becomings 239; immanent practices 11; immanent temporalities 238; immanent transformations 1; space as immanent 4; time as immanent 4; as world political time 4
immigrants 226–9, 235
immigration 27–8, 222, 227–9
imperial eye 16, 45–59
imperialism 14, 32–3, 45, 213, 223, 225; global-imperial order 135; imperial colonial linkages 212; US imperialism 90
'impolitical mandate' 119–20
Inayatullah, Naeem 1, 4, 14, 26, 190–4, 235
indeterminacy 3, 25, 57, 153, 168
indexicality 108
India 246
indigenous peoples: colonization of 52–3; *Coming to Light* (Makepeace) 114; commodification of originary cultures 105–6; Kwakwaka'wakw 104–17; *In the Land of the Head Hunters* (Curtis) 104–5, 107–9, 112–17; *In The Land of The War Canoes* 112–13; *The North American Indian* (Curtis) 105–7; as referent for natural liberty 7; rights of 53; self-representation of 111–12; slavery and 27
individuation 136
infantilizing; child-like 213; infantilizing the present 214–16
injury 24, 28, 30, 246
innocence 90, 92, 99, 211, 213, 214, 218
insecurity 76, 82
'In Situ' 181
institutionalized racism 248
Intergovernmental Panel on Climate Change 195
internalization 31, 176, 197–9
internal security 229
international relations 1, 23, 24, 32, 45, 46, 47, 48, 49, 50, 51, 58, 174, 233, 236
international relations theory 1, 2, 16, 24, 32, 45–51, 58, 76, 174, 224, 233, 236: narrative theorizing 5–6, 8–10; practices in 77–9; 'practice turn' in 76, 77; specter of time and temporality for 2–10
interpretation 78, 83–4, 93, 97, 104, 108, 170; universal interpretation 191; historical interpretation 193; religious interpretation 206; interpretations of fatalism 260
interventions: child-like 212; child-oriented 211–12; discursive practices; interventions of cultural symbols 84; Israeli Interventions 55; legal interventions 210; military interventions 49; programmatic interventions 216; Solomon, Ty 81, 84; timely interventions 214
interventions: 84; Israeli 55; 'just' use of violence and 50; purpose of 49; right to intervene 50
invention 39; Agathangelou Anna and Kyle Killian 13, 14, 24, 31–3, 39; Fanon 13, 24, 32–3; histories of the invention 212; invention as affirmation 65; invention as creativity 3; invention of racial blackness 65; invention in time 31; invention into existence 32; Jared Sexton 65; real leap as invention 13, 14, 24; reinvention 253; Opondo, Sam 212
Iraq 38, 55
Irish Republican Army (IRA) 87–9, 94
Irish Republican paramilitaries 94–6
Isabella I, Queen of Spain 52
Israeli army 138
Israeli interventions 55
Israeli occupation 131, 135
Israeli-Palestinian conflict 53
Iweala, Uzodinma 210

Jabir, Johari 252
Jackson, Jonathan 91
Jackson, Mahalia 252
Jaji, Tsitsi 19, 284–9
Jamaica 212
James, Charlie 109
James, Chifundo 'Mercy' 211
'Janjaweed Wife' (Osondu) 206, 209–11
Japan 172–84
Jaques, Horacio 165
Jewison, Norman 61
Jiang Zemin 198
Jonaitis, Aldona 109, 110
Jones, Donna 64, 65
Journal of Negro History 65
Jung, Carl 100
Junichiro, Take 183

kairos 237
kakusa shakai (divided society) 172
Kant, Immanuel 10, 32, 48, 53, 191
Kazimi, Ali 115; *Shooting Indians* 115

334 *Index*

Keeling, Kara 63
Ki-Moon, Ban 189
King Leopold's Rule in Africa (Morel) 213
Koolhaas, Remment L. "Rem" 262
Kopytoff, Igor 256
Kordela, K. 242
Krishna and postcolonial imaginary 223
Kwakwaka'wakw: *In the Land of the Head Hunters* 104–5, 107–10, 112–17; *In the Land of the Head Hunters* reconstruction 112–15; *In The Land of The War Canoes* 112–13; maintaining complexity for 115–16; *The North American Indian* 110
Kyle D. Killian i, xix, 1–42
Kyoto Protocol 198–9

labor 160–4, 240–2; socially necessary labor time 161–2, 164, 168–9, 241–2; labor time 25, 161–2, 241–2
labor as social mediation 161
Lacanian analytic encounter 102
Lacanian theory of subjectivity 80–2
Lacan, Jacques 76, 80, 82, 85, 95, 96
Lacan's notion of retroactive causality 79
Lacan's taxonomy of the unconscious 99–100
Lacan's theory of the subject 97–8
Lacan's theory of the unconscious 98–101
Land of the Head Hunters, In the (Curtis) 104–5, 107–9, 112–17
Land of The War Canoes, In The 112–13
language 49, 78, 98
law 30, 50, 61; 62, 70, 73, 92, 93, 147; emergency law 228; Japanese construction law 182; law international 54, 58, 153; law natural 47, 49; laws scientific 45; laws timeless 237; laws of value eternal 242; the New Homeless Law 179; no rights before the law 30; rule-of-law 135, 139
Leander, Anna 78–9
Lee, Shelton Jackson "Spike" 248, 256, 257
legal institutions 49
legitimate commerce 49
Leo III, Pope of the Roman Catholic Church 46
Leopold II, King of Belgium 213
Leviathan (Hobbes) 6
life 4–6, 10, 12–19, 24–5, 27, 35, 36, 46–51, 53–9, 63–73, 89, 91, 92, 96–7, 99, 101, 106, 108–10, 114, 119, 129, 145, 162–3, 169, 175, 176, 181–3, 198, 200, 205, 209, 211–18, 222, 228, 233, 235, 237, 241, 242, 250–5, 257, 262, 263

life insurance 212
'linear time' 199–200
'lingering present' 151
Locke, John 48, 52, 53
Longfellow, Henry Wadsworth 108
Long Way Gone, A (Beah) 210
Lo Porto, Giovanni 55
Lose Your Mother (Hartman) 63
lost decades (*ushinatta nijugonen*) 172
low-income housing 179

Machiavelli, Niccolo 48, 55
Mac Stíofáin, Seán 88
Madonna 211
mai homeism 179
mai homu shugi 179
Makepeace, Anne 110, 114
Malawi 214
Mamdani, Mahmood 207
Man, attributes of 52
Mandela, Nelson 198
Manichean 32, 34, 35, 37
manifest destiny 111
Marriott, David 63, 65
Martin Luther King Jr. (MLK) Day Laborers Center 160, 165, 166, 169
Marxist paramilitaries 88
Marx, Karl 25–6, 32, 64, 239–40
masculine 4, 8, 26
Massey, Doreen 175
material, materiality 1–3, 11, 14, 16, 18, 24–7, 34, 38, 40, 49, 50, 53, 71, 76–9, 82–3, 112, 135, 141, 150, 160, 162–3, 173, 181–2, 197, 200, 207, 209, 217, 234, 239, 243, 248
materiality: critical theory 240; historical materialism 239; Marx, Karl 25–6, 239
McClintock, Ann 29
material wealth 241
May, Jon 260
Mbeki, Thabo 197–8
Mbembe, Achille 36, 63, 131, 148
meaning 76–7, 79–85
meaning-making 80–2, 84–5
mechanical reproduction 105–6
Medina, Edgar 165
Mediterranean region, European security practices/policies in 221–2, 226–9
Memory: figuration 131, 136, 142, 144–5, 150; visual memory 131, 142
merchant capitalism 29
'Messianic time' 252
metaphor: analogy 24

Index

Michael J. Shapiro xxii, 13, 18, 211, 238, 246–59
middle-class society 36–7, 172
Middle East and North Africa region (MENA) 3, 36
Middle Passage 25, 26, 30
migrant day laborers: temporalities of work and 159, 164–8; violence and 168–70
military-style equipment deployments 55
military technology 54, 56, 57
Miracle Year of 1492 52
miscegenation 112
mobile phone advertisements 142
Modern imperialism 45, 223; imperial eye 16; imperial vision 238
modernity: capitalism and 25–6; capitalist modernity 234, 238–42; death and 11; governmental machinery and 12; indigenous peoples and 107, 110–12, 115–16; slavery and 24, 29, 33, 35–6, 38, 90; temporal discourse of 191–3, 199; temporal Othering and 190; time and 14, 26, 175, 243
modernity as time machine 90, 243; Anna M. Agathangelou and Kyle Killian 10–14, 24–6, 29, 33, 35–6, 38; ontological disposition of modernity 29
monogeny 7, 191
moral: ethics 47, 51, 54; morality 34, 45, 46, 49–51, 55, 58, 91, 209, 214; moral judgements 91, 196
Moore, Mike 214
Morel, E.D. 213
Morgenthau, Hans 190
Moten, F. 62–3, 67, 71, 73
Moynihan, Daniel Patrick 63
musical narrative 254–5
mutual benefits 49
My House (Tsutsumi) 181–2
myth 38, 49, 59, 70, 82, 106, 182, 280–2

Nanibush, Wanda 104–18
narrative: coherent narrative of childhood 210; narrativization 8, 9–10
'narratives of arrival' 27–8
narrative theorizing 5–6, 8–10; developmental narrative 197; dominant narratives 84; narrative activity 5, 8; narrative of temporal activity 8–10; narratives of time 4; narrative order 8; narrative timing project 5; narrative vocation 5
Nashef, Ismail 132

nationalism 37
national origins 82
Native Americans 93
native populations *see* indigenous peoples
natural liberty 7
Negri, Antonio 240
Négritude 35, 38, 64
neoliberalism 65, 159, 164, 172, 207, 214; analog photography and 269; homelessness and 172–84; humanitarianism in age of 214; ideals of 265; internalization of neoliberal policies 176; metanarrative of control 261; migrant day laborers and 164, 169–70; neoliberal forms of governmentality 176; neoliberalism and necropolitics 207; neoliberal time and violent work 159–60; Palestinian politics and 131, 152; role of technology in 264; slavery and 65; timespace and 262; violence of neoliberalism 164
Neumann, Iver B. 77
new; as future; as present
New Deal 249
New Homeless Law 179
New Orleans, Louisiana 246, 247–57
New Republic 66
New York Times 247
Nicolson, Marianne 115–16
Niebuhr, Reinhold 190
Nietzsche, Friedrich 64
nihonjinron (Japaneseness) 174
Non-Aligned Movement 197
non-existence 69; existence 36, 69, 100
North American Indian, The (Curtis) 105–7, 110
nostalgia 107
Nyers, Peter 229

object: the slave as object 105–7; the structure of time as object 17
Official Irish Republican Army (OIRA) 94
Ogawa, Tetsuo 183
'ontological resistance' 97
Opondo, Sam Okoth xxi, 17, 205–20
oppression 33
order 2–9, 10–12, 15, 19, 23, 26, 31, 45–7, 48–50, 132, 135, 139, 140, 147, 161, 169, 181–4, 210, 233, 252
Order of Things, The (Foucault) 10
ordinary decent criminals (ODCs) 94
Organisation for Economic Co-operation and Development (OECD) 178
Organization of African Unity 198

336 *Index*

Orphée noir (Sartre) 35
Oslo Accords 131, 132
Osondu, E.C. 205–9
Other, the: as commodity 34; Native Americans as 93, 109; recognition/predetermined misrecognition of 35; temporal Othering 190–5, 199–200; time(s) of the Self and 191–3; value and 29
ownership 30, 182, 241

Pacific Northwest 159
Palestine: declaration of statehood 151; perpetual present of 152–3
Palestinian: being Palestinian 281; darker 281; exiled 282; hijab 281
Palestinian Liberation Organization (PLO) 132
Palestinian National Authority (PNA) 131, 132, 137, 139, 148
Palestinian politics: dilemmas of derivative authority 137–40; discourse, aesthetics, and the political subject of 129–53; emergent political order 132–7; entanglement and the politics of visibility 140–8; the present and its absences 150–3
Palestinian security forces 138
part-time employees (*freeters*) 178
past 38, 150, 151, 153, 173, 176, 192, 193, 223, 262, 269; as another culture 223; belonging to the 221; closed 153; cultural 116, 256; distant 113; Enlightenment and 190; European 191, futures 152; Hindess 223; horrific 214; liquidate the past 38; musical 253; New Orleans 252; past ancestral 104; past irrecoverable 82; past primitivized 107; past primordial 107, 115, 116; relegating to the 229; revolutionary 135; Selves 194; sound 254; traditions 110; vestiges 159; 223, 227; violence of the 207; 'as a whole continent of different countries' 223
Patriot Act 58
Patterson, Orlando 65–7, 89, 97
peace 2, 3, 9, 46, 48, 54, 212, 293; as end 2; as linearity 3; as permanence 3; as time 212
Peepoople 217
peepoo technology 217
Perera, Suvendrini 17, 119–28
performance 77, 83
perpetual present 38, 152–3, 262

phenomenology of individual consciousness 254
Phenomenology of Internal Time Consciousness (Husserl) 254
philosophico-anthropological discourses 238
photographic print 260, 265, 269
photography: analog photography 260, 264–5, 269; digital photography 260, 264–5, 269; photographic print 265, 269; street photographers 263–4
Picasso, Pablo 55
Pickford, Mary 112
pictorialist aesthetic 105
Piri, Luke 214
plantation system 249
poetic intervention: Anna M. Agathangelou and Kyle Killian 19
poetics 12, 19, 138
Poitier, Sidney 61
police violence 256–7
political action 38
political prisoners 88, 91, 92, 94–6
political temporality 238
politics of global security 235–6
politics of refusal 94–5
politics of time: homelessness and 180; labor, capital and 160–4; lived condition of blackness and 33; socially constituted time and 240–2; temporality of global politics and 233–43; toward a politics of time in a time of violence 168–70; world politics 234–9
polygeny 7
population management 224
'Position of the Unthought, The' (Hartman and Wilderson) 63
postcolonial 1, 2, 10, 13, 15–16, 24–6, 38, 87–90, 130, 135–6, 151–3, 193, 214, 221, 223–6, 235, 240; postcolonial theory 1; the tragedy of the postcolonial 151
postcolonial paramilitaries 88
Postcolony, On the (Mbembe) 63
Post-Fordism: post-Fordist conditions 163
Postone, Moishe 160, 234, 240–1
poststructuralists 79
Pouliot, Vincent 77–8, 82–4; practice theory 76; 'practice turn' 76, 77
'poverty business' 179
Powell, Colin 55
power 49, 69–70, 71
practices: black studies 62–3, 65, 67, 68, 71–3; as 'competent performances' 76, 78, 83; components of 77; constituent aspects of 83; definition of 78, 83;

discursive practices 84; emotion-based approach 85; in international relations theory 77–9; as performances of subjectivity 83; temporality and 82–4; theory of meaning for 78–9
practice theory 76
'practice turn' 76, 77; Pouliot, Vincent 77–8, 82–4
Prashad, Vijay 50
Preemption: economic preemption 36; military preemption 38; politics of preemption 233
preemptive deterrence 58
pre-ordainment 49–50
present: as continual 269; as debt deferred promises 1; defatal 17; digital 19, 269; as eternal 14; as eternalized 12; exceeds its conditions 34; as historicism 2; History as property of the 27; indefinite finality 150–3; as inhabited 3; as liquidating the past 38; living 34, 99; and the now 10; Palestinian 129, 154; perpetually in motion 38; as political 7; as politics of memory 233; as ruptured 15; as a shadowy history 2; violence of the 207; as vulnerable space i
'primitive accumulation' 25
prison time 95
productive ambivalences: Abourahme, Nasser 17, 129–55
profits 19, 25–6, 36, 182, 240, 242–3, 284; money 247
property 182, 241; private property 182, 241
prosaic 17, 206, 208, 216
'protention' 254
public parks 178, 182–3
public rental housing 179

Qalandiya Refugee Camp 150
Quayson, A. 31
Quimby, George 112–13

Racial Discourses of Life Philosophy, The (Jones) 64
raciality 27; global raciality 24, 33
racism 33, 38, 88, 111, 112, 248, 256
Radio Gaza (Handal) 278–80
radical alternatives: as alternative futures 229; Anna M. Agathangelou and Kyle Killian introduction 1–19, 23–40; David Marriott 63; dissident 190, 199; evacuation 216–18, 248; Frantz Fanon 63; Hartman 63; indeterminacy 3, 25, 57, 153, 168; as laughter 88, 114, 211, 218; Sam Opondo 17; temporality as lived experience 4; tomba thinking politics differently 243; *see also* Chalkivik, Asli
radical: radically alternative 162; radically alternatives ix; radically different temporal experiences i; radical new beginnings i
Raheja, Michelle H. 111
Ramallah 138
Rancière, Jacques 207
'raw life' 63; 'Raw Life' (Sexton and Copeland) 63
Read, Jason 242
real leap 13, 14, 24, 31–9; Fanon 24
reconstruction 71, 104, 107, 108, 113, 114, 183, 197, 247
redemption: antinomies of 24, 38; childhood suffering and 205–10, 213–14; class redemption 91; humanitarian conception of 218; 'just' use of violence and 50; personal redemption 91
redemptive discourses 206–7, 210
Red, White and Black (Wilderson) 63
refugees 120, 178
Regis, Helen 254
relation 69–70
Renaissance 53
'representational disenchantment' 173
reproduction 2, 8, 27, 36, 105–6, 108, 139, 146, 173, 175, 240, 242, 243, 255, 269; Anna M. Agathangelou and Kyle Killian 2, 8, 36; Caklivik, Asli 240, 242, 243; heterosexual reproduction 27; mechanical reproduction 105–6; reproduction of collectivity 173, 175; reproduction of global capitalism 36; reproduction of reality 108; Ritu Vij 173, 175; symbolic reproduction 139; Wanda Nanibush 105–6, 108
Reservation Reelism (Raheja) 111
resistance: active resistance 260; black 31, 73; counterpower resistance 192, 194; indigenous peoples 17, 52–3, 104; migrant day laborers and 167; 'ontological resistance' 97; Palestinian 139, 148; of paramilitary organizations 87–102
resonance 98
restoring dignity 49
Res, van Muenster 233
'retention' 254

retroactive time 80–2
revolution: zero publics-practice for revolution 184n
rights 207
Rio Declaration 195, 196, 198
risk: risk-taking 176
Robinson, Tony Terrell 256
Roll, Jordan, Roll (Genovese) 66
Romeo and Juliet (Shakespeare) 108
ruptures 8, 24, 28
Russ, A.R. 25, 26, 31
Russell, Catherine 110
Rwanda 207

Saarto, Ari 181
Said, Edward 140
Sakaguchi, Kyohei 181
salto mortale 32; Karl Marx 32; Agathangelou and Killian 32
salvage ethnography: agency and self-representation 110–12; cinema as a technology of 107–10; colonial archives and 115–17; reconstructed *Head Hunters* 112–15; temporality and 'object' of 105–7
salvation 49
Sartre, Jean Paul 33, 35
Saussure, Ferdinand de 80
savages 7, 52, 192 *see also* indigenous peoples
Save Darfur Coalition 207
Scenes of Subjection (Hartman) 63
Schiller, Johann Christoph Friedrich 193
Scott, Dred 92–4, 95
Second Assembly of the Global Environment 198
Second Intifada 132
secular 6, 10–13, 46–7, 52, 55, 190
secular finitude 10
secularization 14, 137; Anna M. Agathangelou and Kyle Killian introduction 10, 14; fatal 13; fatalism 260; fate 54–5; God 10, 11
security: citizenship and 224–6; European security practices/policies in Mediterranean region 221, 226–9; external security 229; internal security 229; monopoly on coercive means and 137–8; politics of global security 235–6
Seeman, Annette 16, 119–28
self-interest 176
self-representation 110–12
sentimentality 105, 206, 211–14
settler-colonialism 144

Sexton, Jared 61–75
sexuality 27, 53, 212
Shakespeare, William 108
Shakur, Assata 91
Shapiro, Michael 238
Sharpe, Christina 70
Shilliam, Robbie xix, 26
Shinjuku Park 183
Shooting Indians (Kazimi) 115
Siba N. Grovogui 45–60
similitude 177
Simon, David 252, 253, 256, 257
Simon Gikandi 33–4
singular 2, 27, 28, 71, 190, 223, 227, 260–2
slavery 25–6, 28–30, 34, 65, 67, 70, 89–90; *Slavery and Social Death* (Patterson) 65; slaves 27–30, 34, 95, 212–13; slave ships 26–7, 31; slave trade 12, 26, 28, 30–1, 49, 90
smart bombs 55
SnapChat 264
social: sociality 69, 177, 180, 183–4, 240; normative sociality 179
social classification 177
social death 64–7, 72–3, 89–90, 93, 96, 99–101, 261, 262–3
social integration 176
social life 61–73, 89, 182, 254, 269
socially necessary labor time 161–2, 164, 168–9, 241–2
social recognition 77, 83
social time 174, 180–1
Solidarity 152, 163, 164, 169, 177, 179; external solidarity 145
Solomon, Ty 76–86
Song of Hiawatha, The (Longfellow) 108
Sontag, Susan 260, 264, 269
South Africa 198
sovereignty: Patriot Act 58; as political fiction 137; secular appropriation of time and 46; violence and 6–8, 23
space: spatiality 5, 260, 261
Spain 52, 222
Spanish Civil War 55
speculation 25–31, 32, 36, 38, 269; speculative capital 32
speed 236, 238
Spillers, Hortense 73
Spivak, Gayatri Chakravorty 238, 240
statehood 151
stasis 87, 218
'statism' 151
stasis 87, 218; Opondo 218

St. Cyr, Lillian (Princess Red Wing) 111–12
Steele, Brent 189, 194
Stieglitz, Alfred 105
street photographers 263–4
structure: historical materialism 239; temporal structures 234, 239
subject 7, 11, 12, 16, 24, 25, 27, 30
subject formation 80–2
subjectivity: alienation and 97–8; atemporality and 173–4; black subjectivity 33–5, 102; death and 96; 'desiring subjectivity' 179; dialectic of subjectivity and history 34–5; difference and 80–2; *fiction of time* and 14; of indigenous peoples 107, 109; meaning and 76–7, 79–85; Palestinian political subjectivity 153; political subjectivity 131; relations of time, empire, and 46–7; slave ship as birthplace of modern subjectivity 26; sovereignty and 23; technology and 54–5; temporality and 176; value and 29
Suicide (Durkheim) 261
suprema potestas 47
surveillance 58, 235–6

tabula rasa: Frantz Fanon 39
Taipei Times 246
Taney, Roger B. 93–4, 95, 101
techne 47
technical assistance 49
technologies of power 49
technology
technology 15, 25, 45, 47–9, 53–9, 92, 107, 112, 161, 217, 227, 228, 233, 235–6, 255, 264: aesthetic experiences and 56–9; cinema as a technology of salvage ethnography 107–10; drone technology 54; as governing temporal modality 58; impact on war-making 236; law as 92; military technology 54, 56, 57; subjectivity and 54–5; violence and 53–6
technostrategy 236
television aesthetic 253
temporal coherence 95, 96, 98, 100, 148, 238
temporal discourse 189, 193, 197–9
temporality as device 107; as discourse 189–90, 193, 197–9; as institution of governance 4; as lived experience 4, 238; as metaphysics 15
temporality: atemporality and 95; capital as 25; capitalism and 160–4;
'coeval temporalities' 175–6; culture preservation and 113; disjunctive temporalities 209–11; economy of progress and 12; heterotemporality 238; of imagination 110; 'linear time' 199–200; 'lingering present' 151; modernity and 190, 191–3, 199; of musical narrative 254–5; 'object' of salvage ethnography and 105–7; as phenomenological experience of speed, 236, 240; practices and 82–4; retroactive temporality 80–2, 84–5; role in the performative constitution of the subject 83–5; role of emotions and 85; of slavery 29; socialized horizon of 176; of subjectivity 82; temporal discourse 189, 193, 197–9; temporalizing difference 221, 222–3, 229; 'temporalizing security' 221, 222, 227, 229; as tied to the unthought of modernity 35–6, 38; timespace 260, 261–2; violence of abstraction by political and economic 238; of work for migrant day laborers 164–8; of world-political time 237–8 *see also* time
temporalization 19, 160, 176, 214, 221–3, 234, 239, 242
'temporalizing security' 221, 222, 227, 229
temporal Othering: environmental retorts of 194–9; human development 193; time(s) of the Self and the Other 191–3; universalizing history 190–1
Thatcher, Margaret 94–5
threat: foreigners as 229; right to respond to 58
Thrift, Nigel 260
time: African time 238; aspects of 237; atemporality 173–4; blackness and 39; in capitalist modernity 234; children's time 213; as *chronos* 237; clock time 242; colonialism 13; cosmic time 7; durational time 176, 183; family time 209–11; as force 13, 24; global politics and 234–9; historical materialist account of 239–40; historical time 243; homogeneous time 11; 'homogenous empty time' 151; as *kairos* 237; Kantian view on 237; labor time 25, 161–2, 241–2; as linear movement 25; 'linear time' 199–200; 'Messianic time' 252; modernity and 13, 175, 243; perpetual present and 262; political temporality 238; politics of global times 239–42; 'postmodern problematic' of 239;

prison time 95; as a problem of time 24; religious connotations of 46; retroactive time 80–2; secular appropriation of 46; of the Self and the Other 191–3; socially constituted time 240–2; socially necessary labor time 161–2, 164, 168–9, 241–2; *social time* 174, 180–1; speed and 236; of suffering children 205–8; technology and 58; timespace 260, 261–2; toward a politics of time in a time of violence 168–70; unitary time 200; universal time 56; world-political time 237–8 *see also* politics of time; temporality
Time and World Politics (Hutchings) 237
timelessness 4, 9, 12, 26, 31–2, 71, 174–5, 269
Time Magazine 246
Time of the City, The (Shapiro) 238
timespace: defatalizing 265; fatalization of individual agency and 260; perpetual present and 261–2
Tomba, Massimiliano: thinking politics differently 243
Toshikoshi Hakenmura (New Year's Eve village for dispatched workers) 172
tourists 120
tradition 105
transcendence 32
transcendental 4, 10, 12, 26, 237
Transformation: amputating the transformation of the present 36; dialectical transformation 35; genuine transformation 38; historical transformation 34; modern transformation of slavery 65; secular transformation 11; social transformation 19, 34, 163; transformation in security practices 17; zero degree of transformation 69; *see also* Jared Sexton; transformational politics
transnational adoption 211–12
Treme (Simon) 252–6
Trinh T. Minh-ha 113
Tsutsumi, Yukihiko 181–2, 183
Tunisia 228
Turki, Fawaz 151

Ueno Park 183
U'mista Cultural Society 110
uncertainty 36
unconscious: eternal time of 62; Freudian discovery of the unconscious 98; Lacan's first and second elements of 95; Lacan's taxonomy of the unconscious 99–100; Lacan's theory of the unconscious 98–101
undeveloped states 196–7
unhinging time 34–9
Union Carbide Corporation 246–7
unitary time 200
United Nations Climate Change Working Group 195
United Nations Conference on Environment and Development (UNCED) 195
United Nations Environment Programme (UNEP) 189
United Nations (UN) 198, 210
United States: discourses of childhood innocence 214; drone warfare 55; Hurricane Katrina 246, 247–57; invasion of Iraq 55; lives of slave women in 28–9; manifest destiny 111; military-style equipment deployments 55; policy in the Persian Gulf 236; self-identity in 194
universal history 193, 243
universal time 14, 56
unthought 28, 35–6, 38, 68; Hartman and Frank Wilderson 63; locus of non-positive value 28; zero degree of social conceptualization 27
urbanization 64, 107, 111; suburbanization 135, 147
used clothes 207
use of children 211–14
utopia: askesis 12; counter-sites 177; Michel Foucault 177

Valenzuela, Abel, Jr. 166
valorizing 240, 241, 242
Valverde, Mariana 5
value: common denominator of 241; as violence 29; as death limit 66; exchange value 181–2; surplus value 162, 168
Vancouver Island 108
van Fossen, A. 25
Vij, Ritu xxii, 17, 172–88
violence: of abstraction by political and economic temporality 238; acceptability/unaccesability of 11; of confrontation 53–4; defatalizing violence 1, 84, 260–1; divine violence 48–50; fatalism 1, 260–1, 263; at homeless people 180–1; humanitarian critique of 213; humanitarianist mode of sensing 207; against indigenous

inhabitants of Congo Free State 213–14; 'just' use of 50; metaphoric violence 97–8; migrant day laborers and 168–70; oppression and 33; photography and 265; police violence 256–7; of racism 33; sacred violence 46; slavery and 89–90, 97; of socially necessary labor time 162; sovereignty and 6–8, 23; sovereign violence 46; as technique of life 46–7; technology and 53–6; toward a politics of time in a time of 168–70
Virilio, Paul 236
Virno, Paolo 240
visibility: politics of 140–9; problem of homelessness 178
visual memory 131, 142
Vitalis, Robert 26
void: void sovereignty 131
VOZ Worker Rights and Education Project 160, 169–70
vulnerability 24, 39, 70, 72, 97, 165, 168, 200, 247; vulnerability in the present 269

Waiting for Godot (Beckett) 206
'Waiting' (Osondu) 205–9, 211, 217–18
Walker, Rob 1, 4, 8, 233–5
'Walking to New Orleans' (Domino) 251
war 2, 8, 13, 17, 23, 54, 55, 56, 58, 87, 92, 102, 100, 107, 190, 207, 236

War on Terror 207
Weather Underground 90
Webster, Gloria Cranmer 110, 115
Weinstein, Warren 55
West and the rest 31
West Bank 55, 135
West, Kanye 247
When the Levees Broke (Lee) 248–52, 256, 257
White Fawn's Devotion (Young Deer) 112
Wilderson, Frank B. 27–8, 61, 63, 67, 71–2, 73, 87–103
Williams, Evelyn 91
Witch's Flight, The (Keeling) 63
Woman, Native, Other (Minh-ha) 113
world-political time 237–8
Wretched of the Earth, The (Fanon) 33–4, 39

yoseba (day labor market) 178, 181
Young Deer, James 111–12
Yoyogi Park 183

zenkoku Komuniti Yunion Rengokai (National Federation of Community unions) 172
'Zero Yen Houses' 181–3
Zimbabwe 214
Žižek, Slavoj 76, 81–3, 84, 85
Zong case 27